I finally bought my first pair of glasses!! Pulling so many all-nighters was bad for my eyes, so the optometrist recommended I get glasses. And now, after 39 years, I finally have obtained my first pair of glasses ever!! When I put them on, my first thought was, "I should've gotten these sooner!" I can see!! I can see almost too well!! Glasses are incredible. I'm so invincible, I could pull off a whole week of all-nighters.
(My current weight...65 kg!! Woo-hoo!! I did it!! My reformed eating habits are paying off!!)

—Mitsutoshi Shimabukuro, 2014

Mitsutoshi Shimabukuro made his debut in **Weekly Shonen Jump** in 1996. He is best known for **Seikimatsu Leader Den Takeshi!**, for which he won the 46th Shogakukan Manga Award for children's manga in 2001. His current series, **Toriko**, began serialization in Japan in 2008.

TORIKO

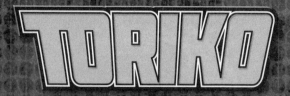

TORIKO VOL. 33
SHONEN JUMP Manga Edition

STORY AND ART BY **MITSUTOSHI SHIMABUKURO**

Translation/Christine Dashiell
Weekly Shonen Jump Lettering/Erika Terriquez
Graphic Novel Touch-Up Art & Lettering/Elena Diaz
Design/Matt Hinrichs
Weekly Shonen Jump Editor/Hope Donovan
Graphic Novel Editor/Marlene First

Printed in the U.S.A.

Published by VIZ Media, LLC
P.O. Box 77010
San Francisco, CA 94107

10 9 8 7 6 5 4 3 2 1
First printing, April 2016

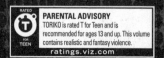

TORIKO

Story and Art by
Mitsutoshi Shimabukuro

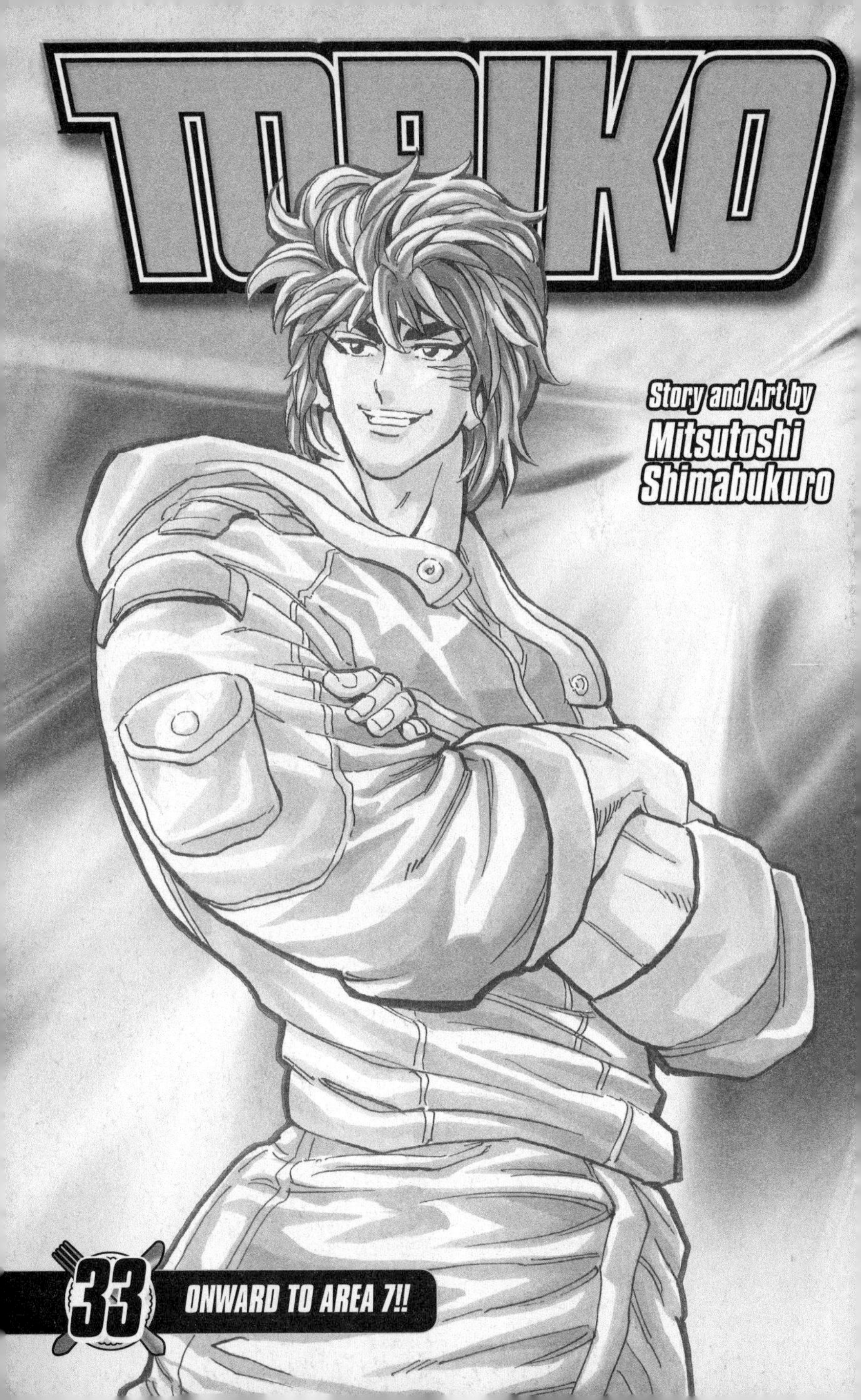

33
ONWARD TO AREA 7!!

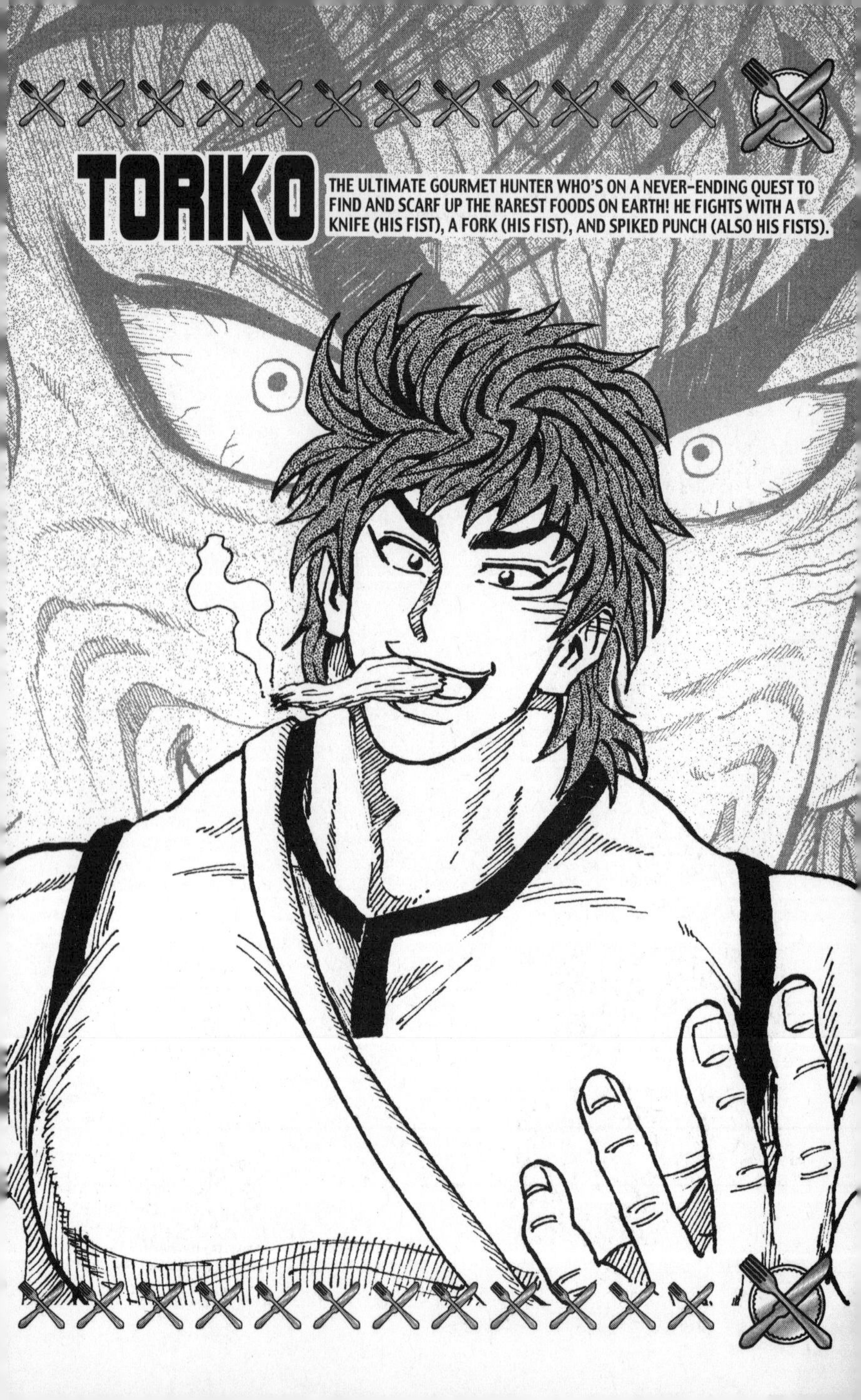
TORIKO
THE ULTIMATE GOURMET HUNTER WHO'S ON A NEVER-ENDING QUEST TO FIND AND SCARF UP THE RAREST FOODS ON EARTH! HE FIGHTS WITH A KNIFE (HIS FIST), A FORK (HIS FIST), AND SPIKED PUNCH (ALSO HIS FISTS).

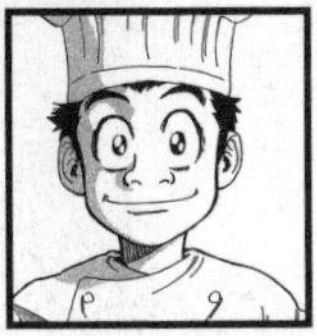

●KOMATSU
TALENTED IGO HOTEL CHEF AND TORIKO'S #1 FAN.

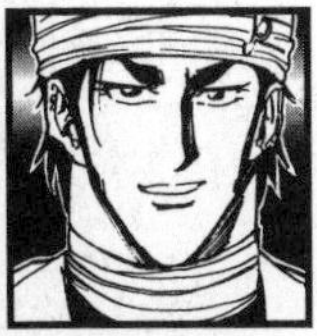

●COCO
ONE OF THE FOUR KINGS, THOUGH HE IS ALSO A FORTUNETELLER. SPECIAL ABILITY: POISON FLOWS IN HIS VEINS.

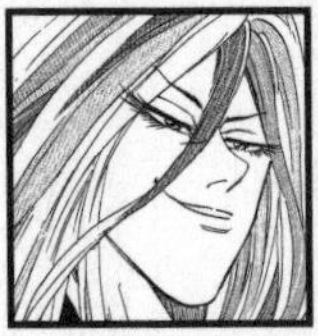

●SUNNY
ONE OF THE FOUR KINGS. SENSORS IN HIS LONG HAIR ENABLE HIM TO "TASTE" THE WORLD. OBSESSED WITH ALL THAT IS BEAUTIFUL.

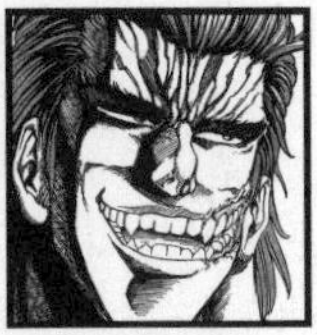

●ZEBRA
ONE OF THE FOUR KINGS. A DANGEROUS INDIVIDUAL WITH SUPERHUMAN HEARING AND VOCAL POWERS.

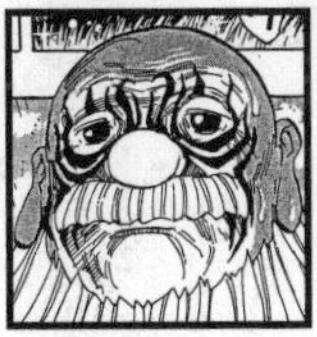

●DARUMA
THE MAYOR OF HEX FOOD WORLD. HE'S THE ONLY PERSON WHO KNOWS HOW TO PROPERLY PREPARE AIR.

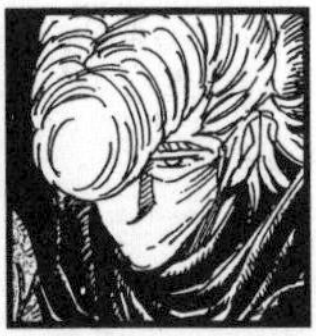

●TEPPEI
FORMER GOURMET REVIVER. HE WAS "PREPARED" BY JOJE AND IS NOW JOIE'S PUPPET.

WHAT'S FOR DINNER

THE AGE OF GOURMET IS DECLARED OVER. IN ORDER TO GET KOMATSU BACK FROM GOURMET CORP., TORIKO VENTURES INTO THE GOURMET WORLD ON HIS OWN! EIGHTEEN MONTHS LATER, THE PAIR RETURNS HOME ALONG WITH A MASSIVE AMOUNT OF PROVISIONS TO FEED THE HUMAN WORLD. UPON THEIR RETURN, THE TWO ARE COMMISSIONED BY THE NEW IGO PRESIDENT, MANSOM, TO SEARCH FOR THE REMAINDER OF ICHIRYU'S FULL COURSE MEAL. JOINING FORCES WITH THE OTHER FOUR KINGS—COCO, SUNNY AND ZEBRA—THEY SUCCEED IN RETRIEVING THE MIRACLE INGREDIENT THAT WILL SAVE HUMANITY FROM STARVATION: THE BILLION BIRD.

IN ORDER TO REVIVE THE AGE OF GOURMET, THE FIVE OF THEM TAKE AN ENORMOUS ORDER! THEY MUST TRAVEL TO THE GOURMET WORLD AND FIND ACACIA'S FULL-COURSE MEAL! ARMED WITH THE INFORMATION AND THE OCTOMELON CAMPER MONSTER GIVEN TO THEM BY ICHIRYU'S MYSTERIOUS FRIEND CHICHI, THE FIVE MEN SET THEIR SIGHTS ON THE GOURMET WORLD.

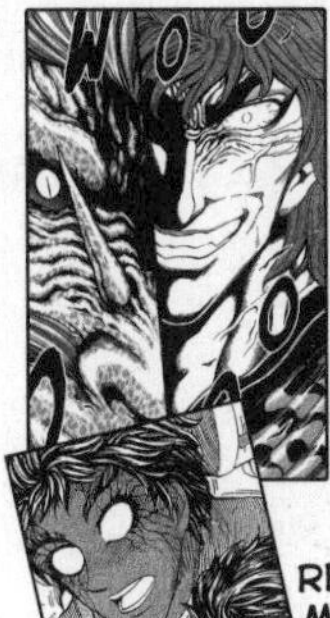

THEIR FIRST STOP IS AREA 8, WHERE TORIKO MUST FACE OFF AGAINST THE RULER OF THE CONTINENT, NIGHTMARE HERCULES, IN ORDER TO OBTAIN ACACIA'S SALAD, AIR. BUT THE OVERWHELMING DIFFERENCE IN STRENGTH LEAVES TORIKO ON THE BRINK OF DEATH.

MEANWHILE, KOMATSU REACHES AIR AND USES HIS MASTERFUL CULINARY SKILLS TO PREPARE IT. THIS MAGNIFICENT FEAT SAVES THE NIGHTMARES AND ALL OF AREA 8! AT LAST, TORIKO AND HIS FRIENDS SAMPLE AIR AND TORIKO EVEN ADDS IT TO HIS FULL-COURSE MEAL AS THE SALAD.

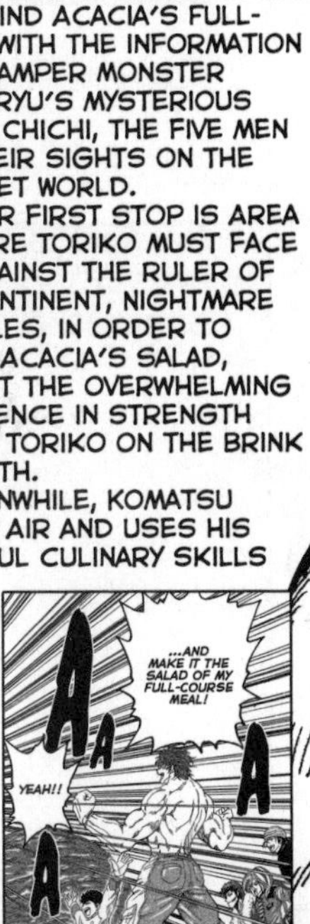
...AND MAKE IT THE SALAD OF MY FULL-COURSE MEAL!
AAAAA
YEAH!!

Contents

TORIKO

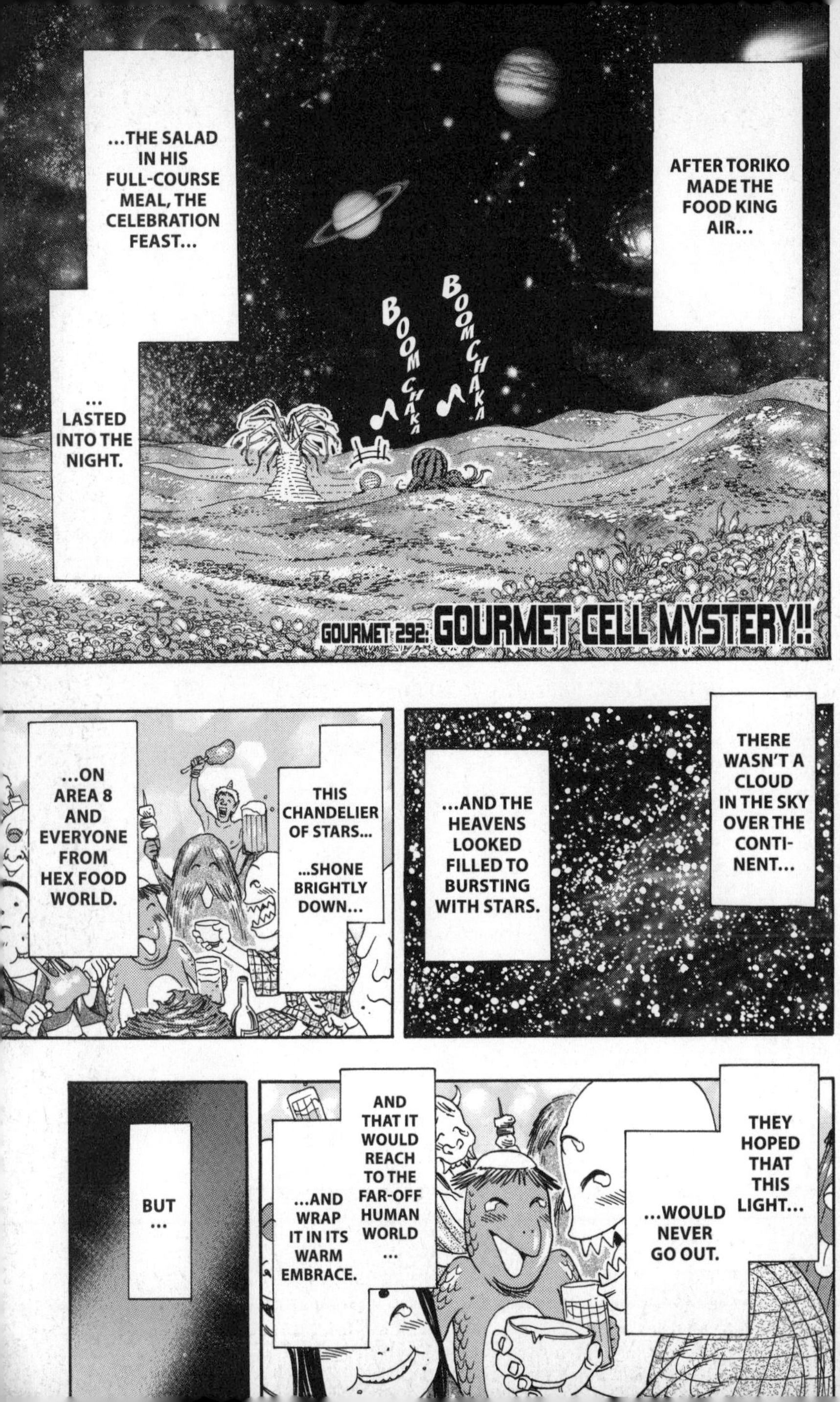
AFTER TORIKO MADE THE FOOD KING AIR...
...THE SALAD IN HIS FULL-COURSE MEAL, THE CELEBRATION FEAST...
BOOM CHAKA
BOOM CHAKA
...LASTED INTO THE NIGHT.
GOURMET 292: GOURMET CELL MYSTERY!!
THERE WASN'T A CLOUD IN THE SKY OVER THE CONTI- NENT...
...AND THE HEAVENS LOOKED FILLED TO BURSTING WITH STARS.
THIS CHANDELIER OF STARS...
...SHONE BRIGHTLY DOWN...
...ON AREA 8 AND EVERYONE FROM HEX FOOD WORLD.
THEY HOPED THAT THIS LIGHT...
...WOULD NEVER GO OUT.
AND THAT IT WOULD REACH TO THE FAR-OFF HUMAN WORLD...
...AND WRAP IT IN ITS WARM EMBRACE.
BUT...

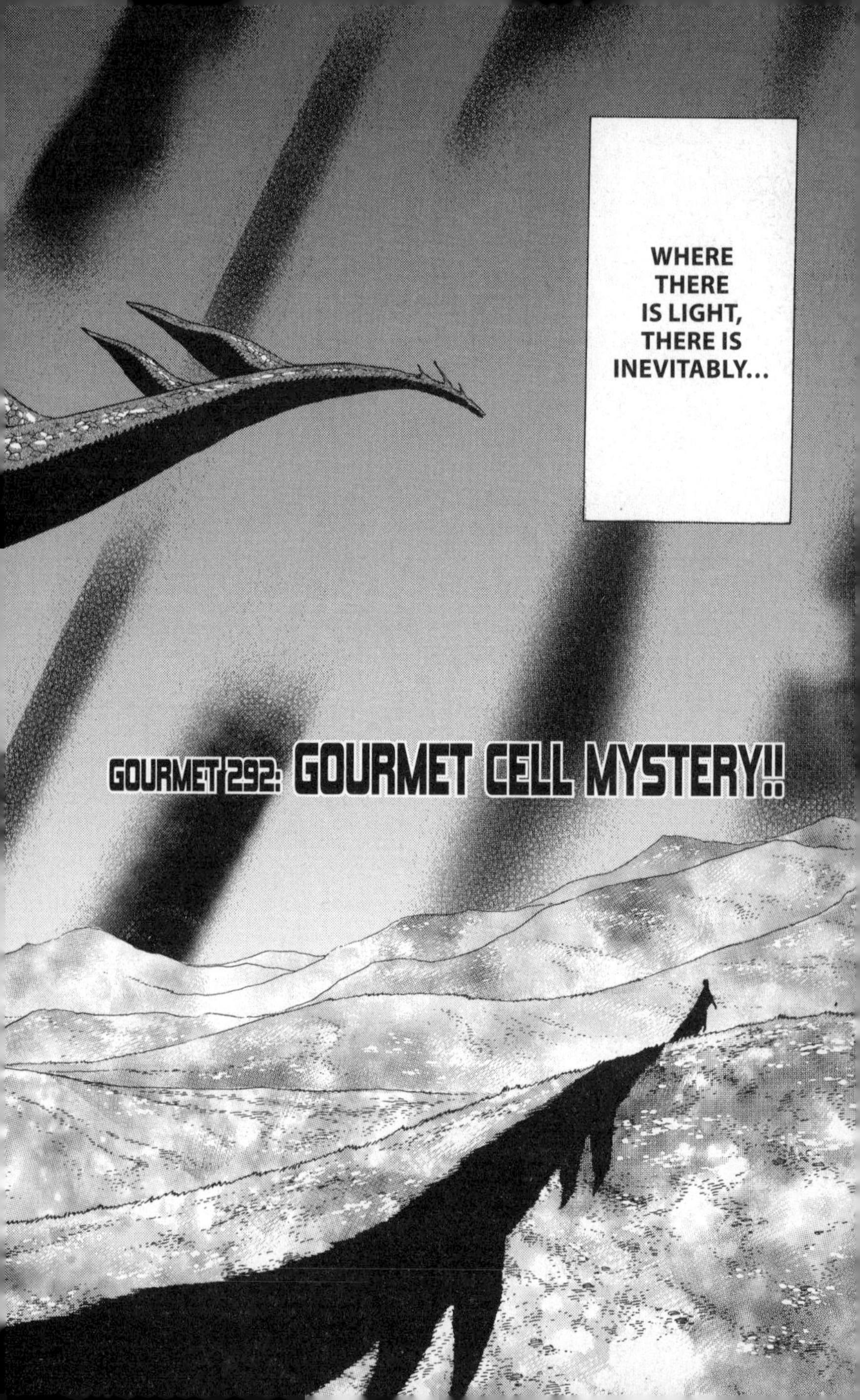
WHERE THERE IS LIGHT, THERE IS INEVITABLY...
GOURMET 292: GOURMET CELL MYSTERY!!

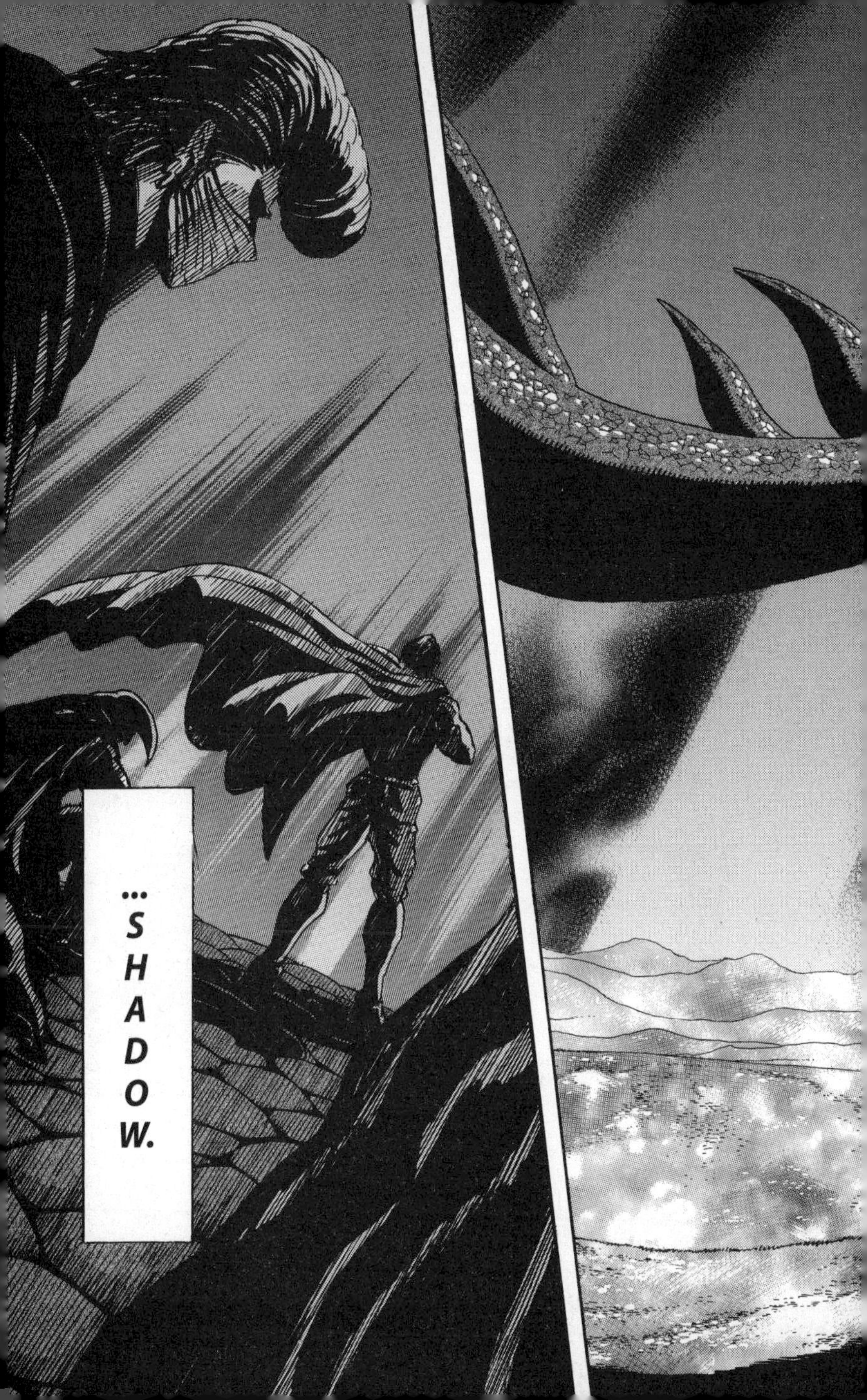
...SHADOW.

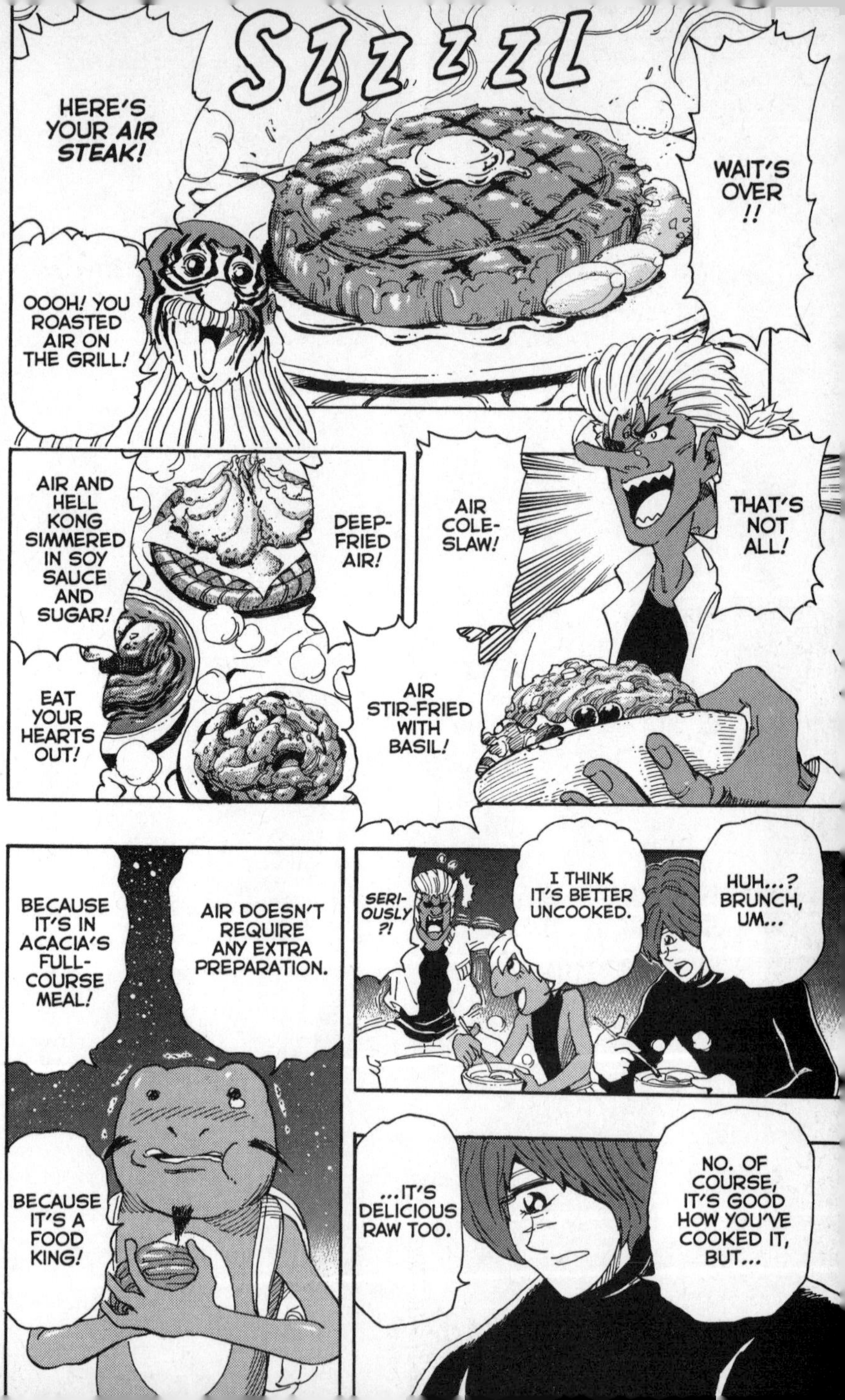
SZZZZL
WAIT'S OVER!!
HERE'S YOUR AIR STEAK!
OOOH! YOU ROASTED AIR ON THE GRILL!
THAT'S NOT ALL!
AIR COLE-SLAW!
AIR STIR-FRIED WITH BASIL!
DEEP-FRIED AIR!
AIR AND HELL KONG SIMMERED IN SOY SAUCE AND SUGAR!
EAT YOUR HEARTS OUT!
HUH...? BRUNCH, UM...
I THINK IT'S BETTER UNCOOKED.
SERIOUSLY?!
NO. OF COURSE, IT'S GOOD HOW YOU'VE COOKED IT, BUT...
...IT'S DELICIOUS RAW TOO.
AIR DOESN'T REQUIRE ANY EXTRA PREPARATION.
BECAUSE IT'S IN ACACIA'S FULL-COURSE MEAL!
BECAUSE IT'S A FOOD KING!

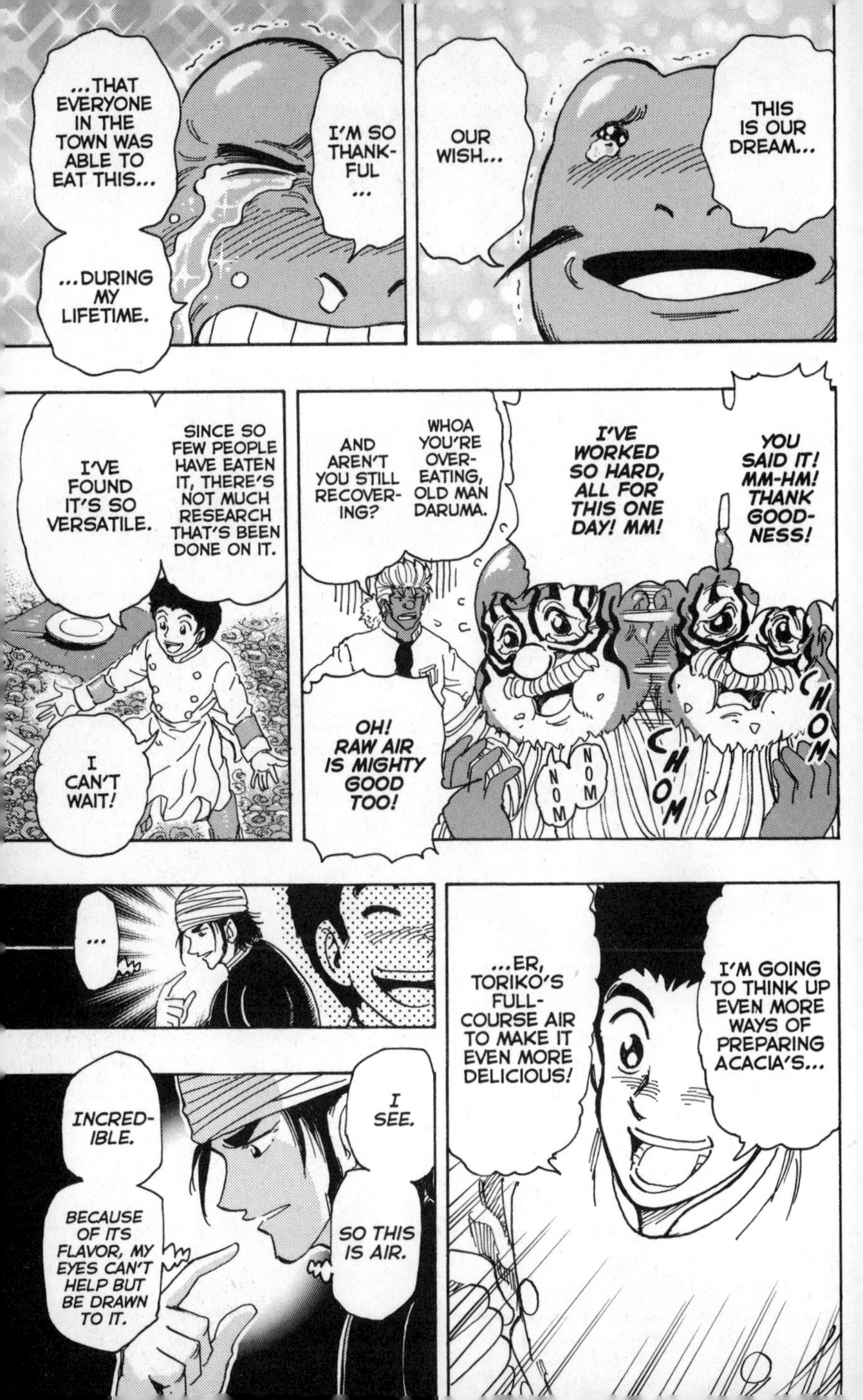
THIS IS OUR DREAM...
OUR WISH...
I'M SO THANKFUL...
...THAT EVERYONE IN THE TOWN WAS ABLE TO EAT THIS...
...DURING MY LIFETIME.
YOU SAID IT! MM-HM! THANK GOODNESS!
I'VE WORKED SO HARD, ALL FOR THIS ONE DAY! MM!
WHOA YOU'RE OVER-EATING, OLD MAN DARUMA.
AND AREN'T YOU STILL RECOVERING?
CHOM CHOM
NOM NOM
OH! RAW AIR IS MIGHTY GOOD TOO!
SINCE SO FEW PEOPLE HAVE EATEN IT, THERE'S NOT MUCH RESEARCH THAT'S BEEN DONE ON IT.
I'VE FOUND IT'S SO VERSATILE.
I CAN'T WAIT!
I'M GOING TO THINK UP EVEN MORE WAYS OF PREPARING ACACIA'S...
...ER, TORIKO'S FULL-COURSE AIR TO MAKE IT EVEN MORE DELICIOUS!
...
I SEE.
SO THIS IS AIR.
INCREDIBLE.
BECAUSE OF ITS FLAVOR, MY EYES CAN'T HELP BUT BE DRAWN TO IT.

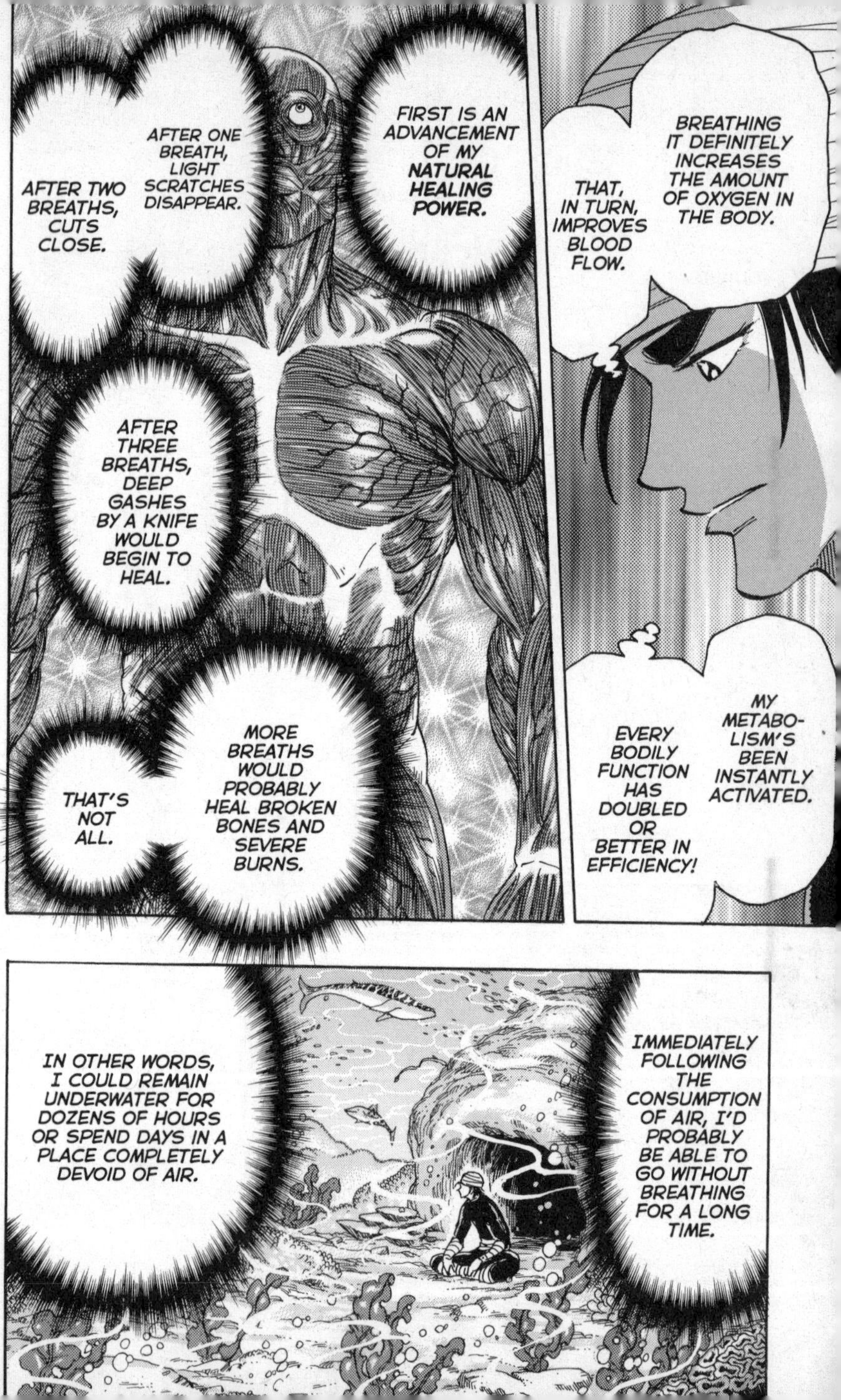
BREATHING IT DEFINITELY INCREASES THE AMOUNT OF OXYGEN IN THE BODY.
THAT, IN TURN, IMPROVES BLOOD FLOW.
MY METABOLISM'S BEEN INSTANTLY ACTIVATED.
EVERY BODILY FUNCTION HAS DOUBLED OR BETTER IN EFFICIENCY!
FIRST IS AN ADVANCEMENT OF MY **NATURAL HEALING POWER.**
AFTER ONE BREATH, LIGHT SCRATCHES DISAPPEAR.
AFTER TWO BREATHS, CUTS CLOSE.
AFTER THREE BREATHS, DEEP GASHES BY A KNIFE WOULD BEGIN TO HEAL.
MORE BREATHS WOULD PROBABLY HEAL BROKEN BONES AND SEVERE BURNS.
THAT'S NOT ALL.
IMMEDIATELY FOLLOWING THE CONSUMPTION OF AIR, I'D PROBABLY BE ABLE TO GO WITHOUT BREATHING FOR A LONG TIME.
IN OTHER WORDS, I COULD REMAIN UNDERWATER FOR DOZENS OF HOURS OR SPEND DAYS IN A PLACE COMPLETELY DEVOID OF AIR.

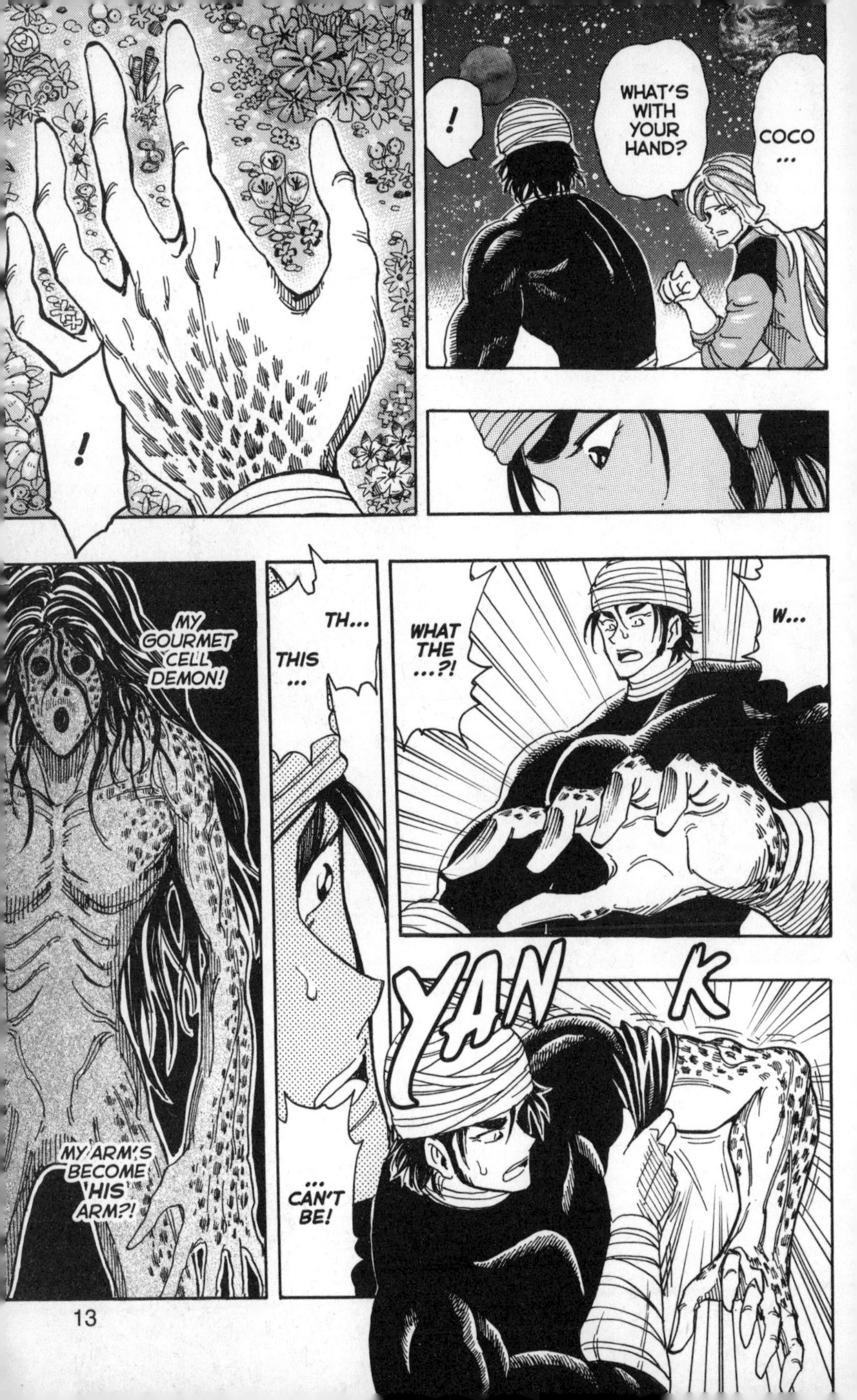
COCO...
WHAT'S WITH YOUR HAND?
!
!
W...
WHAT THE ...?!
YANK
TH...
THIS...
...CAN'T BE!
MY GOURMET CELL DEMON!
MY ARM'S BECOME HIS ARM?!

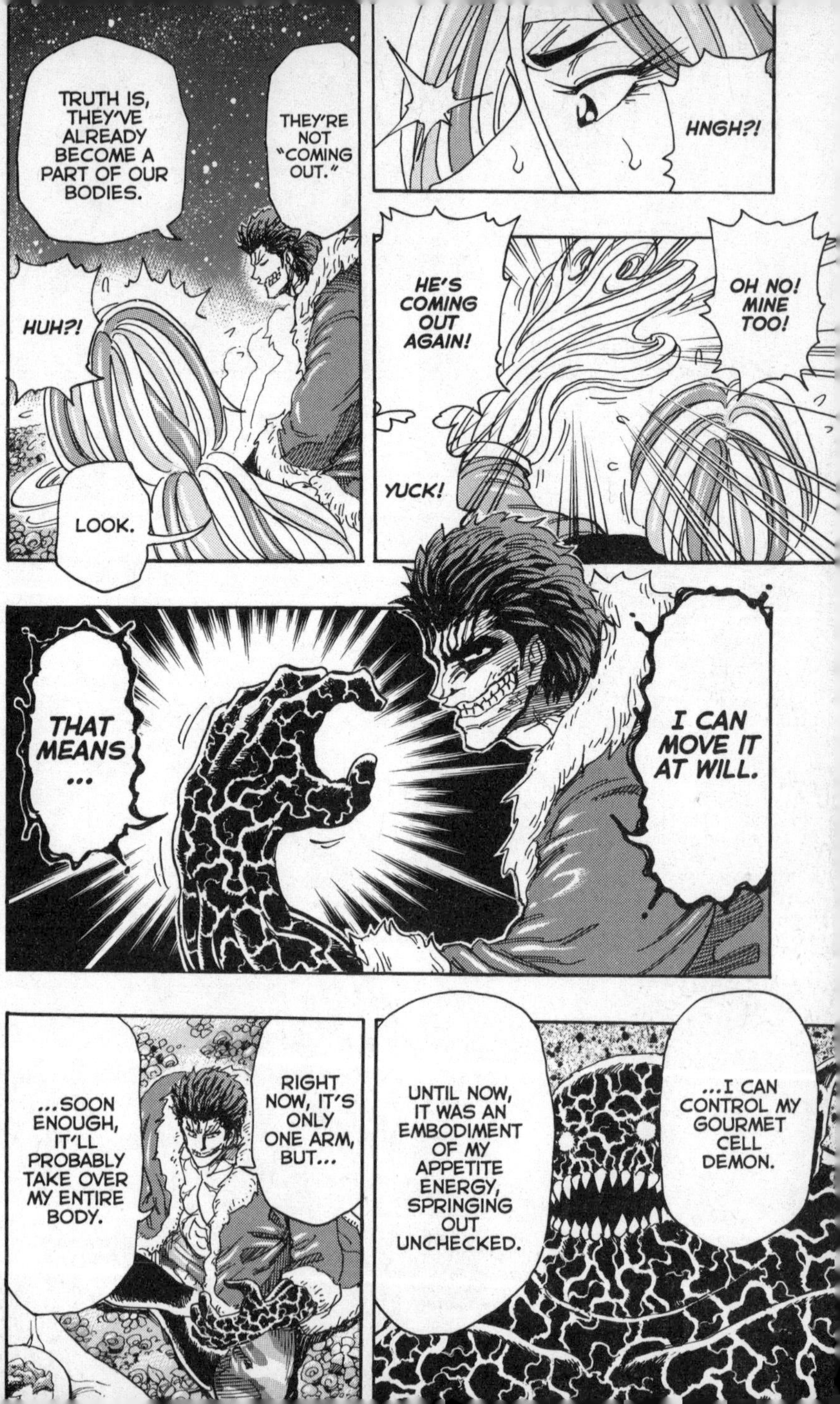
HNGH?!
OH NO! MINE TOO!
HE'S COMING OUT AGAIN!
YUCK!
THEY'RE NOT "COMING OUT."
TRUTH IS, THEY'VE ALREADY BECOME A PART OF OUR BODIES.
HUH?!
LOOK.
I CAN MOVE IT AT WILL.
THAT MEANS...
...I CAN CONTROL MY GOURMET CELL DEMON.
UNTIL NOW, IT WAS AN EMBODIMENT OF MY APPETITE ENERGY, SPRINGING OUT UNCHECKED.
RIGHT NOW, IT'S ONLY ONE ARM, BUT...
...SOON ENOUGH, IT'LL PROBABLY TAKE OVER MY ENTIRE BODY.

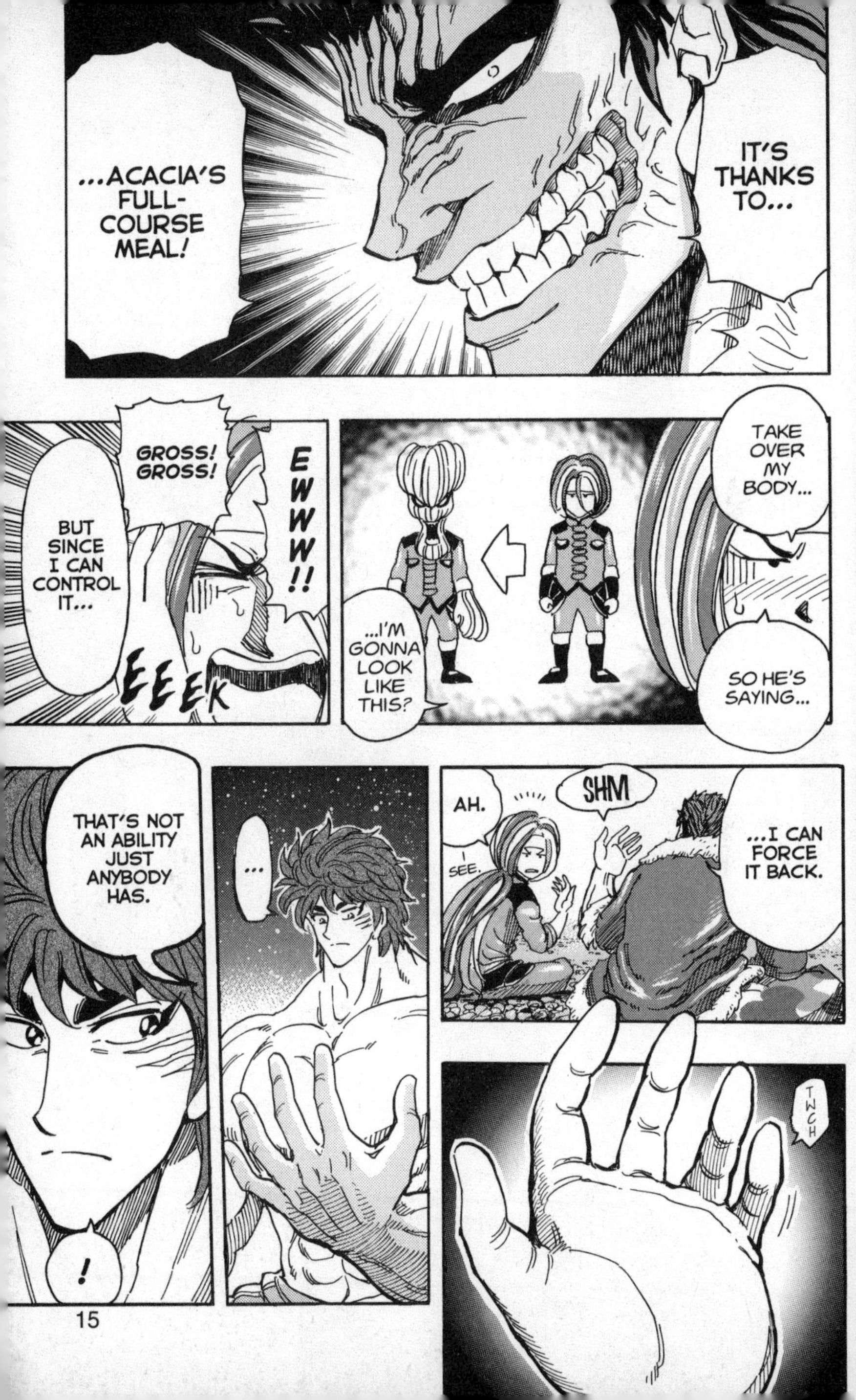
IT'S THANKS TO...
...ACACIA'S FULL-COURSE MEAL!
TAKE OVER MY BODY...
SO HE'S SAYING...
...I'M GONNA LOOK LIKE THIS?
GROSS! GROSS!
EWWWW!!
BUT SINCE I CAN CONTROL IT...
EEEK
...I CAN FORCE IT BACK.
SHM
AH.
I SEE.
TWCH
...
THAT'S NOT AN ABILITY JUST ANYBODY HAS.
!

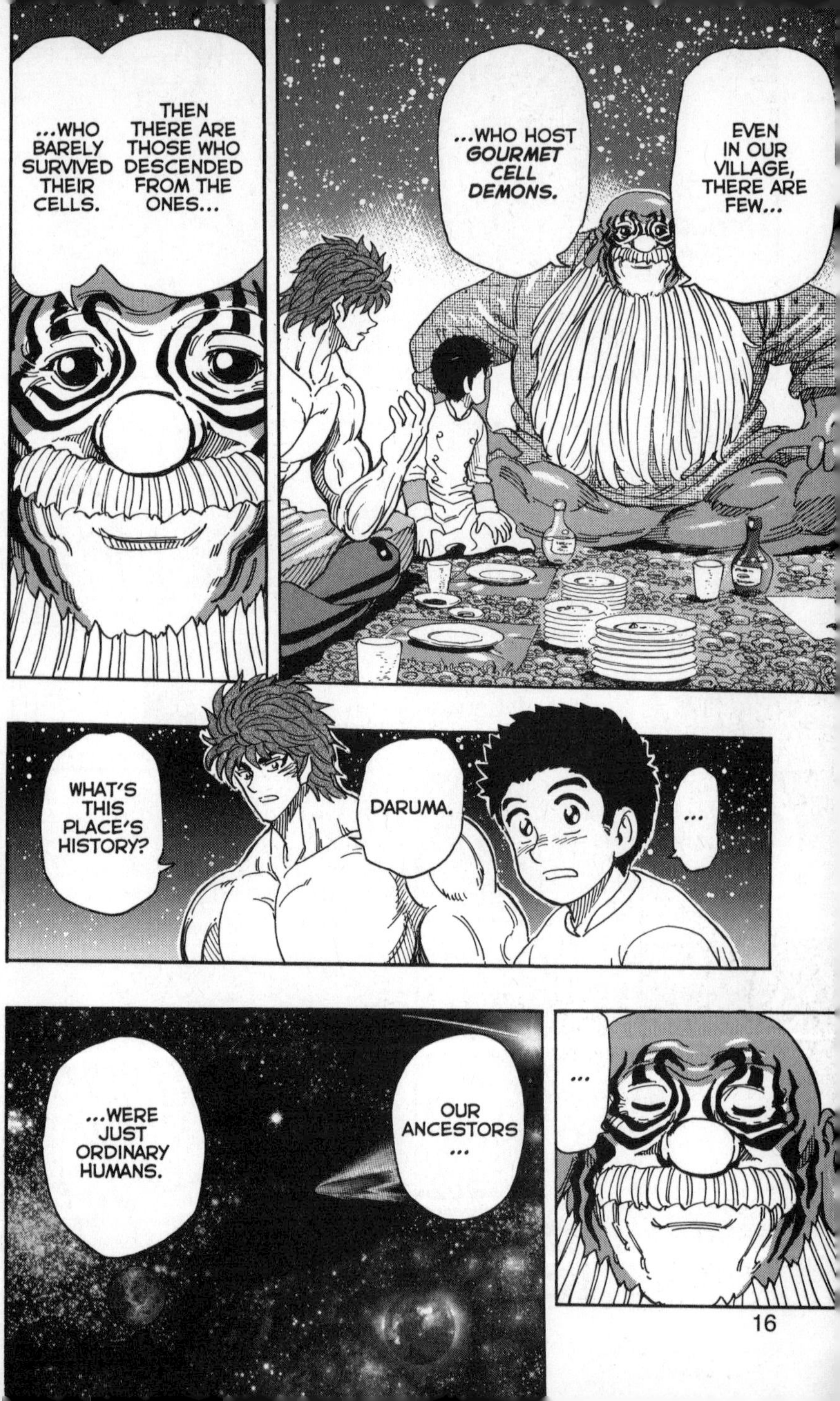

EVEN IN OUR VILLAGE, THERE ARE FEW...
...WHO HOST GOURMET CELL DEMONS.
THEN THERE ARE THOSE WHO DESCENDED FROM THE ONES...
...WHO BARELY SURVIVED THEIR CELLS.
...
DARUMA.
WHAT'S THIS PLACE'S HISTORY?
...
OUR ANCESTORS ...
...WERE JUST ORDINARY HUMANS.

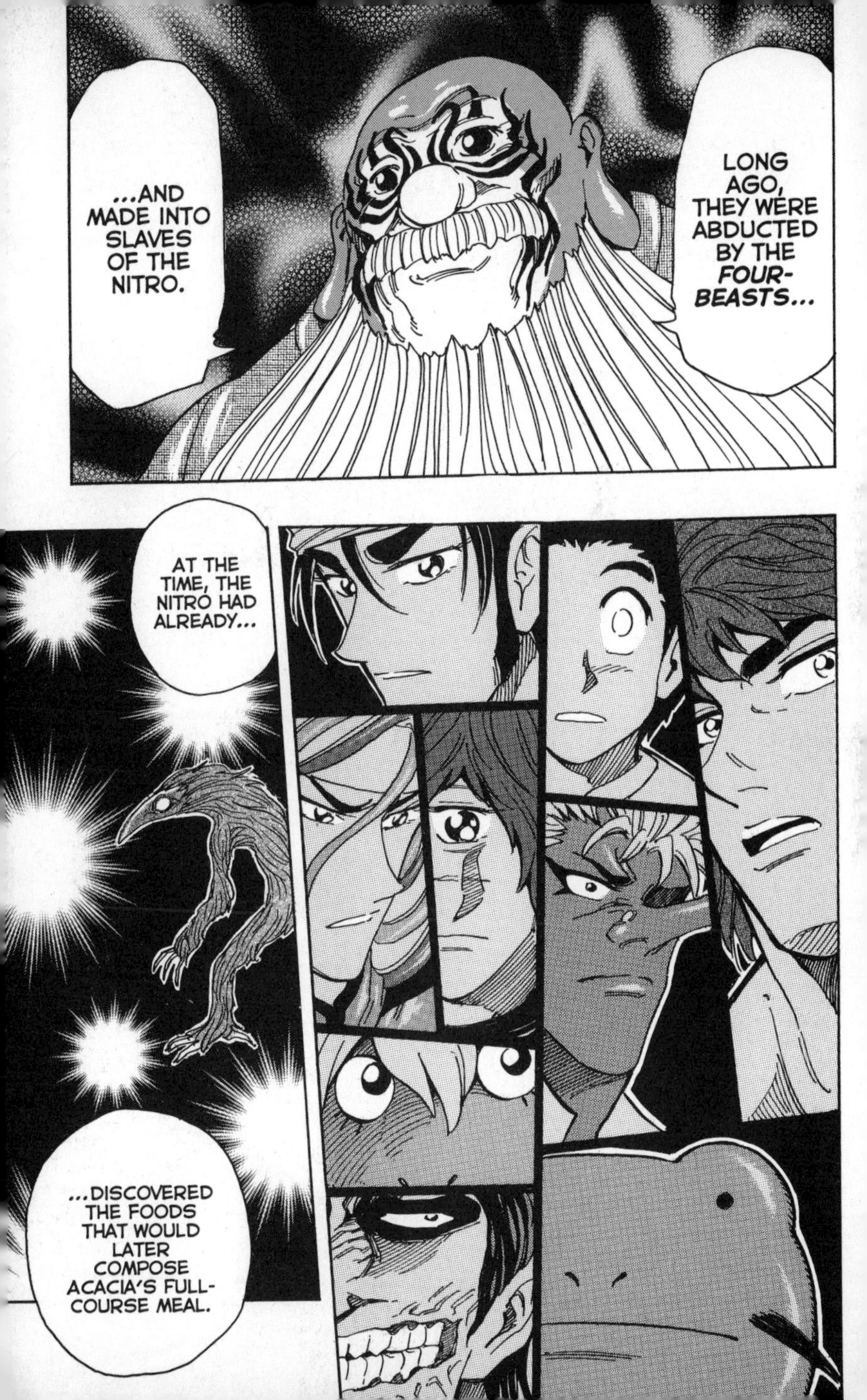
LONG AGO, THEY WERE ABDUCTED BY THE *FOUR-BEASTS*...
...AND MADE INTO SLAVES OF THE NITRO.
AT THE TIME, THE NITRO HAD ALREADY...
...DISCOVERED THE FOODS THAT WOULD LATER COMPOSE ACACIA'S FULL-COURSE MEAL.

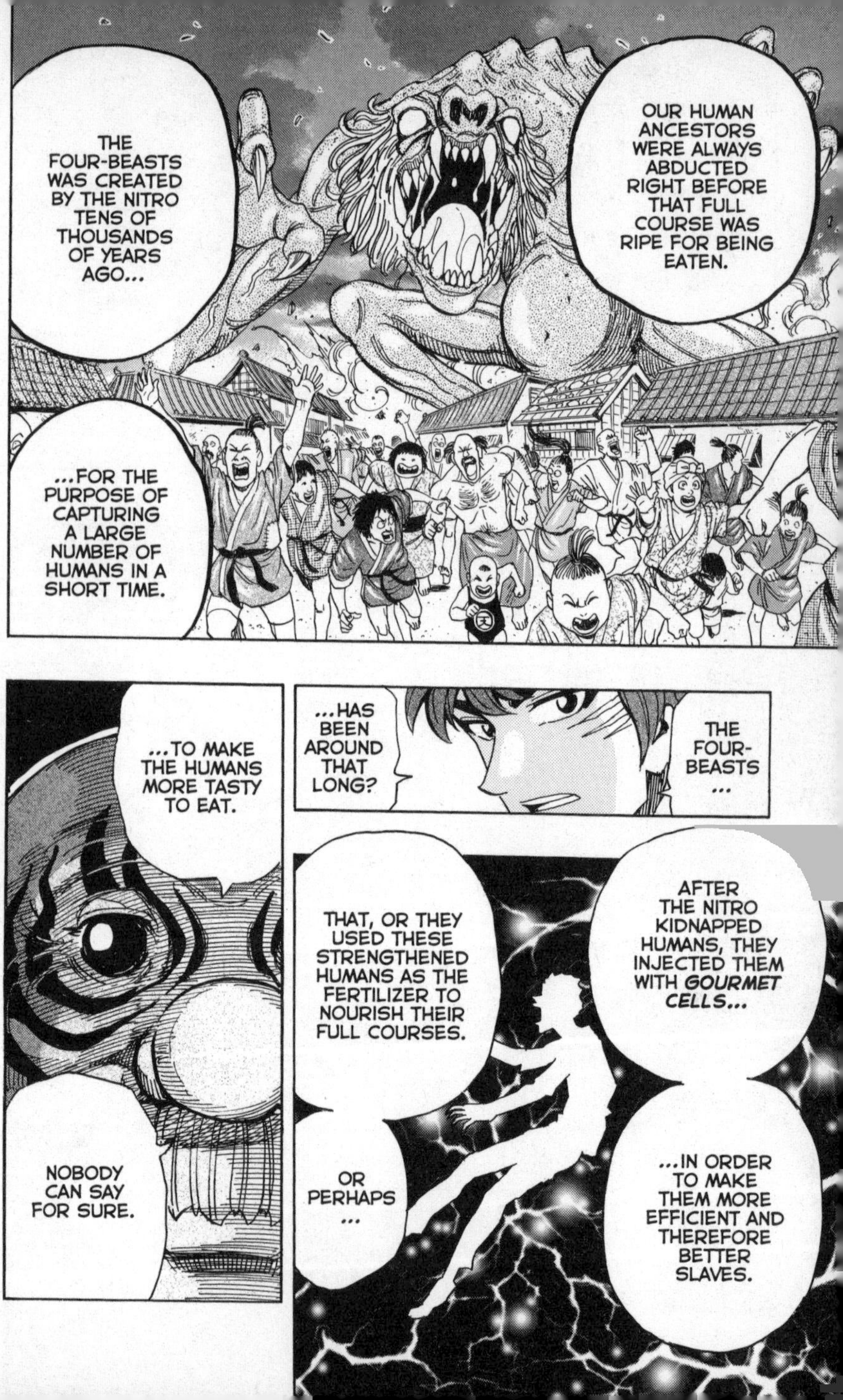
OUR HUMAN ANCESTORS WERE ALWAYS ABDUCTED RIGHT BEFORE THAT FULL COURSE WAS RIPE FOR BEING EATEN.
THE FOUR-BEASTS WAS CREATED BY THE NITRO TENS OF THOUSANDS OF YEARS AGO...
...FOR THE PURPOSE OF CAPTURING A LARGE NUMBER OF HUMANS IN A SHORT TIME.
THE FOUR-BEASTS...
...HAS BEEN AROUND THAT LONG?
AFTER THE NITRO KIDNAPPED HUMANS, THEY INJECTED THEM WITH *GOURMET CELLS*...
...IN ORDER TO MAKE THEM MORE EFFICIENT AND THEREFORE BETTER SLAVES.
THAT, OR THEY USED THESE STRENGTHENED HUMANS AS THE FERTILIZER TO NOURISH THEIR FULL COURSES.
OR PERHAPS...
...TO MAKE THE HUMANS MORE TASTY TO EAT.
NOBODY CAN SAY FOR SURE.

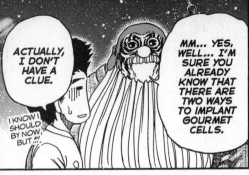

H... HOW DID THEY...
...IMPLANT THE GOURMET CELLS?
MM... YES, WELL... I'M SURE YOU ALREADY KNOW THAT THERE ARE TWO WAYS TO IMPLANT GOURMET CELLS.
ACTUALLY, I DON'T HAVE A CLUE.
I KNOW I SHOULD BY NOW, BUT...
1) INGESTION. BY EATING THE CELLS A LITTLE AT A TIME, THE BODY ADAPTS TO AND GROWS ACCUSTOMED TO THEM.
2) INJECTION. THE CELLS ARE DIRECTLY INJECTED INTO THE BODY.
THE MERIT TO THE FIRST METHOD, INGESTION, IS THAT IT'S SAFE.
THE DRAWBACK IS THAT IT TAKES TIME AND MORE OFTEN THAN NOT IT DOESN'T RESULT IN ADAPTATION.
THE MERIT TO THE SECOND METHOD, INJECTION, IS THAT ADAPTATION OCCURS QUICKLY.
THE DRAWBACK IS THAT IF THE HUMAN CAN'T ADAPT, THEY ARE OVERWHELMED BY THE GOURMET CELLS AND TURN INTO A MONSTER. IN THE WORST-CASE SCENARIO, THEY DIE.
...
A... AND THE ANCESTORS OF THE TOWN?
NATURALLY, THEY WERE THE LATTER.
!

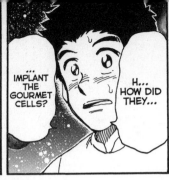

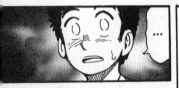

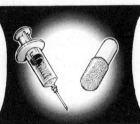

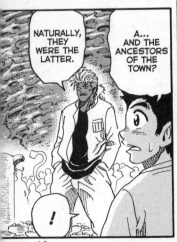

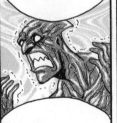

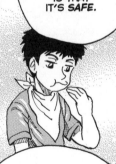

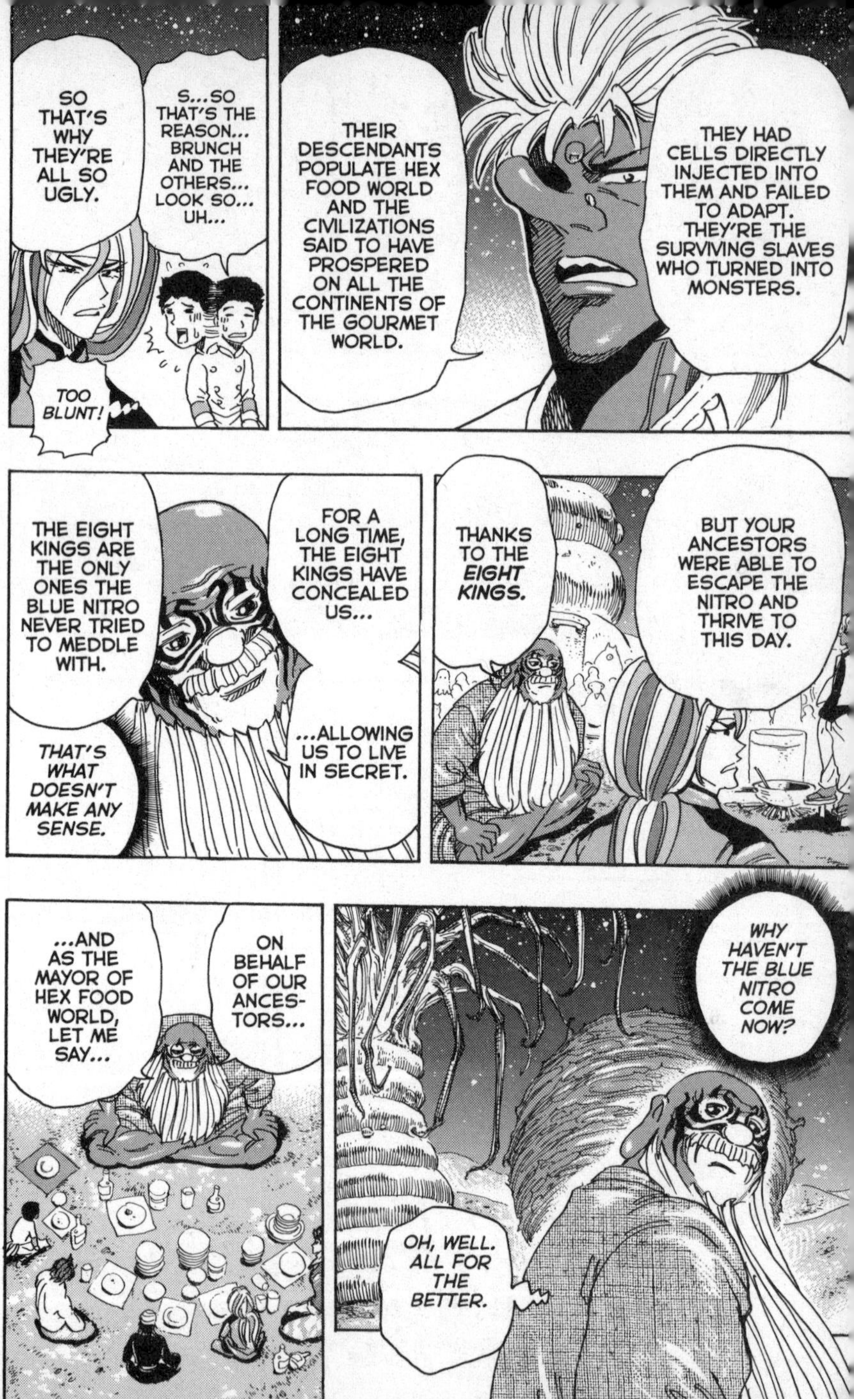
THEY HAD CELLS DIRECTLY INJECTED INTO THEM AND FAILED TO ADAPT. THEY'RE THE SURVIVING SLAVES WHO TURNED INTO MONSTERS.
THEIR DESCENDANTS POPULATE HEX FOOD WORLD AND THE CIVILIZATIONS SAID TO HAVE PROSPERED ON ALL THE CONTINENTS OF THE GOURMET WORLD.
S...SO THAT'S THE REASON... BRUNCH AND THE OTHERS... LOOK SO... UH...
SO THAT'S WHY THEY'RE ALL SO UGLY.
TOO BLUNT!
BUT YOUR ANCESTORS WERE ABLE TO ESCAPE THE NITRO AND THRIVE TO THIS DAY.
THANKS TO THE *EIGHT KINGS.*
FOR A LONG TIME, THE EIGHT KINGS HAVE CONCEALED US...
...ALLOWING US TO LIVE IN SECRET.
THE EIGHT KINGS ARE THE ONLY ONES THE BLUE NITRO NEVER TRIED TO MEDDLE WITH.
THAT'S WHAT DOESN'T MAKE ANY SENSE.
WHY HAVEN'T THE BLUE NITRO COME NOW?
OH, WELL. ALL FOR THE BETTER.
ON BEHALF OF OUR ANCES-TORS...
...AND AS THE MAYOR OF HEX FOOD WORLD, LET ME SAY...

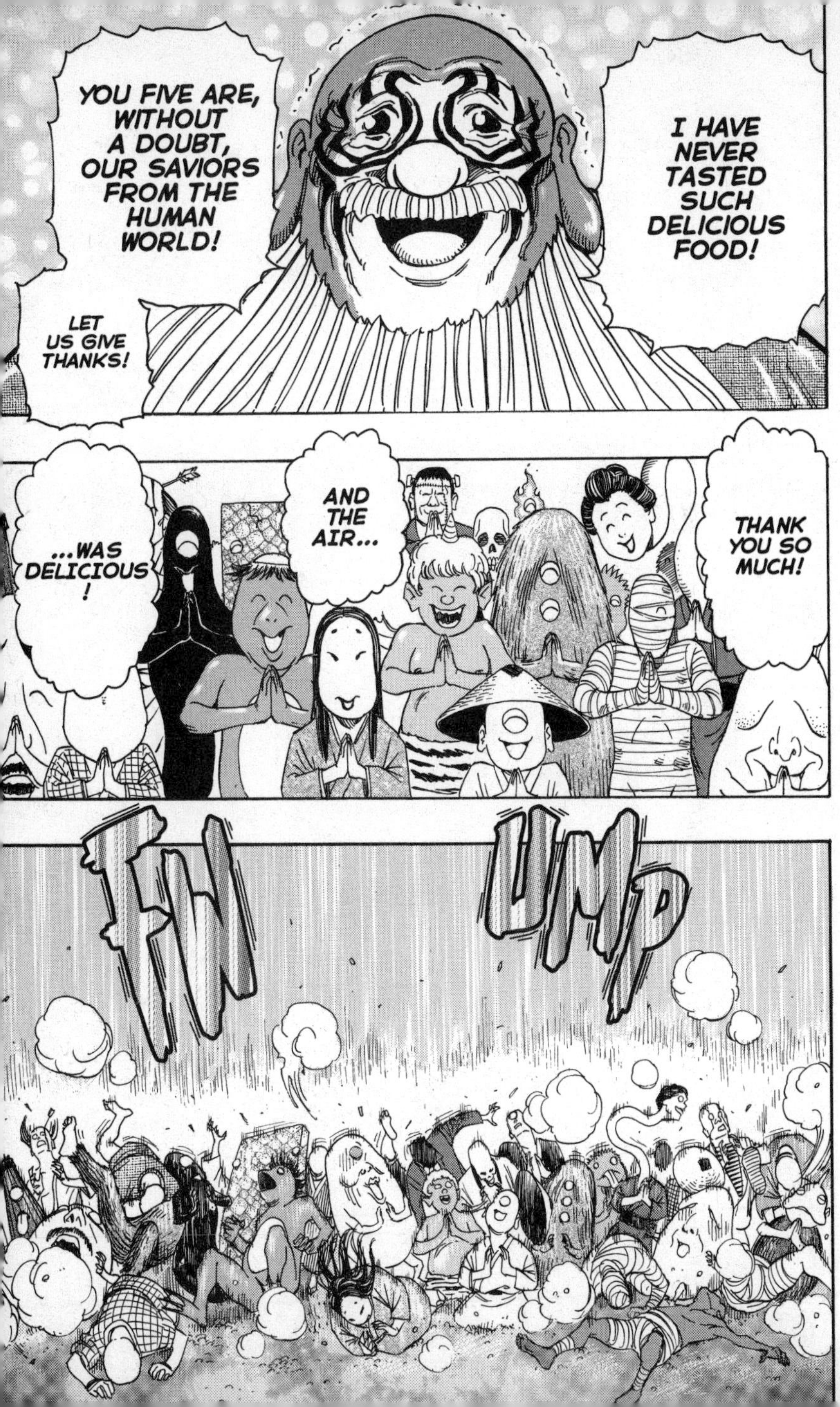
I HAVE NEVER TASTED SUCH DELICIOUS FOOD!
YOU FIVE ARE, WITHOUT A DOUBT, OUR SAVIORS FROM THE HUMAN WORLD!
LET US GIVE THANKS!
THANK YOU SO MUCH!
AND THE AIR...
...WAS DELICIOUS!
FWUMP

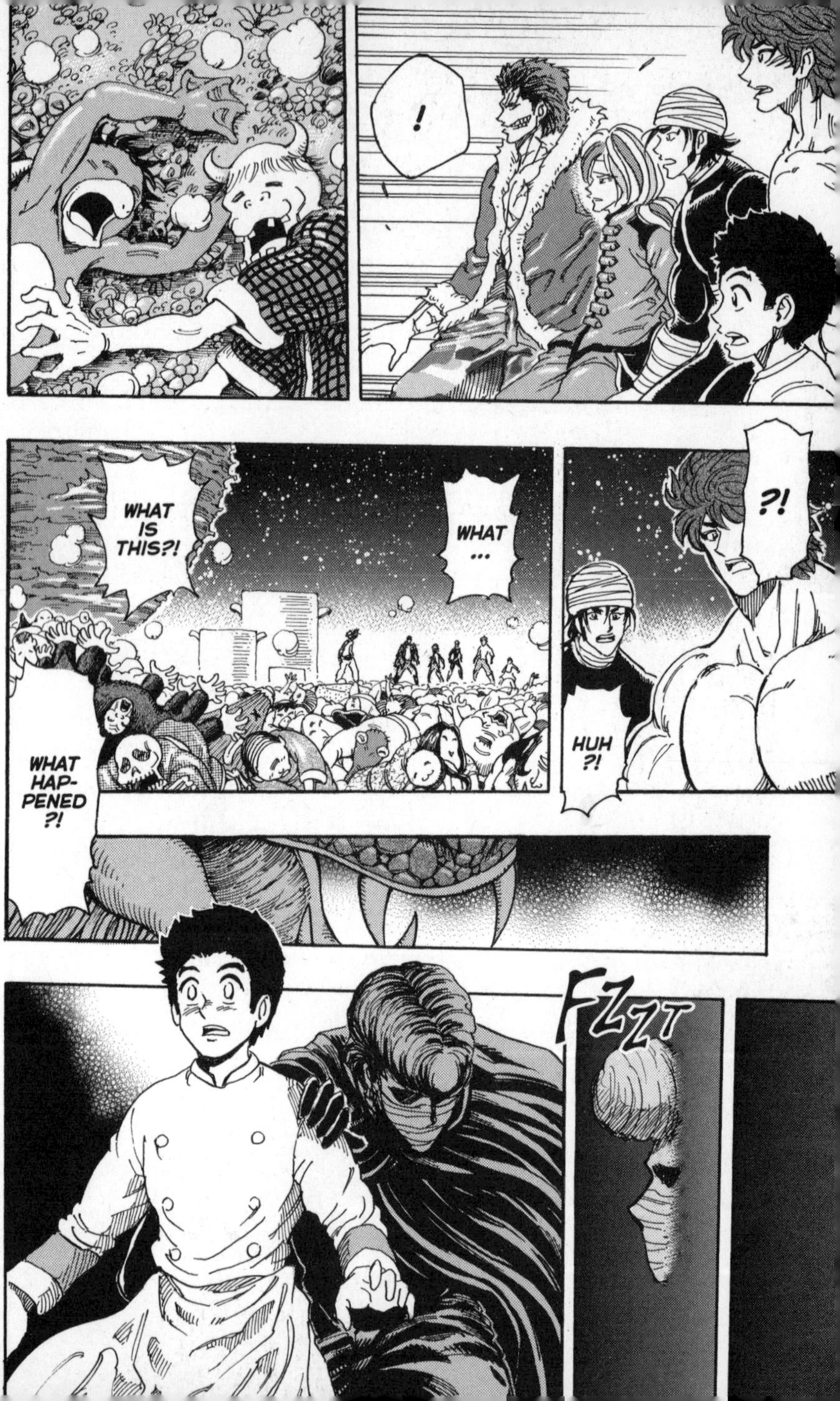
!
?!
HUH ?!
WHAT ...
WHAT IS THIS?!
WHAT HAP-PENED ?!
FZZT

BE A GOOD BOY...

...AND GO TO SLEEP.

THO

K

HUH?!

KOMA...

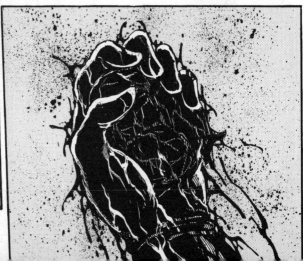

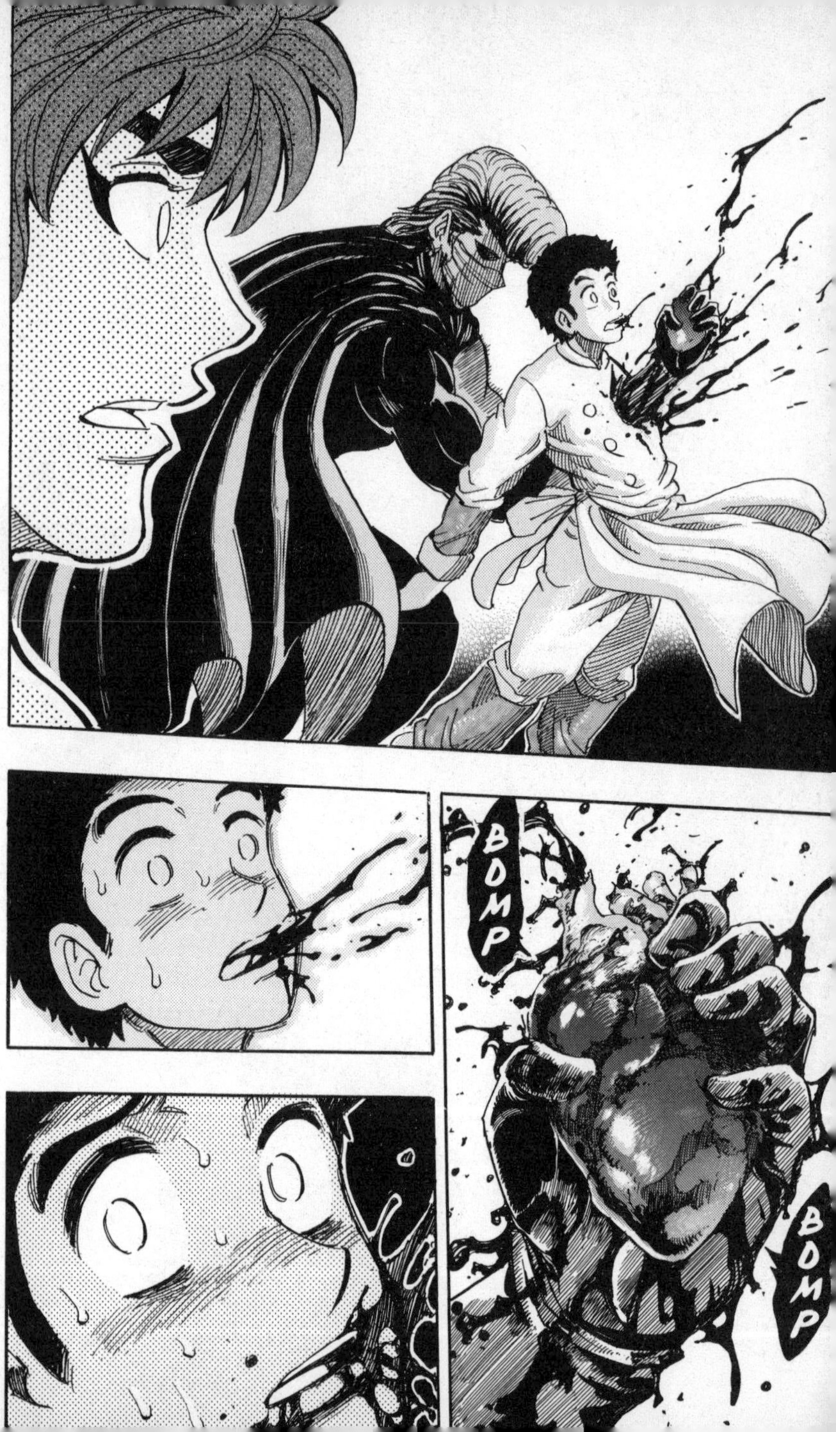
BDMP
BDMP

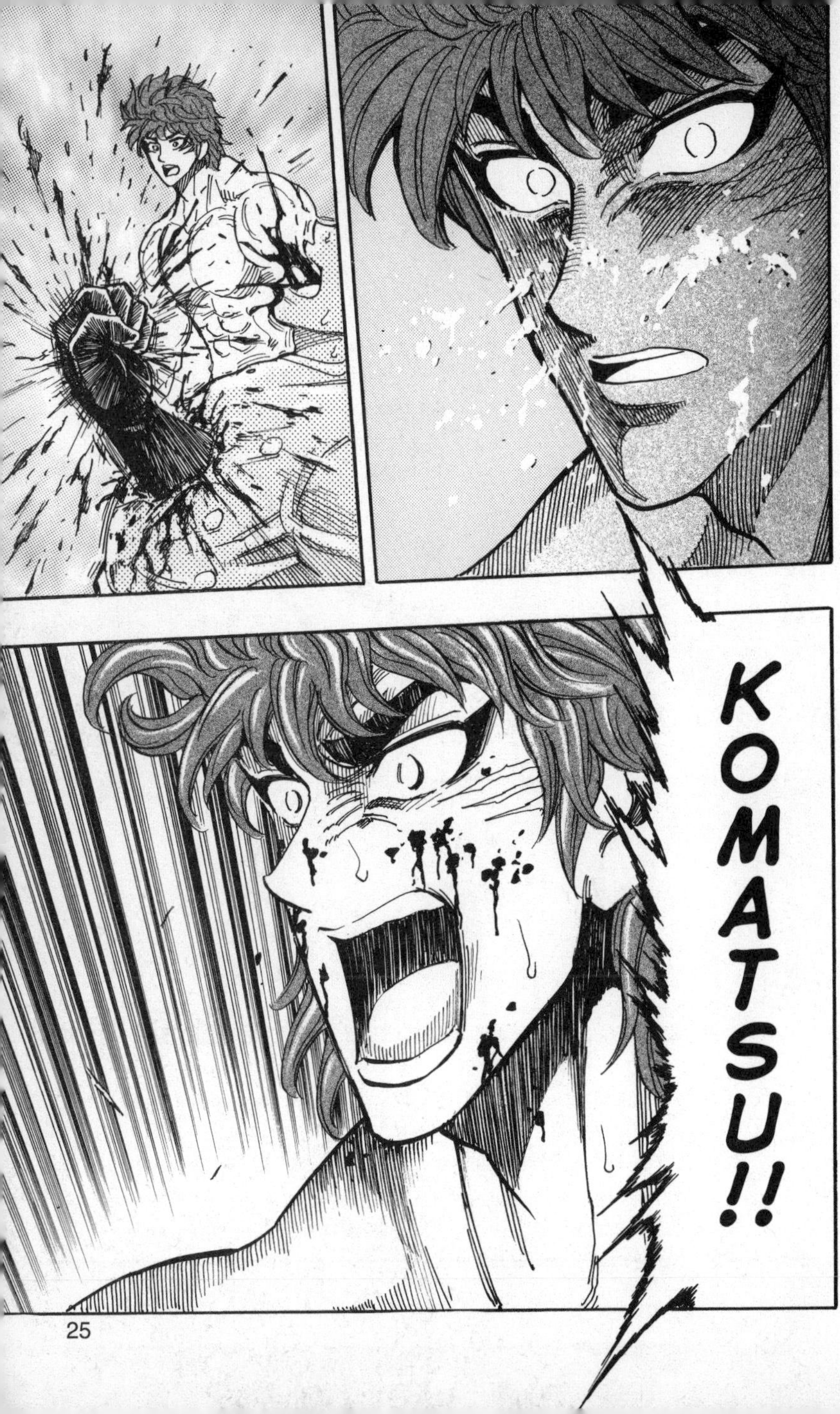
KOMATSU!!

TORIKO

GOURMET CHECKLIST
Vol. 317

BUTTER WALNUT
(FRUIT)

CAPTURE LEVEL: 17
(WHEN IT STILL EXISTED)
HABITAT: RESURRECTED BY
PUKIN
SIZE: 15 CM
HEIGHT: ---
WEIGHT: 1 KG
PRICE: 2,000,000 YEN PER NUT

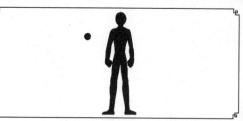

SCALE

A PHANTOM HIGH-CALORIE INGREDIENT THAT WAS REVIVED BY GOURMET REVIVER PUKIN. SINCE IT CAN MOVE FREELY WITH ITS LEGLIKE ROOTS, IT IS DIFFICULT TO CAPTURE, MAKING IT VERY EXPENSIVE. IT HAS A HARD SHELL, BUT ONCE HEATED IT WILL MELT AWAY SO YOU CAN EAT THE MEAT. IF A REGULAR PERSON EATS JUST ONE OF THESE GUYS, THEY CAN GO TEN DAYS WITHOUT HAVING TO EAT ANYTHING ELSE-- THAT'S HOW NUTRITIONALLY DENSE THIS INGREDIENT IS.

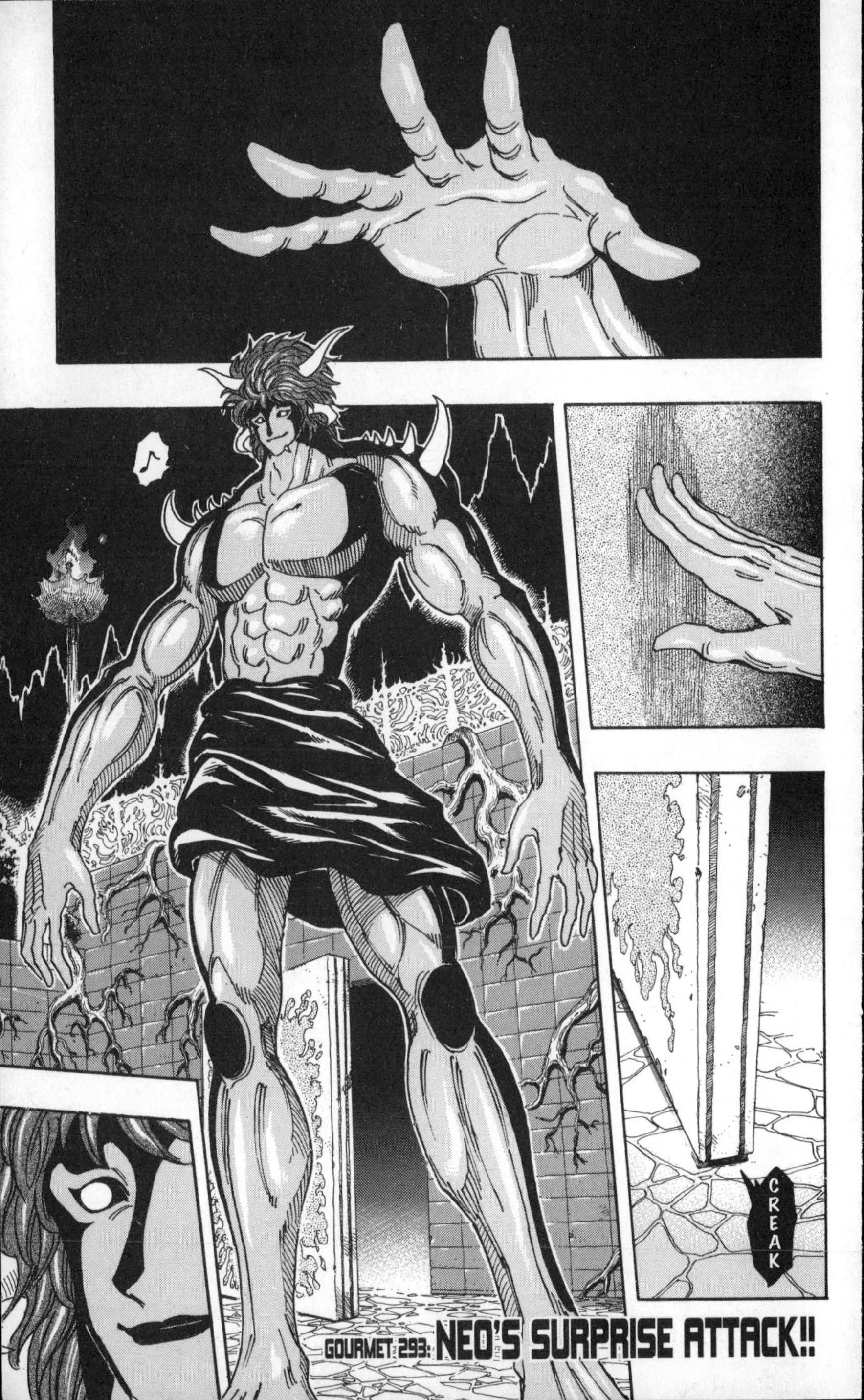

♪
CREAK
GOURMET 293: NEO'S SURPRISE ATTACK!!

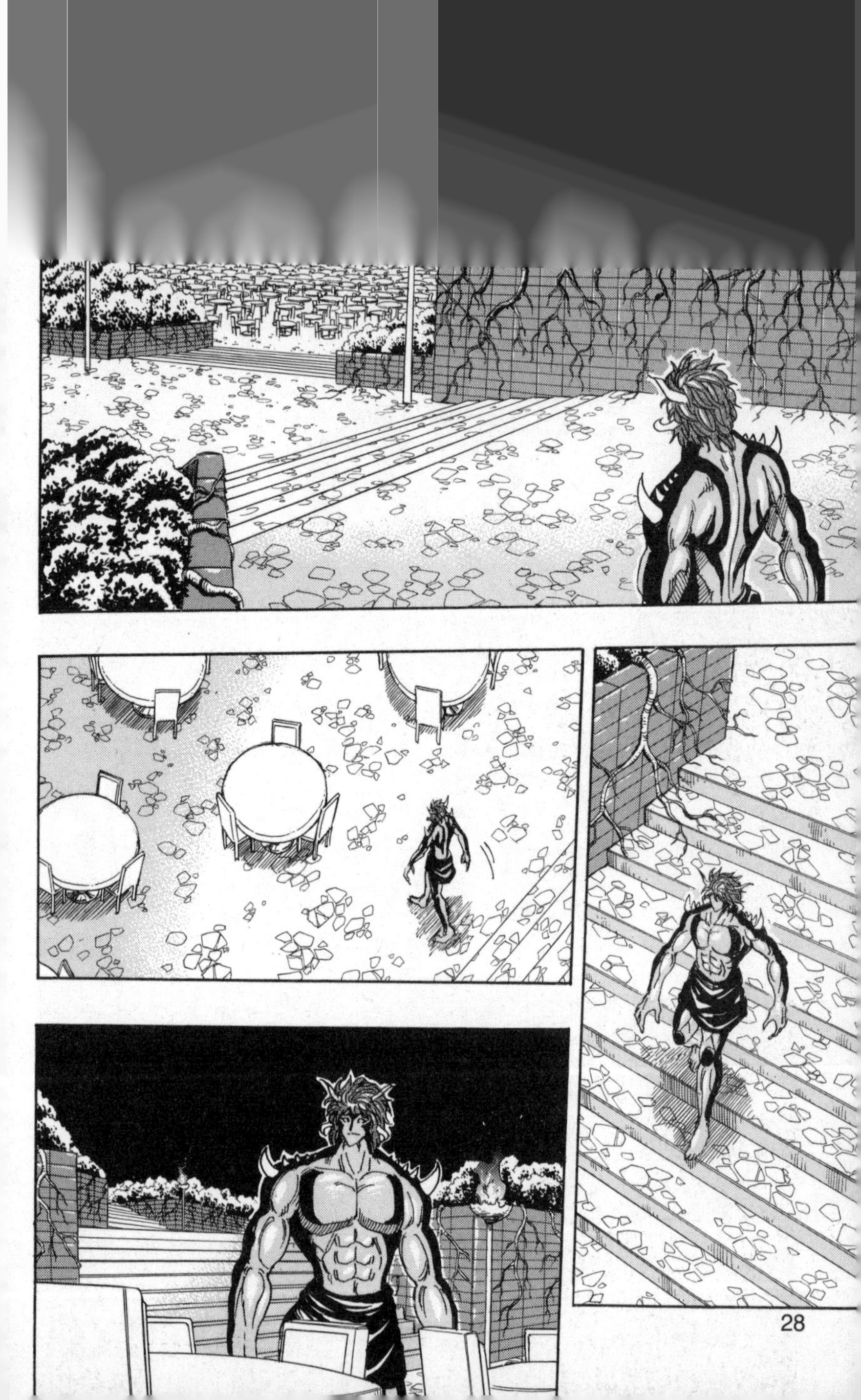

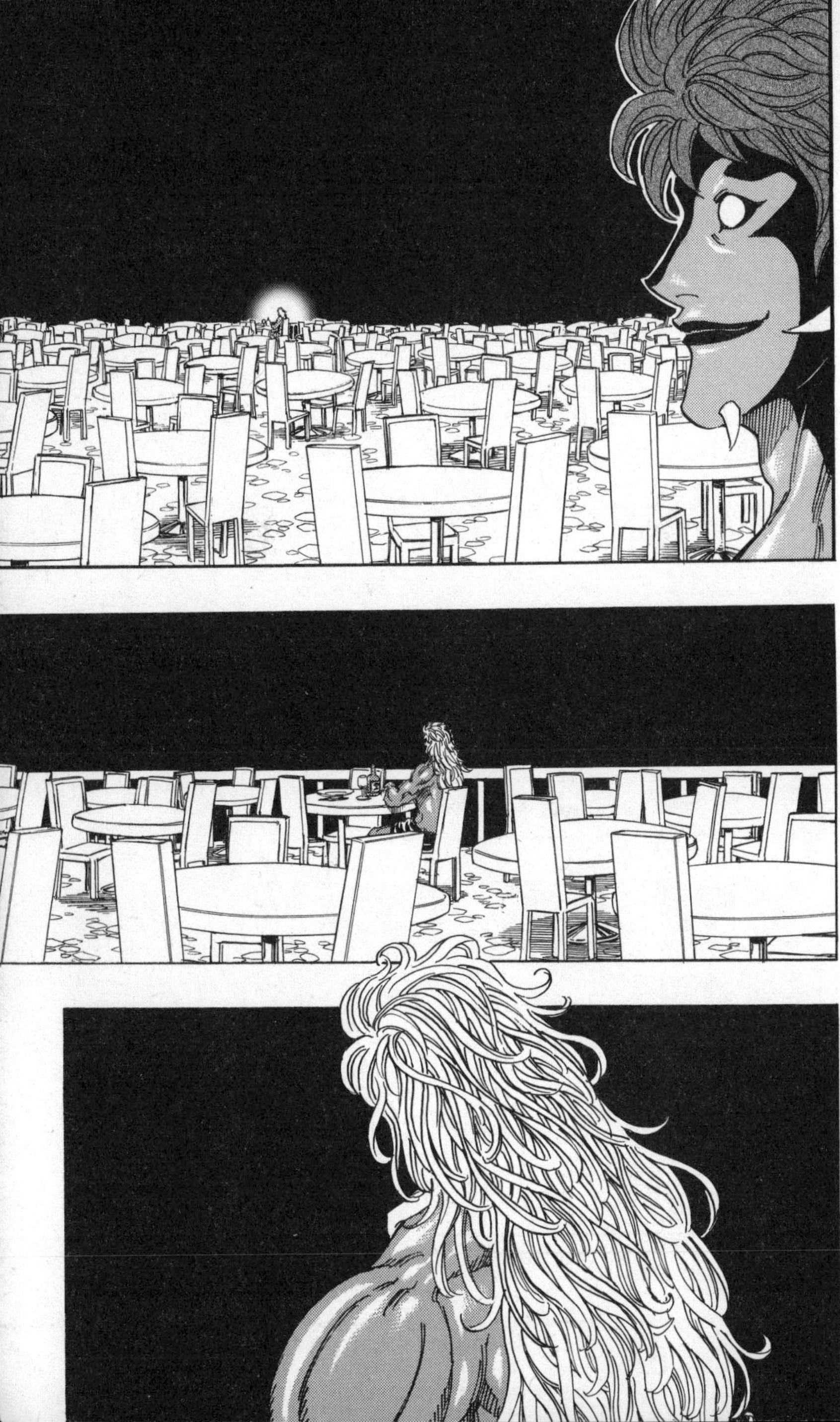

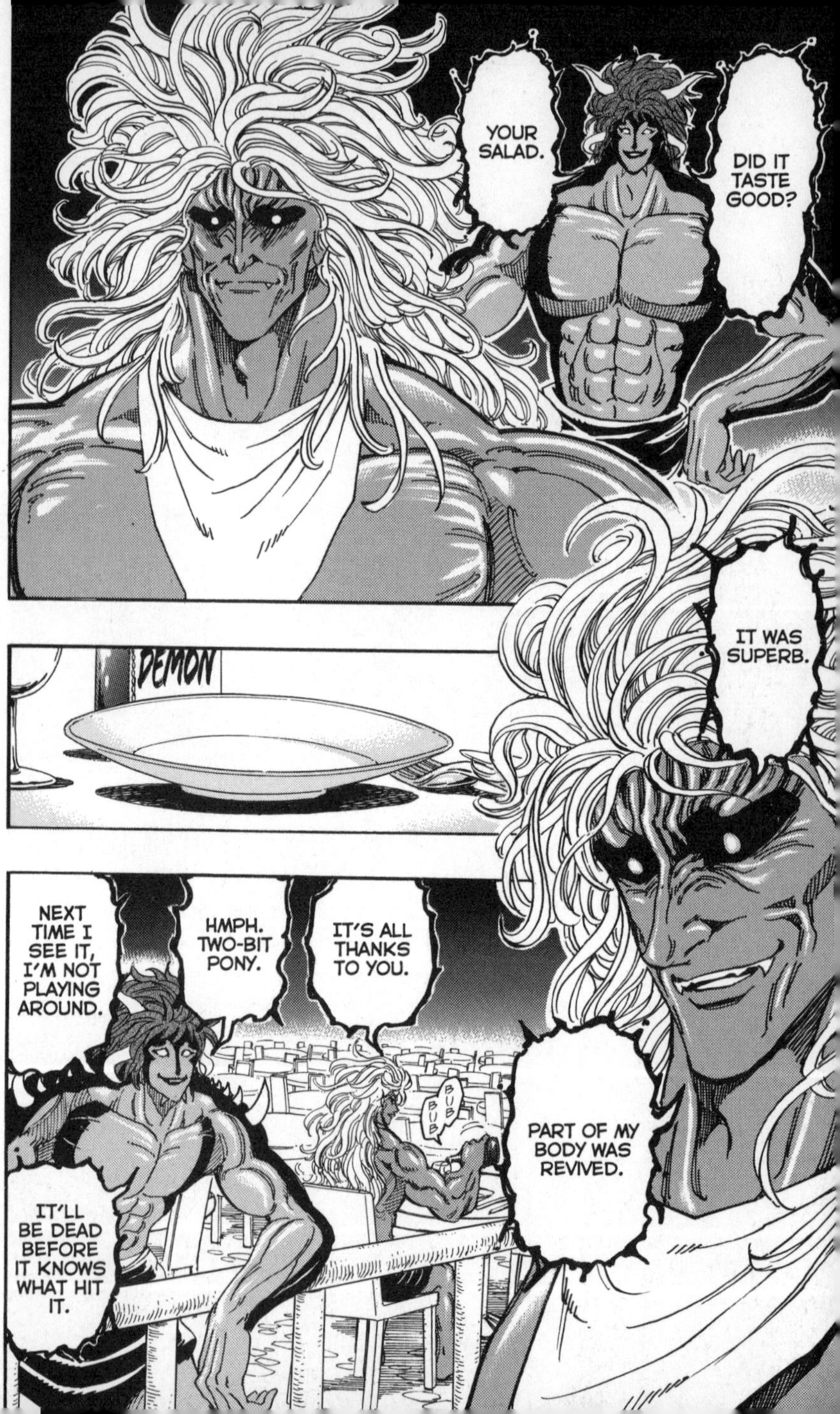
DID IT TASTE GOOD?
YOUR SALAD.
IT WAS SUPERB.
PART OF MY BODY WAS REVIVED.
DEMON
IT'S ALL THANKS TO YOU.
BUB BUB BUB
HMPH. TWO-BIT PONY.
NEXT TIME I SEE IT, I'M NOT PLAYING AROUND.
IT'LL BE DEAD BEFORE IT KNOWS WHAT HIT IT.

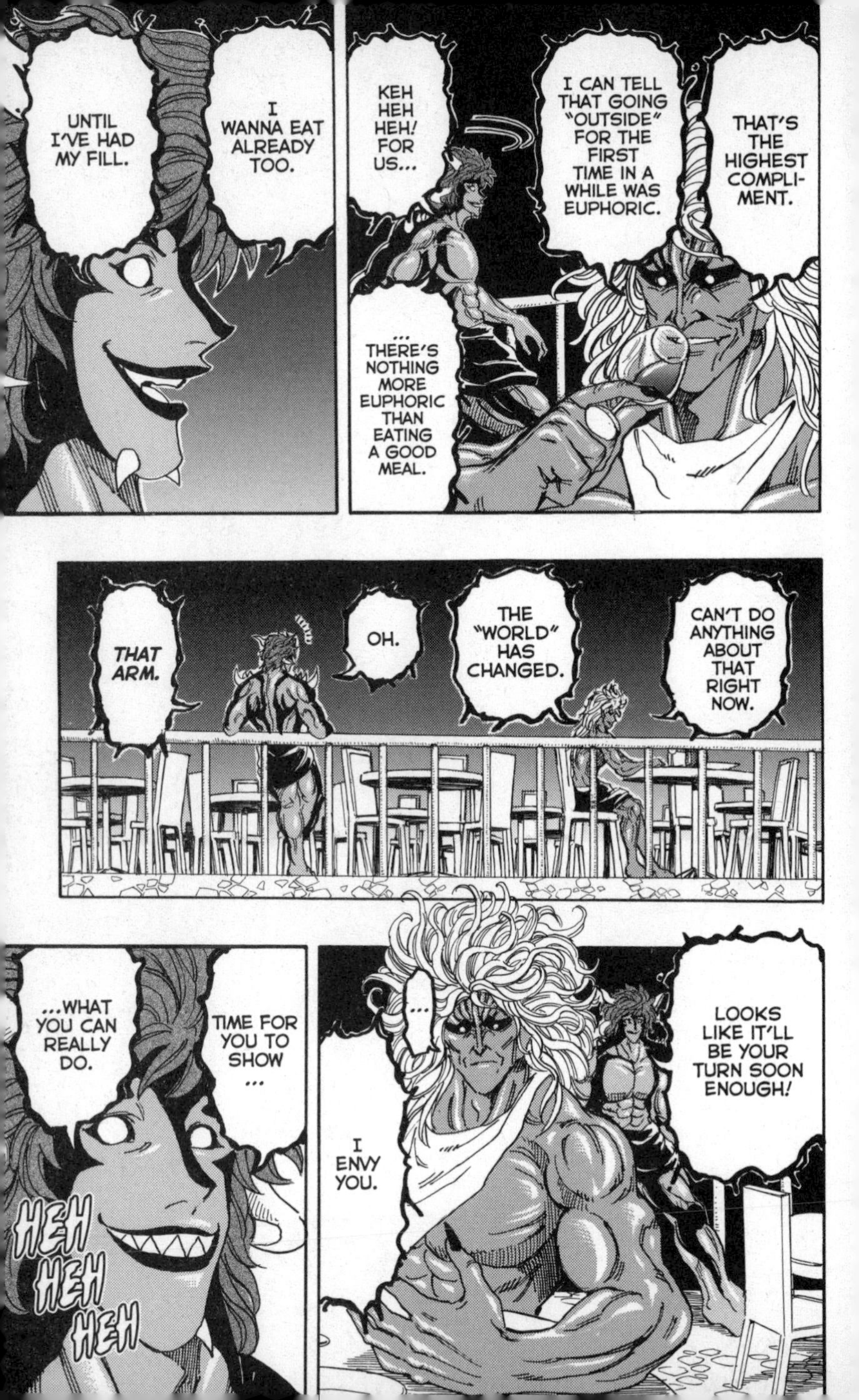
THAT'S THE HIGHEST COMPLIMENT.
I CAN TELL THAT GOING "OUTSIDE" FOR THE FIRST TIME IN A WHILE WAS EUPHORIC.
KEH HEH HEH! FOR US...
...THERE'S NOTHING MORE EUPHORIC THAN EATING A GOOD MEAL.
I WANNA EAT ALREADY TOO.
UNTIL I'VE HAD MY FILL.
CAN'T DO ANYTHING ABOUT THAT RIGHT NOW.
THE "WORLD" HAS CHANGED.
OH.
THAT ARM.
LOOKS LIKE IT'LL BE YOUR TURN SOON ENOUGH!
...
I ENVY YOU.
TIME FOR YOU TO SHOW...
...WHAT YOU CAN REALLY DO.
HEH HEH HEH

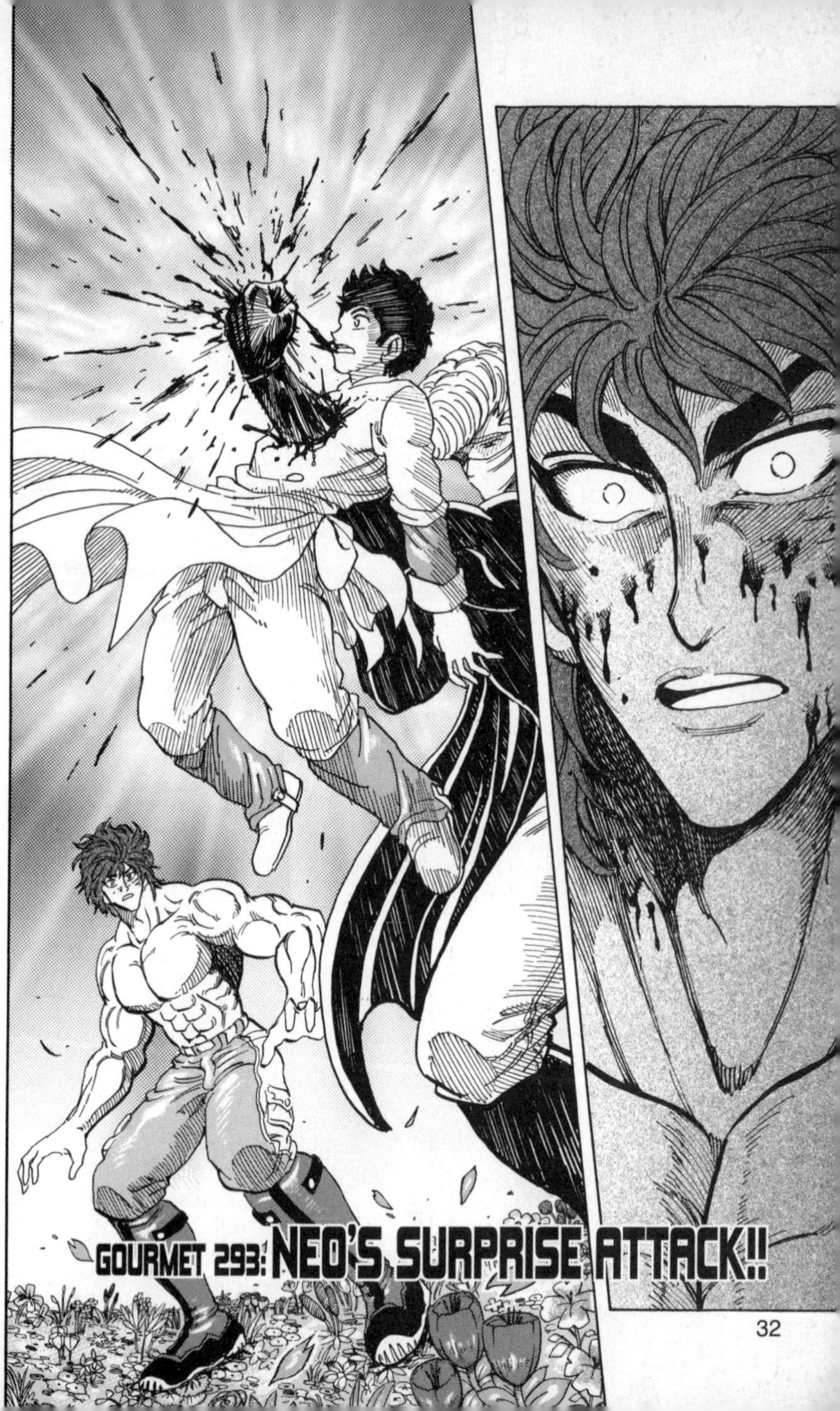
GOURMET 293: NEO'S SURPRISE ATTACK!!

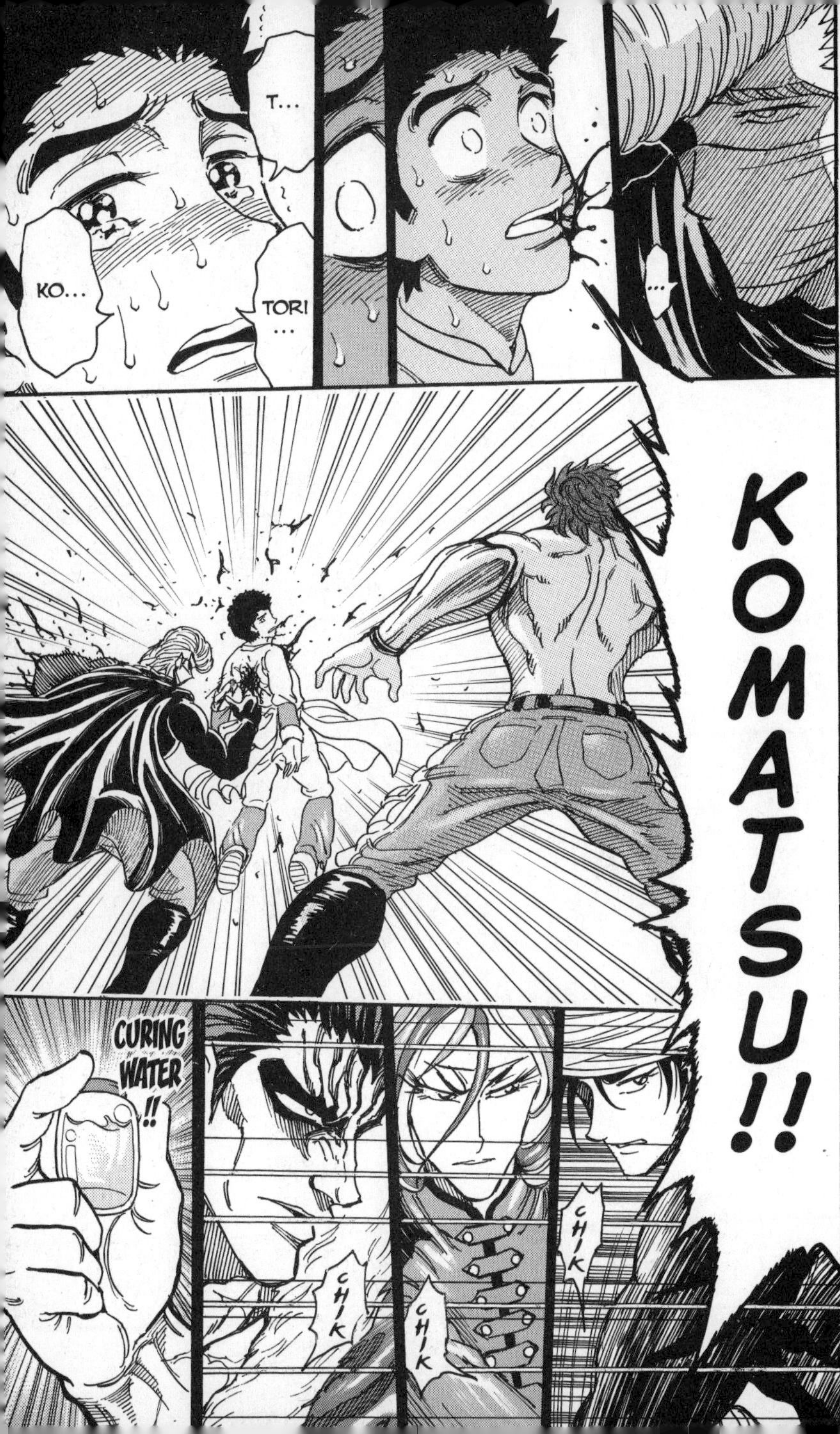
...
T...
TORI ...
KO...
KOMATSU!!
CHIK
CHIK
CHIK
CURING WATER!!

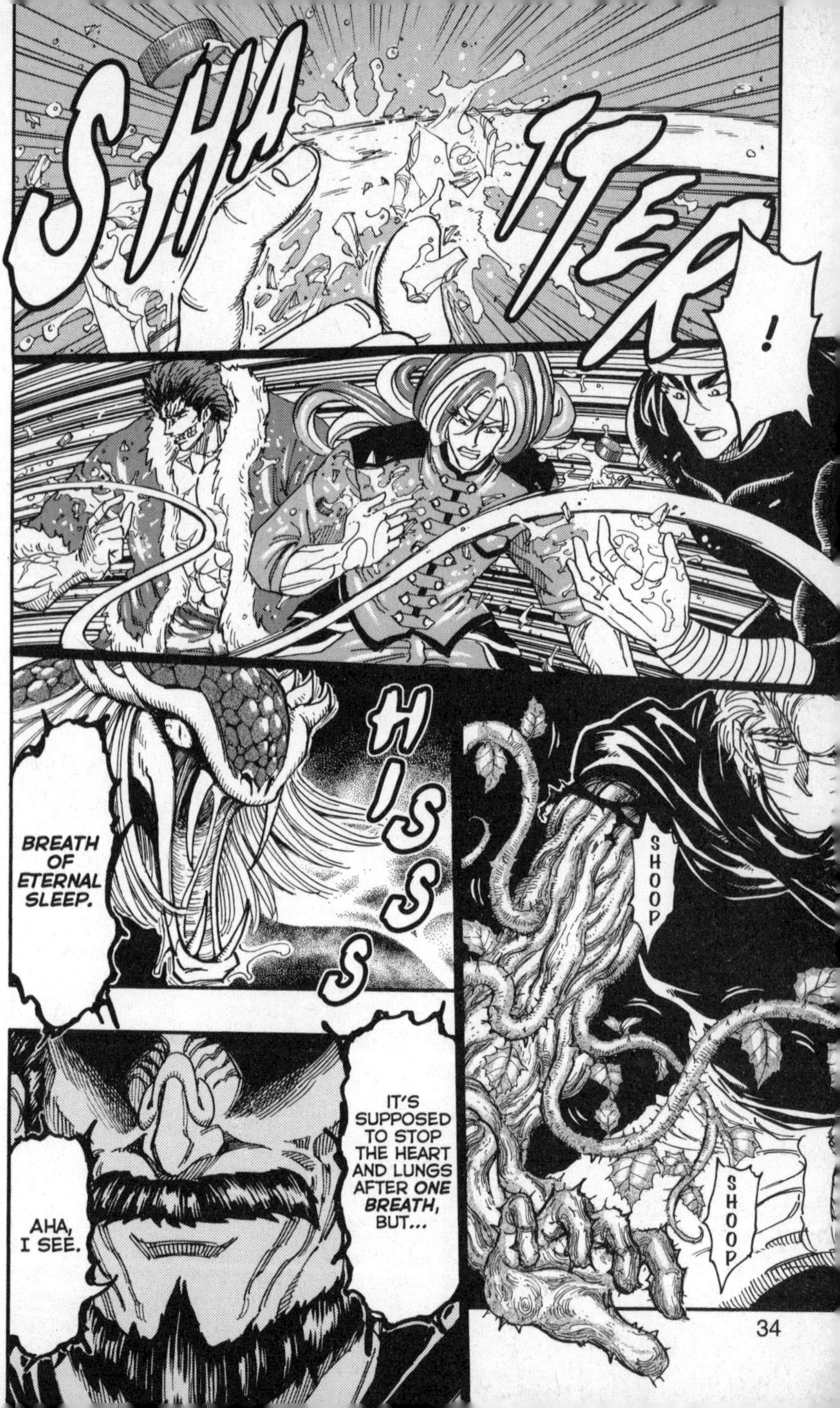
SHATTER
!
SHOOP
SHOOP
HISSS
BREATH OF ETERNAL SLEEP.
IT'S SUPPOSED TO STOP THE HEART AND LUNGS AFTER *ONE BREATH*, BUT...
AHA, I SEE.

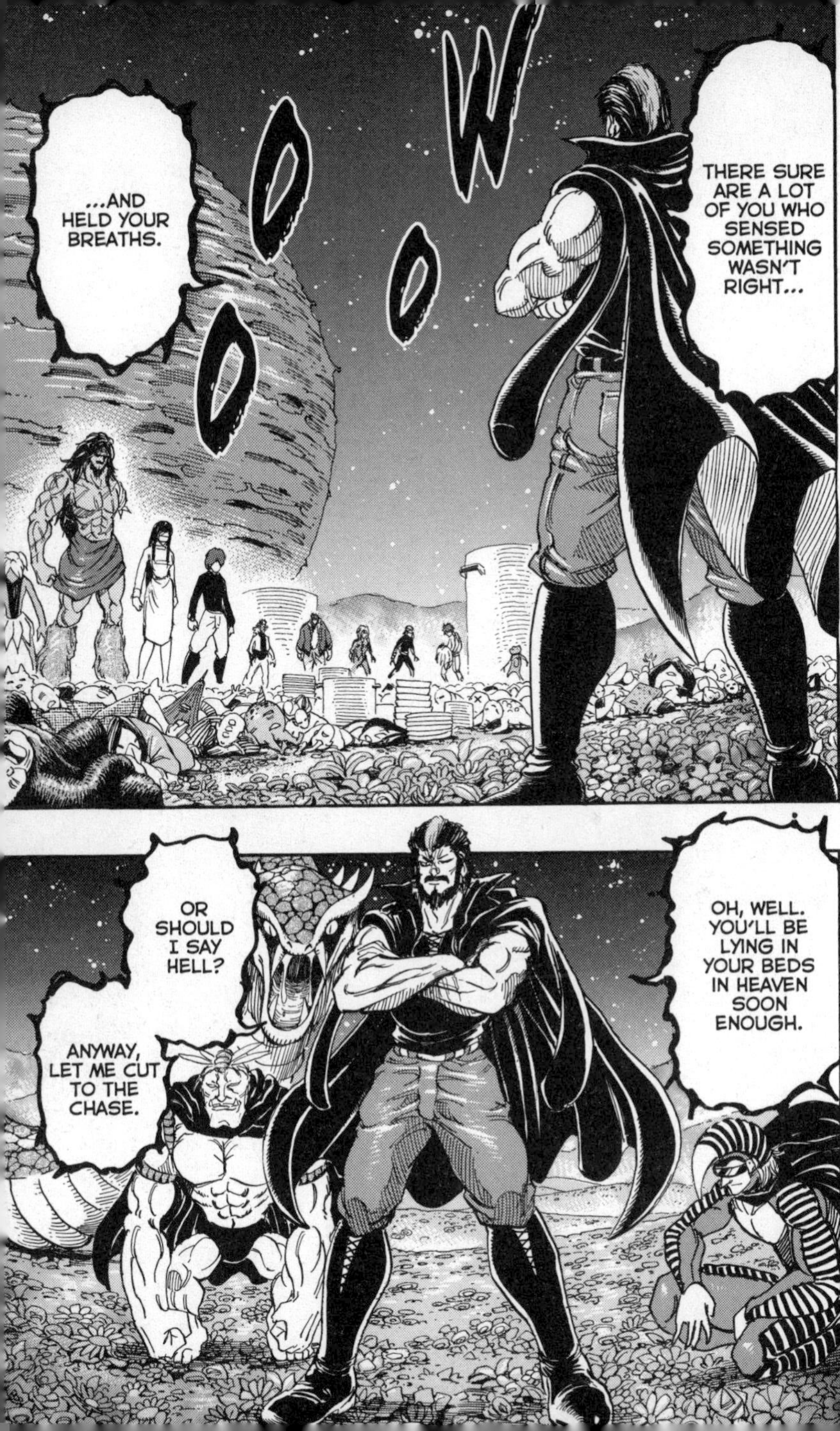
THERE SURE ARE A LOT OF YOU WHO SENSED SOMETHING WASN'T RIGHT...
...AND HELD YOUR BREATHS.
OH, WELL. YOU'LL BE LYING IN YOUR BEDS IN HEAVEN SOON ENOUGH.
OR SHOULD I SAY HELL?
ANYWAY, LET ME CUT TO THE CHASE.

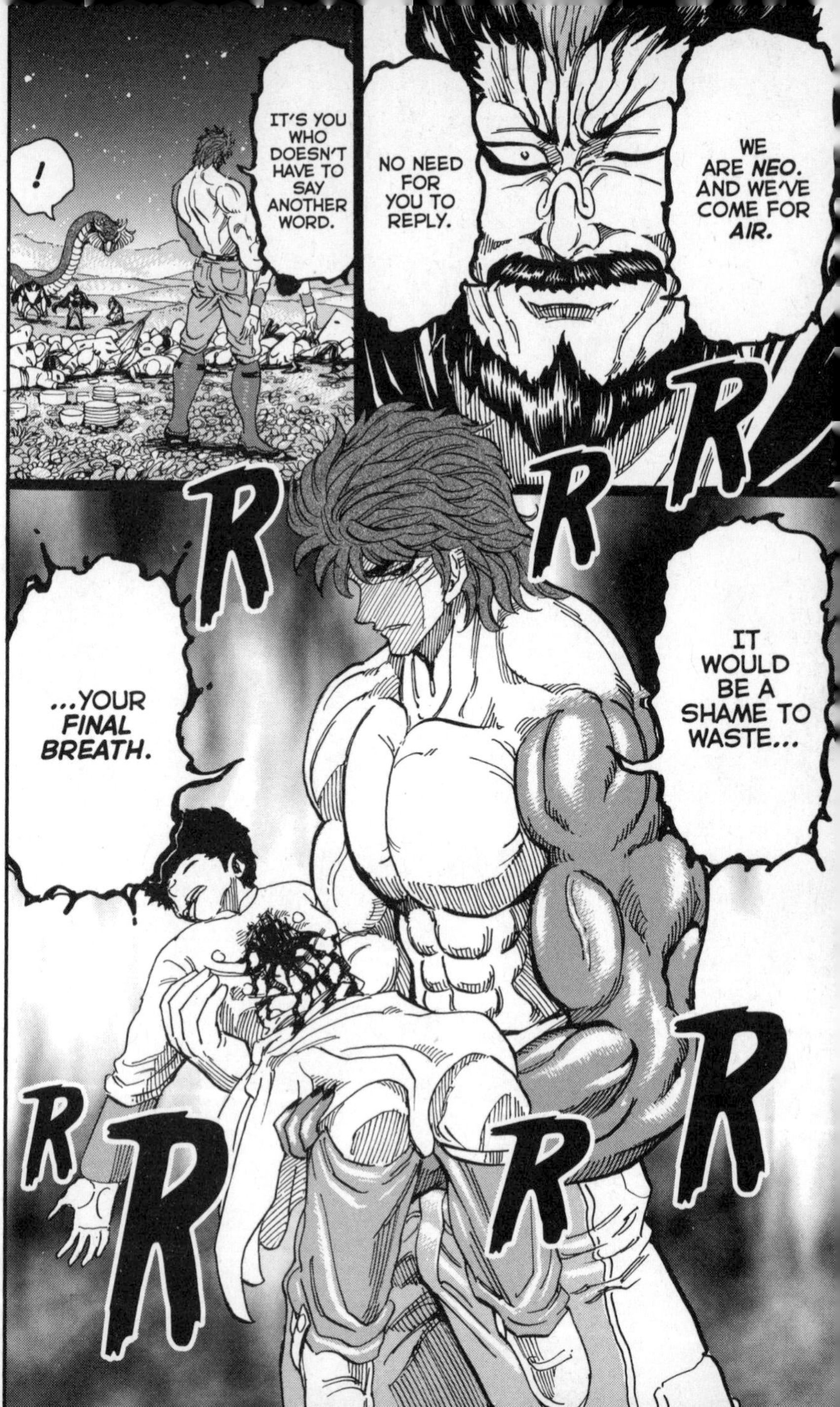
WE ARE NEO. AND WE'VE COME FOR AIR.
NO NEED FOR YOU TO REPLY.
IT'S YOU WHO DOESN'T HAVE TO SAY ANOTHER WORD.
!
RRR
IT WOULD BE A SHAME TO WASTE...
...YOUR FINAL BREATH.
RRRR

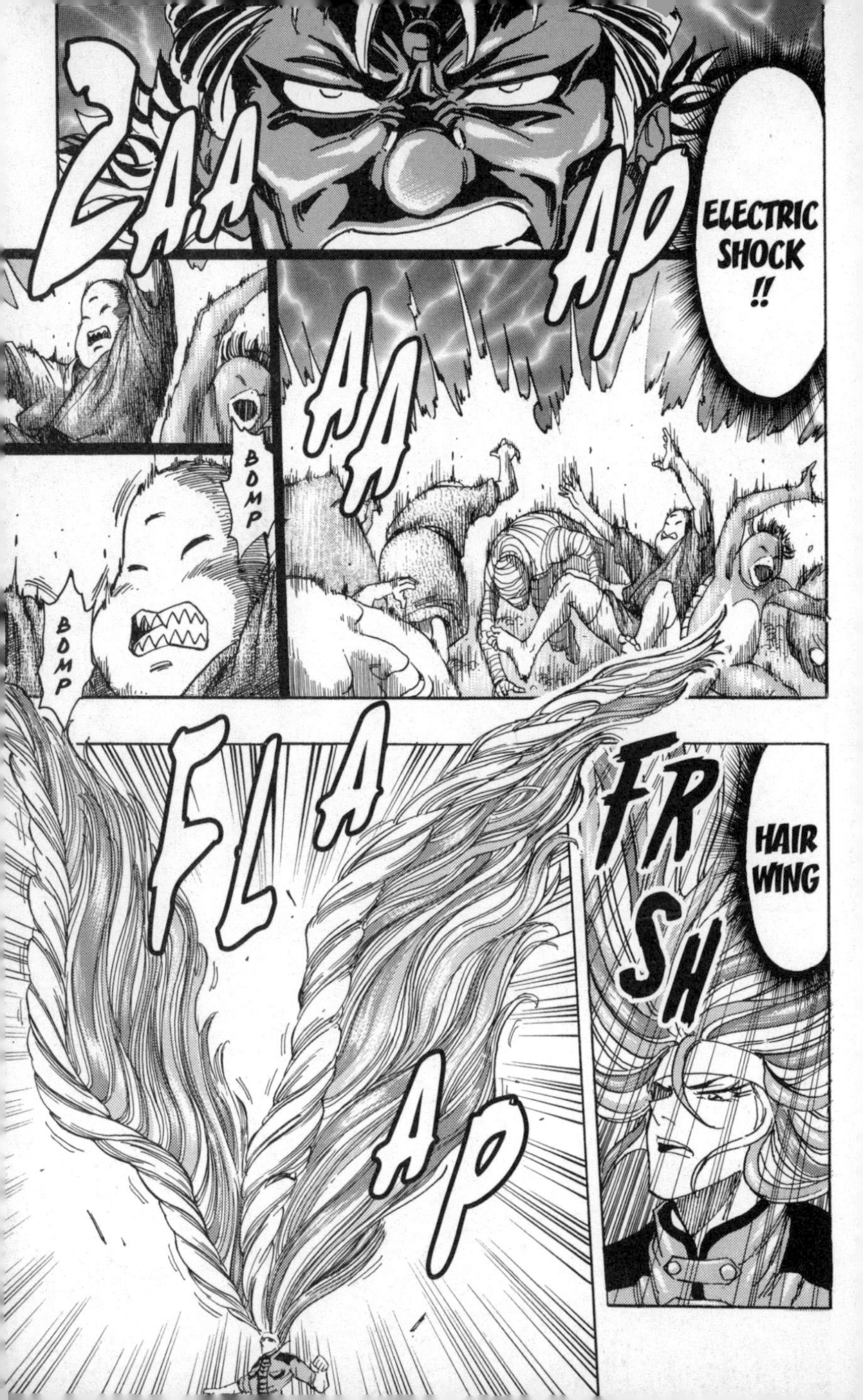
ELECTRIC SHOCK!!
ZAAAAAP
BOMP BOMP
HAIR WING
FRSH
FLAAP

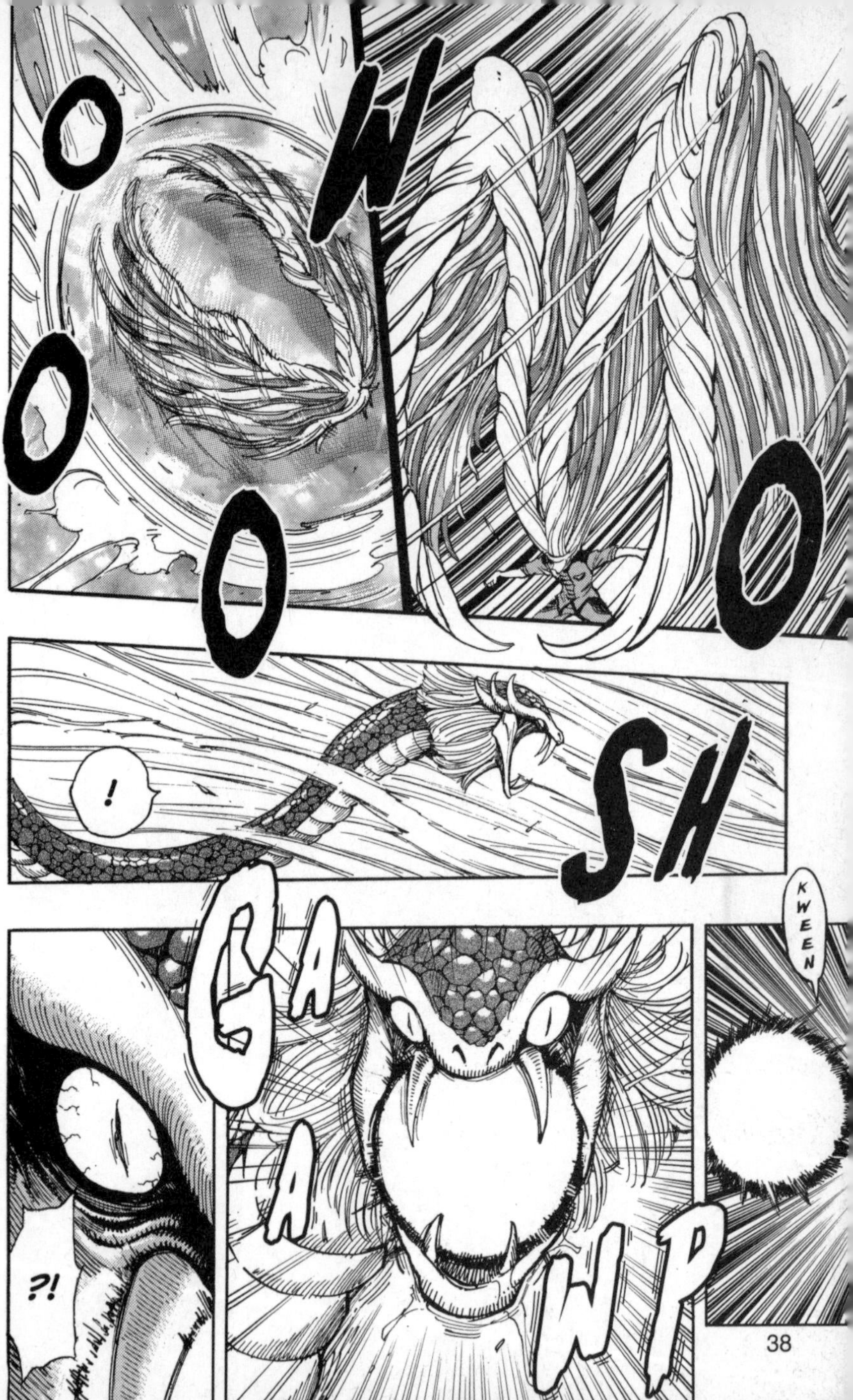

W
O
O
O
O
SH
!
KWEEN
GA
A
WP
?!

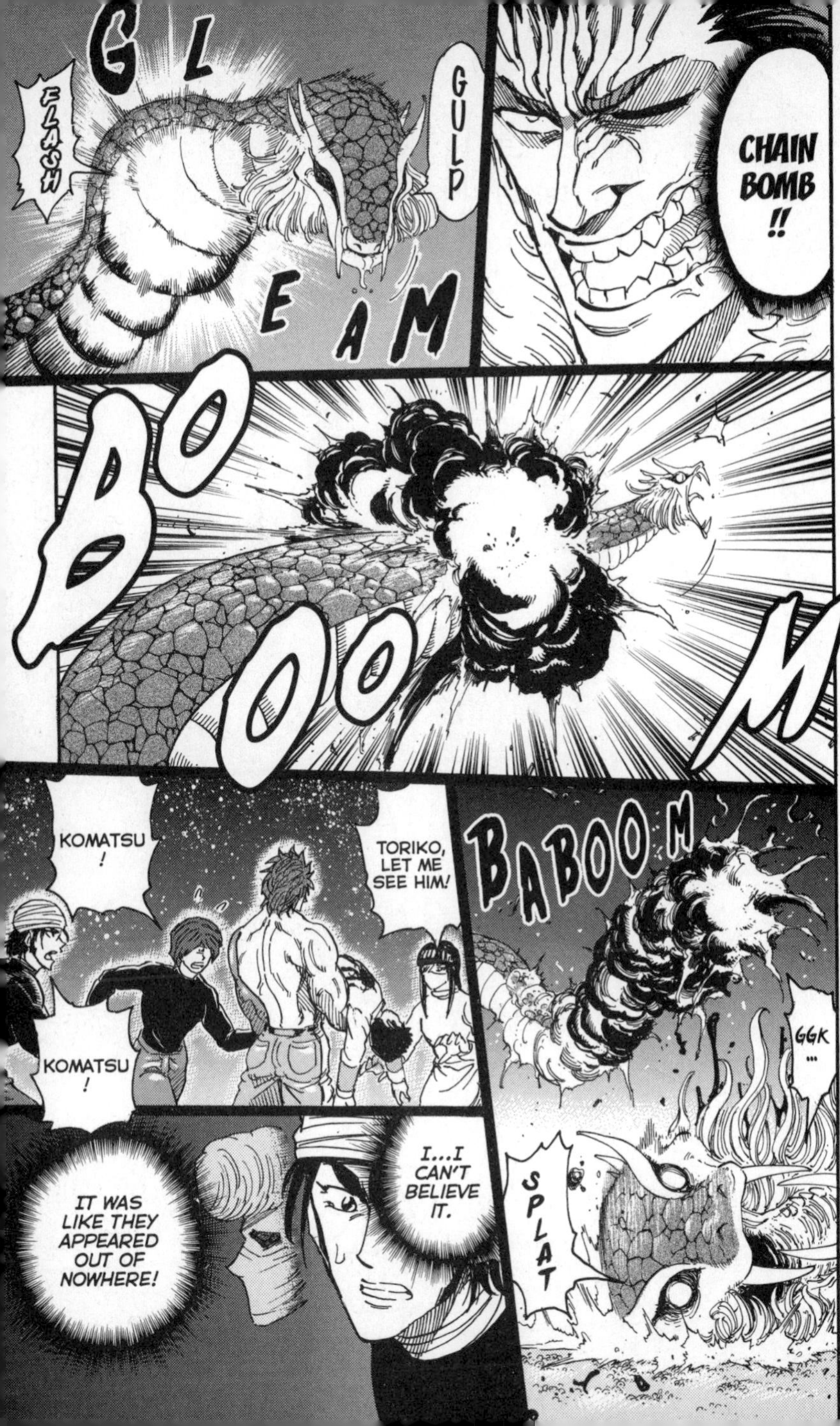
CHAIN BOMB!!
GULP
GLEAM
FLASH
BOOOOM
BABOOM
GGK...
SPLAT
TORIKO, LET ME SEE HIM!
KOMATSU!
KOMATSU!
I...I CAN'T BELIEVE IT.
IT WAS LIKE THEY APPEARED OUT OF NOWHERE!

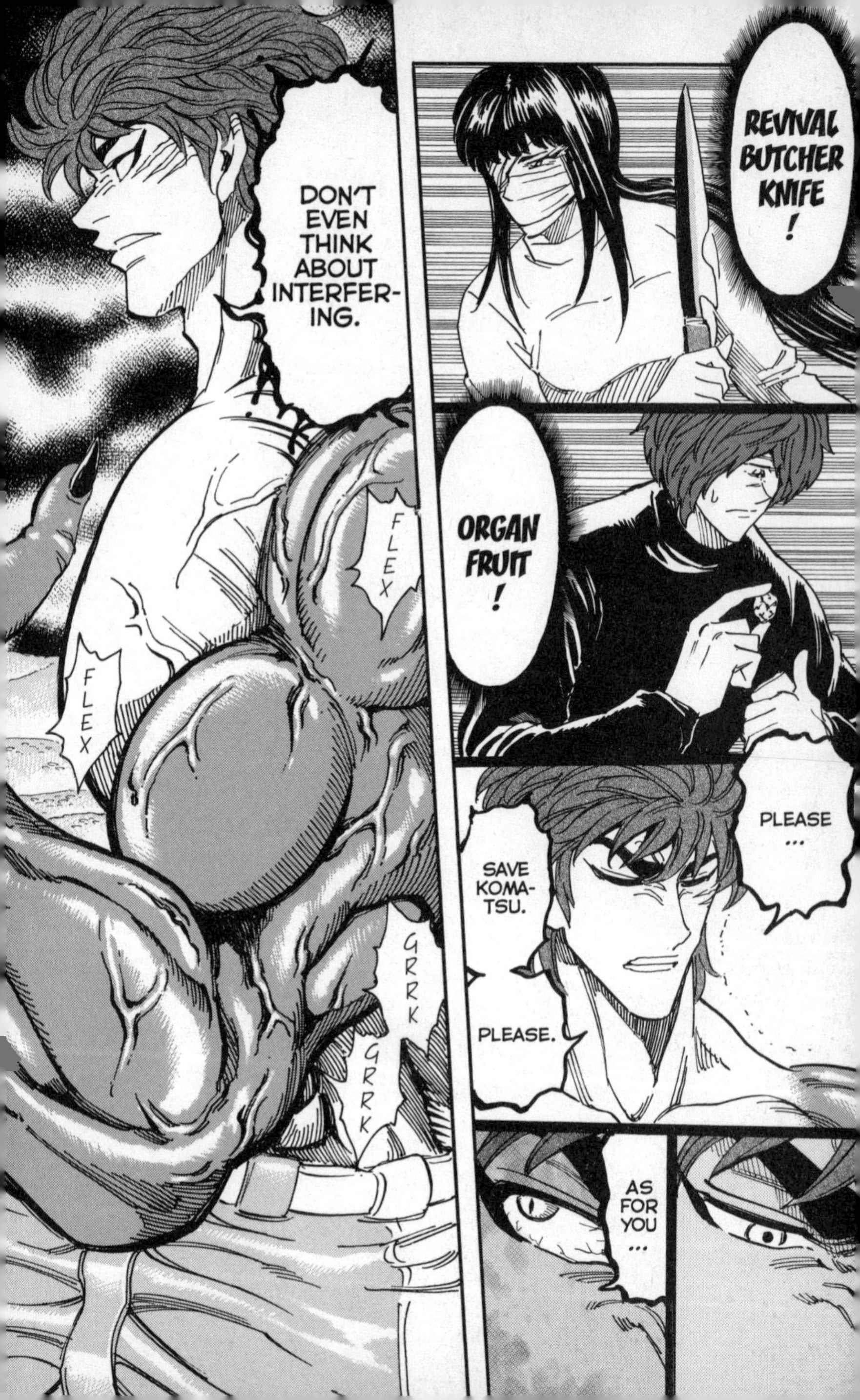
REVIVAL BUTCHER KNIFE!
ORGAN FRUIT!
PLEASE...
SAVE KOMATSU.
PLEASE.
AS FOR YOU...
DON'T EVEN THINK ABOUT INTERFERING.
FLEX
FLEX
GRRK
GRRK

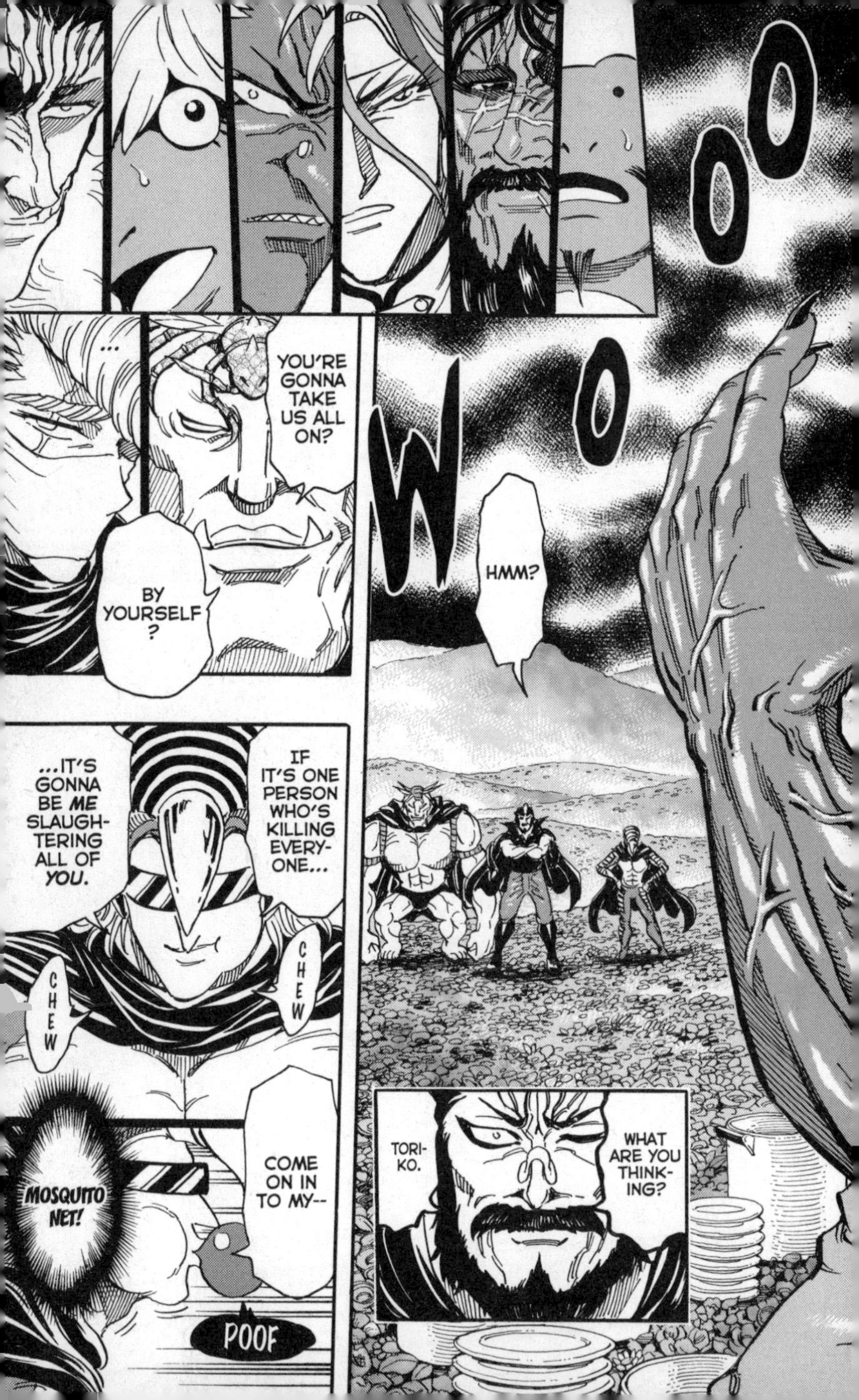
WOOOO
HMM?
...
YOU'RE GONNA TAKE US ALL ON?
BY YOURSELF?
IF IT'S ONE PERSON WHO'S KILLING EVERYONE...
...IT'S GONNA BE *ME* SLAUGHTERING ALL OF *YOU*.
CHEW
CHEW
WHAT ARE YOU THINKING?
TORI-KO.
COME ON IN TO MY--
MOSQUITO NET!
POOF

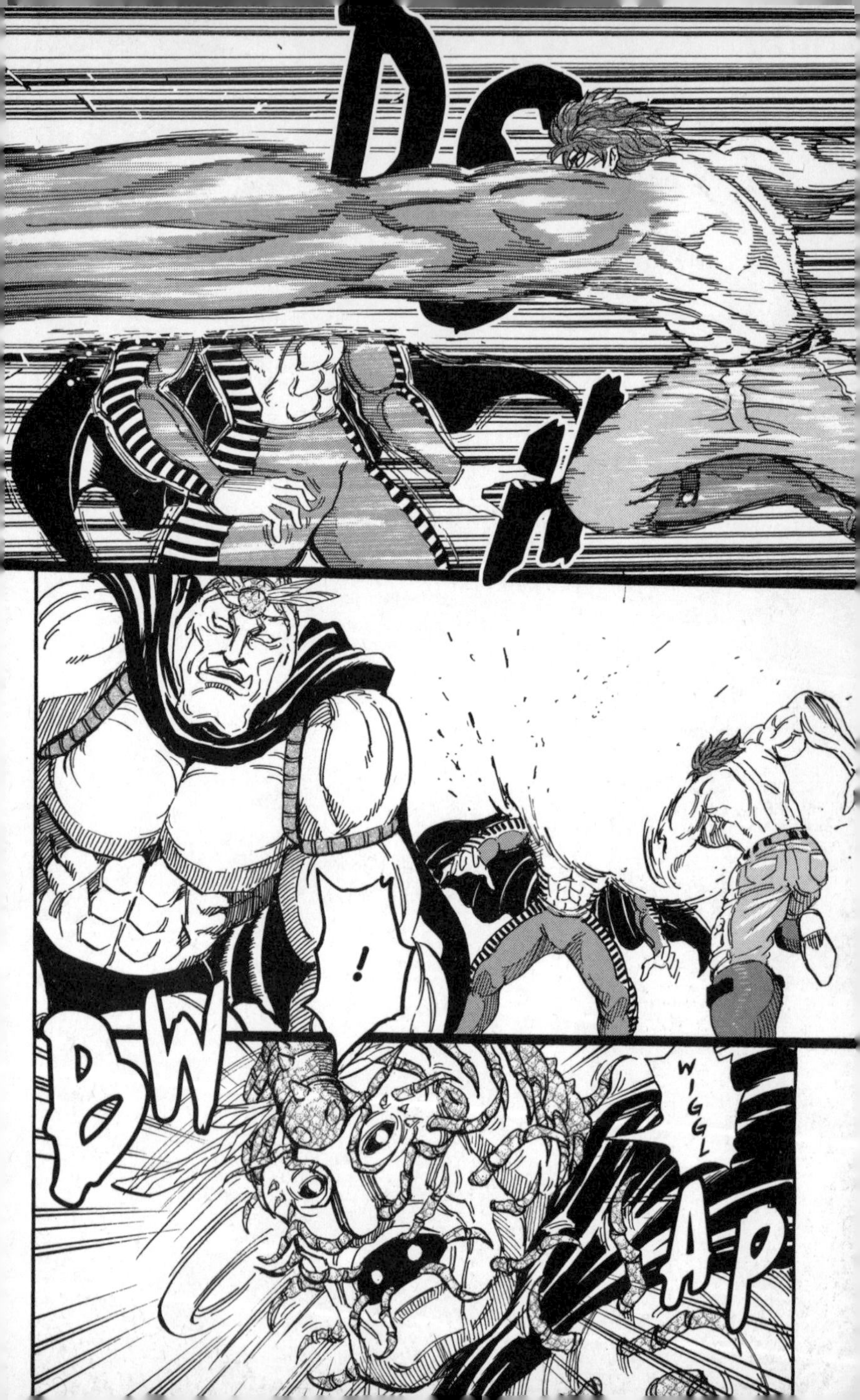
DOK
!
WIGGL
BWAP

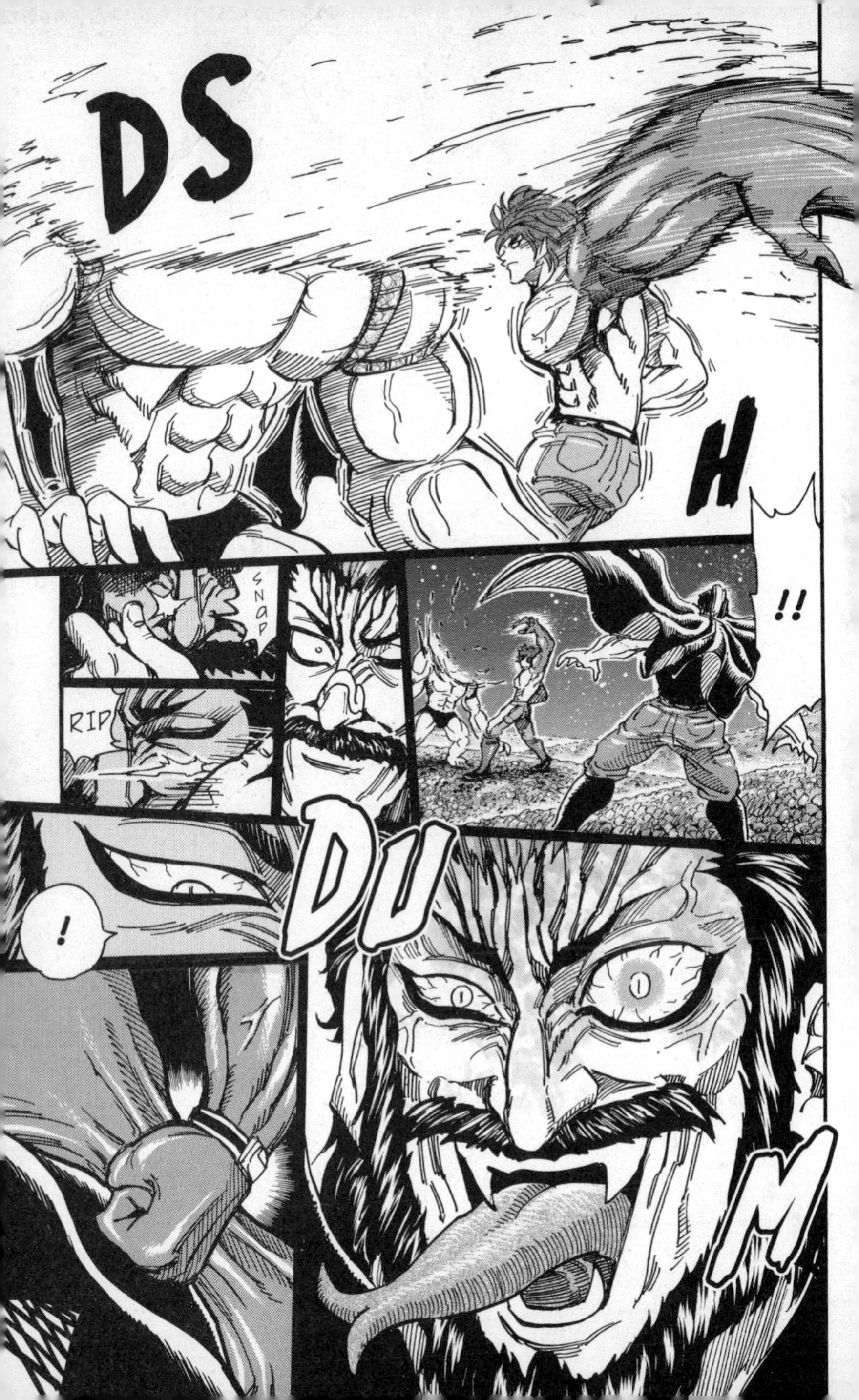
DS
H
!!
SNAP
RIP
DU
M
!

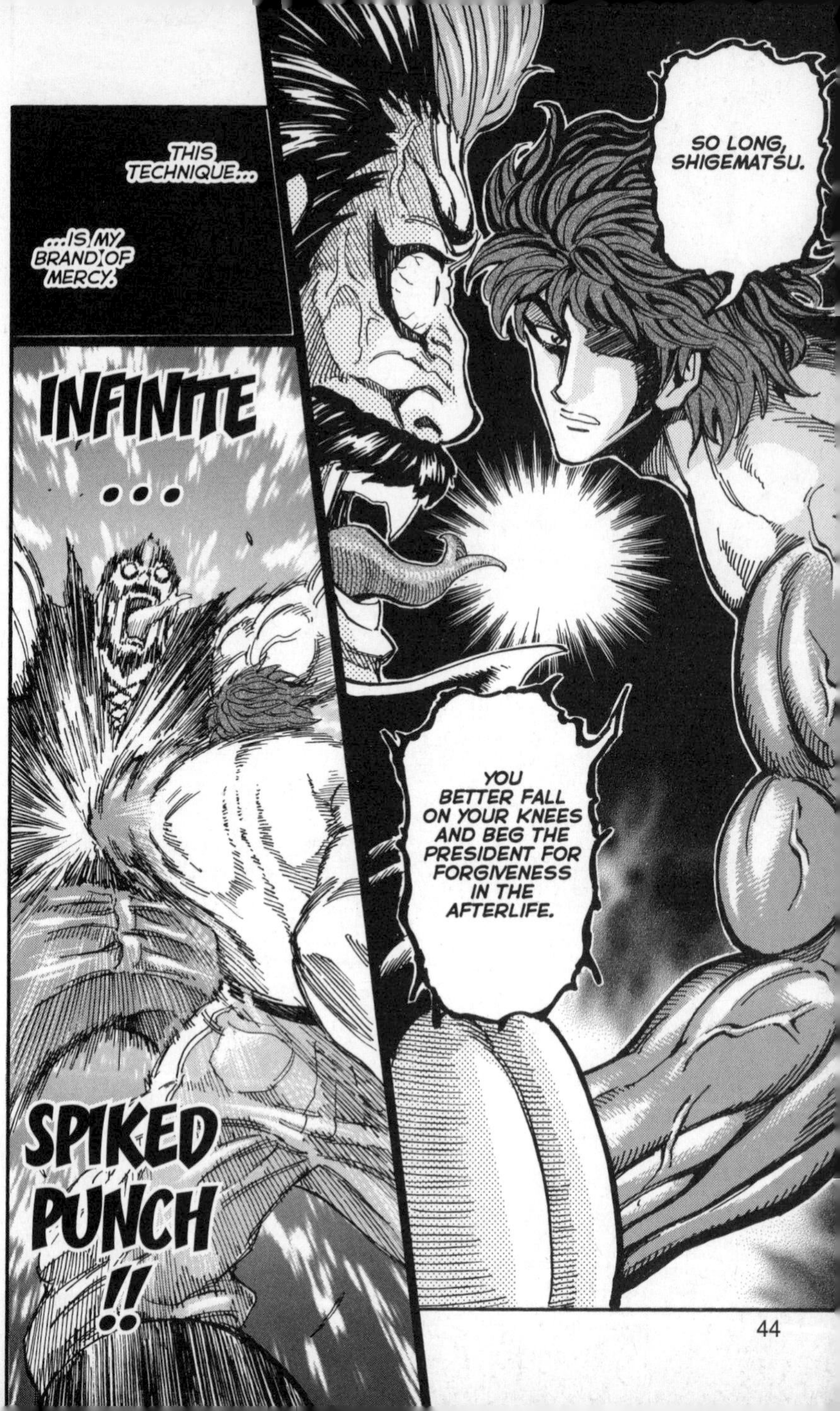
SO LONG, SHIGEMATSU.
YOU BETTER FALL ON YOUR KNEES AND BEG THE PRESIDENT FOR FORGIVENESS IN THE AFTERLIFE.
THIS TECHNIQUE...
...IS MY BRAND OF MERCY.
INFINITE...
SPIKED PUNCH!!

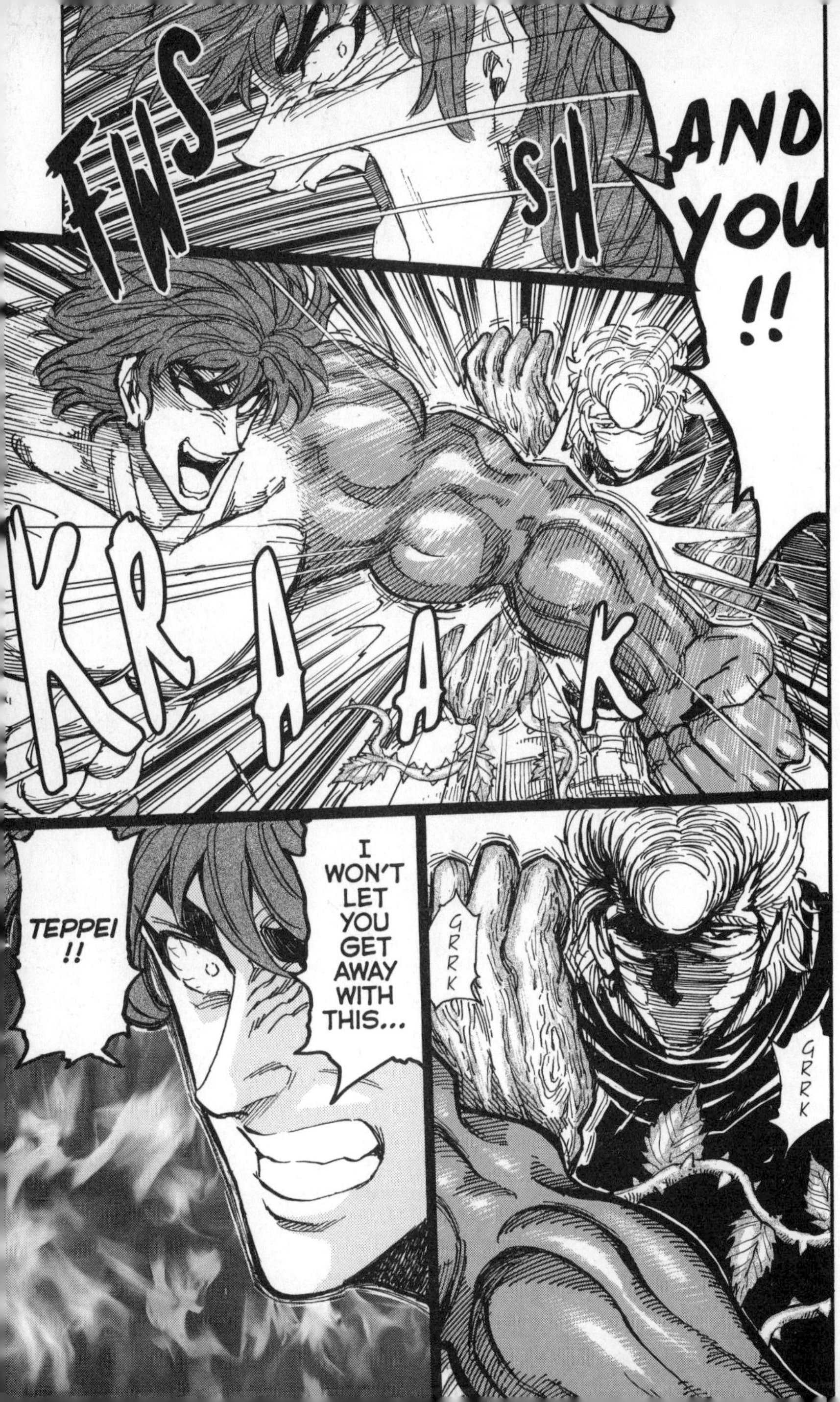
AND YOU!!
FWSSH
KRAAAK
GRRK
GRRK
I WON'T LET YOU GET AWAY WITH THIS...
TEPPEI!!

TORIKO

GOURMET CHECKLIST

Vol. 318

CALORIE BANANA
(FRUIT)

CAPTURE LEVEL: 29 (WHEN IT STILL EXISTED)
HABITAT: RESURRECTED BY PUKIN
SIZE: 25 CM
HEIGHT: ---
WEIGHT: 2 KG
PRICE: 300,000 YEN PER BANANA

...AND CALORIE BANANAS. *

SCALE

EACH BANANA CONTAINS 10,000 CALORIES. WHILE RIPE, IT CAN BE STORED FOR SEVERAL HOURS. IT IS AN INGREDIENT THAT WAS REVIVED BY GOURMET REVIVER PUKIN AND IS A HANDY TRAVEL SNACK DUE TO ITS SMALL SIZE. IT'S THE PERFECT INGREDIENT FOR GOURMET HUNTERS WHO NEED TO CONSTANTLY REPLENISH THEIR ENERGY.

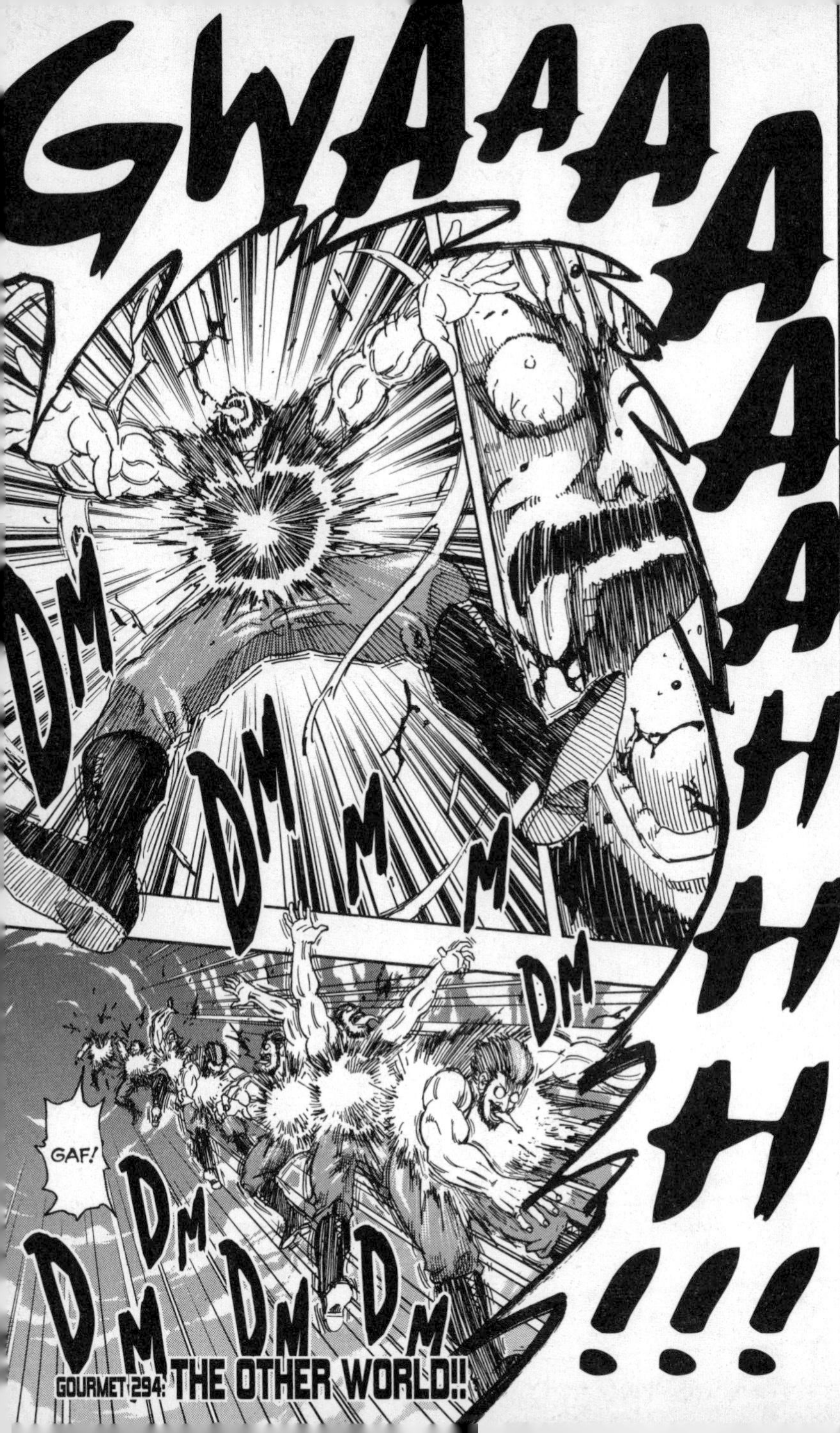
GWAAAAAAAAHHHHH!!!
DM
DM
M
M
DM
GAF!
DM DM DM DM DM DM

GOURMET 294: THE OTHER WORLD!!

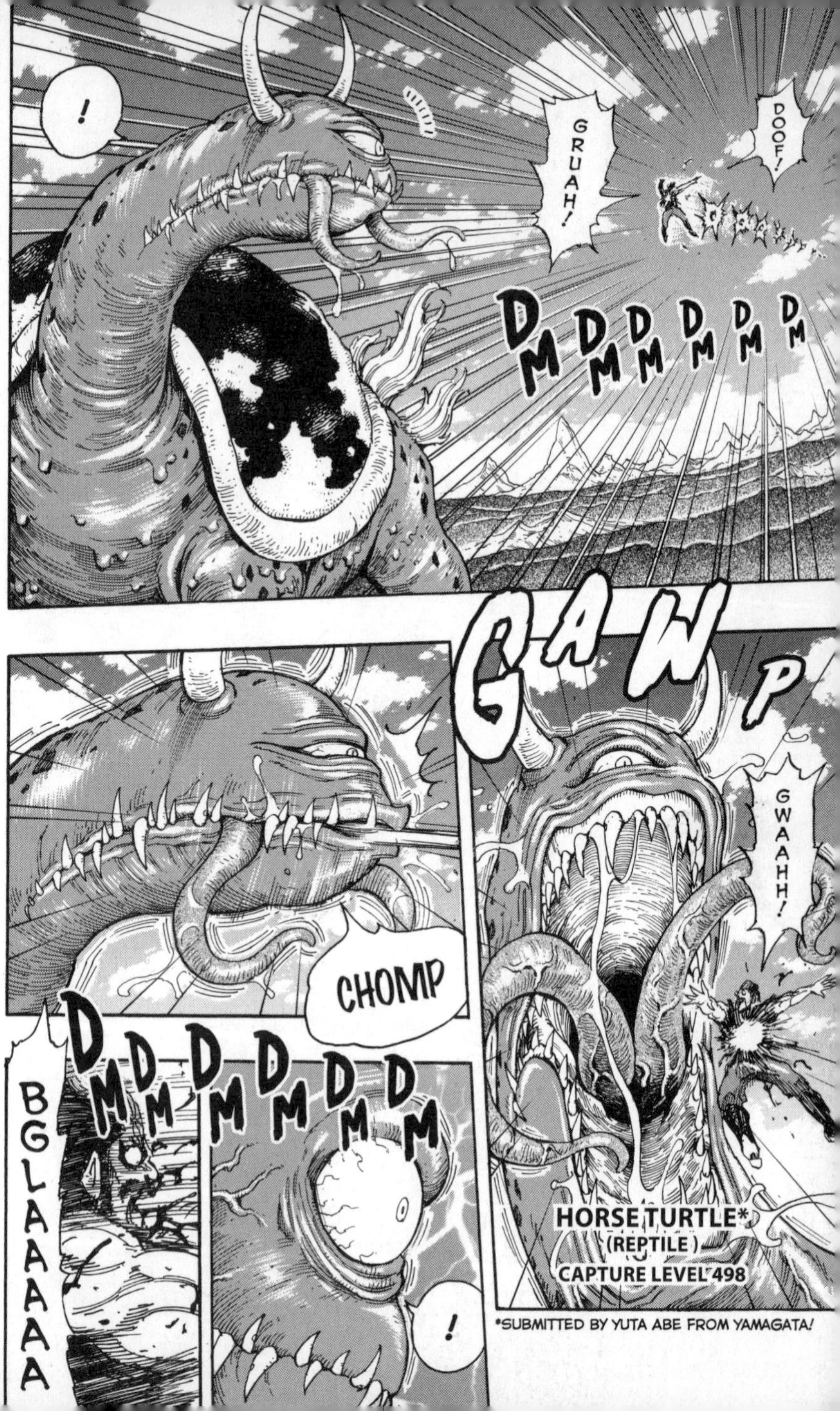
DOOF!
GRUAH!
!
DM DM DM DM DM DM
GAWP
GWAAHH!
HORSE TURTLE*
(REPTILE)
CAPTURE LEVEL 498
*SUBMITTED BY YUTA ABE FROM YAMAGATA!
CHOMP
DM DM DM DM DM DM DM
!
BGLAAAAAA

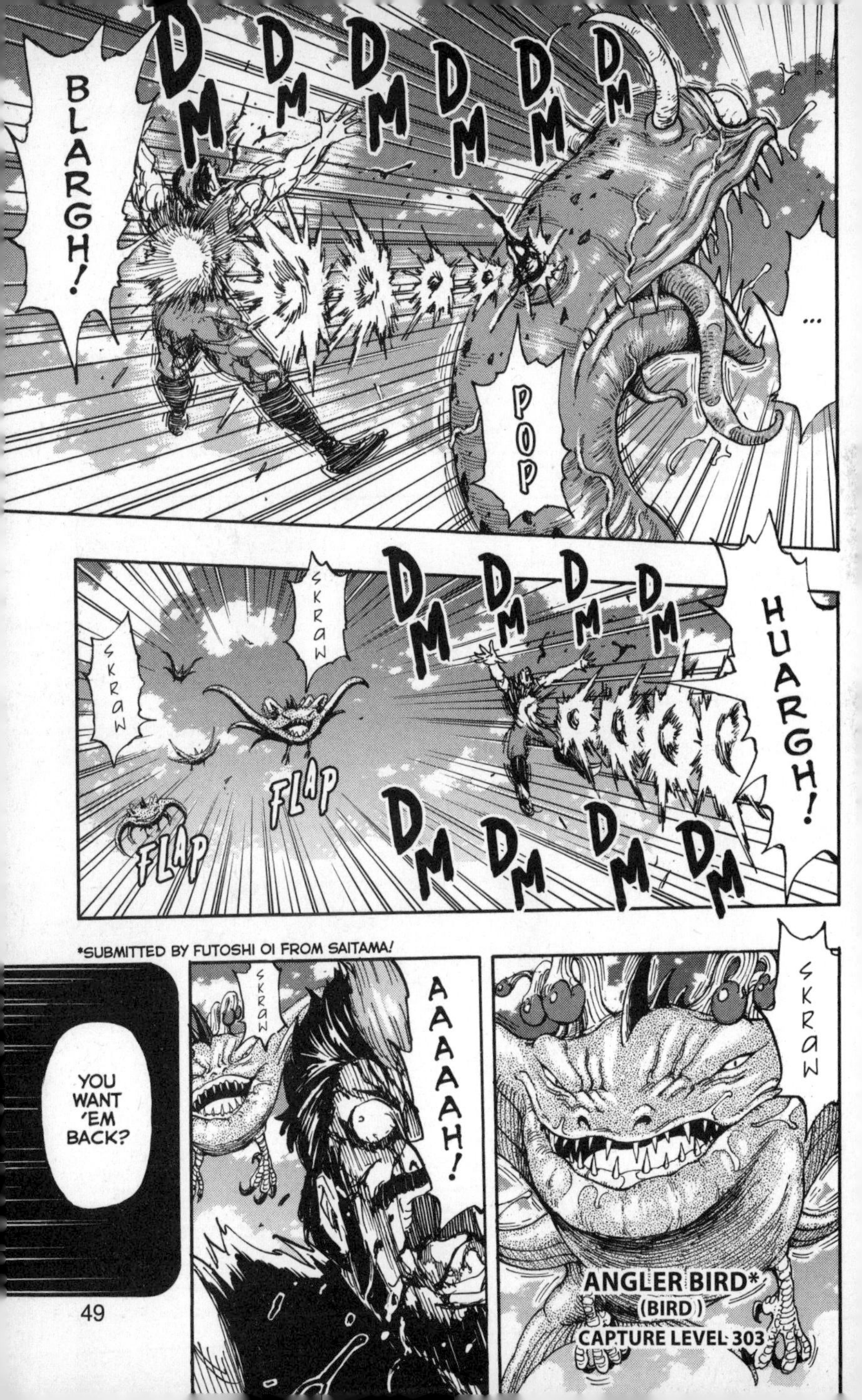
...
POP
DMDMDMDMDMDM
BLARGH!
HUARGH!
DMDMDMDM
DMDMDMDM
SKRAW
SKRAW
FLAP
FLAP
SKRAW
ANGLER BIRD*
(BIRD)
CAPTURE LEVEL 303
AAAAAAH!
SKRAW
YOU WANT 'EM BACK?
*SUBMITTED BY FUTOSHI OI FROM SAITAMA!

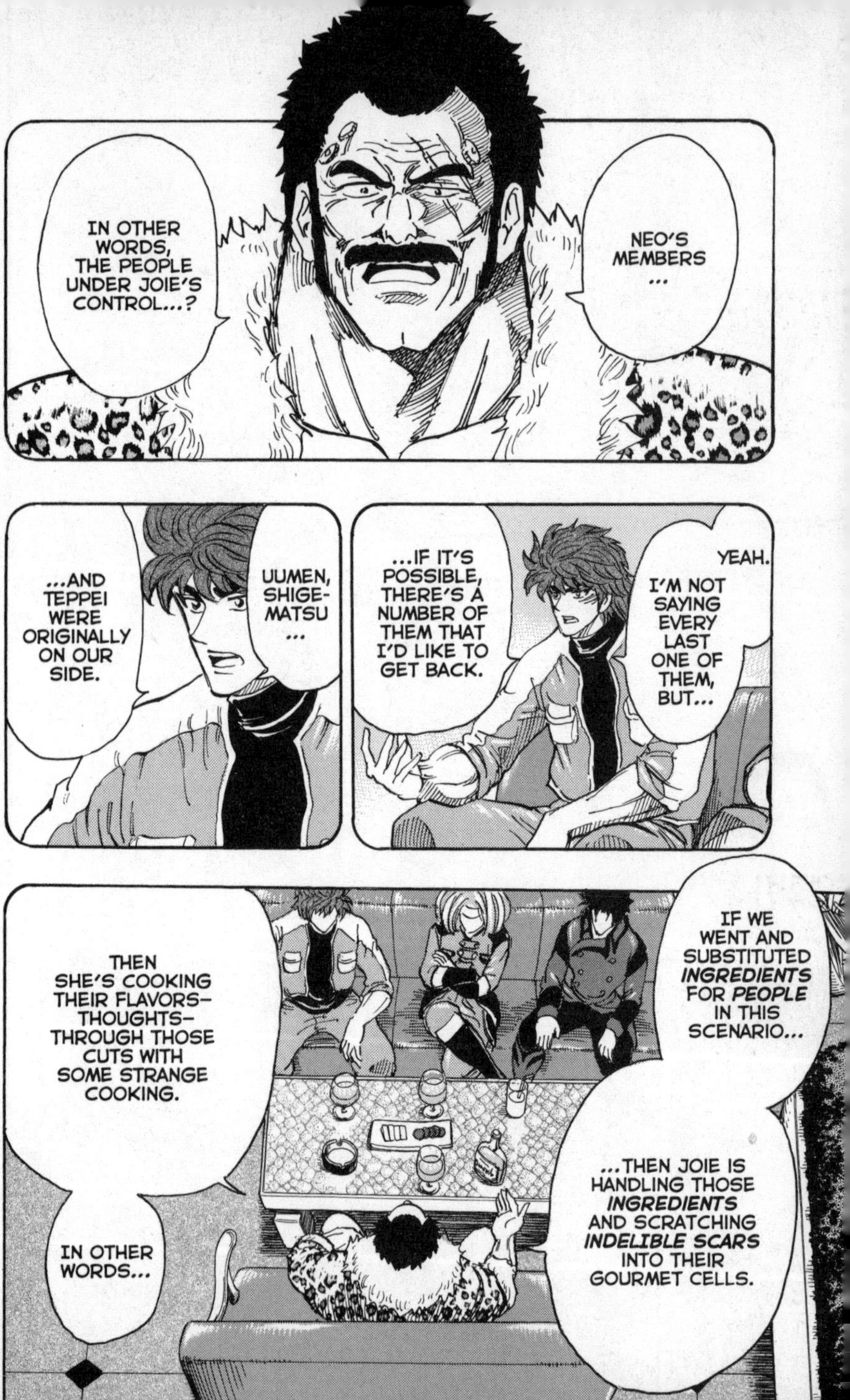
NEO'S MEMBERS ...
IN OTHER WORDS, THE PEOPLE UNDER JOIE'S CONTROL...?
YEAH.
I'M NOT SAYING EVERY LAST ONE OF THEM, BUT...
...IF IT'S POSSIBLE, THERE'S A NUMBER OF THEM THAT I'D LIKE TO GET BACK.
UUMEN, SHIGE-MATSU ...
...AND TEPPEI WERE ORIGINALLY ON OUR SIDE.
IF WE WENT AND SUBSTITUTED *INGREDIENTS* FOR *PEOPLE* IN THIS SCENARIO...
...THEN JOIE IS HANDLING THOSE *INGREDIENTS* AND SCRATCHING *INDELIBLE SCARS* INTO THEIR GOURMET CELLS.
IN OTHER WORDS...
THEN SHE'S COOKING THEIR FLAVORS—THOUGHTS—THROUGH THOSE CUTS WITH SOME STRANGE COOKING.

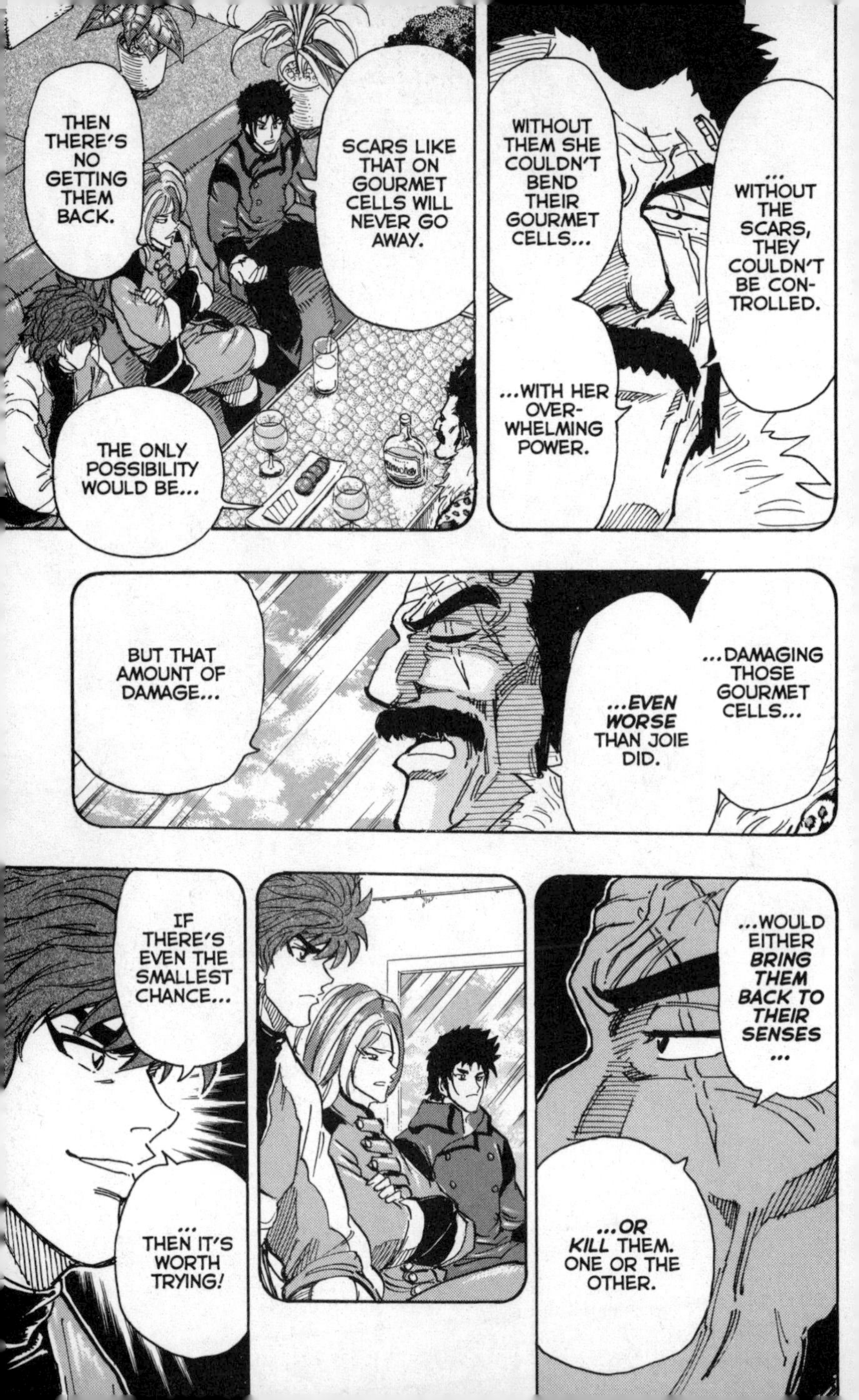
...WITHOUT THE SCARS, THEY COULDN'T BE CON-TROLLED.
WITHOUT THEM SHE COULDN'T BEND THEIR GOURMET CELLS...
...WITH HER OVER-WHELMING POWER.
SCARS LIKE THAT ON GOURMET CELLS WILL NEVER GO AWAY.
THEN THERE'S NO GETTING THEM BACK.
THE ONLY POSSIBILITY WOULD BE...
...DAMAGING THOSE GOURMET CELLS...
...*EVEN WORSE* THAN JOIE DID.
BUT THAT AMOUNT OF DAMAGE...
...WOULD EITHER *BRING THEM BACK TO THEIR SENSES*...
...OR *KILL* THEM. ONE OR THE OTHER.
IF THERE'S EVEN THE SMALLEST CHANCE...
...THEN IT'S WORTH TRYING!

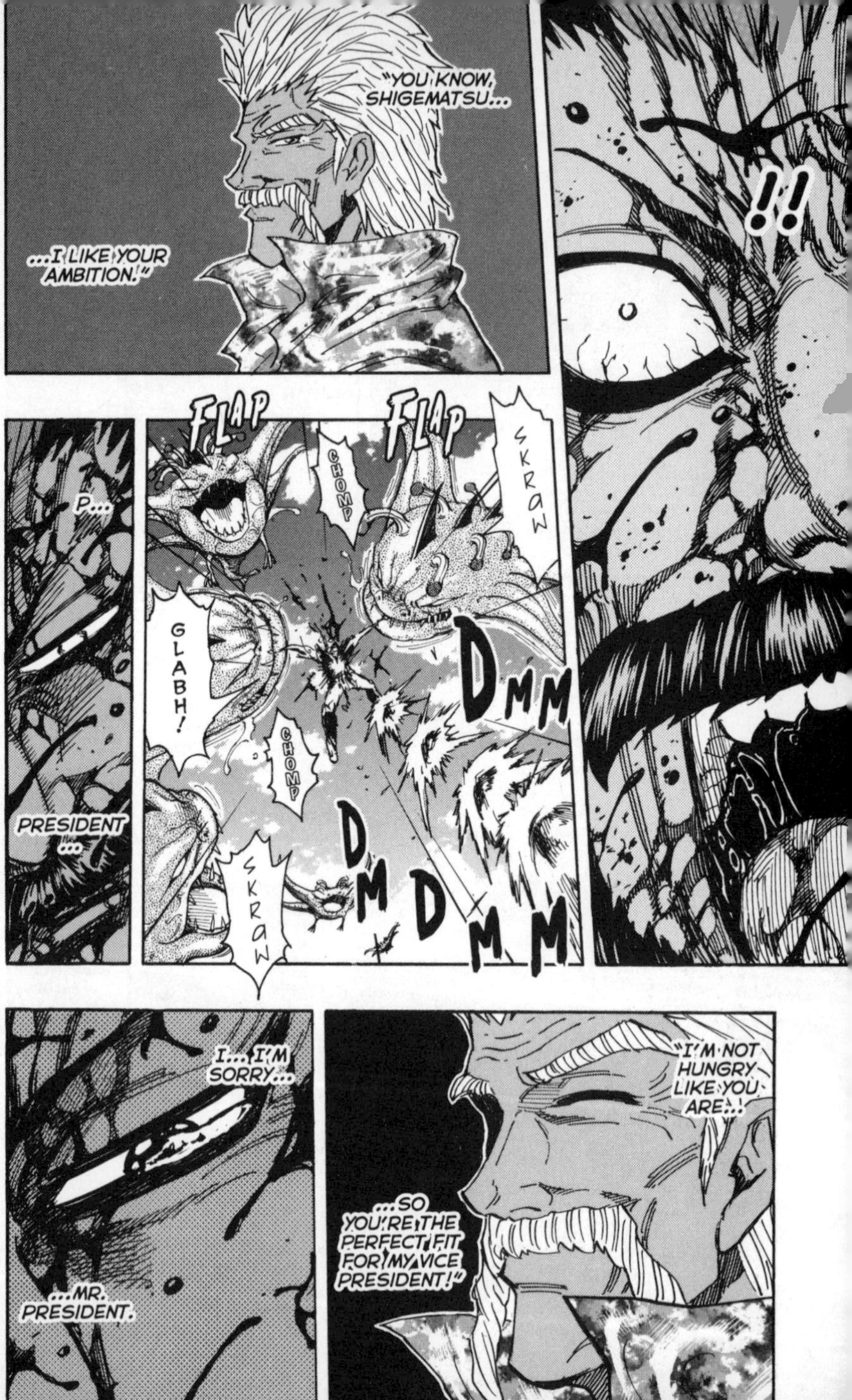
!!
"YOU KNOW, SHIGEMATSU...
...I LIKE YOUR AMBITION."
FLAP
FLAP
SKRAW
CHOMP
GLABH!
DMM
CHOMP
DMDMM
SKRAW
P...
PRESIDENT...
"I'M NOT HUNGRY LIKE YOU ARE..!
...SO YOU'RE THE PERFECT FIT FOR MY VICE PRESIDENT!"
I... I'M SORRY...
...MR. PRESIDENT.

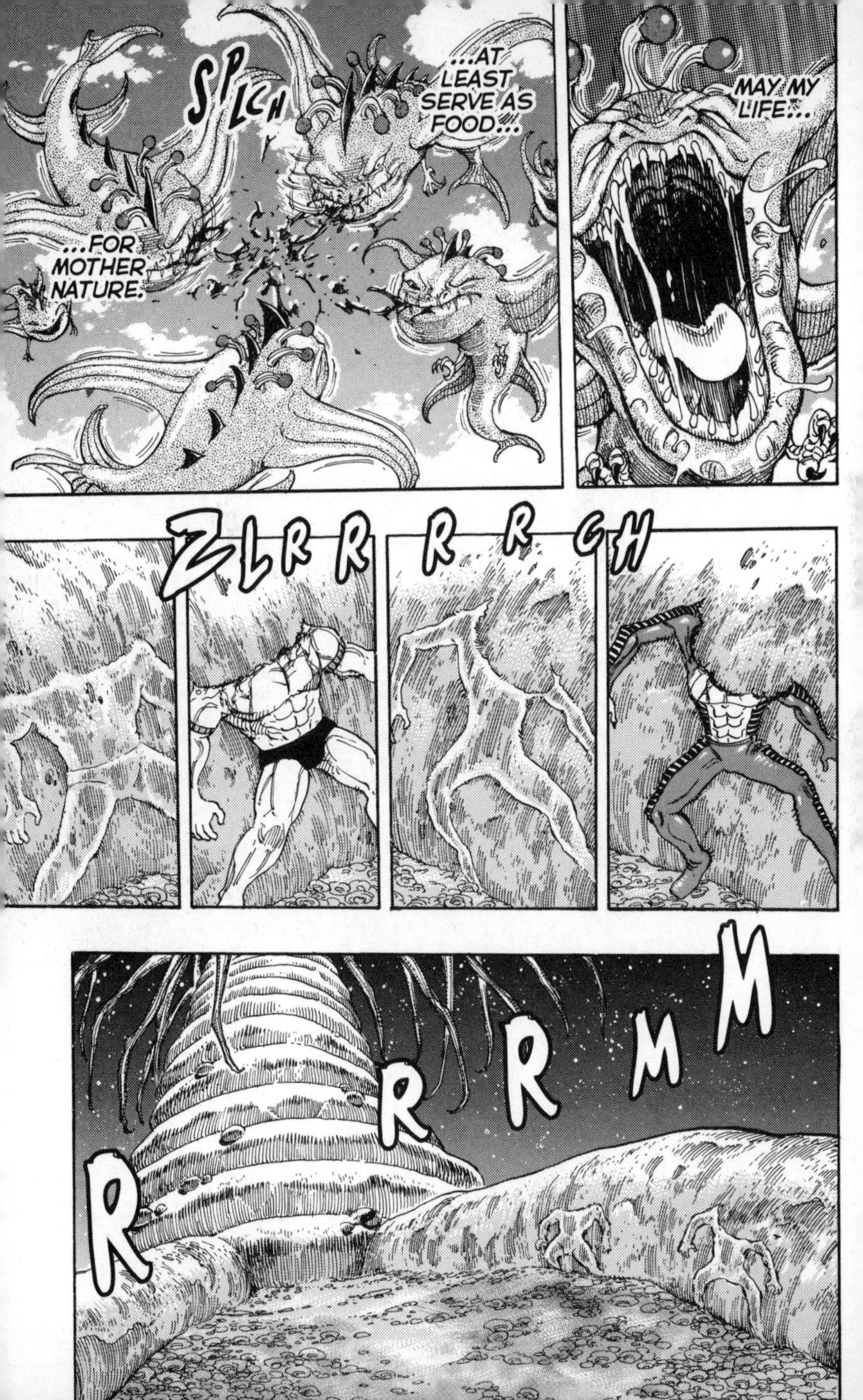
MAY MY LIFE...
...AT LEAST SERVE AS FOOD...
SPLCH
...FOR MOTHER NATURE.
ZLRRRRCH
RRRMMM

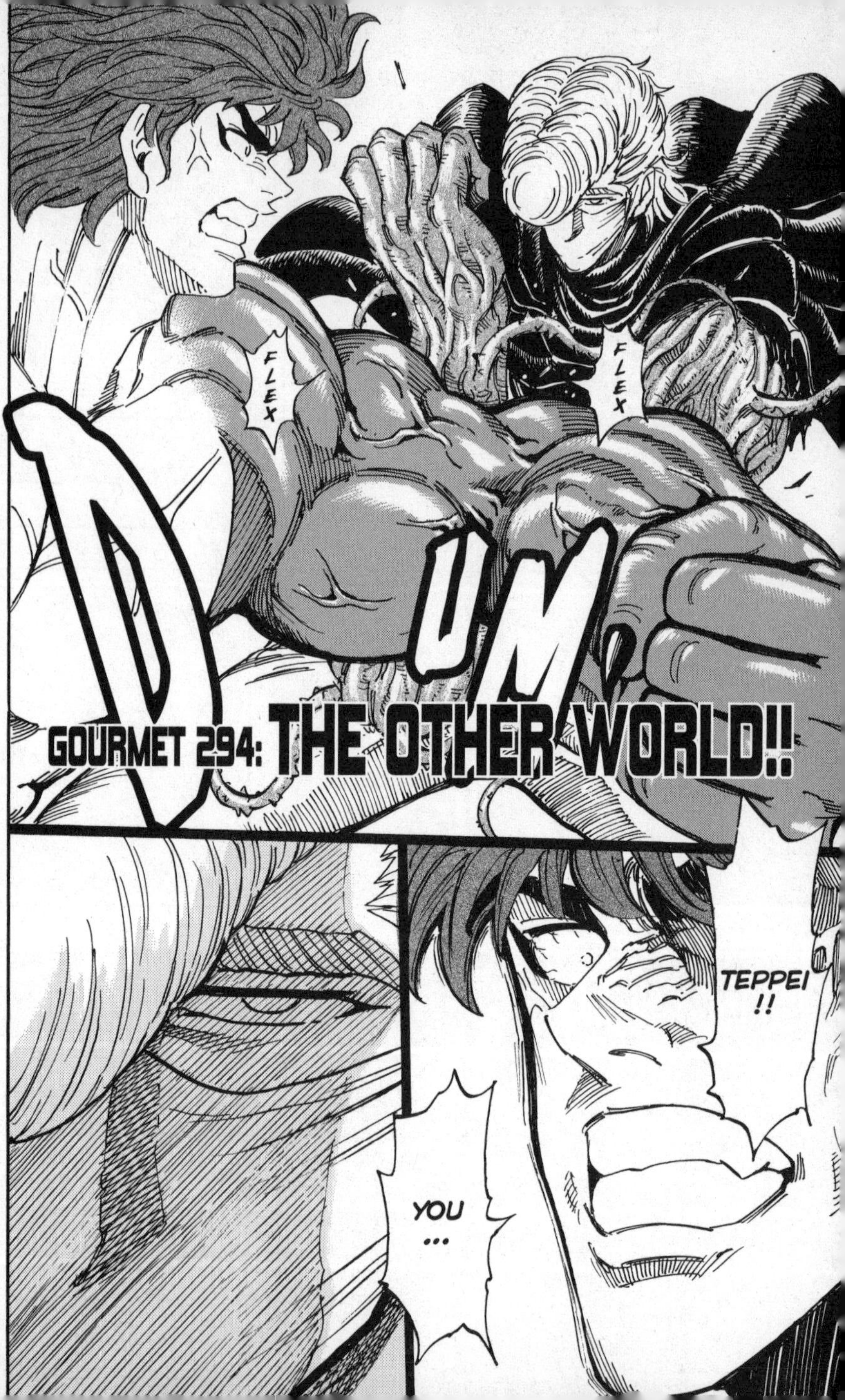
FLEX
FLEX
DOOM
GOURMET 294: THE OTHER WORLD!!
TEPPEI!!
YOU...

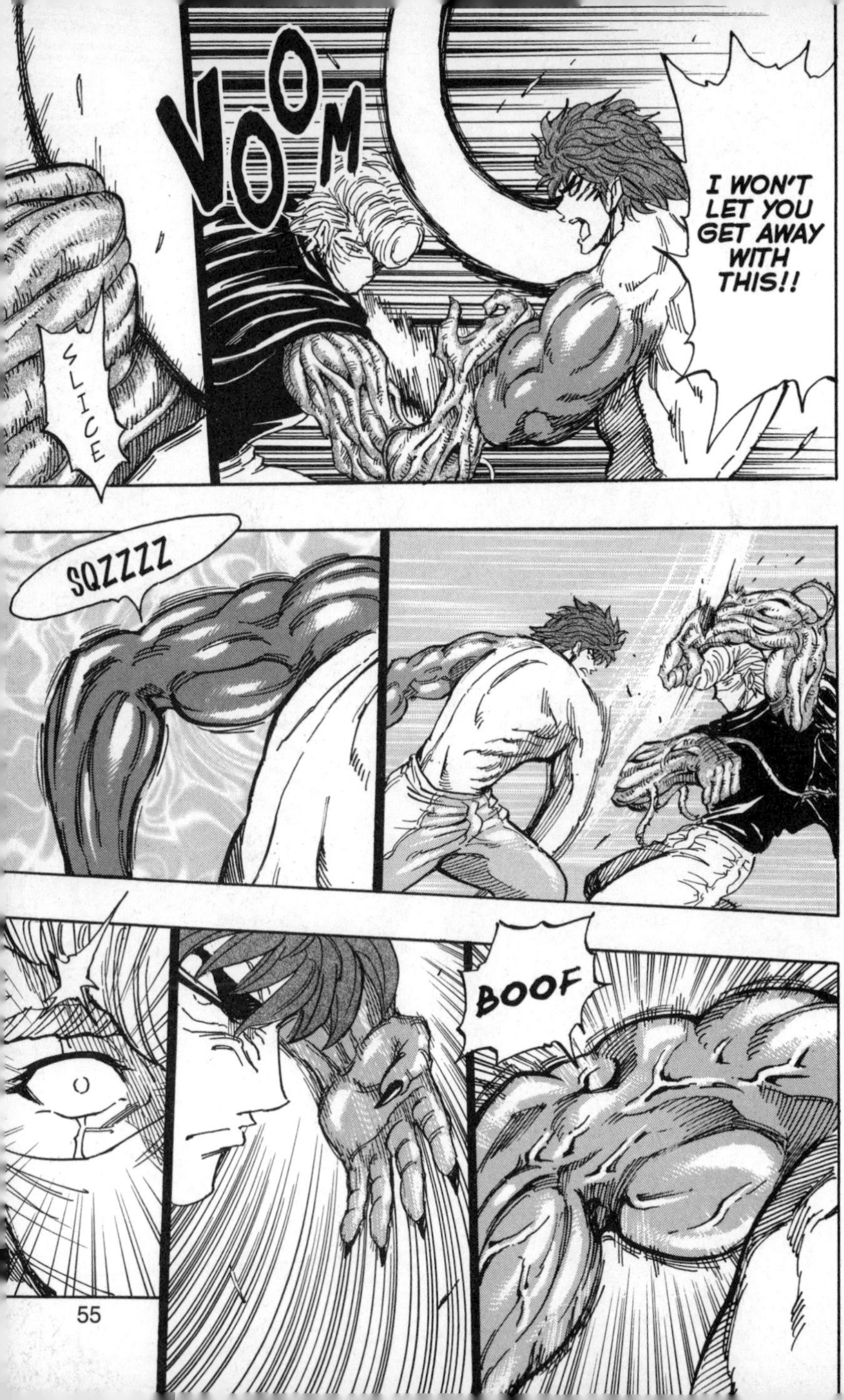
I WON'T LET YOU GET AWAY WITH THIS!!
VOOM
SLICE
SQZZZZ
BOOF

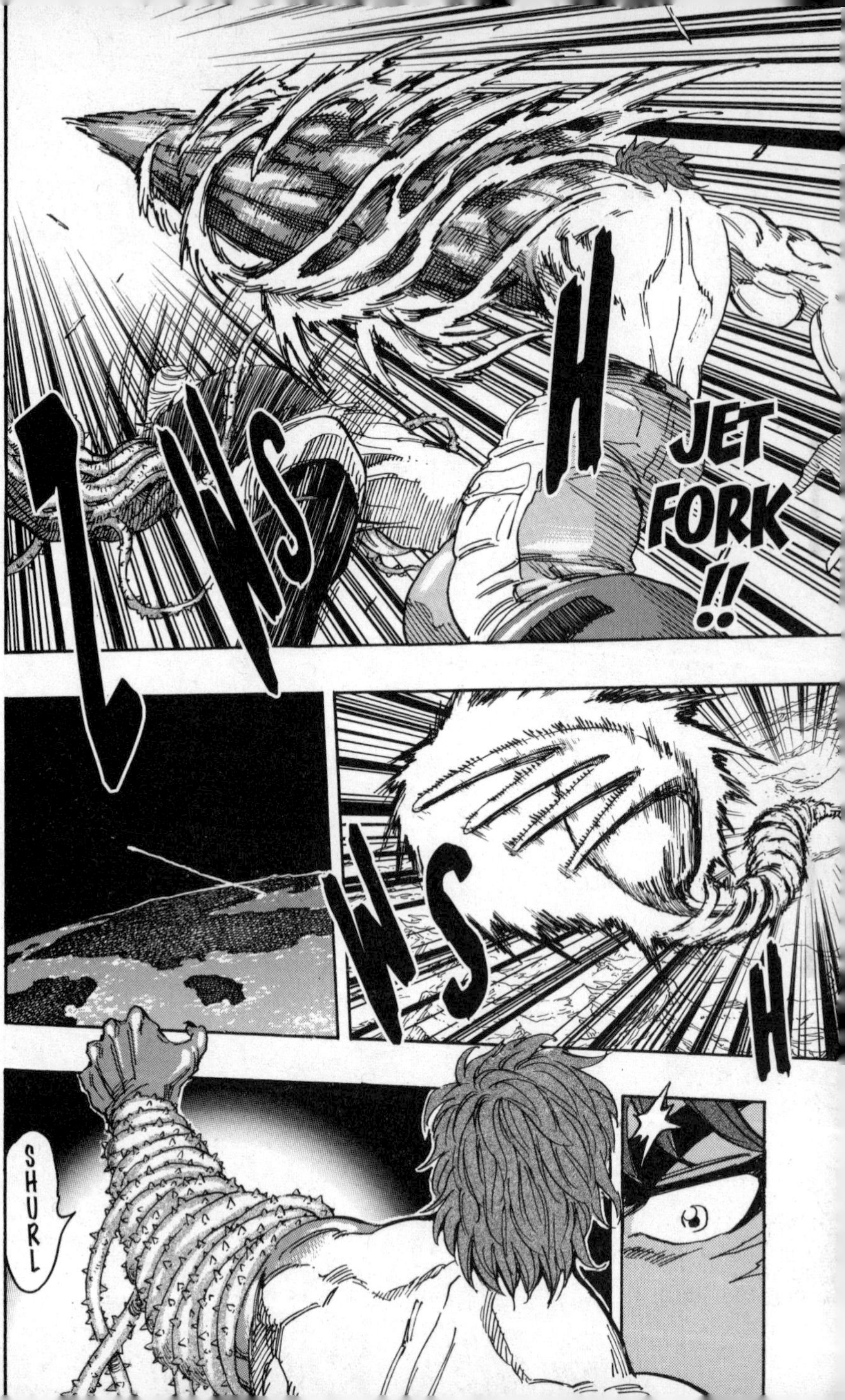
JET FORK!!
ZWSH
WSH
SHURL

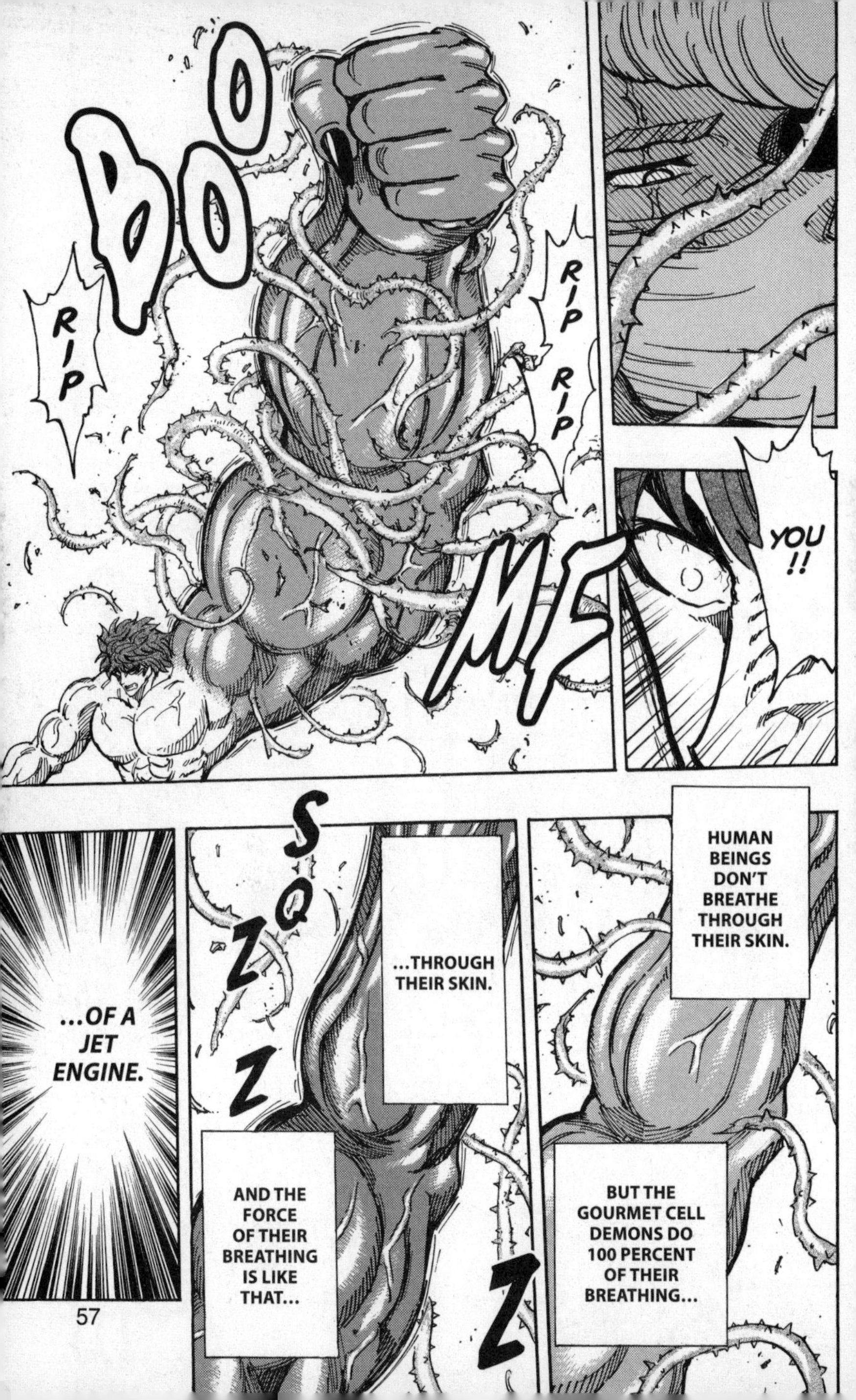
YOU !!
DOOO
RIP RIP
RIP
MF
HUMAN BEINGS DON'T BREATHE THROUGH THEIR SKIN.
BUT THE GOURMET CELL DEMONS DO 100 PERCENT OF THEIR BREATHING...
...THROUGH THEIR SKIN.
SQZZZ
AND THE FORCE OF THEIR BREATHING IS LIKE THAT...
...OF A JET ENGINE.

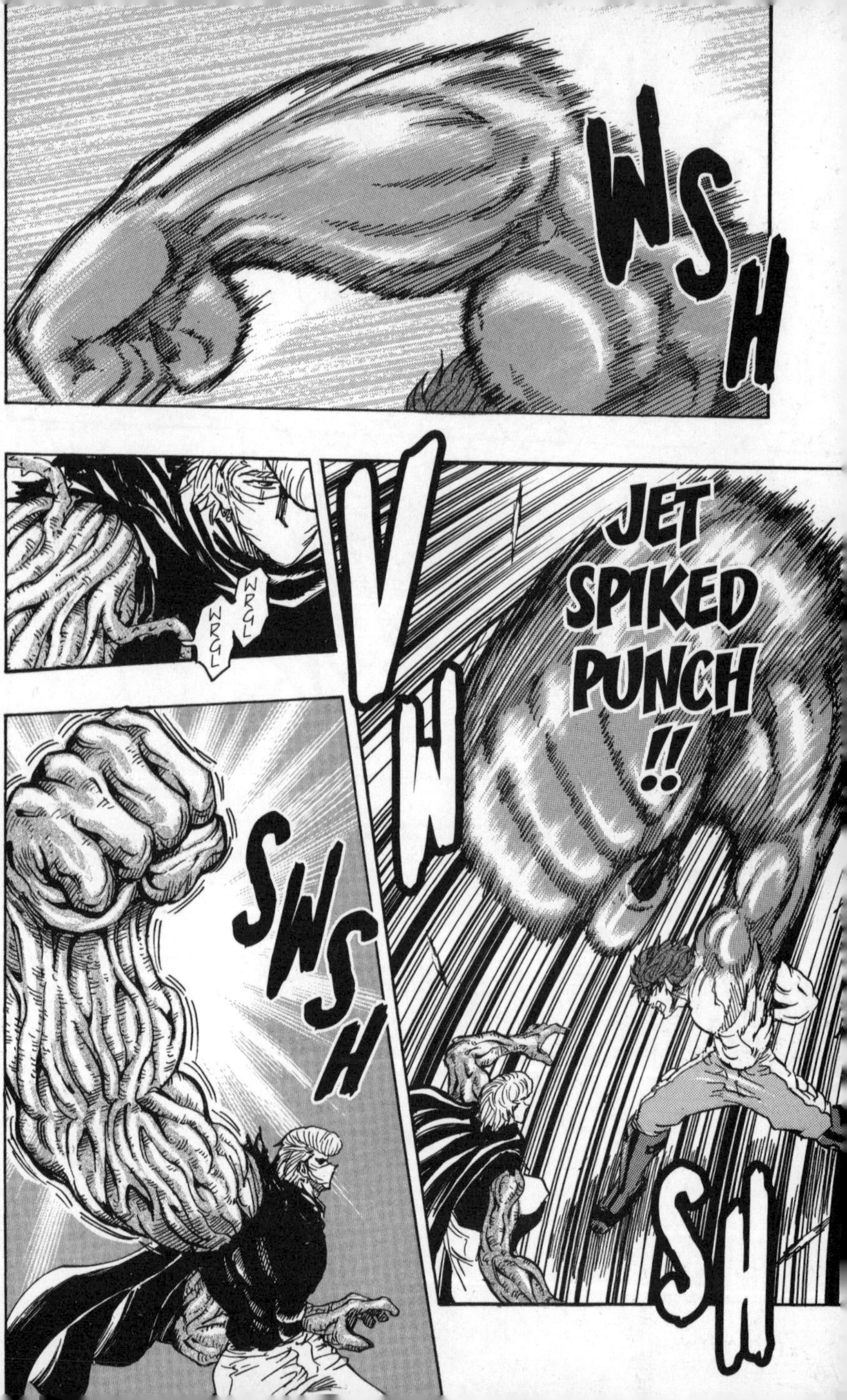
WSH
VW
JET SPIKED PUNCH!!
SH
WRGL WRGL
SWSH

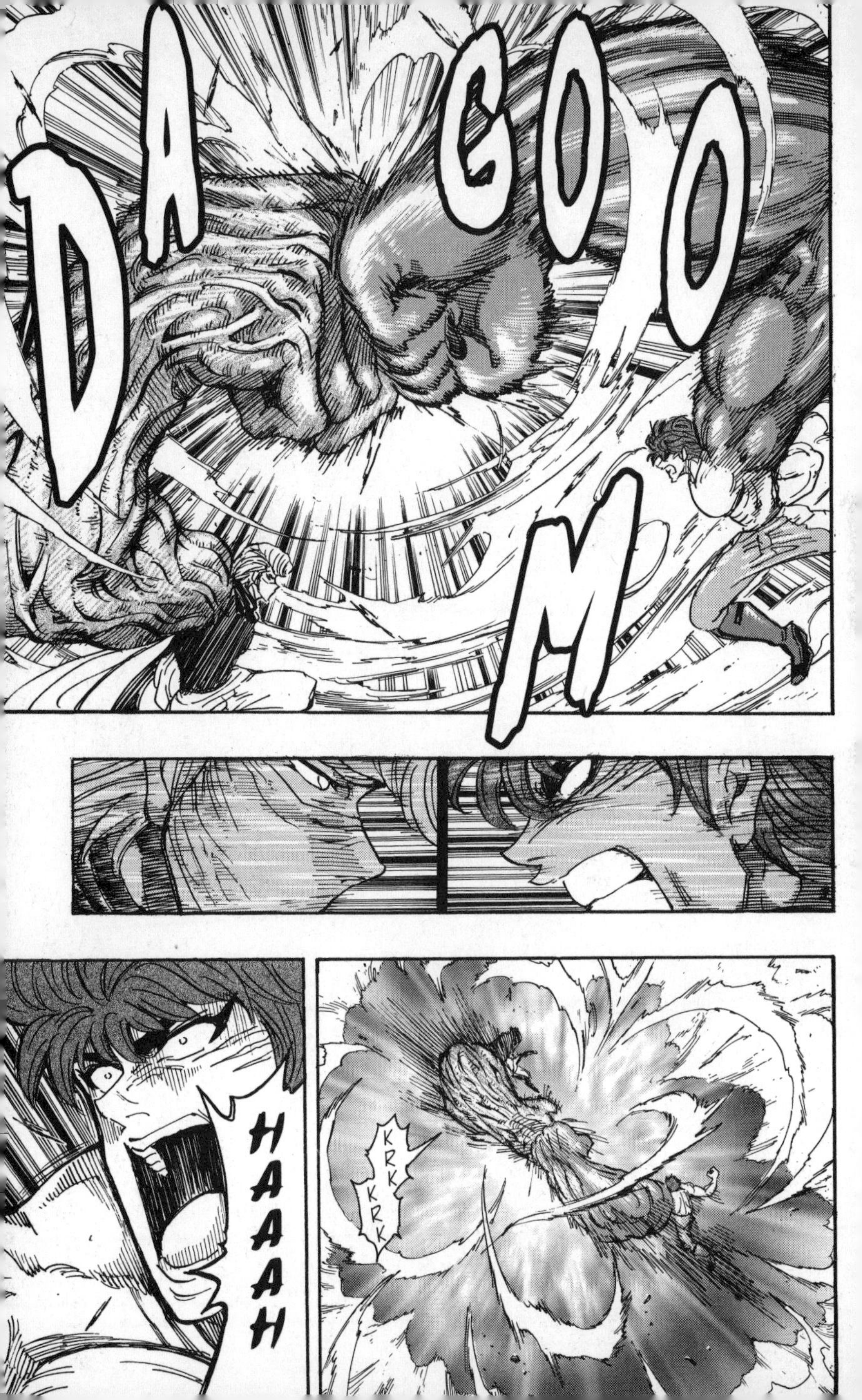
DAGOOM
HAAAAAH
KRK KRK

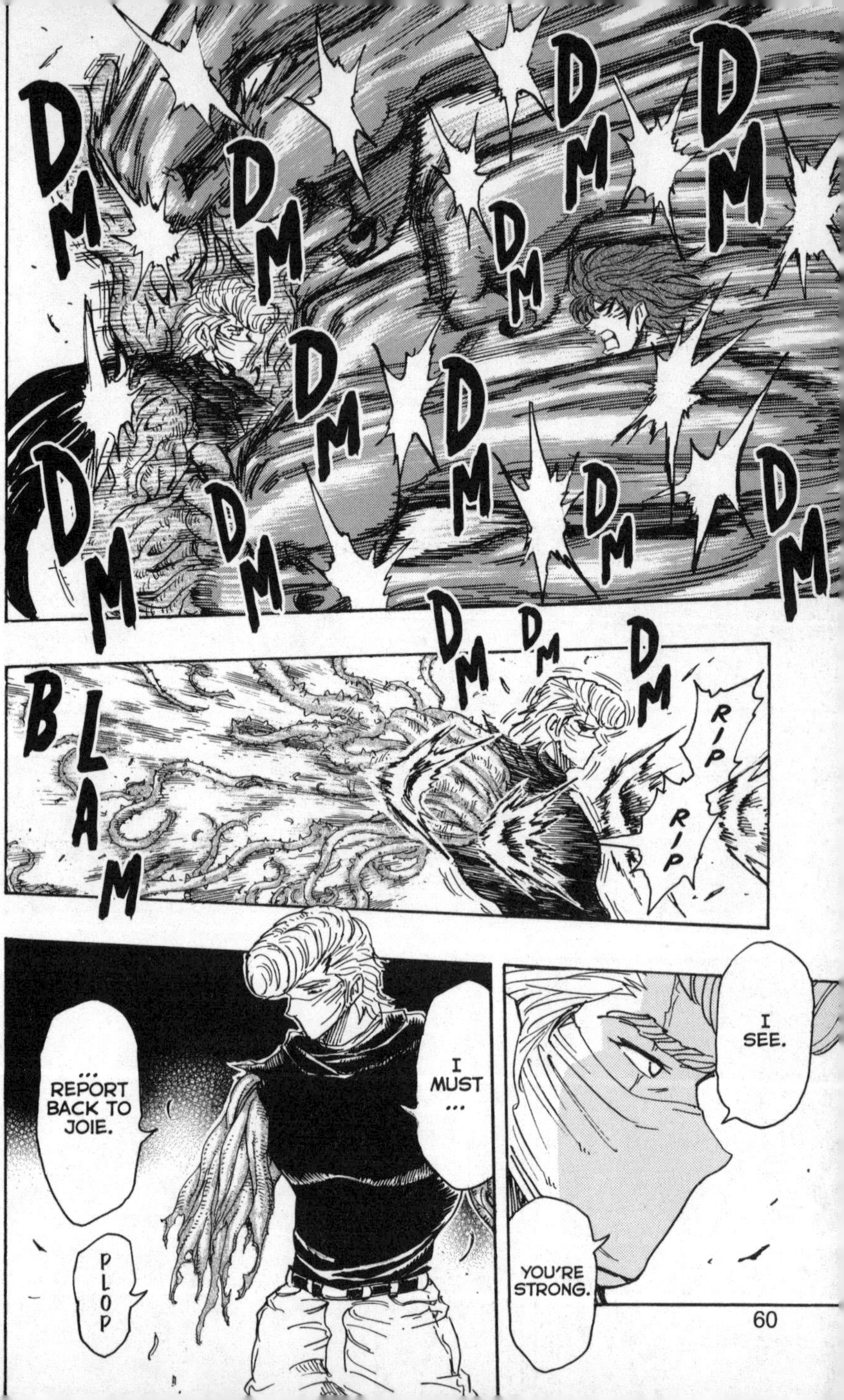
DM DM DM DM DM DM DM DM DM DM DM DM DM DM
DM DM DM
RIP RIP
BLAM
I SEE.
YOU'RE STRONG.
I MUST ...
... REPORT BACK TO JOIE.
PLOP

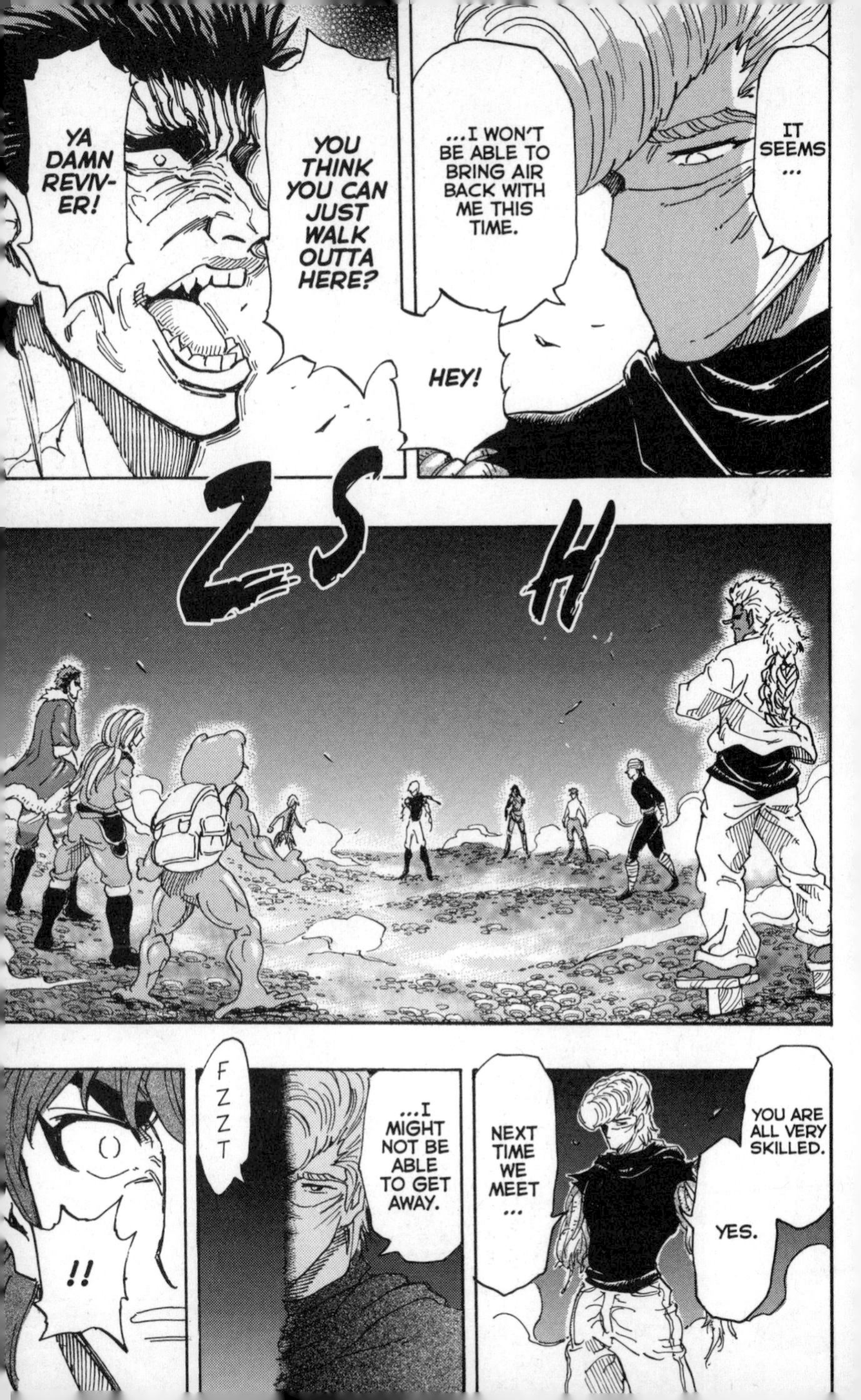
IT SEEMS ...
...I WON'T BE ABLE TO BRING AIR BACK WITH ME THIS TIME.
HEY!
YOU THINK YOU CAN JUST WALK OUTTA HERE?
YA DAMN REVIV-ER!
ZSH
YOU ARE ALL VERY SKILLED.
YES.
NEXT TIME WE MEET ...
...I MIGHT NOT BE ABLE TO GET AWAY.
FZZT
!!

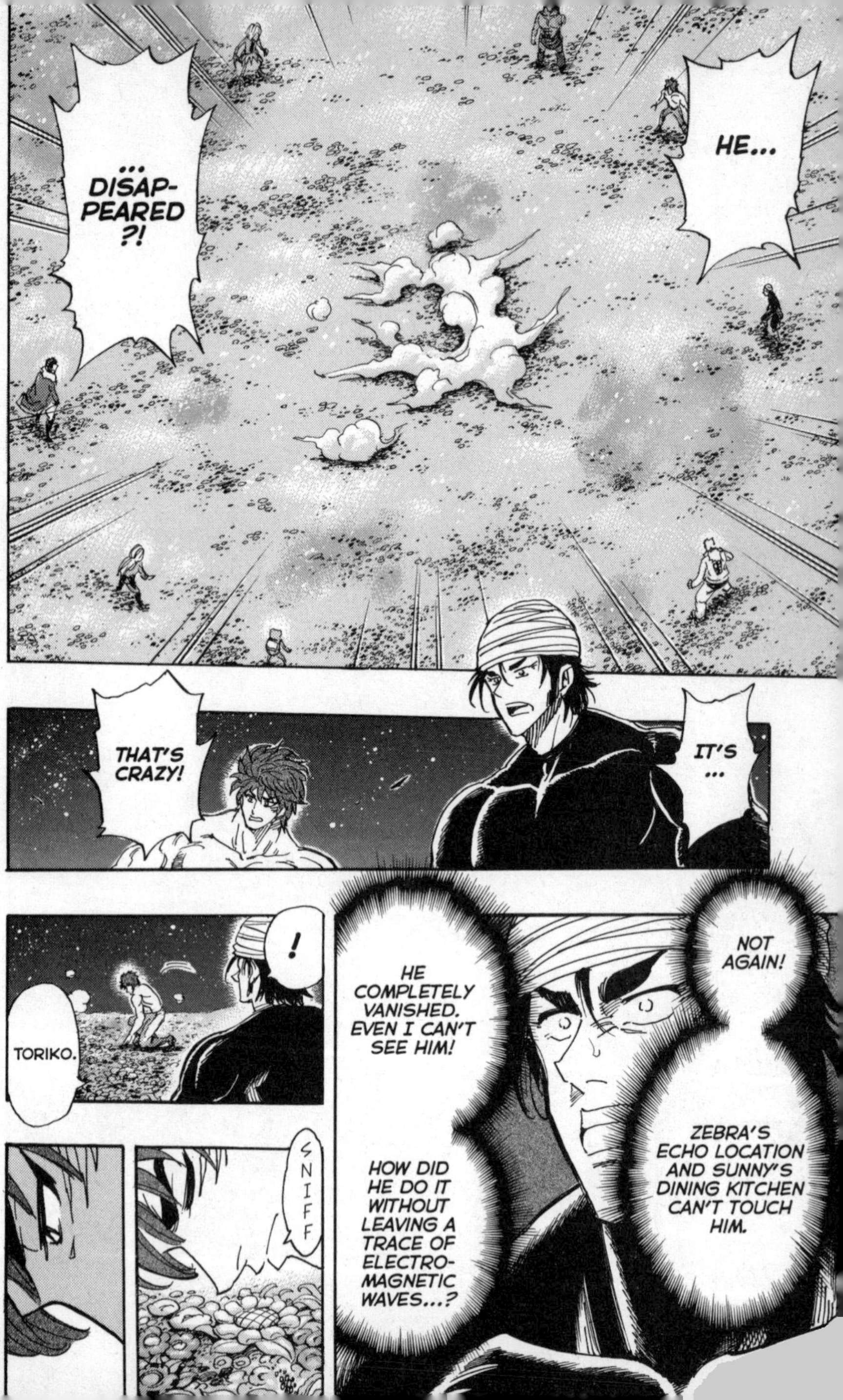
HE...
...DISAP-PEARED?!
IT'S...
THAT'S CRAZY!
NOT AGAIN!
HE COMPLETELY VANISHED. EVEN I CAN'T SEE HIM!
ZEBRA'S ECHO LOCATION AND SUNNY'S DINING KITCHEN CAN'T TOUCH HIM.
HOW DID HE DO IT WITHOUT LEAVING A TRACE OF ELECTRO-MAGNETIC WAVES...?
!
TORIKO.
SNIFF

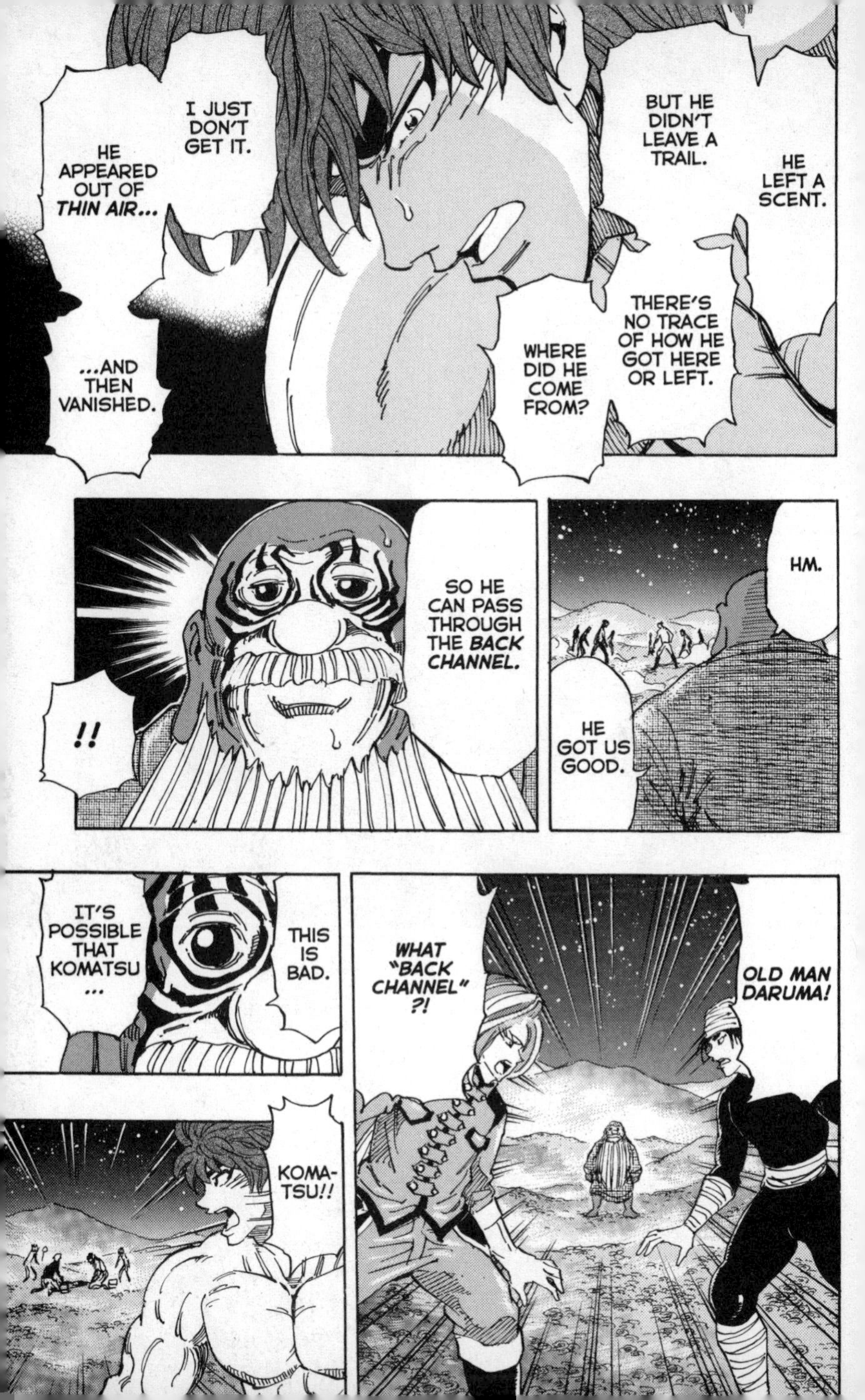
HE LEFT A SCENT.
BUT HE DIDN'T LEAVE A TRAIL.
THERE'S NO TRACE OF HOW HE GOT HERE OR LEFT.
WHERE DID HE COME FROM?
I JUST DON'T GET IT.
HE APPEARED OUT OF THIN AIR...
...AND THEN VANISHED.
HM.
HE GOT US GOOD.
SO HE CAN PASS THROUGH THE BACK CHANNEL.
!!
OLD MAN DARUMA!
WHAT "BACK CHANNEL"?!
THIS IS BAD.
IT'S POSSIBLE THAT KOMATSU...
KOMATSU!!

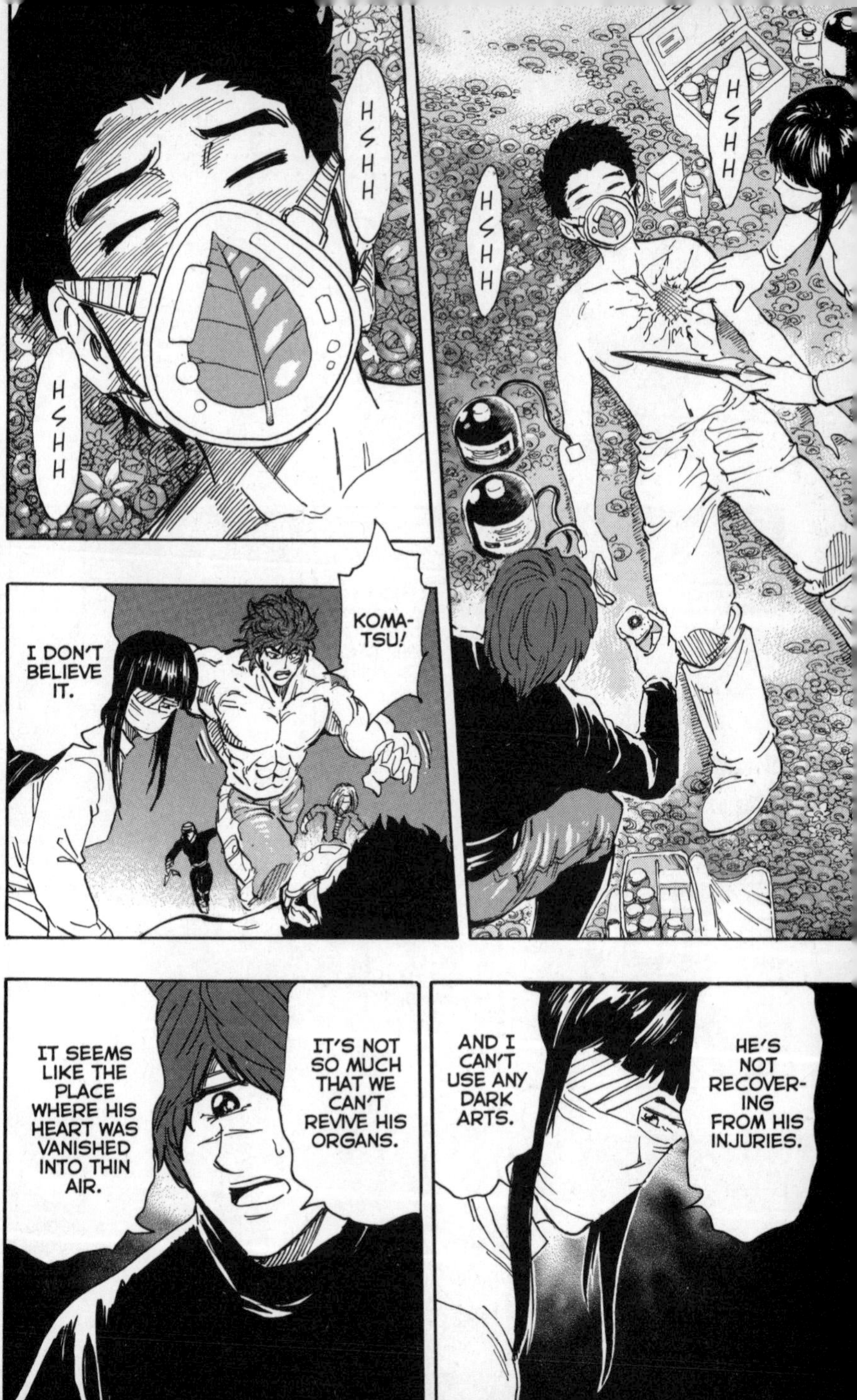

HSHH
HSHH
HSHH
HSHH
KOMA-TSU!
I DON'T BELIEVE IT.
HE'S NOT RECOVERING FROM HIS INJURIES.
AND I CAN'T USE ANY DARK ARTS.
IT'S NOT SO MUCH THAT WE CAN'T REVIVE HIS ORGANS.
IT SEEMS LIKE THE PLACE WHERE HIS HEART WAS VANISHED INTO THIN AIR.

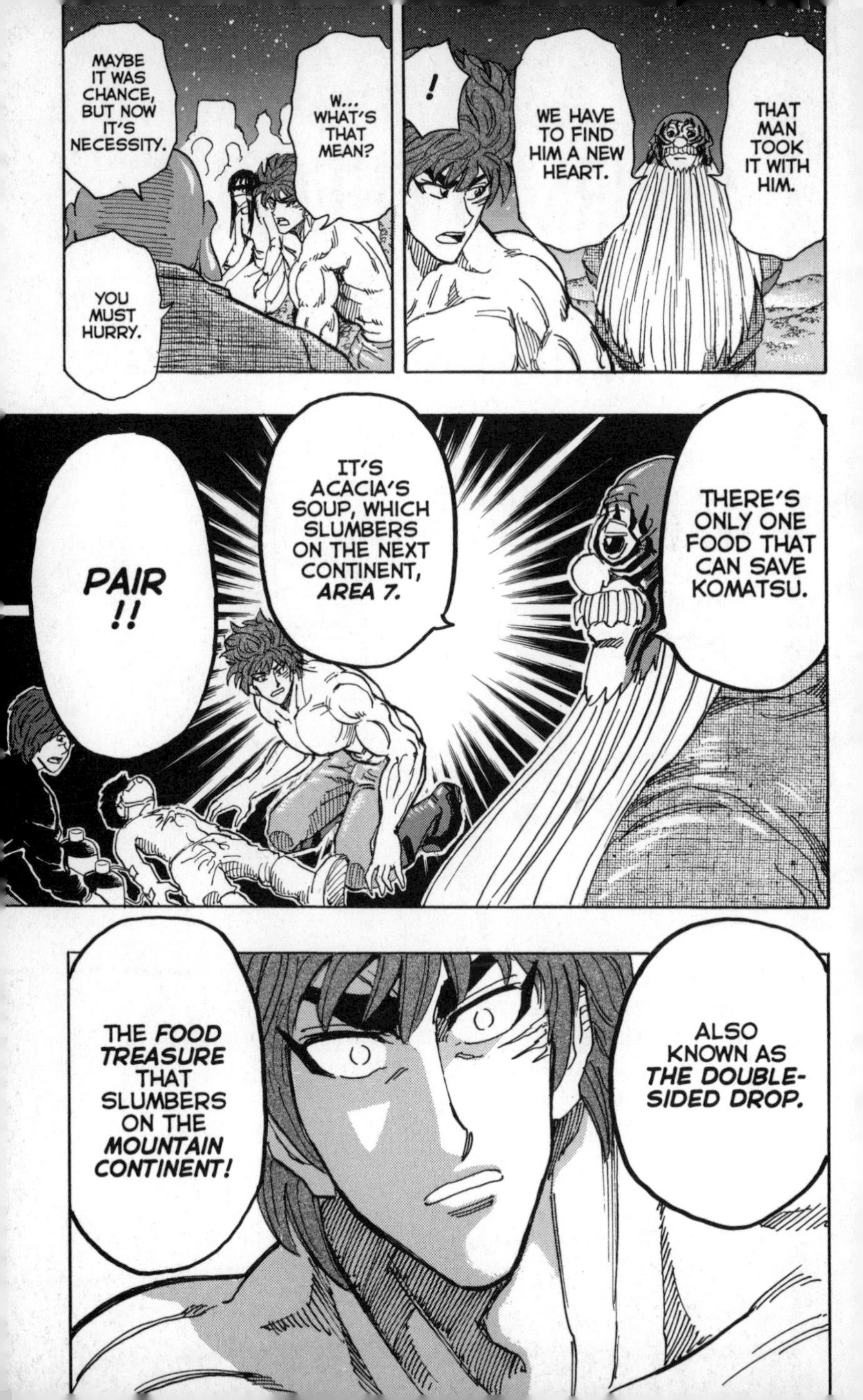
THAT MAN TOOK IT WITH HIM.
WE HAVE TO FIND HIM A NEW HEART.
!
W... WHAT'S THAT MEAN?
MAYBE IT WAS CHANCE, BUT NOW IT'S NECESSITY.
YOU MUST HURRY.
THERE'S ONLY ONE FOOD THAT CAN SAVE KOMATSU.
IT'S ACACIA'S SOUP, WHICH SLUMBERS ON THE NEXT CONTINENT, *AREA 7.*
PAIR!!
ALSO KNOWN AS *THE DOUBLE-SIDED DROP.*
THE *FOOD TREASURE* THAT SLUMBERS ON THE *MOUNTAIN CONTINENT!*

TORIKO

GOURMET CHECKLIST

Vol. 319

BROCCO-SHROOMS
(MUSHROOM)

CAPTURE LEVEL: 40
HABITAT: AROUND SPECIAL PINE TREES
SIZE: 37 CM
HEIGHT: ---
WEIGHT: 1.5 KG
PRICE: 1,600,000 YEN PER BUNCH

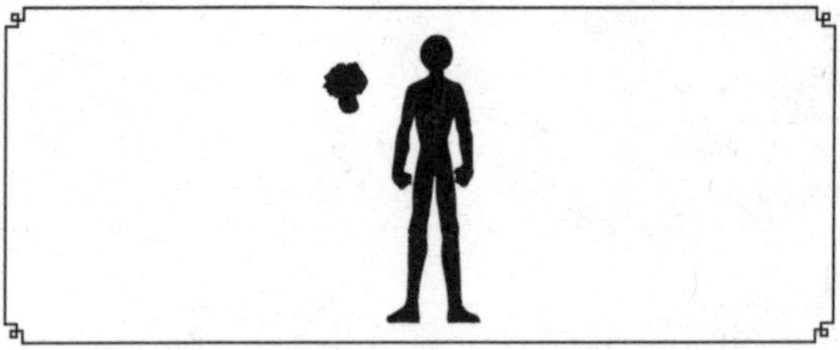

WHOA, BROCCO-SHROOMS*...

SCALE

THEY LET OFF A SWEET SMELL EVERY AUTUMN BUT IF YOU INHALE THEM FOR TOO LONG, BROCCO-SHROOMS WILL GROW ALL OVER YOUR BODY! THAT'S WHY CAPTURING THEM IS A BIT OF A CHALLENGE. THEY ONLY GROW AROUND A SPECIFIC PINE TREE EVERY YEAR, AND THE KEEPERS OF THAT TREE'S MOUNTAIN NEVER TELL ANYONE, NOT EVEN THEIR OWN FAMILY MEMBERS, ITS LOCATION. IT'S A VERY RARE AND EXPENSIVE INGREDIENT.

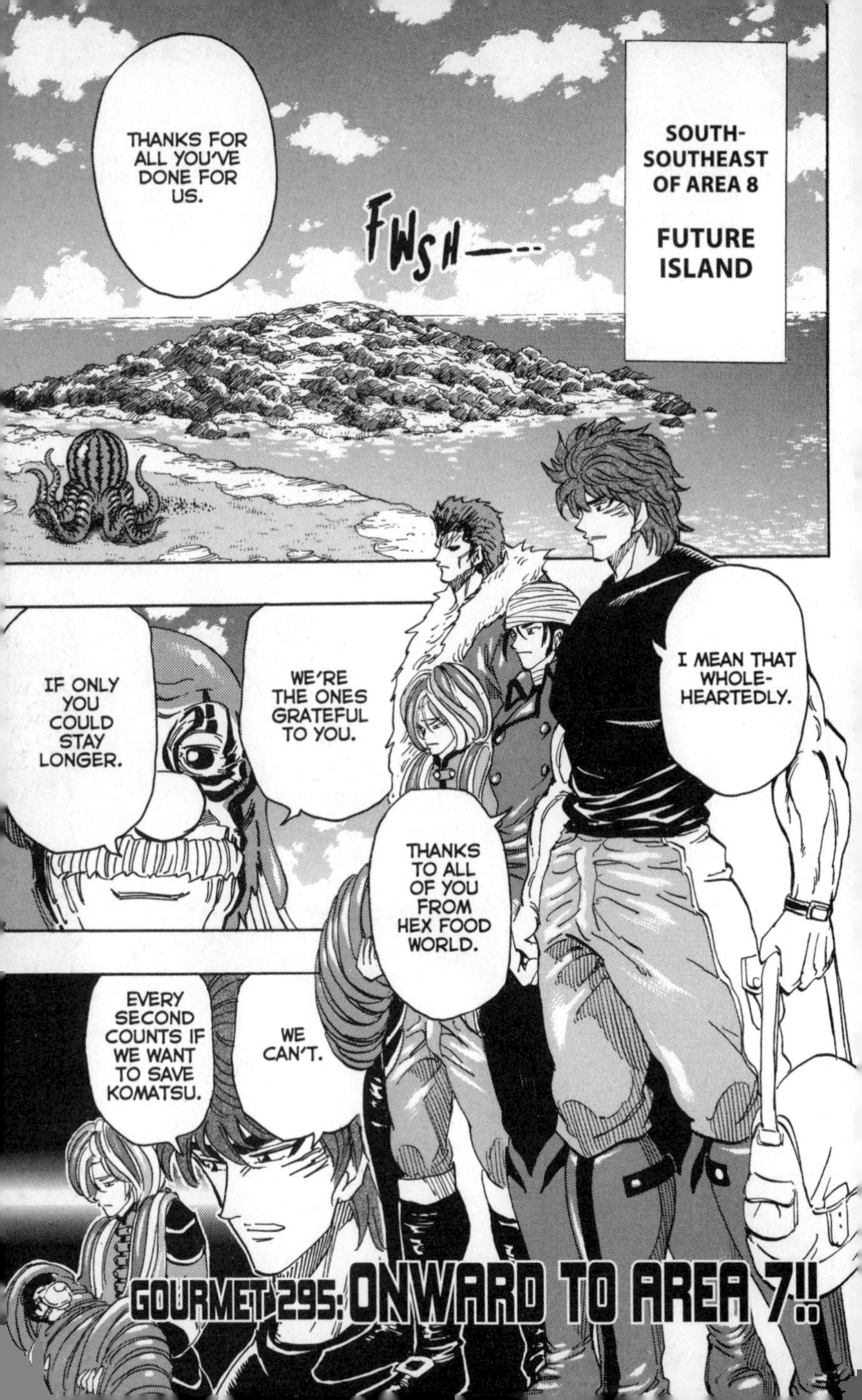
SOUTH-SOUTHEAST OF AREA 8
FUTURE ISLAND
FWSH
THANKS FOR ALL YOU'VE DONE FOR US.
I MEAN THAT WHOLE-HEARTEDLY.
THANKS TO ALL OF YOU FROM HEX FOOD WORLD.
WE'RE THE ONES GRATEFUL TO YOU.
IF ONLY YOU COULD STAY LONGER.
WE CAN'T.
EVERY SECOND COUNTS IF WE WANT TO SAVE KOMATSU.
GOURMET 295: ONWARD TO AREA 7!!

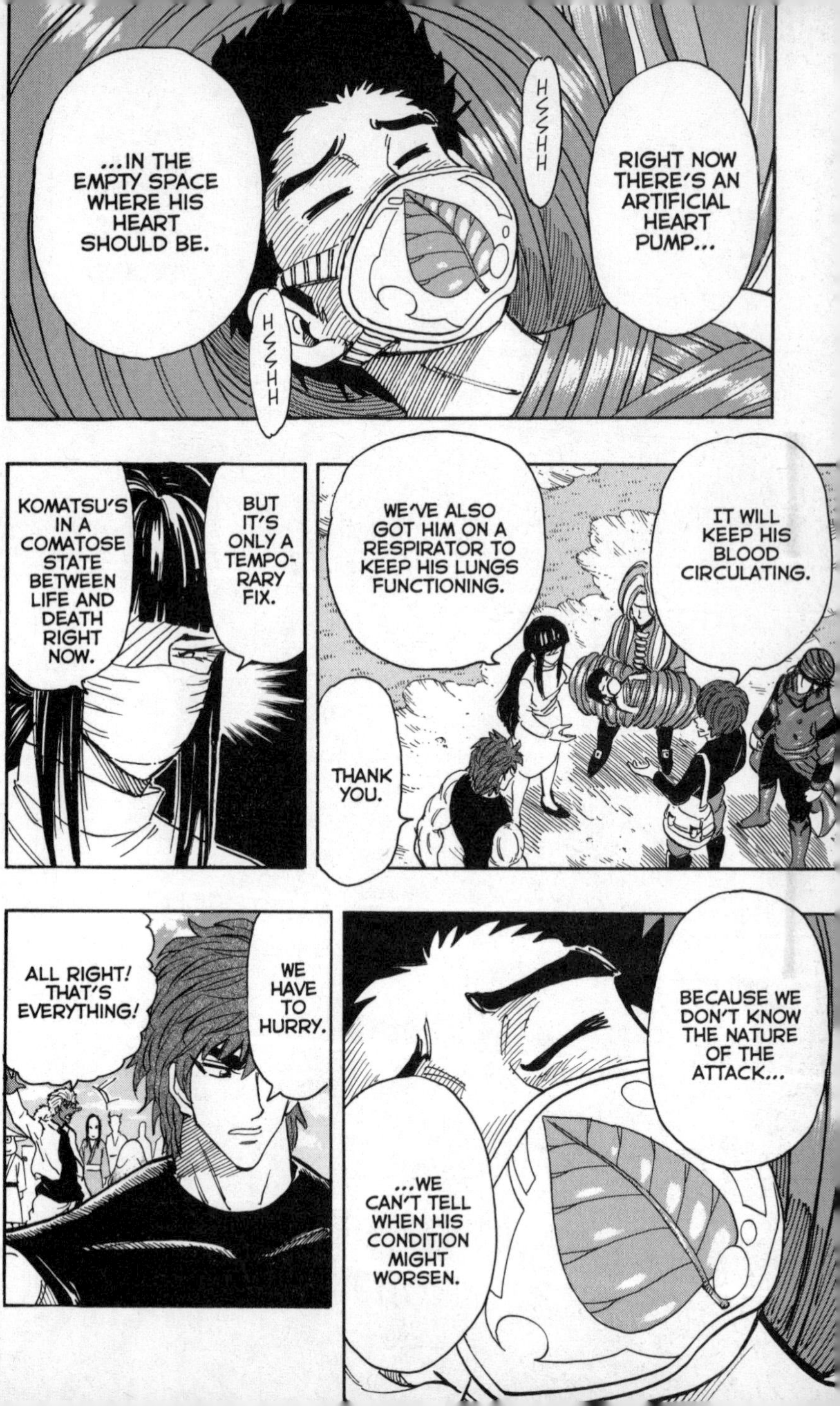
RIGHT NOW THERE'S AN ARTIFICIAL HEART PUMP...
HSSHH
...IN THE EMPTY SPACE WHERE HIS HEART SHOULD BE.
HSSHH
IT WILL KEEP HIS BLOOD CIRCULATING.
WE'VE ALSO GOT HIM ON A RESPIRATOR TO KEEP HIS LUNGS FUNCTIONING.
THANK YOU.
BUT IT'S ONLY A TEMPORARY FIX.
KOMATSU'S IN A COMATOSE STATE BETWEEN LIFE AND DEATH RIGHT NOW.
BECAUSE WE DON'T KNOW THE NATURE OF THE ATTACK...
...WE CAN'T TELL WHEN HIS CONDITION MIGHT WORSEN.
WE HAVE TO HURRY.
ALL RIGHT! THAT'S EVERYTHING!

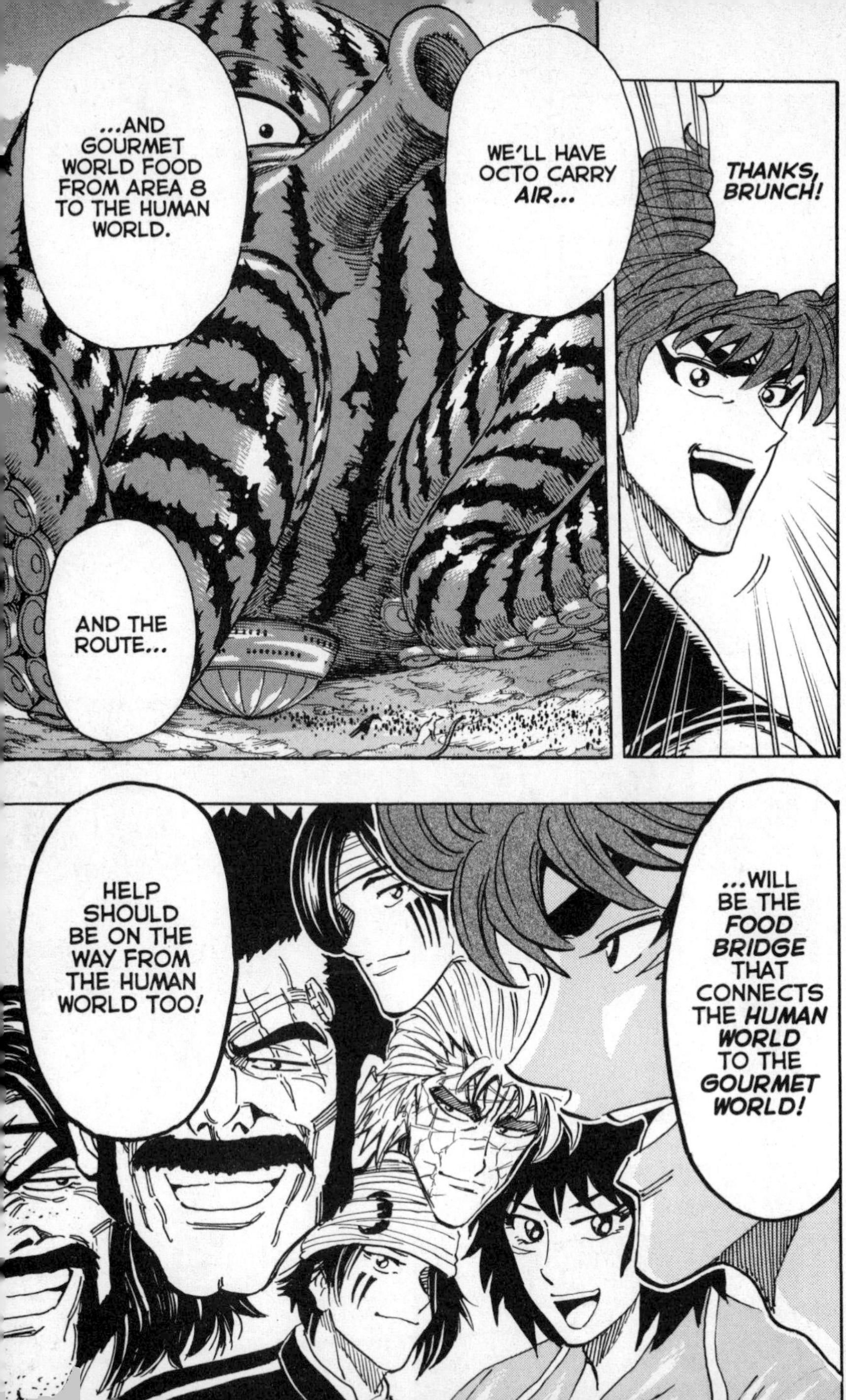
THANKS, BRUNCH!
WE'LL HAVE OCTO CARRY AIR...
...AND GOURMET WORLD FOOD FROM AREA 8 TO THE HUMAN WORLD.
AND THE ROUTE...
...WILL BE THE FOOD BRIDGE THAT CONNECTS THE HUMAN WORLD TO THE GOURMET WORLD!
HELP SHOULD BE ON THE WAY FROM THE HUMAN WORLD TOO!

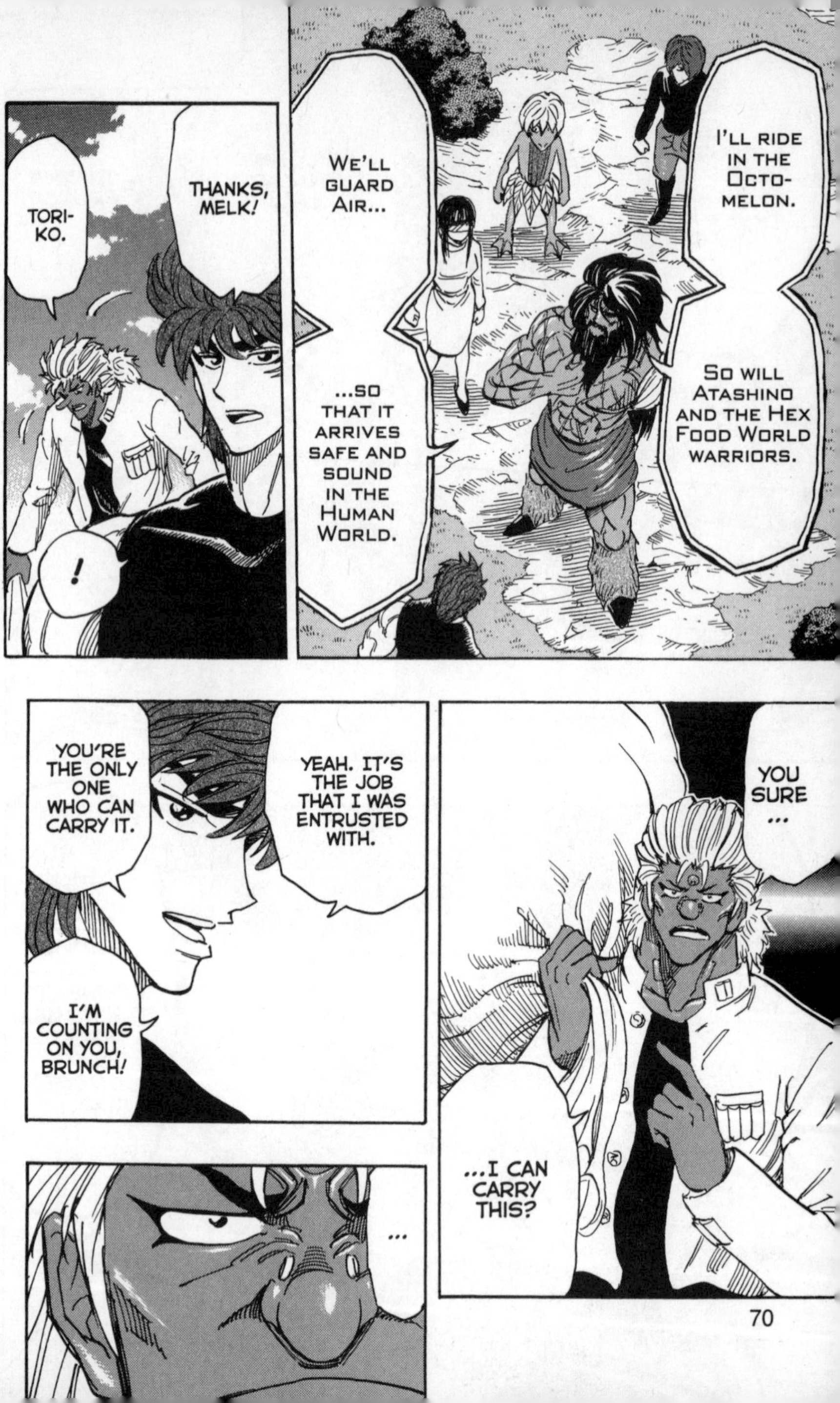
I'LL RIDE IN THE OCTO-MELON.
SO WILL ATASHINO AND THE HEX FOOD WORLD WARRIORS.
WE'LL GUARD AIR...
...SO THAT IT ARRIVES SAFE AND SOUND IN THE HUMAN WORLD.
THANKS, MELK!
TORI-KO.
!
YOU SURE...
...I CAN CARRY THIS?
YEAH. IT'S THE JOB THAT I WAS ENTRUSTED WITH.
YOU'RE THE ONLY ONE WHO CAN CARRY IT.
I'M COUNTING ON YOU, BRUNCH!
...

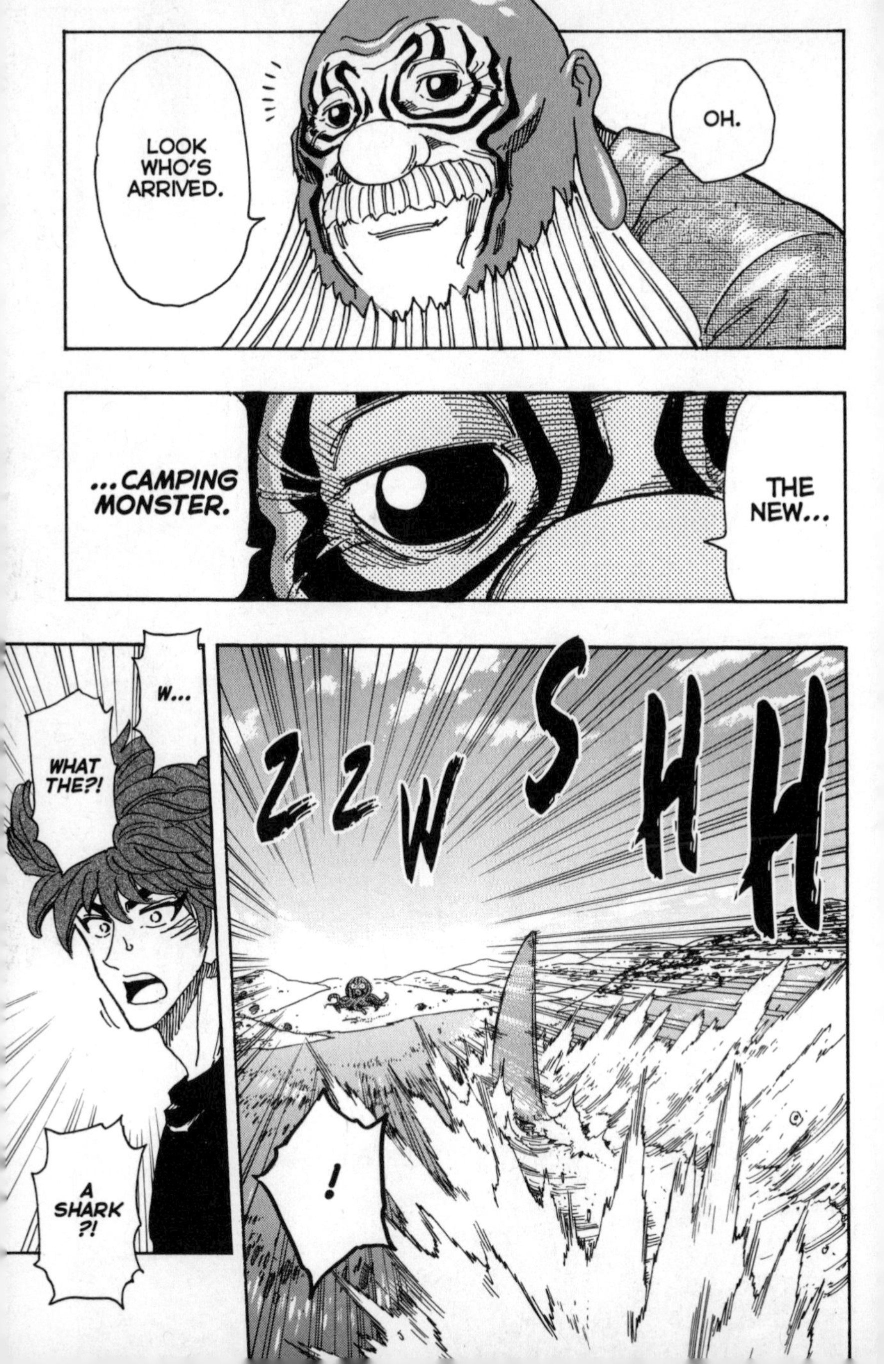
OH.
LOOK WHO'S ARRIVED.
THE NEW...
...CAMPING MONSTER.
ZZWSHH
!
W...
WHAT THE?!
A SHARK ?!

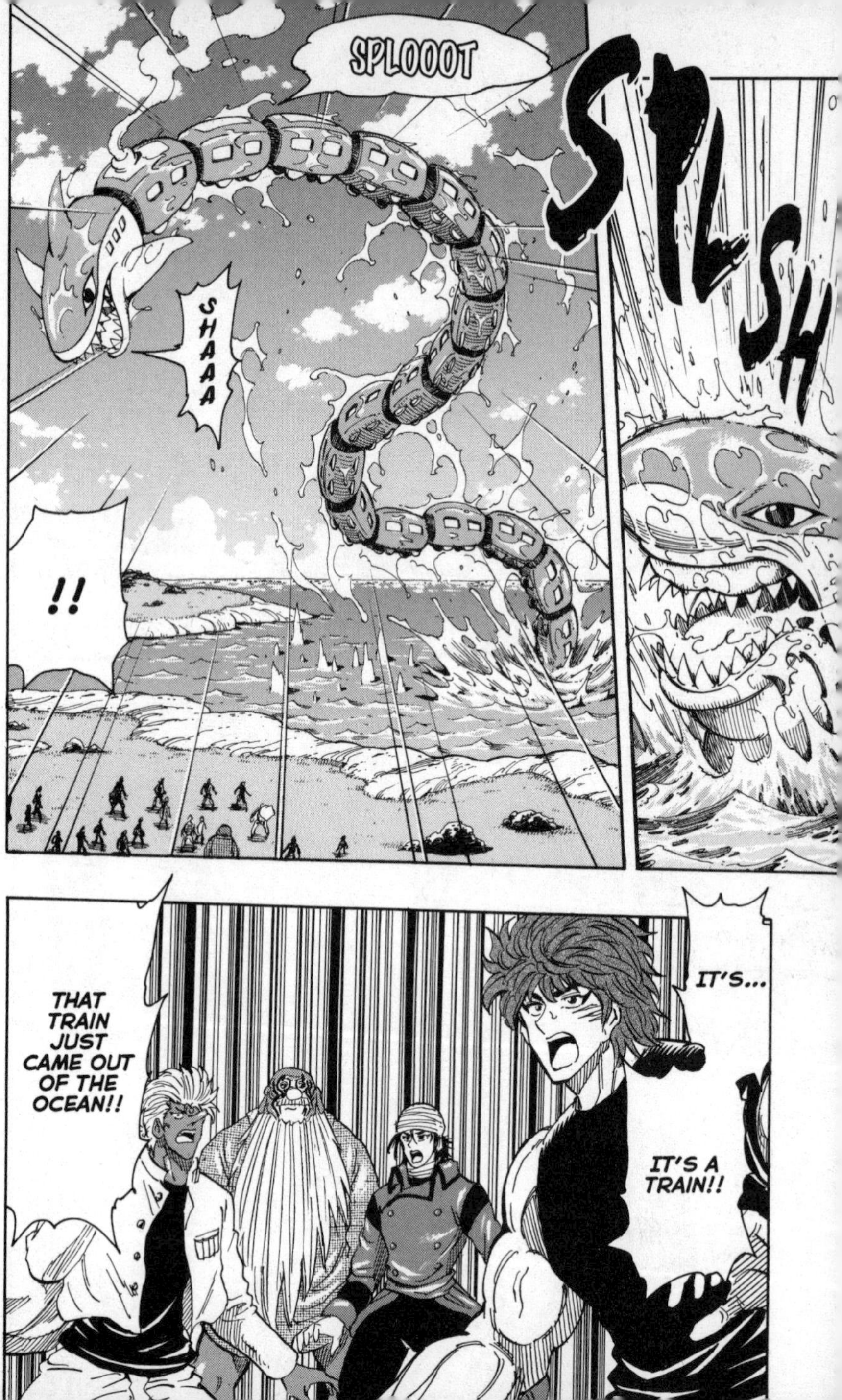
SPLSH
SPLOOOT
SHAAAA
!!
IT'S...
IT'S A TRAIN!!
THAT TRAIN JUST CAME OUT OF THE OCEAN!!

SKREEEE

WHOA...

SO THIS IS...

...OUR NEXT GUIDE.

SHAAA

CHOO-CHOO CHOMPER*
(FISH CRUSTACEAN)
CAPTURE LEVEL 605

*SUBMITTED BY EISHIN YUKI FROM OSAKA!

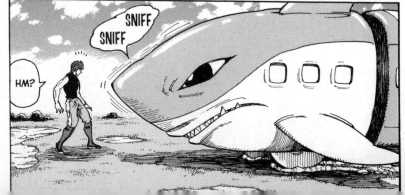

SNIFF
SNIFF

HM?

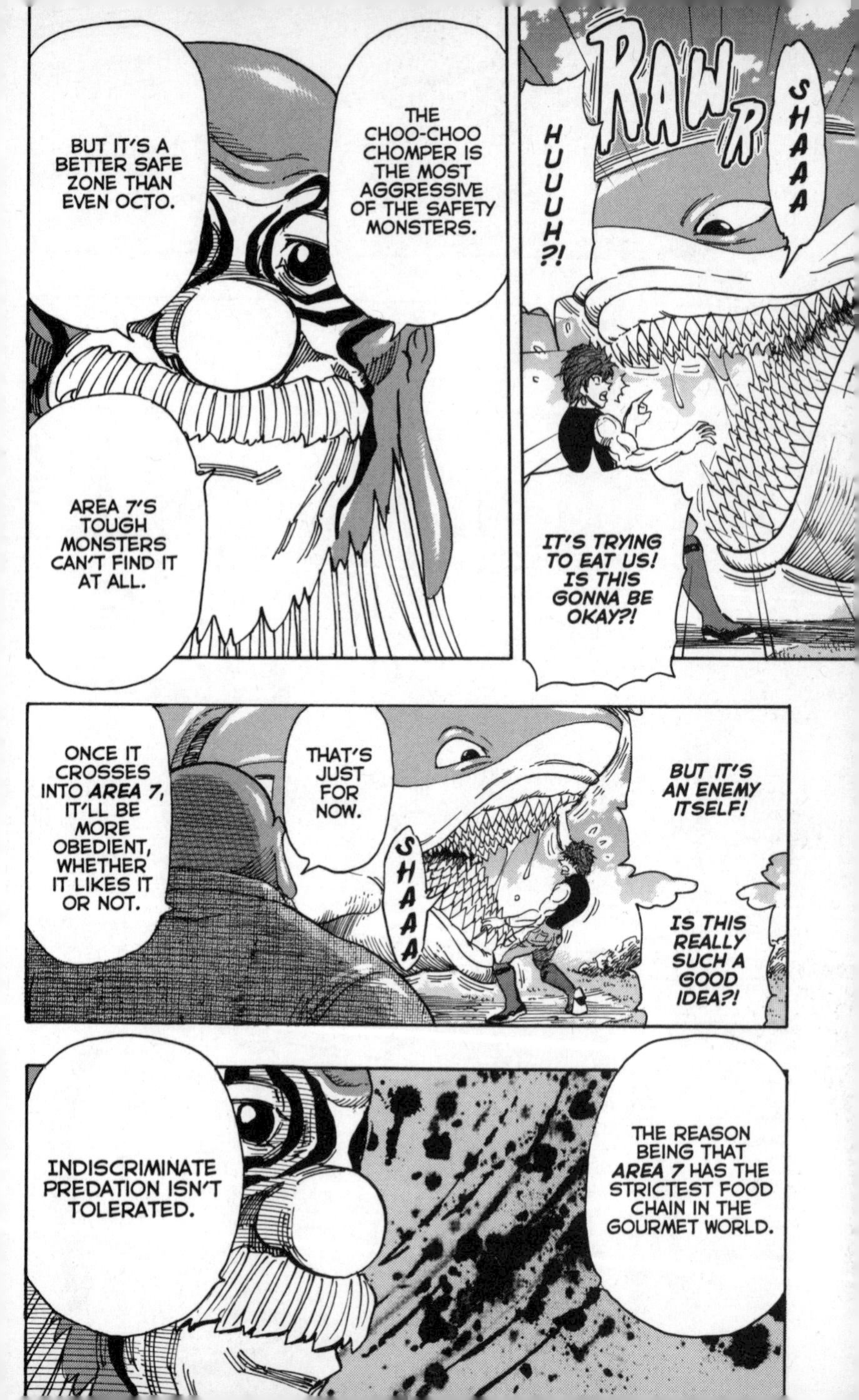
RAWR
SHAAA
HUUUUH?!
IT'S TRYING TO EAT US! IS THIS GONNA BE OKAY?!
THE CHOO-CHOO CHOMPER IS THE MOST AGGRESSIVE OF THE SAFETY MONSTERS.
BUT IT'S A BETTER SAFE ZONE THAN EVEN OCTO.
AREA 7'S TOUGH MONSTERS CAN'T FIND IT AT ALL.
BUT IT'S AN ENEMY ITSELF!
IS THIS REALLY SUCH A GOOD IDEA?!
SHAAA
THAT'S JUST FOR NOW.
ONCE IT CROSSES INTO AREA 7, IT'LL BE MORE OBEDIENT, WHETHER IT LIKES IT OR NOT.
THE REASON BEING THAT AREA 7 HAS THE STRICTEST FOOD CHAIN IN THE GOURMET WORLD.
INDISCRIMINATE PREDATION ISN'T TOLERATED.

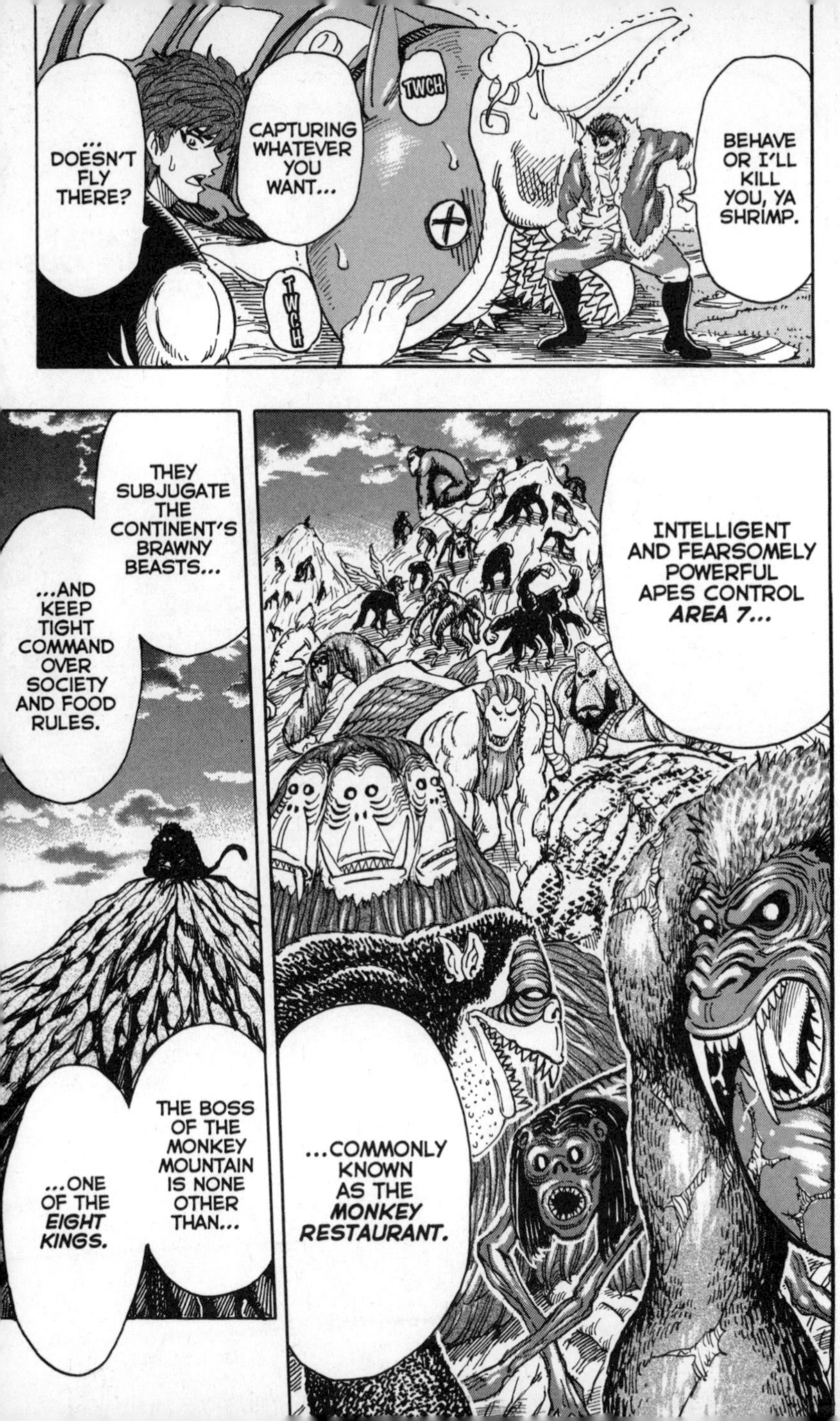
BEHAVE OR I'LL KILL YOU, YA SHRIMP.
TWCH
CAPTURING WHATEVER YOU WANT...
TWCH
...DOESN'T FLY THERE?
INTELLIGENT AND FEARSOMELY POWERFUL APES CONTROL *AREA 7*...
...COMMONLY KNOWN AS THE *MONKEY RESTAURANT*.
THEY SUBJUGATE THE CONTINENT'S BRAWNY BEASTS...
...AND KEEP TIGHT COMMAND OVER SOCIETY AND FOOD RULES.
THE BOSS OF THE MONKEY MOUNTAIN IS NONE OTHER THAN...
...ONE OF THE *EIGHT KINGS*.

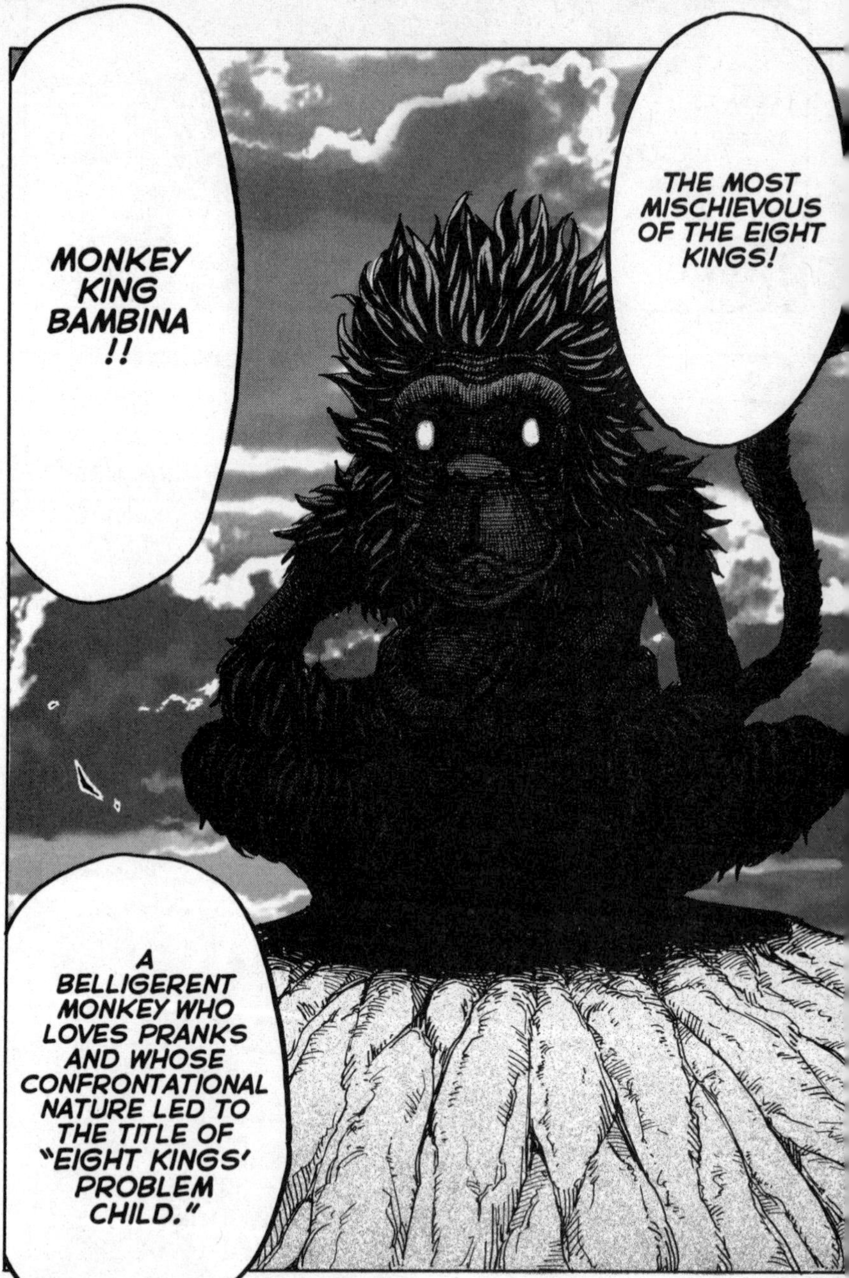
THE MOST MISCHIEVOUS OF THE EIGHT KINGS!
MONKEY KING BAMBINA !!
A BELLIGERENT MONKEY WHO LOVES PRANKS AND WHOSE CONFRONTATIONAL NATURE LED TO THE TITLE OF "EIGHT KINGS' PROBLEM CHILD."

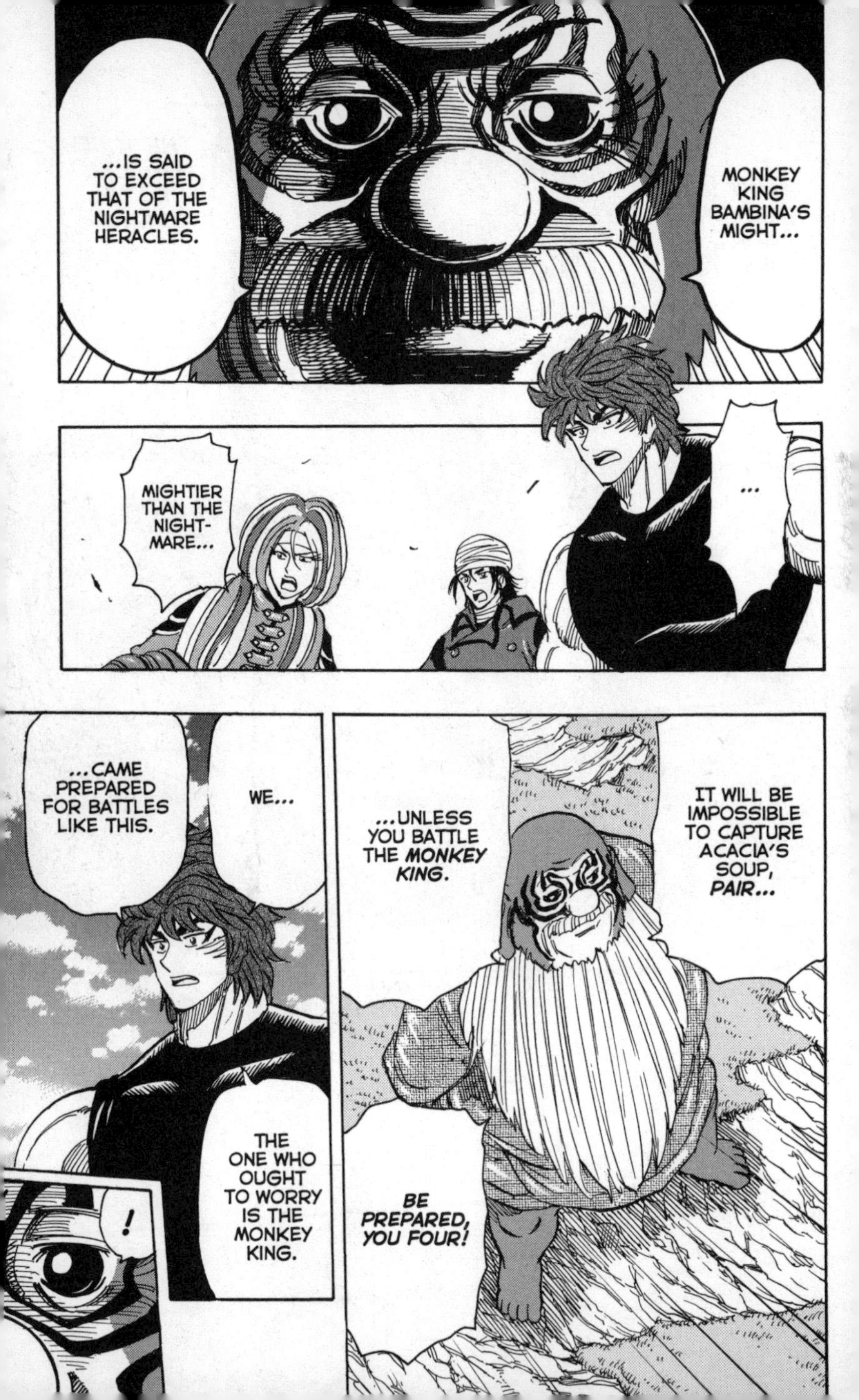
MONKEY KING BAMBINA'S MIGHT...
...IS SAID TO EXCEED THAT OF THE NIGHTMARE HERACLES.
...
MIGHTIER THAN THE NIGHT-MARE...
IT WILL BE IMPOSSIBLE TO CAPTURE ACACIA'S SOUP, *PAIR*...
...UNLESS YOU BATTLE THE *MONKEY KING*.
BE PREPARED, YOU FOUR!
WE...
...CAME PREPARED FOR BATTLES LIKE THIS.
THE ONE WHO OUGHT TO WORRY IS THE MONKEY KING.
!

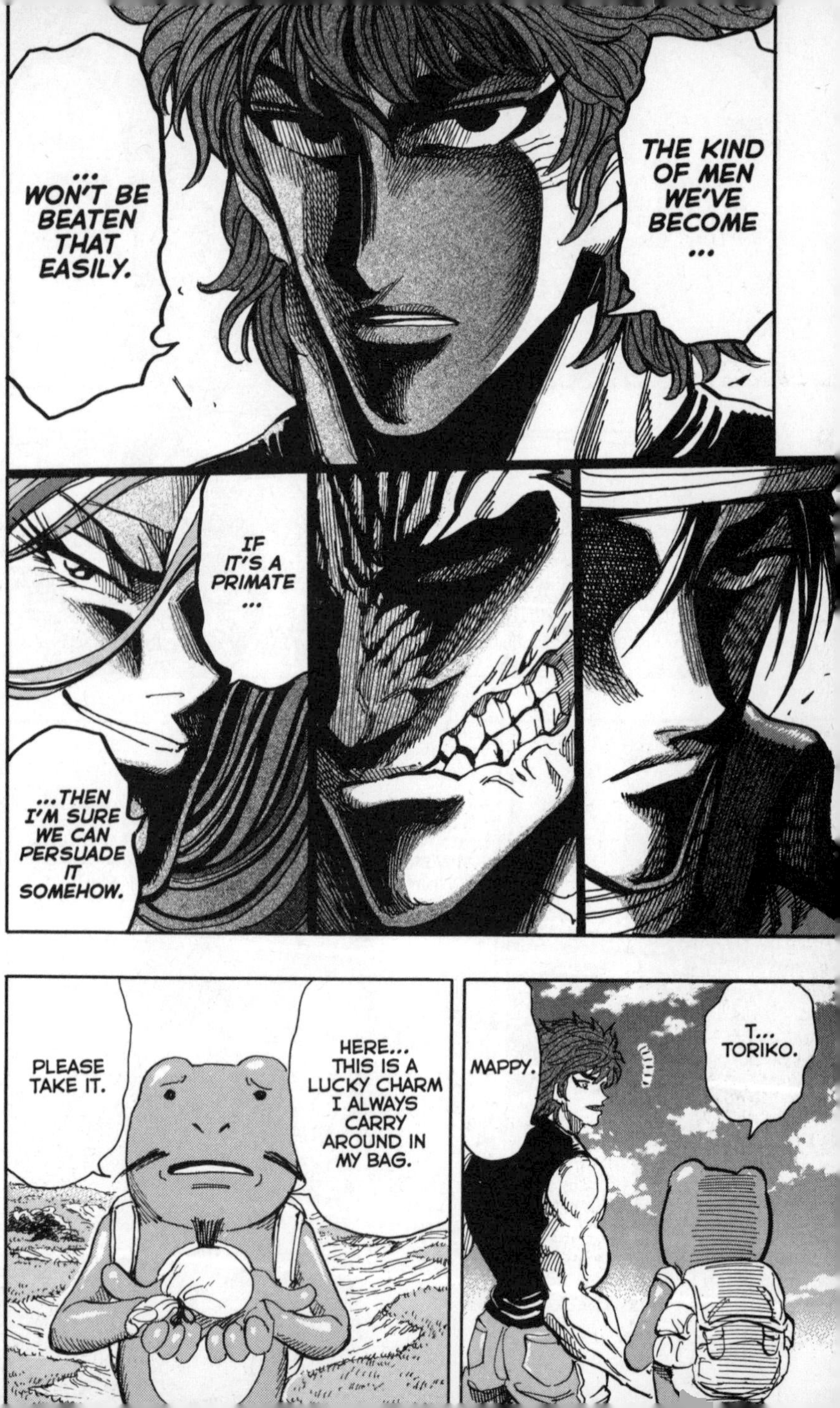
THE KIND OF MEN WE'VE BECOME...
...WON'T BE BEATEN THAT EASILY.
IF IT'S A PRIMATE...
...THEN I'M SURE WE CAN PERSUADE IT SOMEHOW.
T... TORIKO.
MAPPY.
HERE... THIS IS A LUCKY CHARM I ALWAYS CARRY AROUND IN MY BAG.
PLEASE TAKE IT.

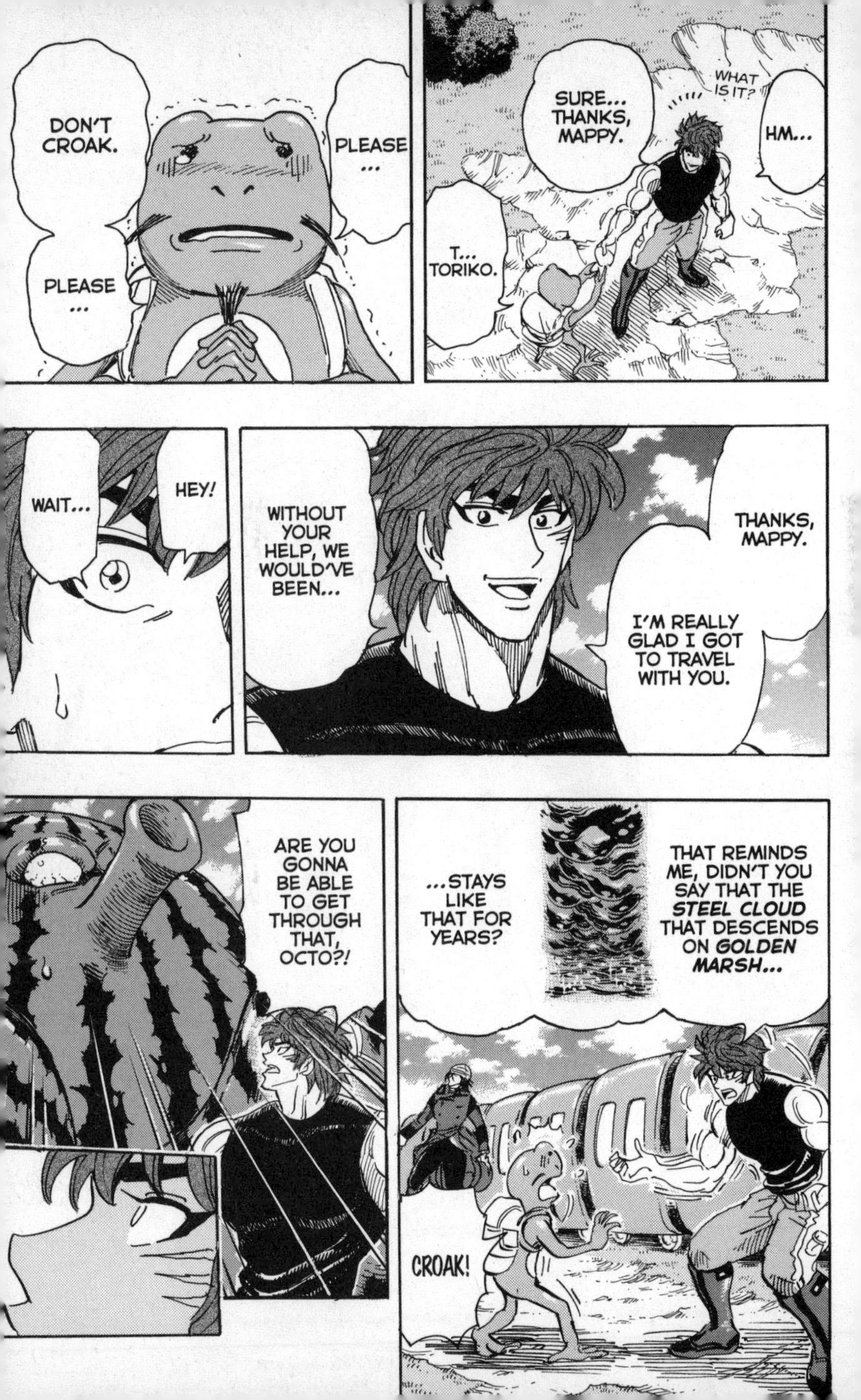
HM...
WHAT IS IT?
SURE... THANKS, MAPPY.
T... TORIKO.
PLEASE ...
DON'T CROAK.
PLEASE ...
THANKS, MAPPY.
I'M REALLY GLAD I GOT TO TRAVEL WITH YOU.
WITHOUT YOUR HELP, WE WOULD'VE BEEN...
HEY!
WAIT...
THAT REMINDS ME, DIDN'T YOU SAY THAT THE *STEEL CLOUD* THAT DESCENDS ON *GOLDEN MARSH*...
...STAYS LIKE THAT FOR YEARS?
CROAK!
ARE YOU GONNA BE ABLE TO GET THROUGH THAT, OCTO?!

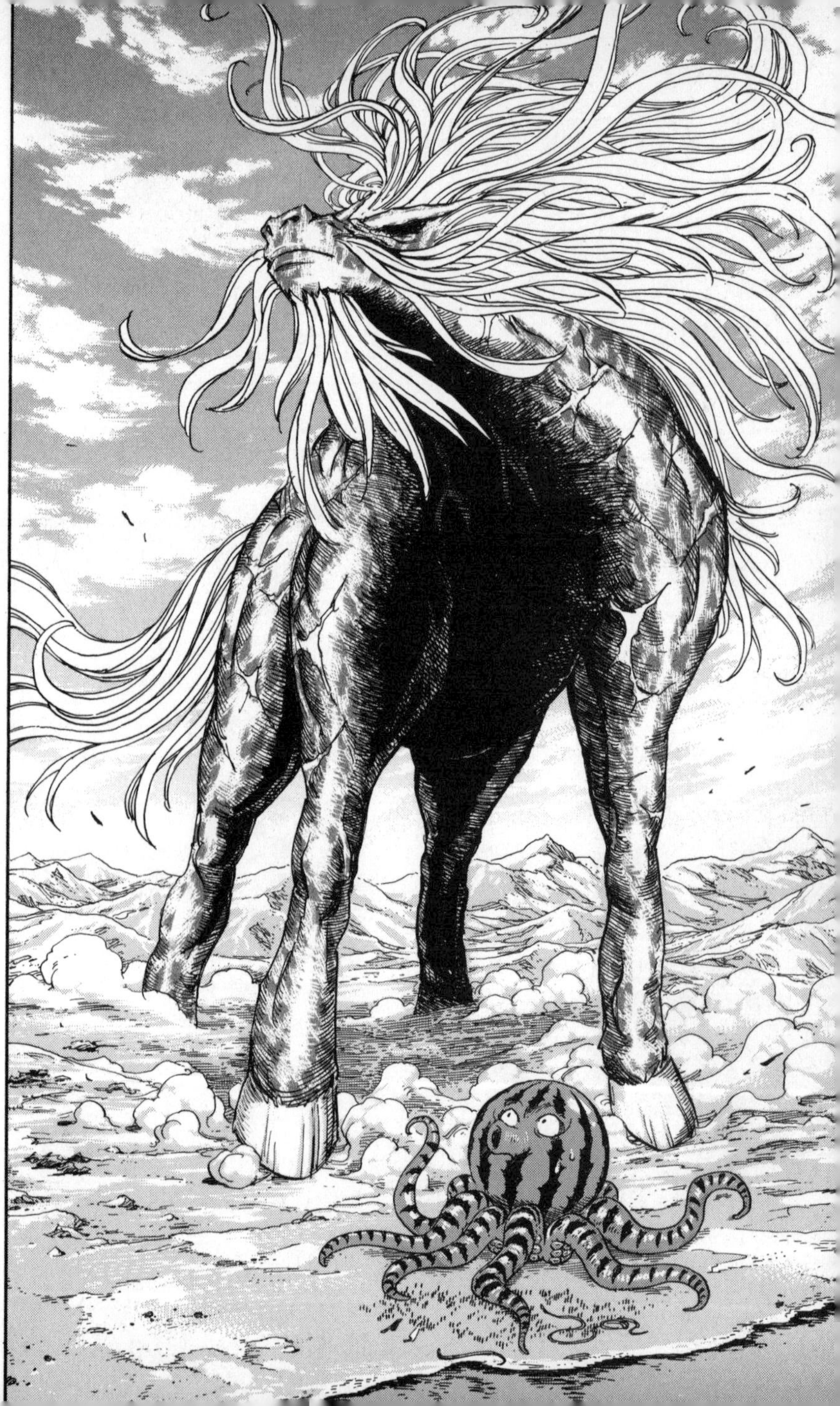

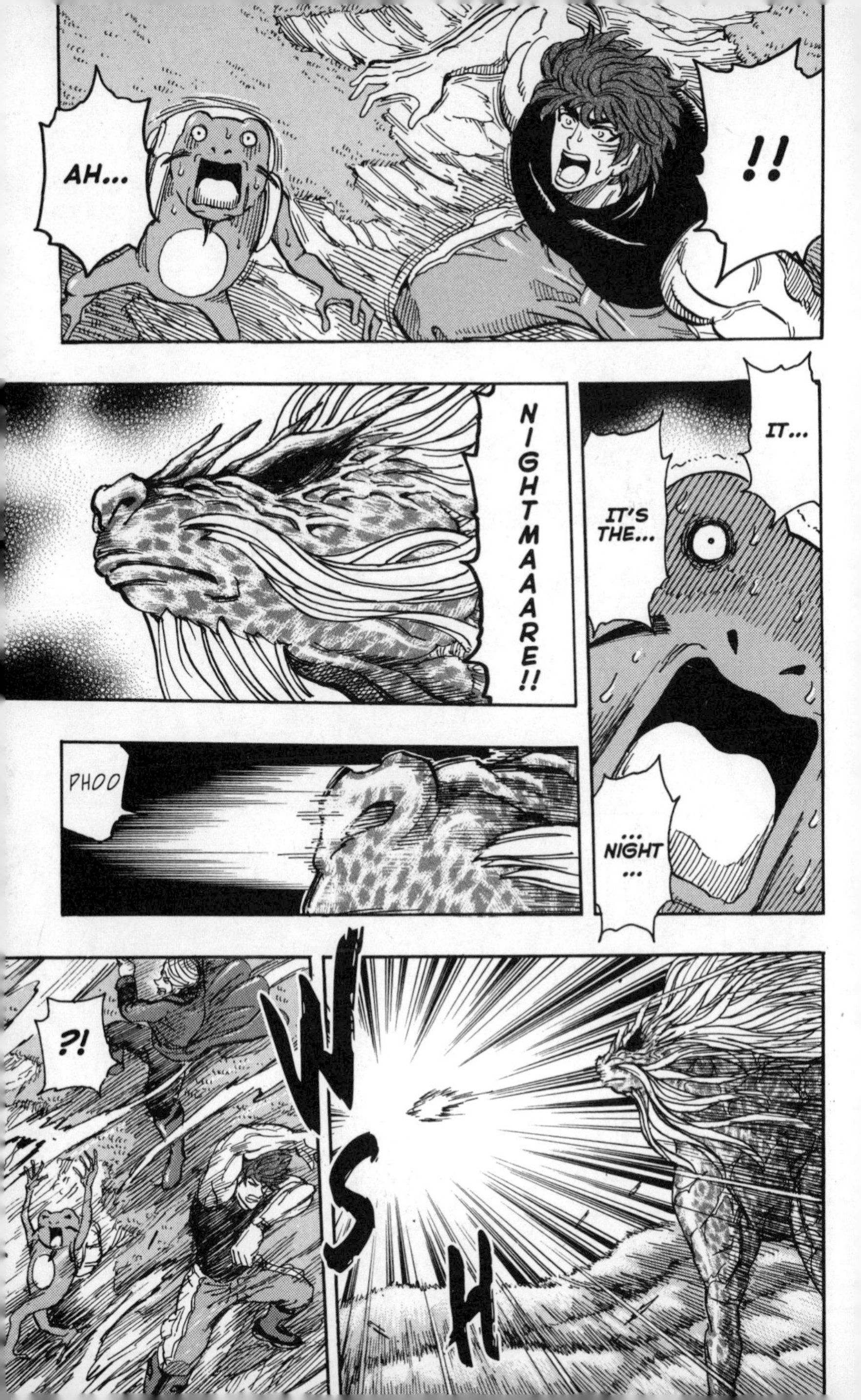
!!
AH...
IT...
IT'S THE...
...NIGHT...
NIGHTMAAAARE!!
PHOO
WSSH
?!

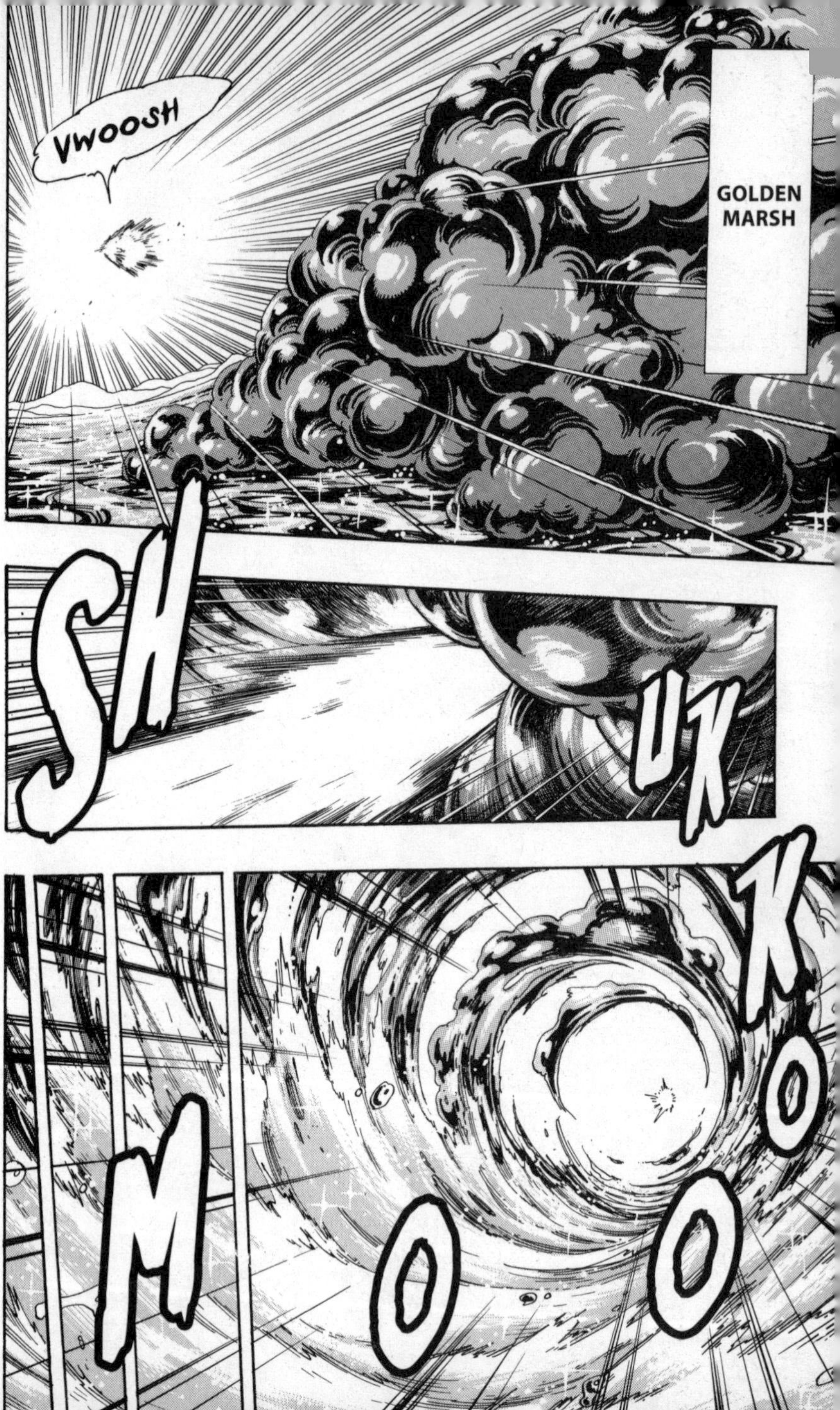
GOLDEN MARSH
VWOOSH
SH
UK
MOOOK

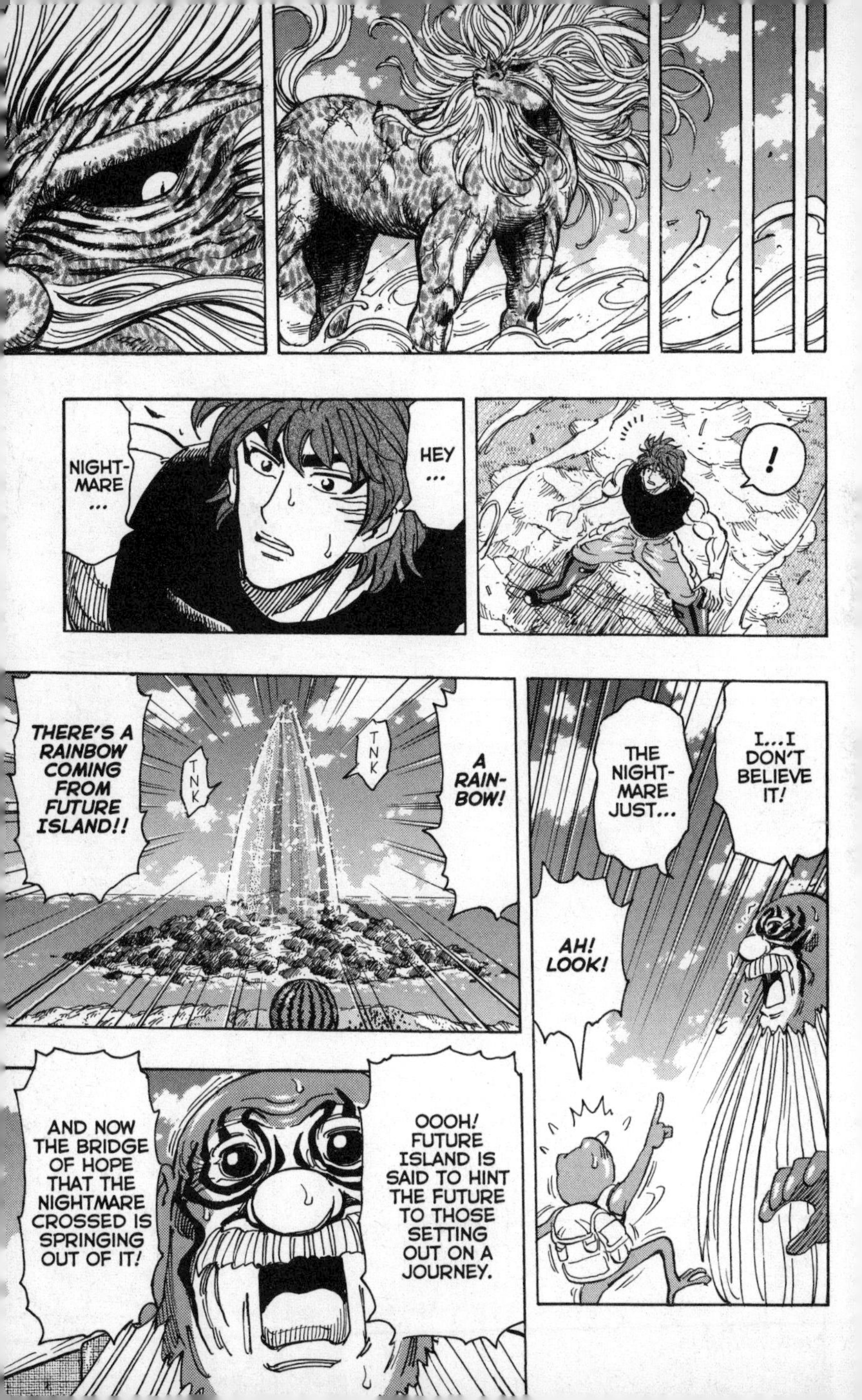
!
HEY ...
NIGHT-MARE ...
I...I DON'T BELIEVE IT!
THE NIGHT-MARE JUST...
AH! LOOK!
A RAIN-BOW!
TNK
TNK
THERE'S A RAINBOW COMING FROM FUTURE ISLAND!!
OOOH! FUTURE ISLAND IS SAID TO HINT THE FUTURE TO THOSE SETTING OUT ON A JOURNEY.
AND NOW THE BRIDGE OF HOPE THAT THE NIGHTMARE CROSSED IS SPRINGING OUT OF IT!

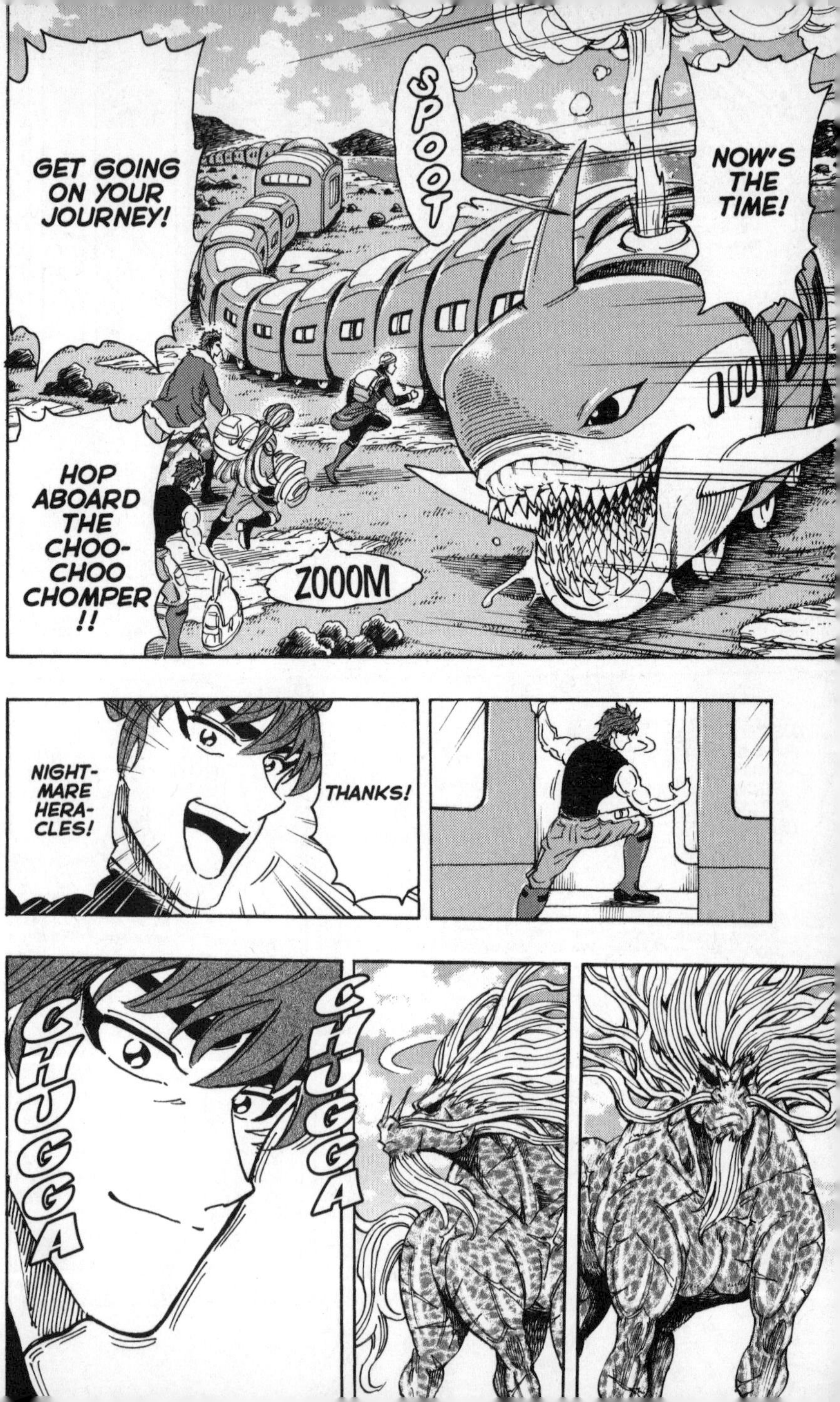
NOW'S THE TIME!
SPOOT
GET GOING ON YOUR JOURNEY!
HOP ABOARD THE CHOO-CHOO CHOMPER!!
ZOOOM
THANKS!
NIGHT-MARE HERA-CLES!
CHUGGA
CHUGGA

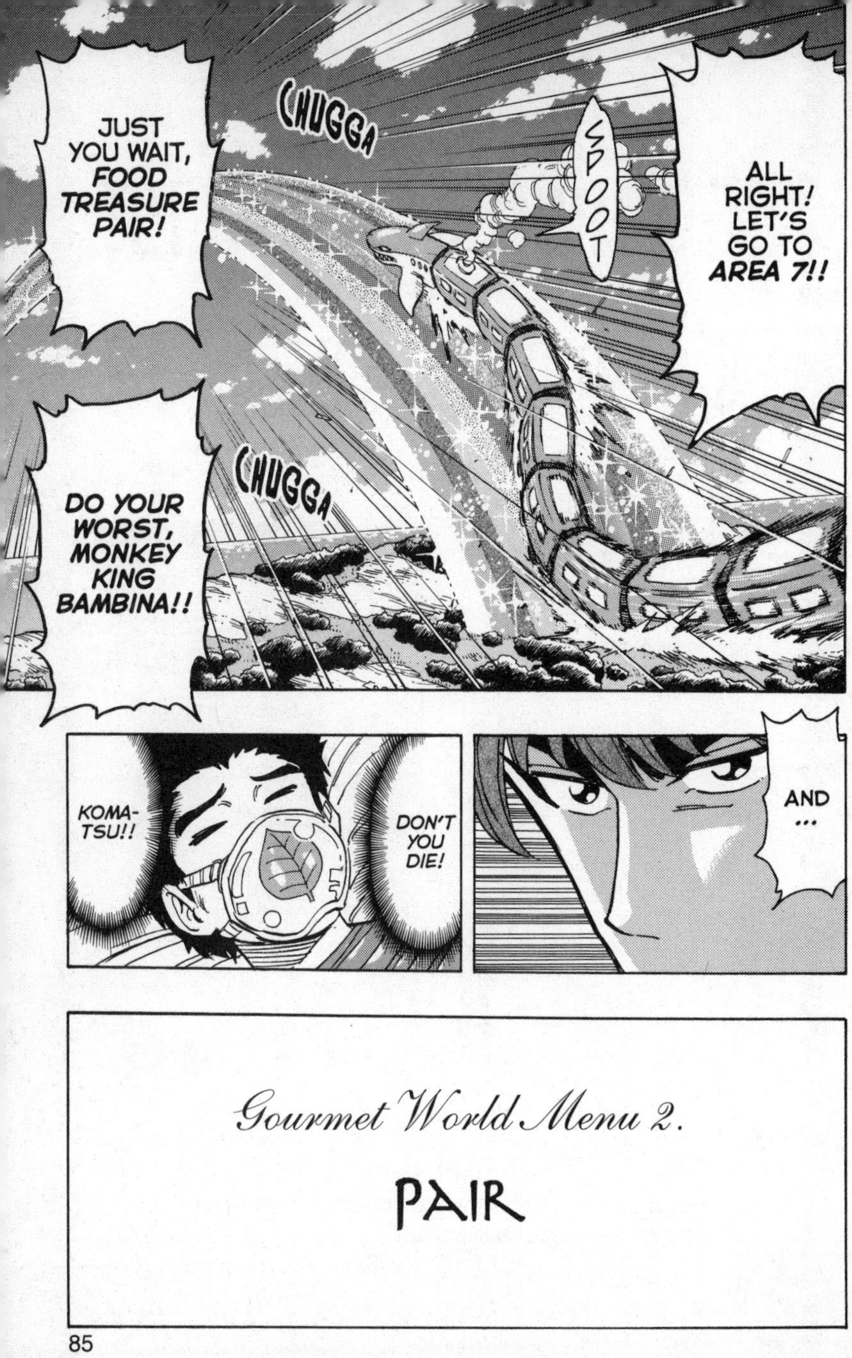

ALL RIGHT! LET'S GO TO AREA 7!!
SPOOT
CHUGGA
JUST YOU WAIT, FOOD TREASURE PAIR!
CHUGGA
DO YOUR WORST, MONKEY KING BAMBINA!!
AND ...
KOMATSU!!
DON'T YOU DIE!

Gourmet World Menu 2.

PAIR

TORIKO

GOURMET CHECKLIST

Vol. 320

CHOCOLATE SEAWEED

(SEA VEGETATION)

CAPTURE LEVEL: 5

HABITAT: LAND THAT USED TO BE OCEAN

SIZE: 55 CM

HEIGHT: ---

WEIGHT: 1.5 KG

PRICE: 120,000 YEN PER STRIP

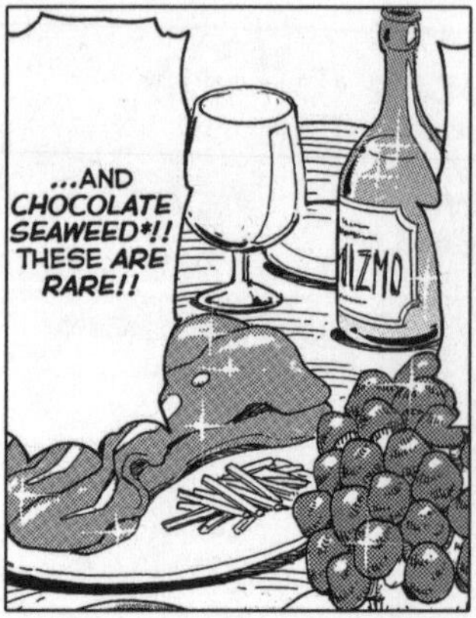
...AND CHOCOLATE SEAWEED*!! THESE ARE RARE!!
MIZMO

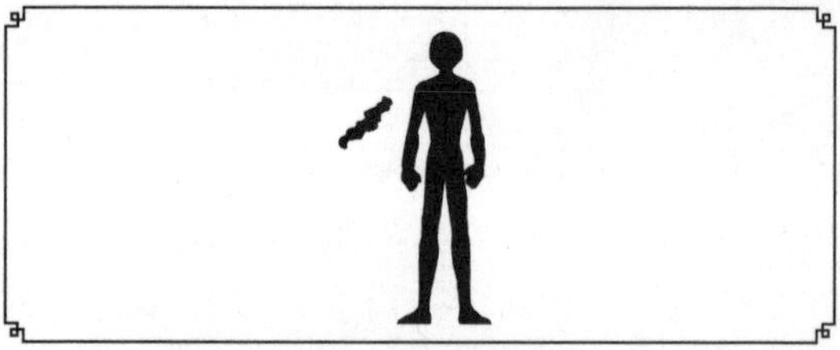

SCALE

A SEAWEED THAT GROWS ON LAND THAT USED TO BE OCEAN. THE SWEET CHOCOLATE FLAVOR IS SLIGHTLY SALTY, MAKING IT REMINISCENT OF ITS FORMER HABITAT. THE CONTRAST OF SWEET AND SALTY IS MOST EXQUISITE AND WORTH THE HIGH PRICE TO PAY FOR GETTING SOME. THIS IS A HIGH-QUALITY INGREDIENT THAT IS POPULAR BOTH AS A SALTY SNACK WITH BEER AND A SWEET TREAT.

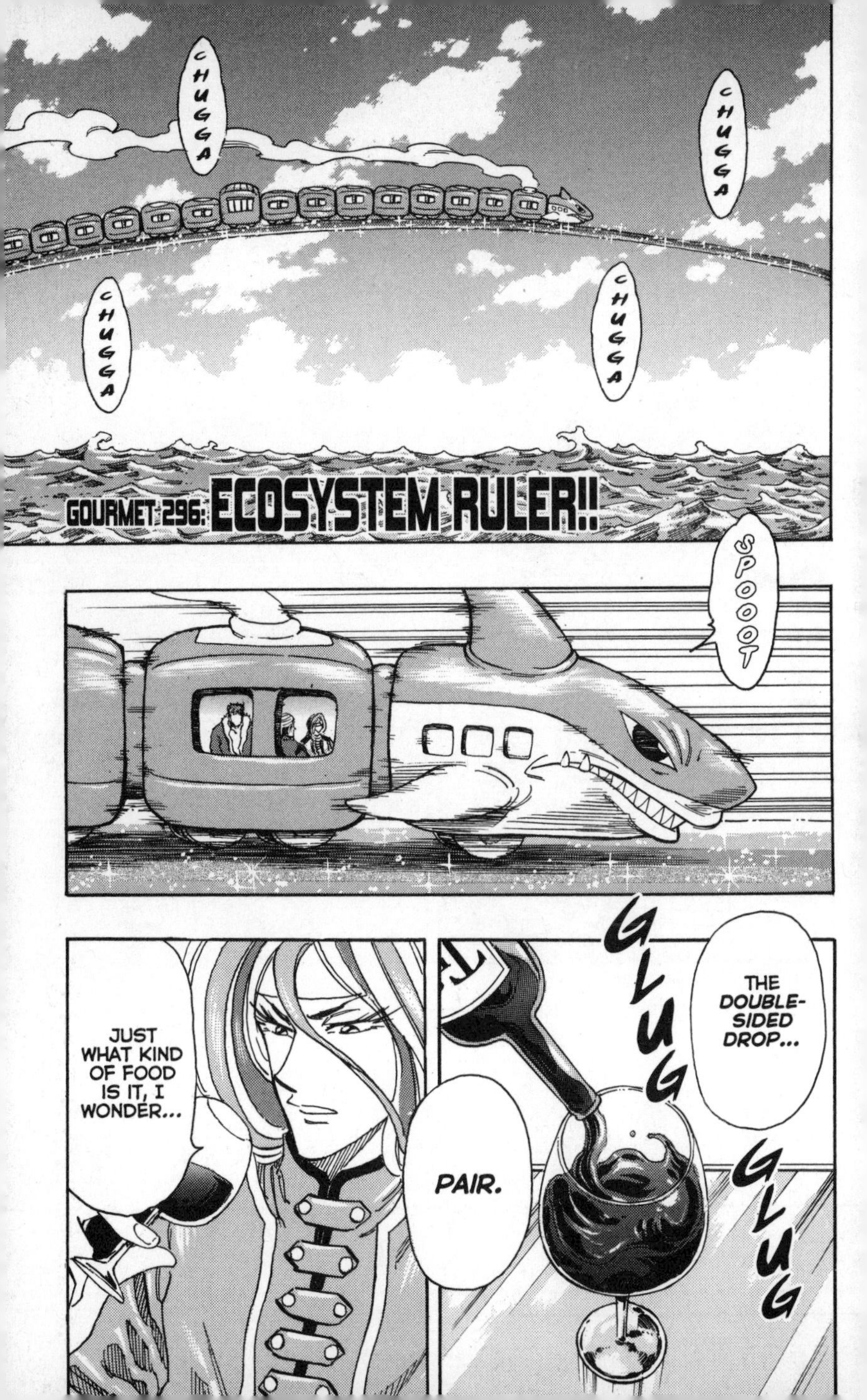
CHUGGA
CHUGGA
CHUGGA
CHUGGA
GOURMET 296: ECOSYSTEM RULER!!
SPOOOOT
GLUG
GLUG
THE DOUBLE-SIDED DROP...
PAIR.
JUST WHAT KIND OF FOOD IS IT, I WONDER...

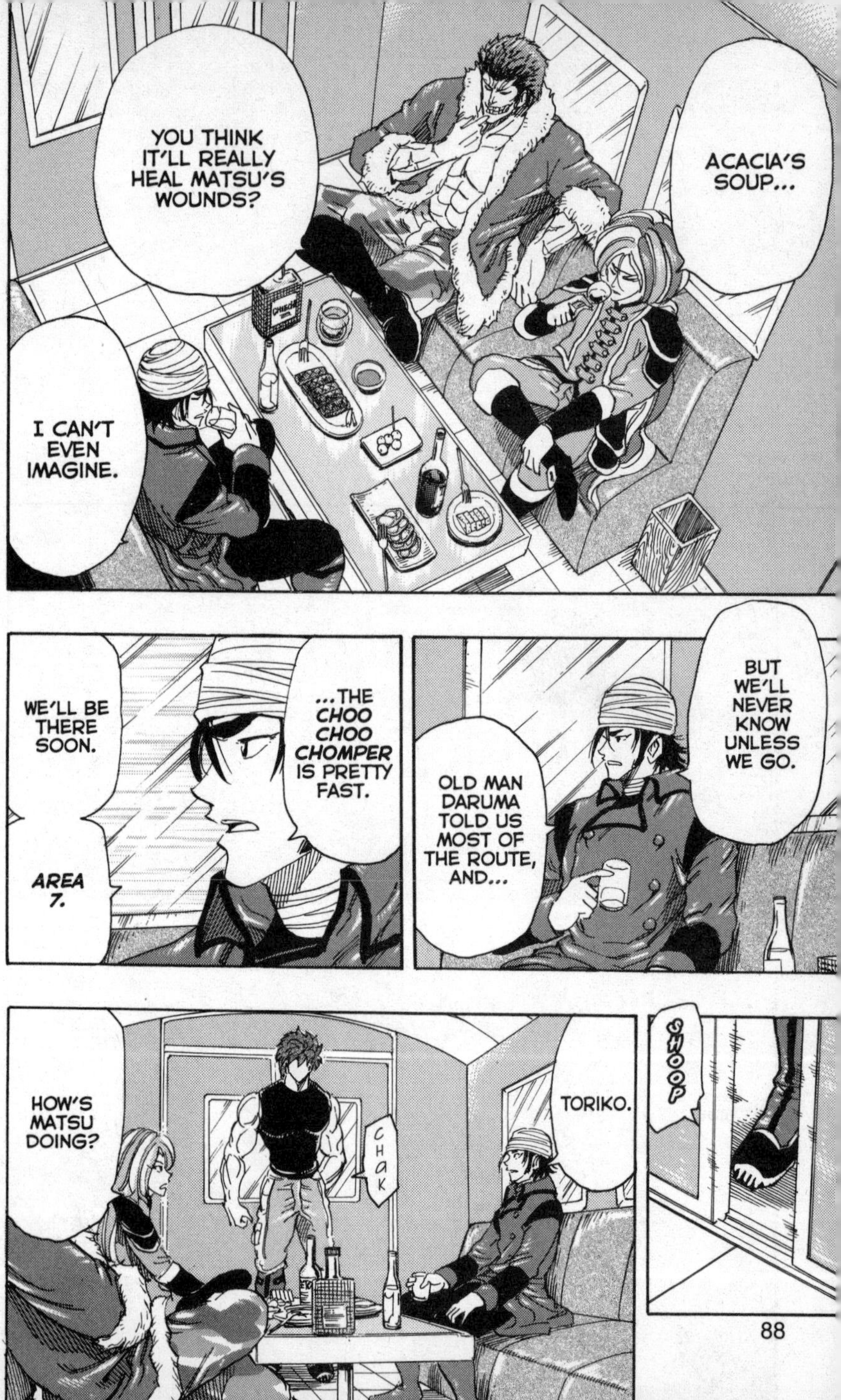
ACACIA'S SOUP...
YOU THINK IT'LL REALLY HEAL MATSU'S WOUNDS?
I CAN'T EVEN IMAGINE.
BUT WE'LL NEVER KNOW UNLESS WE GO.
OLD MAN DARUMA TOLD US MOST OF THE ROUTE, AND...
...THE *CHOO CHOO CHOMPER* IS PRETTY FAST.
WE'LL BE THERE SOON.
AREA 7.
SHOOP
TORIKO.
CHAK
HOW'S MATSU DOING?

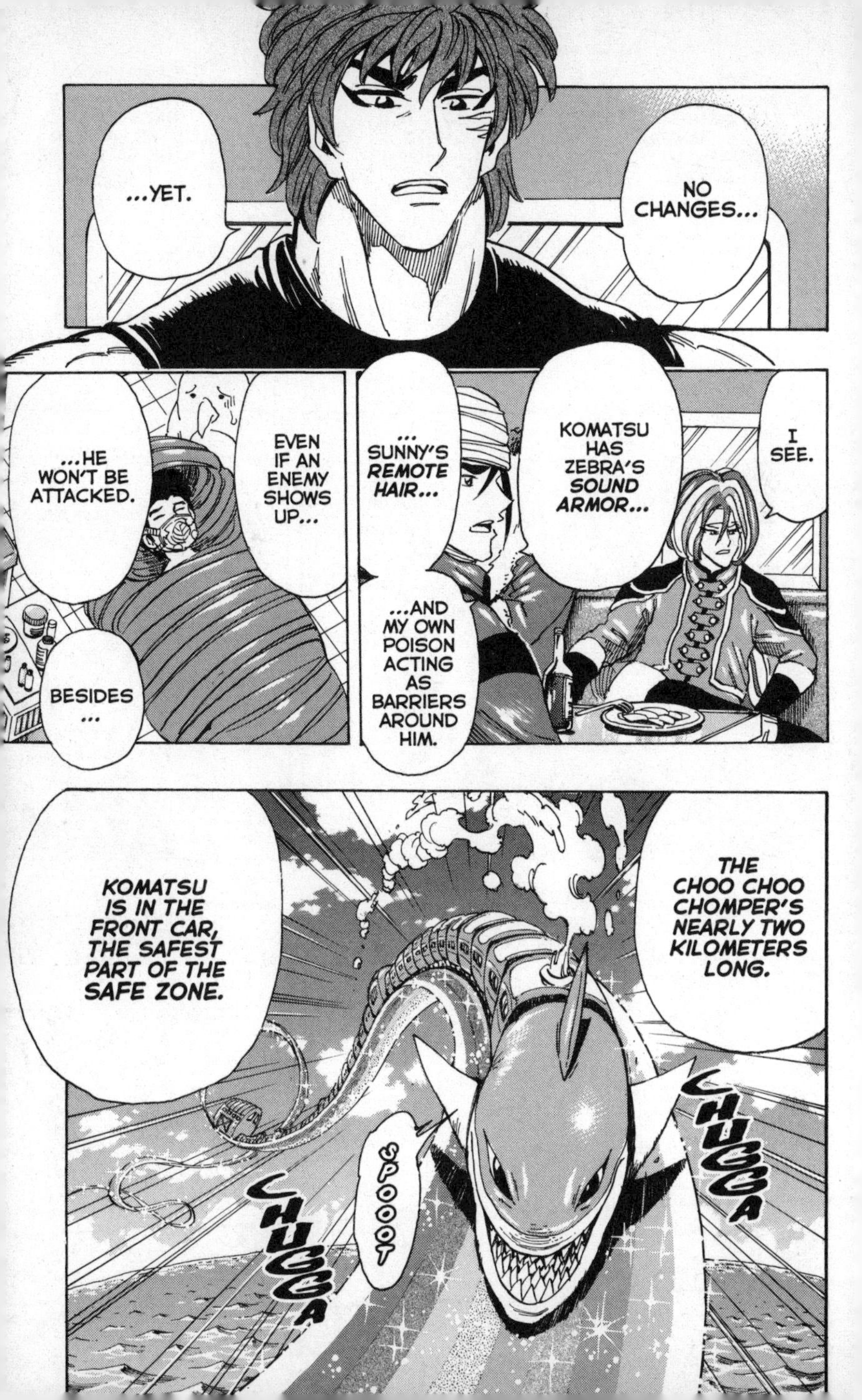
NO CHANGES...
...YET.
I SEE.
KOMATSU HAS ZEBRA'S SOUND ARMOR...
... SUNNY'S REMOTE HAIR...
...AND MY OWN POISON ACTING AS BARRIERS AROUND HIM.
EVEN IF AN ENEMY SHOWS UP...
...HE WON'T BE ATTACKED.
BESIDES...
THE CHOO CHOO CHOMPER'S NEARLY TWO KILOMETERS LONG.
KOMATSU IS IN THE FRONT CAR, THE SAFEST PART OF THE SAFE ZONE.
CHUGGA
SPOOOOT
CHUGGA

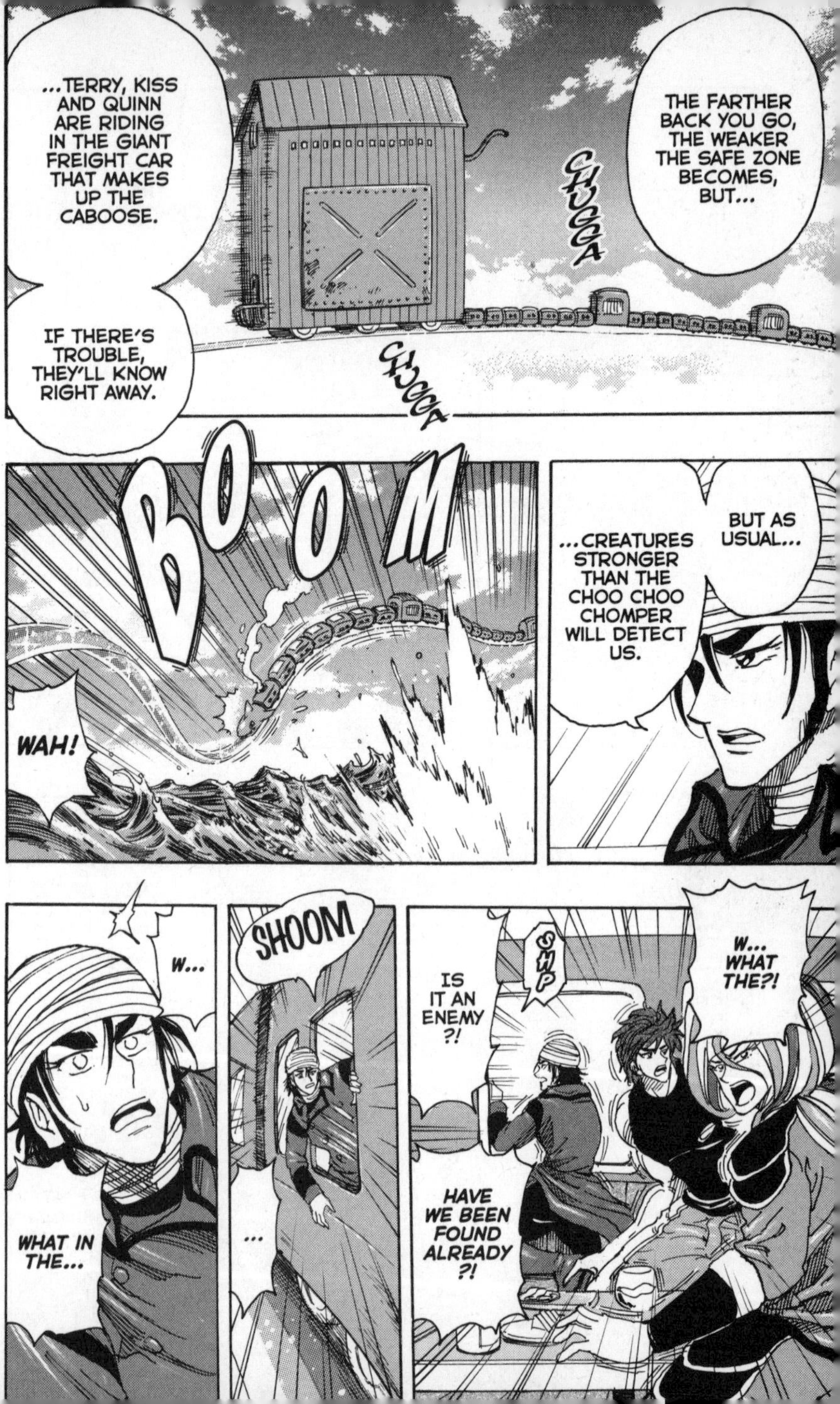
THE FARTHER BACK YOU GO, THE WEAKER THE SAFE ZONE BECOMES, BUT...
CHUGGA
...TERRY, KISS AND QUINN ARE RIDING IN THE GIANT FREIGHT CAR THAT MAKES UP THE CABOOSE.
IF THERE'S TROUBLE, THEY'LL KNOW RIGHT AWAY.
CHUGGA
BUT AS USUAL...
...CREATURES STRONGER THAN THE CHOO CHOO CHOMPER WILL DETECT US.
BOOM
WAH!
W... WHAT THE?!
SHP
IS IT AN ENEMY ?!
HAVE WE BEEN FOUND ALREADY ?!
SHOOM
...
W...
WHAT IN THE...

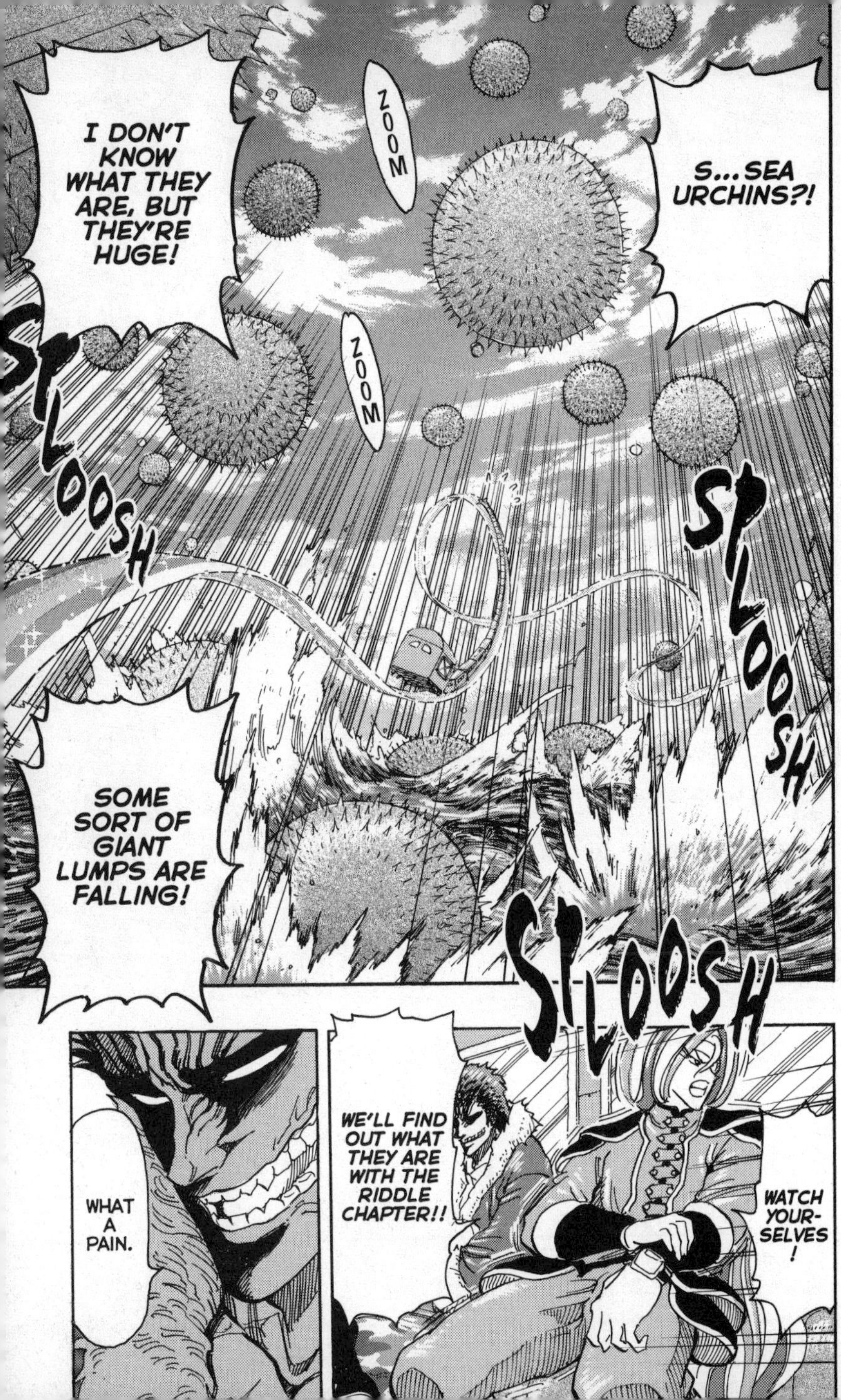
S...SEA URCHINS?!
ZOOM
ZOOM
I DON'T KNOW WHAT THEY ARE, BUT THEY'RE HUGE!
SPLOOSH
SPLOOSH
SOME SORT OF GIANT LUMPS ARE FALLING!
SPLOOSH
WATCH YOURSELVES!
WE'LL FIND OUT WHAT THEY ARE WITH THE RIDDLE CHAPTER!!
WHAT A PAIN.

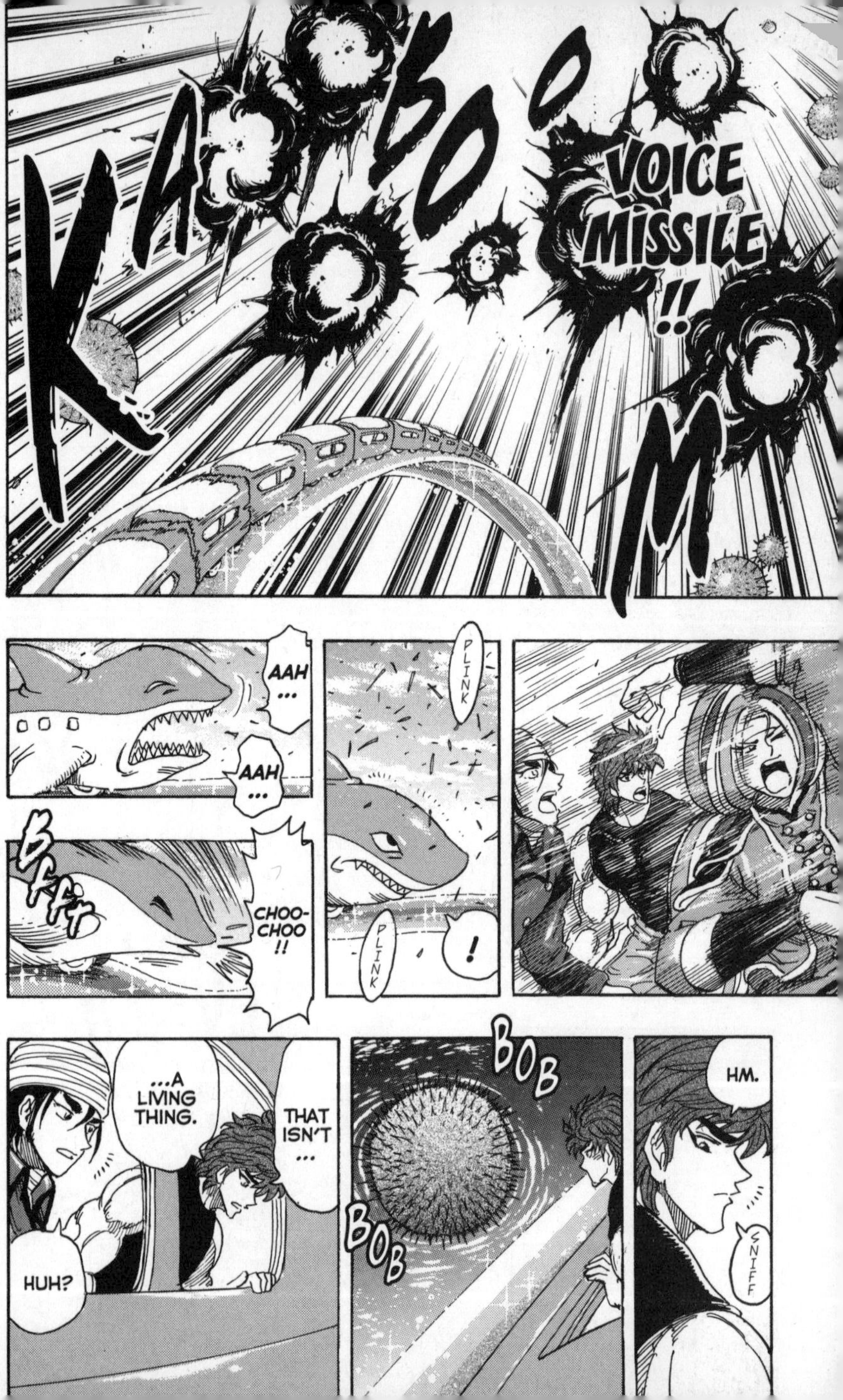

VOICE MISSILE!!
KABOOOM
PLINK
!
PLINK
AAH...
AAH...
CHOO-CHOO!!
HM.
SNIFF
BOB
BOB
THAT ISN'T...
...A LIVING THING.
HUH?

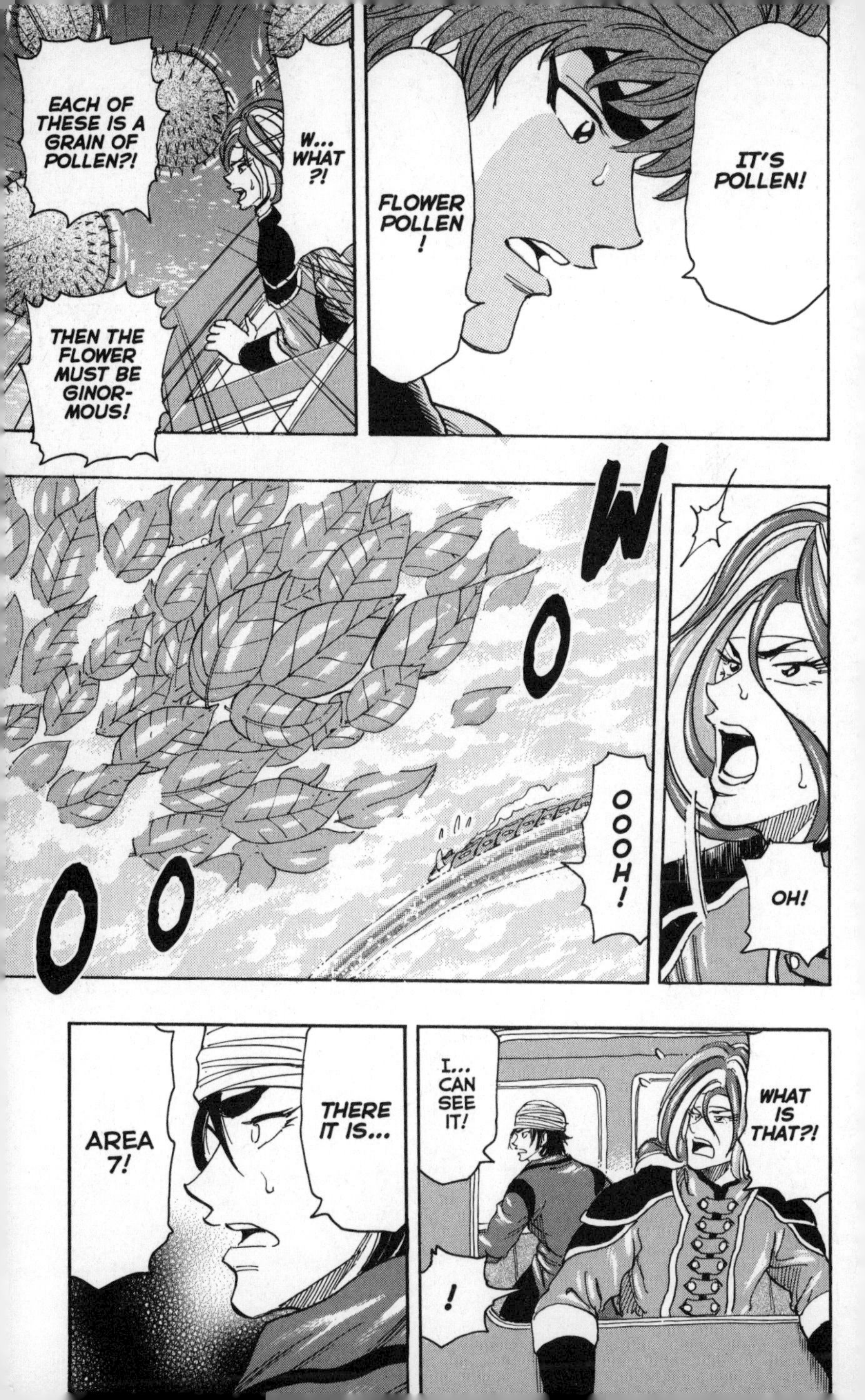
IT'S POLLEN!
FLOWER POLLEN!
W... WHAT?!
EACH OF THESE IS A GRAIN OF POLLEN?!
THEN THE FLOWER MUST BE GINORMOUS!
OH!
WOOOO
OOOOH!
WHAT IS THAT?!
I... CAN SEE IT!
!
THERE IT IS...
AREA 7!

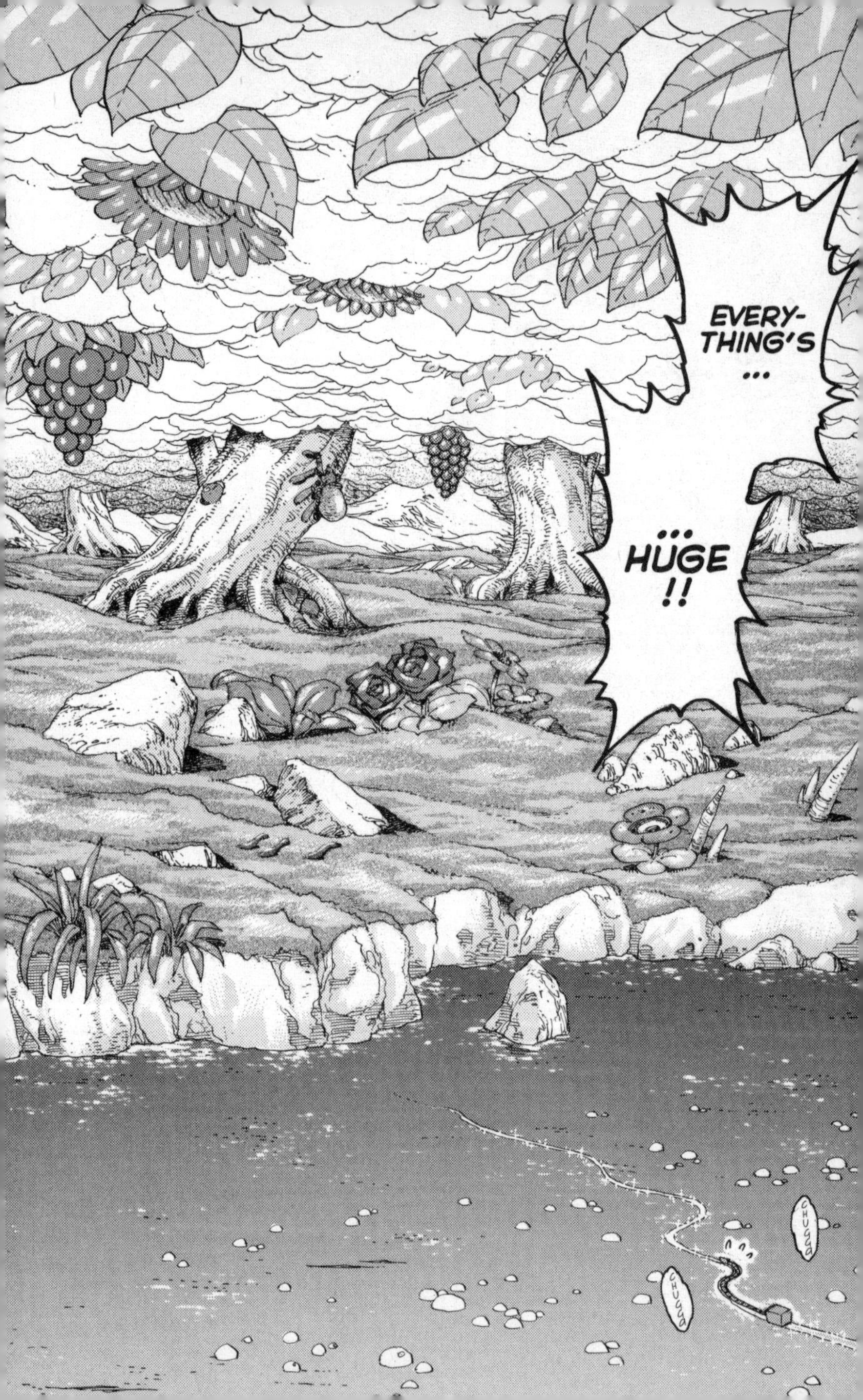
EVERY-THING'S ...
... HÜGE !!
CHUGGG
CHUGGG

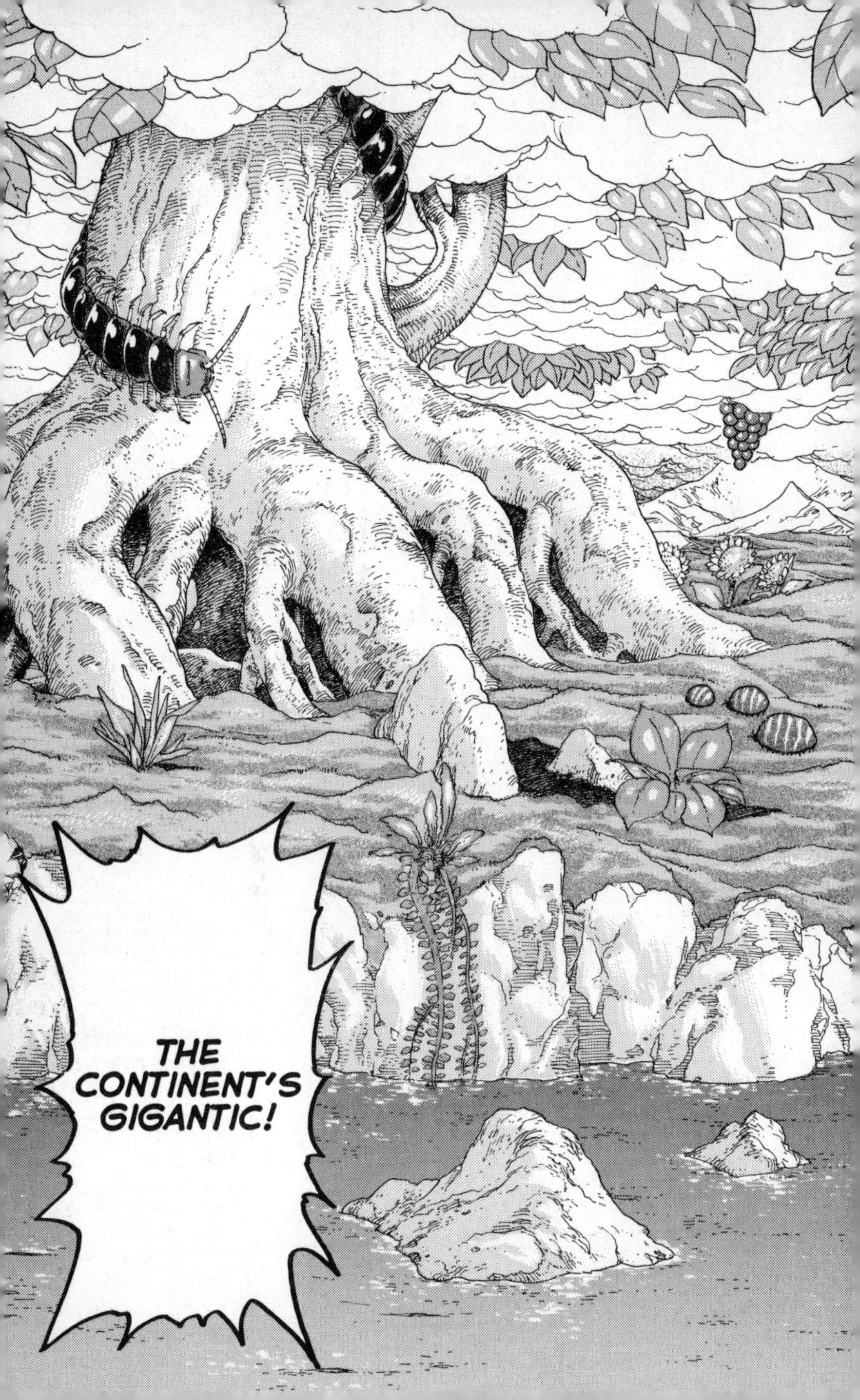
THE CONTINENT'S GIGANTIC!

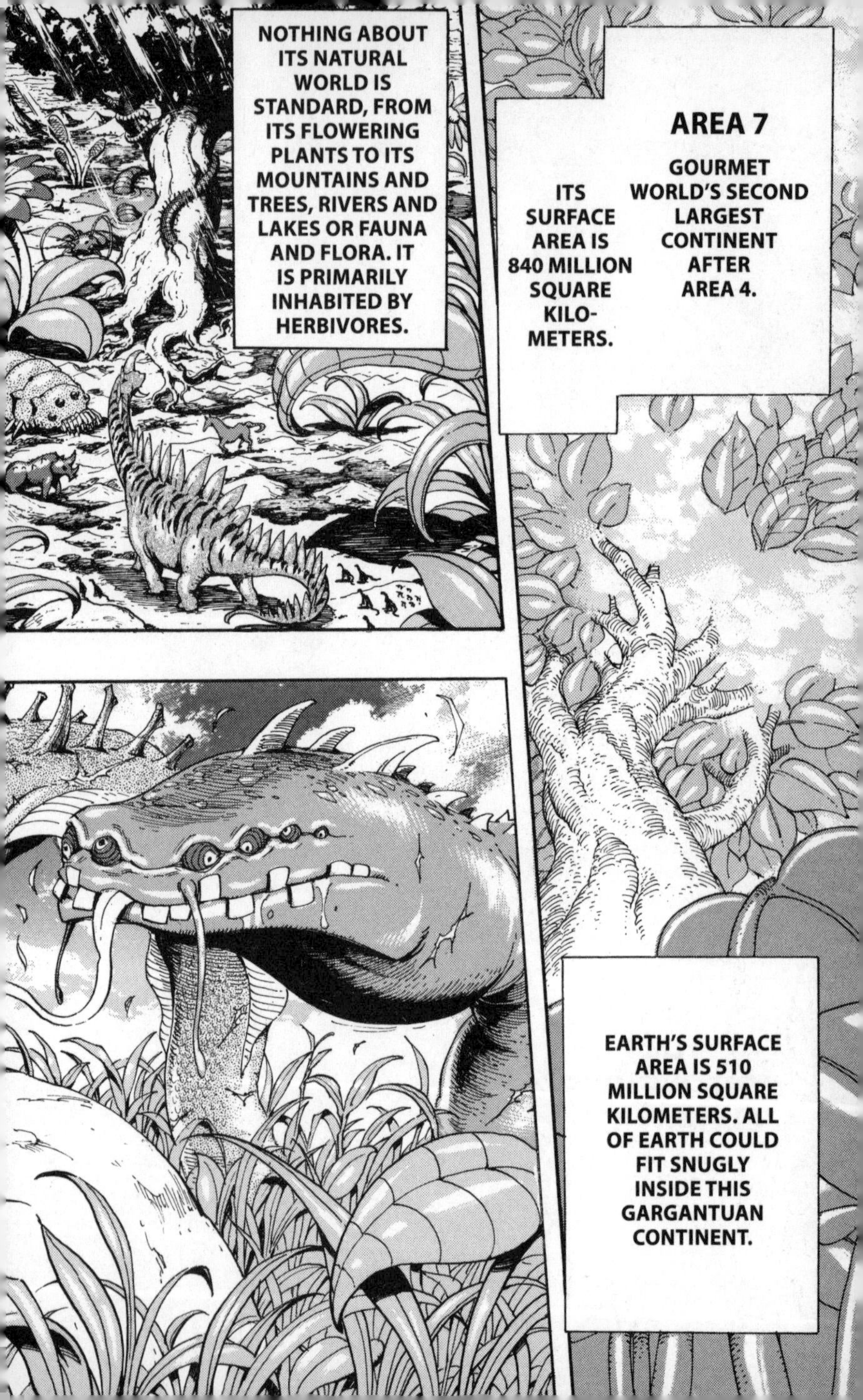
AREA 7
GOURMET WORLD'S SECOND LARGEST CONTINENT AFTER AREA 4.
ITS SURFACE AREA IS 840 MILLION SQUARE KILO-METERS.
EARTH'S SURFACE AREA IS 510 MILLION SQUARE KILOMETERS. ALL OF EARTH COULD FIT SNUGLY INSIDE THIS GARGANTUAN CONTINENT.
NOTHING ABOUT ITS NATURAL WORLD IS STANDARD, FROM ITS FLOWERING PLANTS TO ITS MOUNTAINS AND TREES, RIVERS AND LAKES OR FAUNA AND FLORA. IT IS PRIMARILY INHABITED BY HERBIVORES.

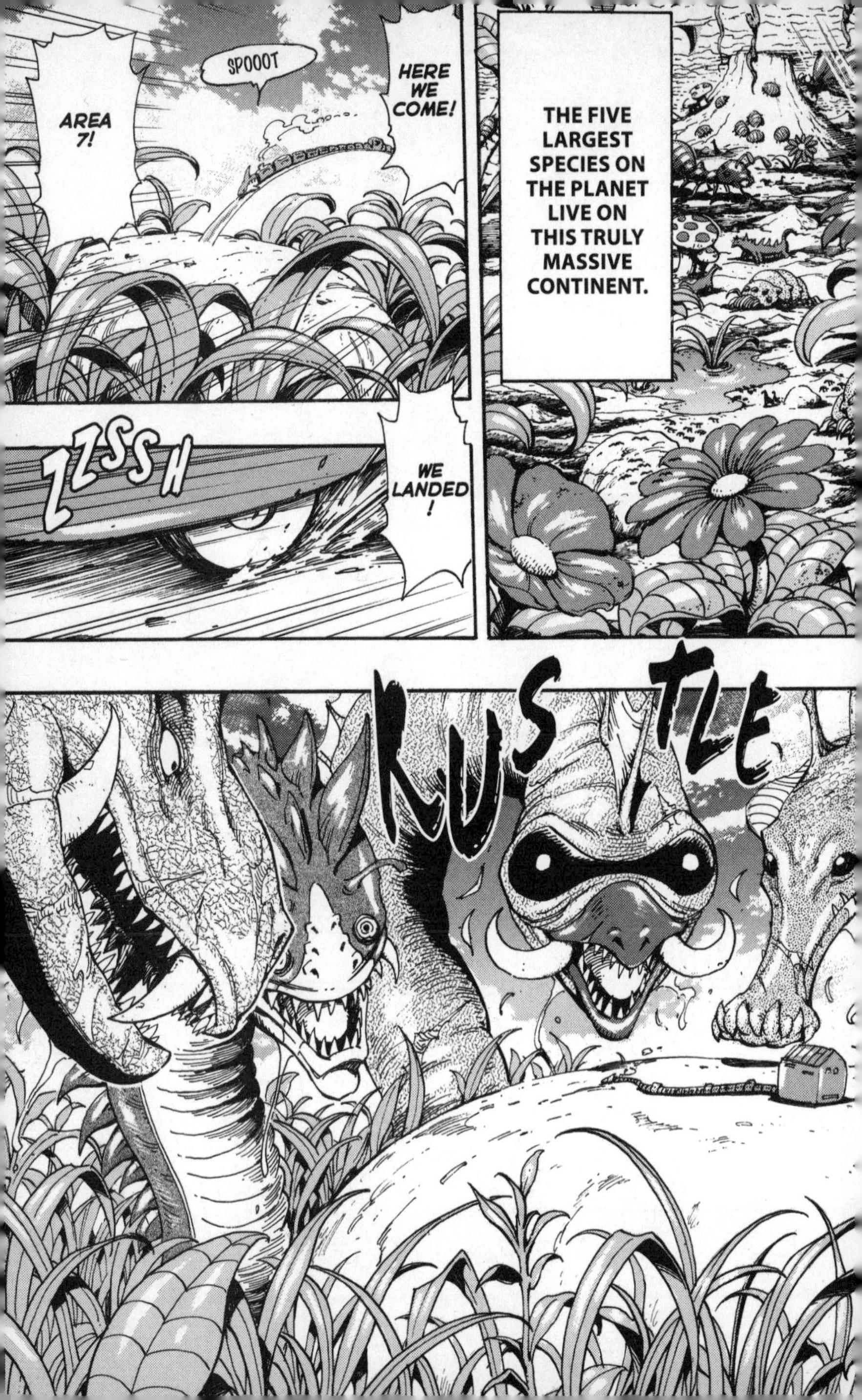
THE FIVE LARGEST SPECIES ON THE PLANET LIVE ON THIS TRULY MASSIVE CONTINENT.
HERE WE COME!
SPOOOT
AREA 7!
WE LANDED!
ZZSSH
RUSTLE

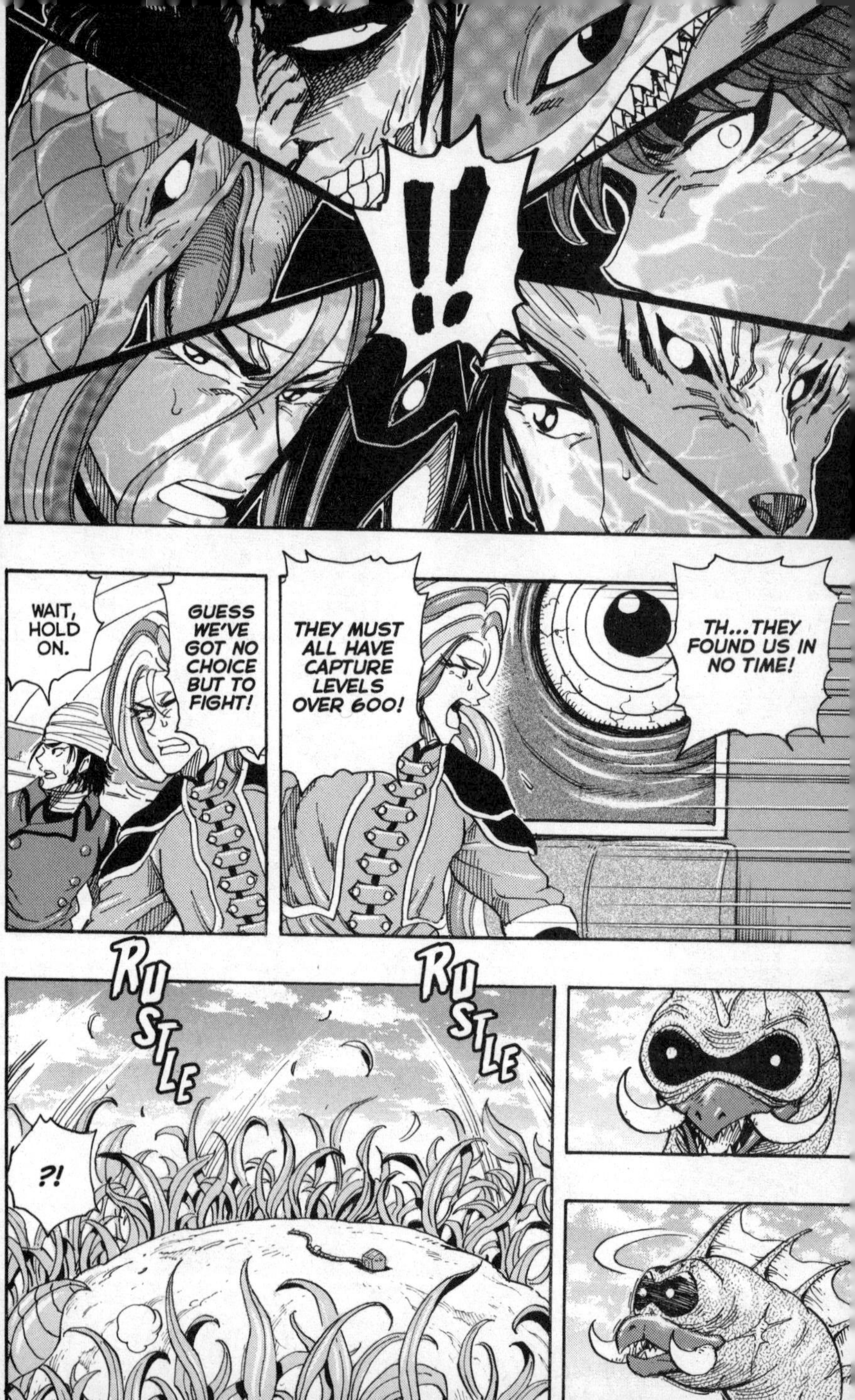
!!
TH...THEY FOUND US IN NO TIME!
THEY MUST ALL HAVE CAPTURE LEVELS OVER 600!
GUESS WE'VE GOT NO CHOICE BUT TO FIGHT!
WAIT, HOLD ON.
RUSTLE
RUSTLE
?!

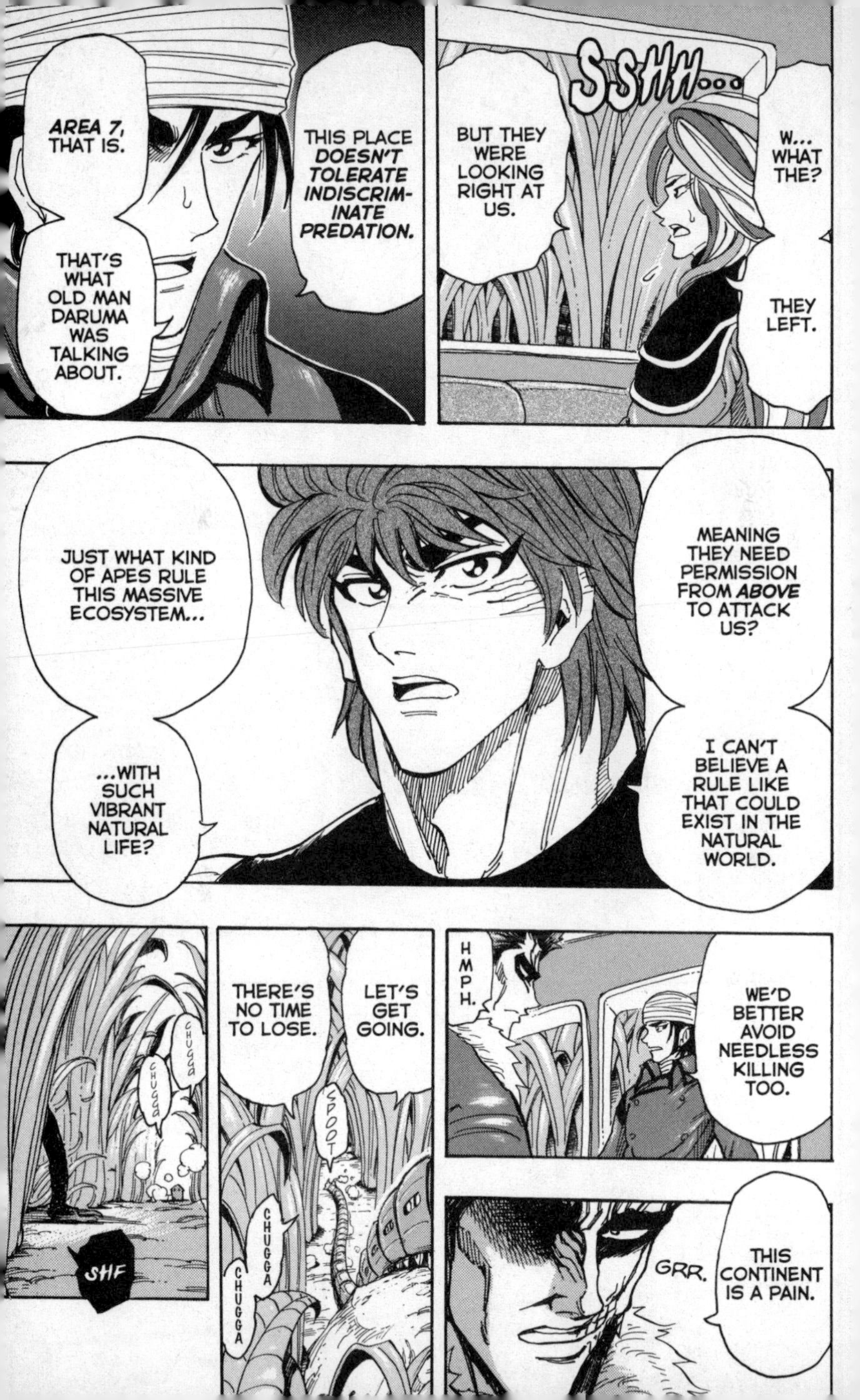
SSHH...
W... WHAT THE?
THEY LEFT.
BUT THEY WERE LOOKING RIGHT AT US.
THIS PLACE *DOESN'T TOLERATE INDISCRIM-INATE PREDATION.*
AREA 7, THAT IS.
THAT'S WHAT OLD MAN DARUMA WAS TALKING ABOUT.
MEANING THEY NEED PERMISSION FROM *ABOVE* TO ATTACK US?
I CAN'T BELIEVE A RULE LIKE THAT COULD EXIST IN THE NATURAL WORLD.
JUST WHAT KIND OF APES RULE THIS MASSIVE ECOSYSTEM...
...WITH SUCH VIBRANT NATURAL LIFE?
WE'D BETTER AVOID NEEDLESS KILLING TOO.
HMPH.
THIS CONTINENT IS A PAIN.
GRR.
LET'S GET GOING.
THERE'S NO TIME TO LOSE.
SPOOT
CHUGGA
CHUGGA
CHUGGA
CHUGGA
SHF

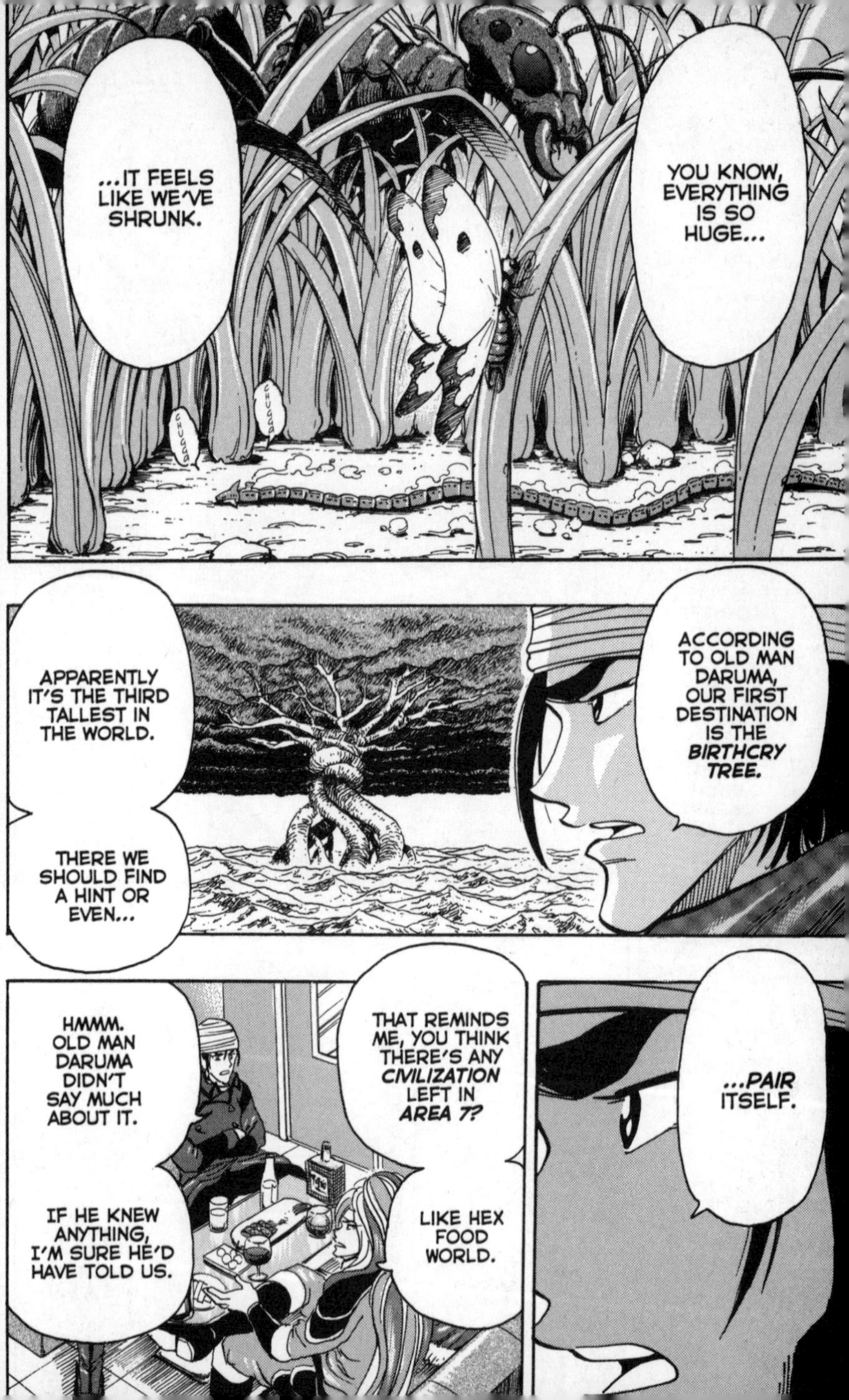
YOU KNOW, EVERYTHING IS SO HUGE...
...IT FEELS LIKE WE'VE SHRUNK.
CHUGGA
CHUGGA
ACCORDING TO OLD MAN DARUMA, OUR FIRST DESTINATION IS THE *BIRTHCRY TREE.*
APPARENTLY IT'S THE THIRD TALLEST IN THE WORLD.
THERE WE SHOULD FIND A HINT OR EVEN...
...PAIR ITSELF.
THAT REMINDS ME, YOU THINK THERE'S ANY *CIVILIZATION* LEFT IN *AREA 7?*
LIKE HEX FOOD WORLD.
HMMM. OLD MAN DARUMA DIDN'T SAY MUCH ABOUT IT.
IF HE KNEW ANYTHING, I'M SURE HE'D HAVE TOLD US.

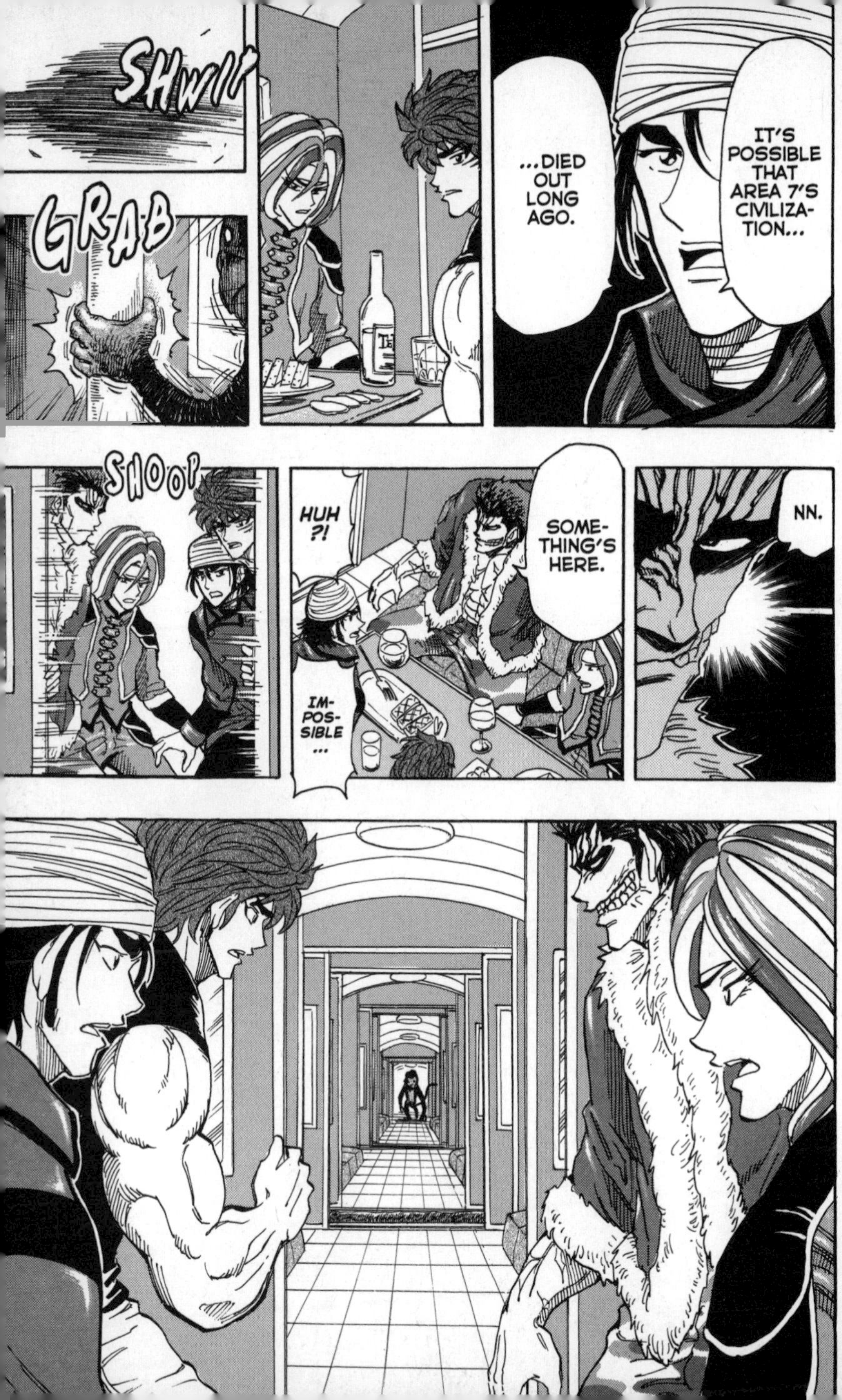
IT'S POSSIBLE THAT AREA 7'S CIVILIZA-TION...
...DIED OUT LONG AGO.
SHWIP
GRAB
NN.
SOME-THING'S HERE.
HUH ?!
IM-POS-SIBLE ...
SHOOP

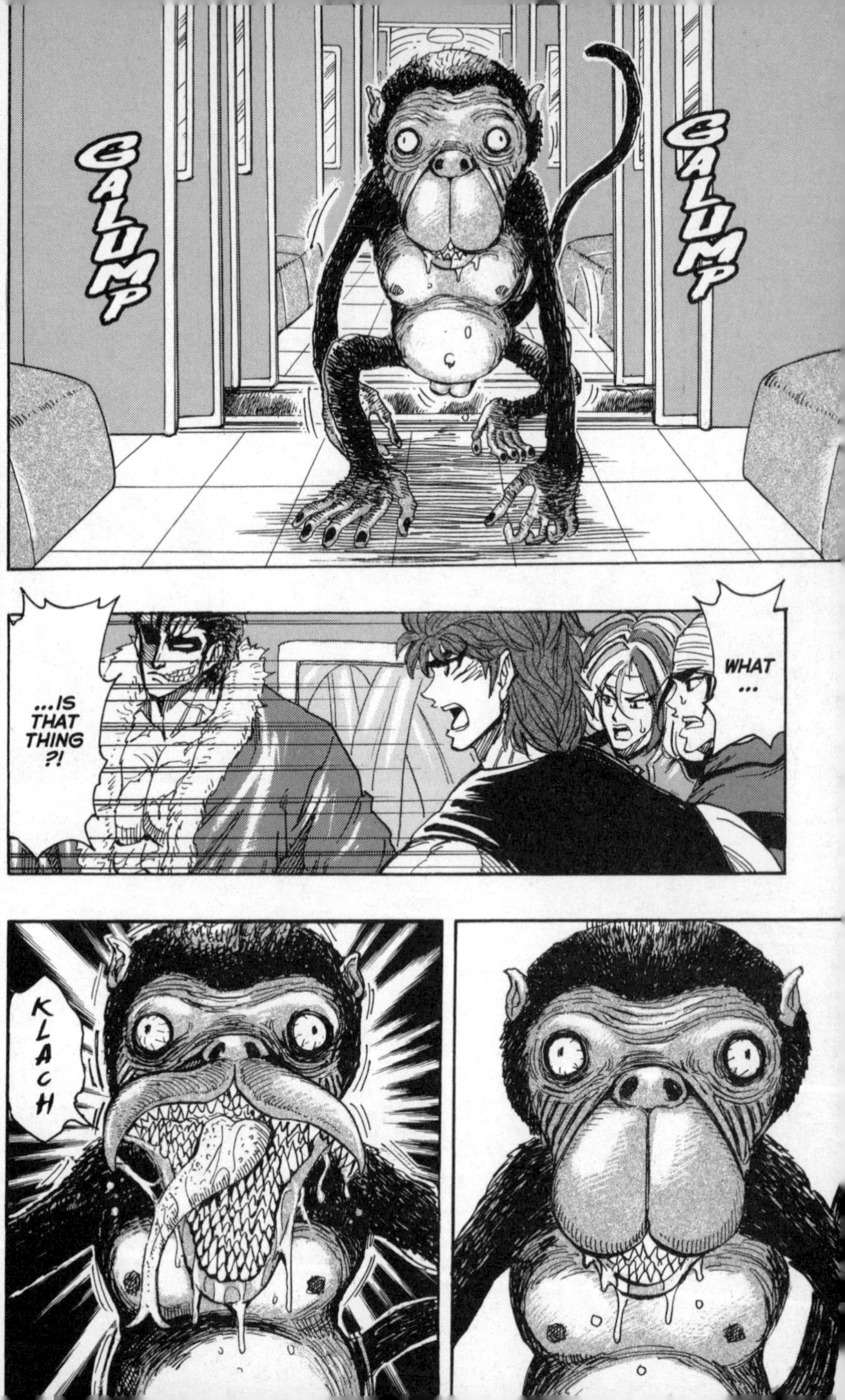
GALUMP
GALUMP
WHAT...
...IS THAT THING?!
KLACH

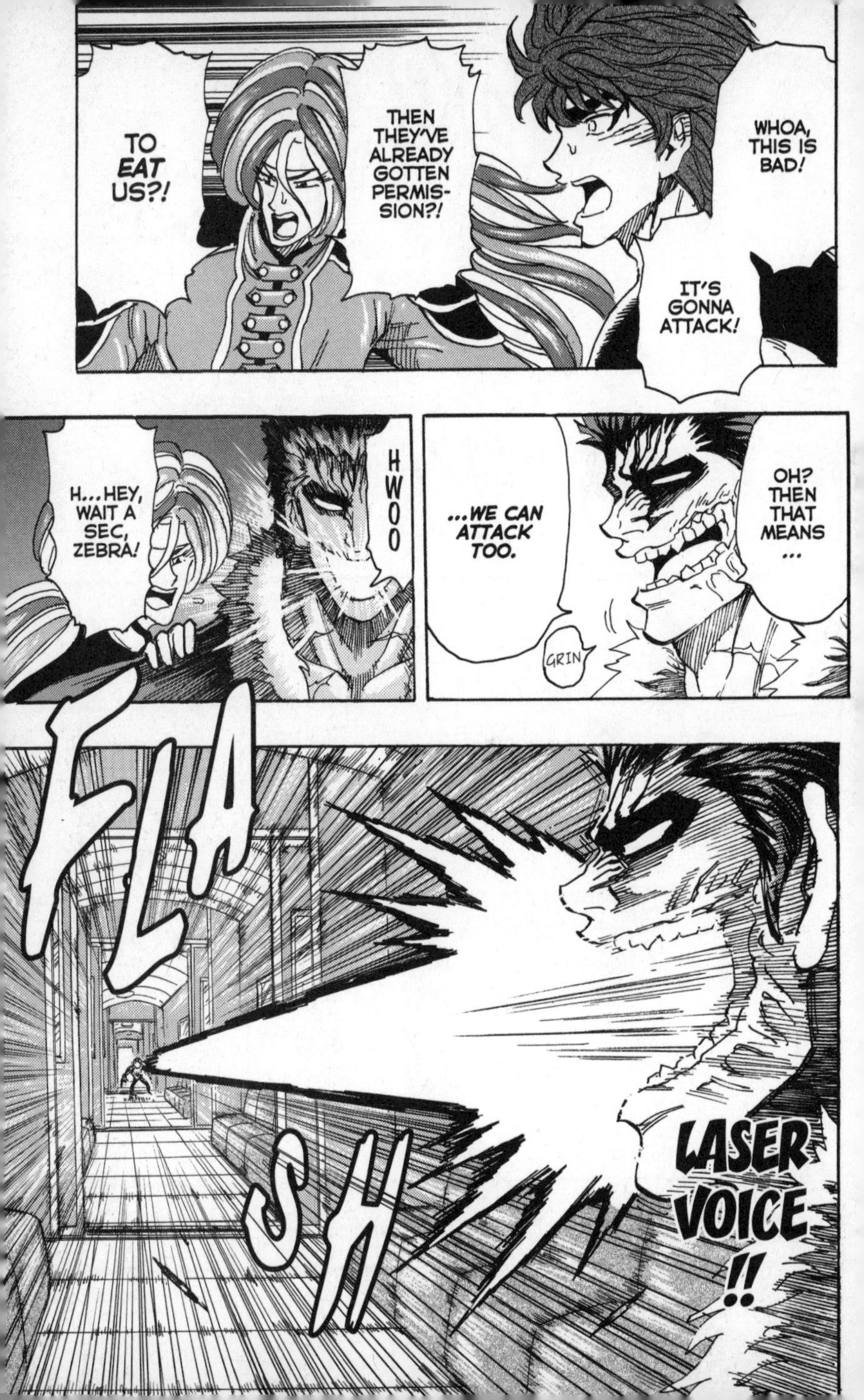
WHOA, THIS IS BAD!
IT'S GONNA ATTACK!
THEN THEY'VE ALREADY GOTTEN PERMIS-SION?!
TO EAT US?!
OH? THEN THAT MEANS ...
...WE CAN ATTACK TOO.
GRIN
HWOO
H...HEY, WAIT A SEC, ZEBRA!
LASER VOICE!!
FLASH

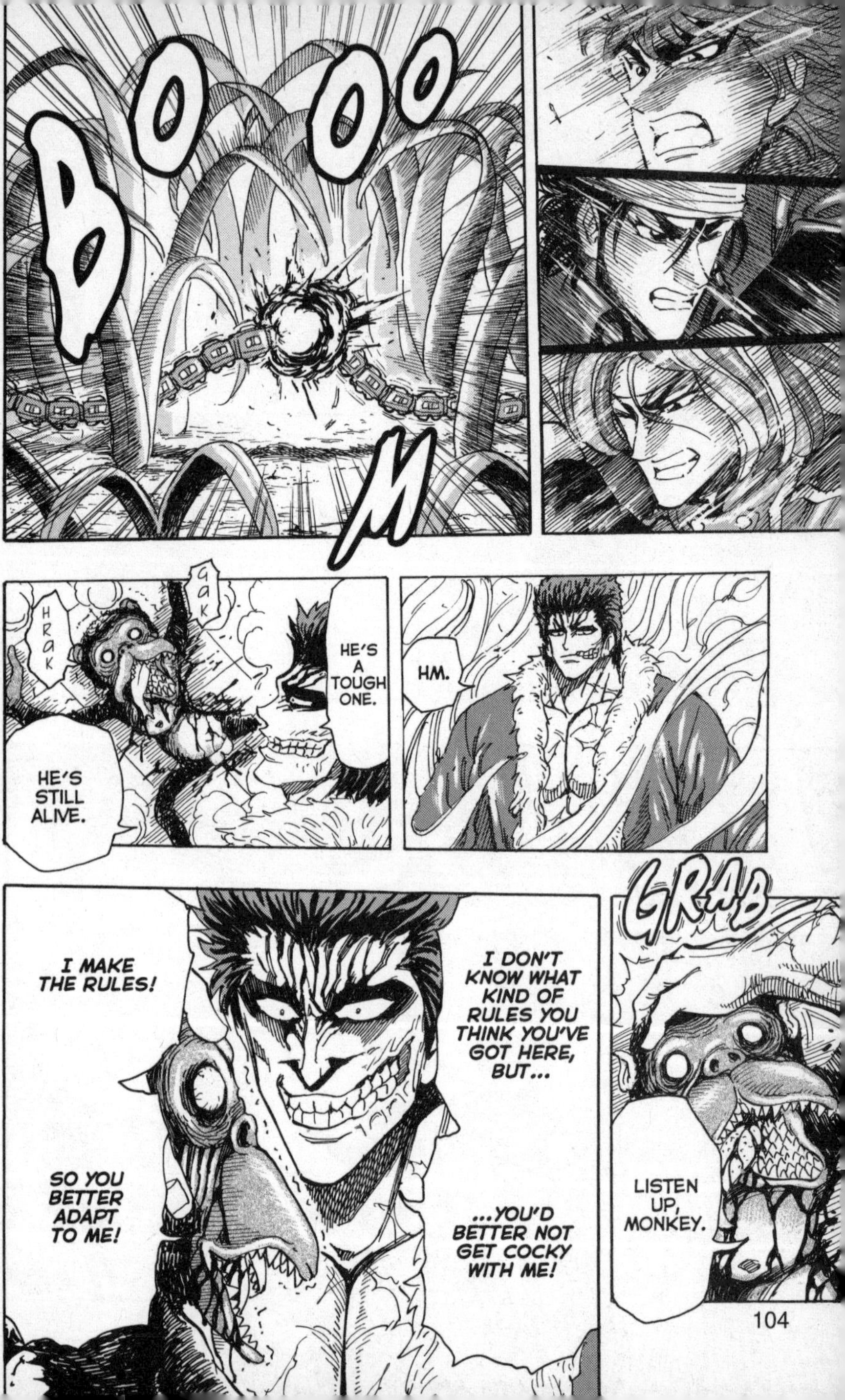

BOOOM
HM.
HE'S A TOUGH ONE.
GAK
HRAK
HE'S STILL ALIVE.
GRAB
LISTEN UP, MONKEY.
I DON'T KNOW WHAT KIND OF RULES YOU THINK YOU'VE GOT HERE, BUT...
...YOU'D BETTER NOT GET COCKY WITH ME!
I MAKE THE RULES!
SO YOU BETTER ADAPT TO ME!

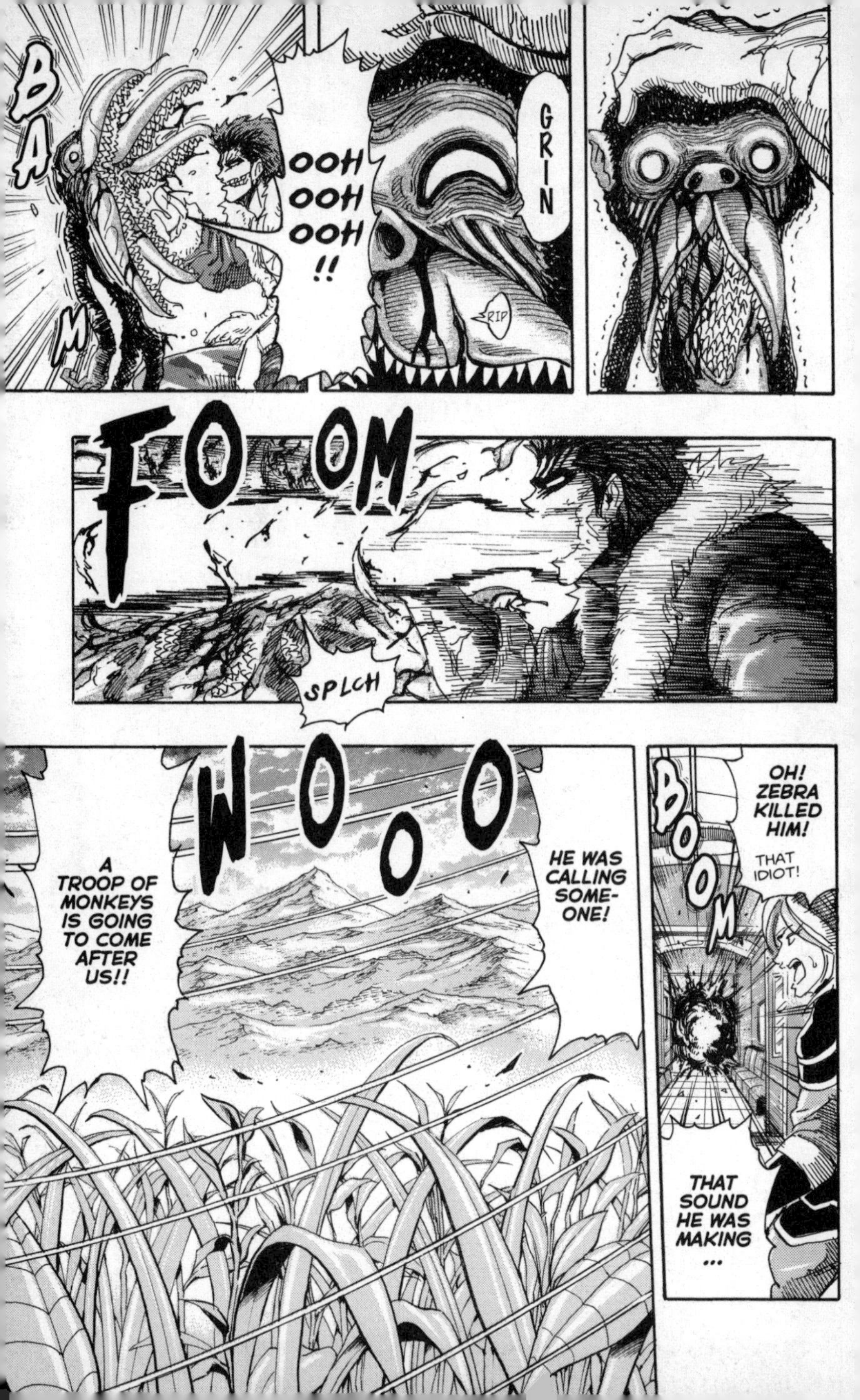
GRIN
OOH OOH OOH!!
RIP
BAM
FOOM
SPLCH
OH! ZEBRA KILLED HIM!
THAT IDIOT!
BOOOM
THAT SOUND HE WAS MAKING...
WOOOO
HE WAS CALLING SOME-ONE!
A TROOP OF MONKEYS IS GOING TO COME AFTER US!!

TORIKO

GOURMET CHECKLIST

Vol. 321

RUBY BEER
(ALCOHOL)

CAPTURE LEVEL: 16

HABITAT: CRUDE MATERIAL THAT COMES FROM CAVES

SIZE: —

HEIGHT: ---

WEIGHT: —

PRICE: 5,000 YEN PER 350 ML CAN

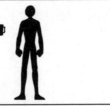

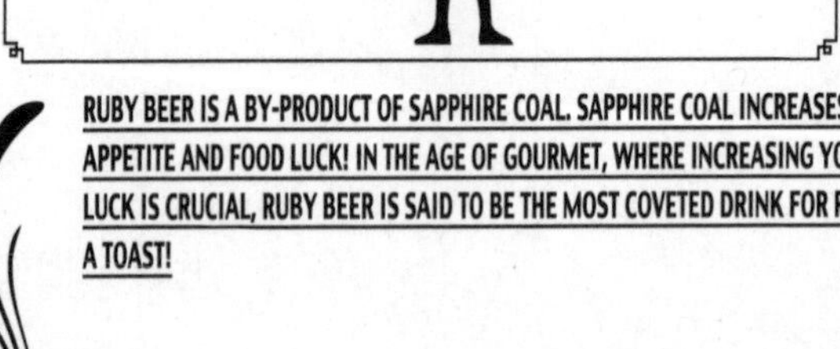

SCALE

RUBY BEER IS A BY-PRODUCT OF SAPPHIRE COAL. SAPPHIRE COAL INCREASES BOTH APPETITE AND FOOD LUCK! IN THE AGE OF GOURMET, WHERE INCREASING YOUR FOOD LUCK IS CRUCIAL, RUBY BEER IS SAID TO BE THE MOST COVETED DRINK FOR RAISING A TOAST!

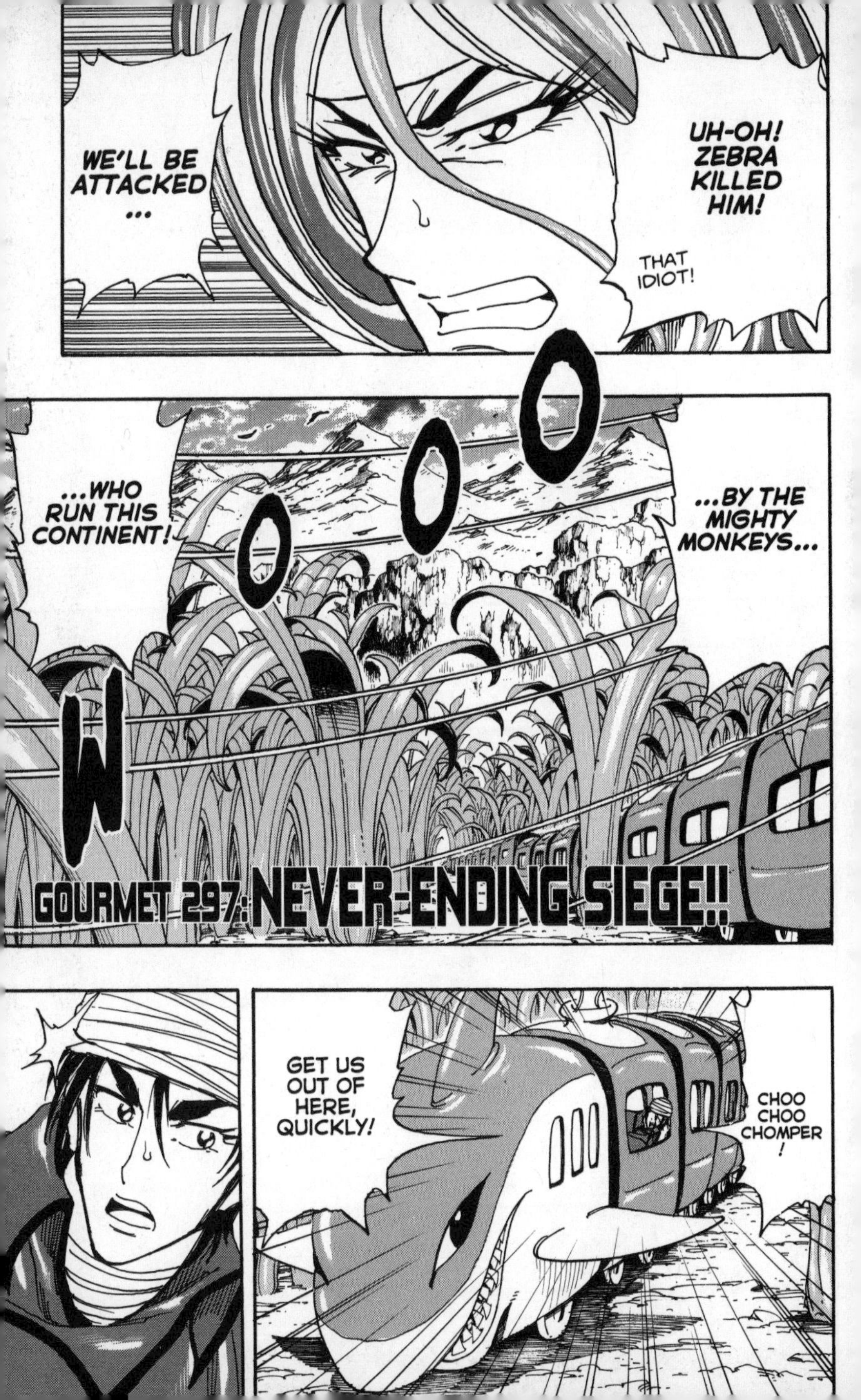
UH-OH! ZEBRA KILLED HIM!
THAT IDIOT!
WE'LL BE ATTACKED ...
...BY THE MIGHTY MONKEYS...
...WHO RUN THIS CONTINENT!
W
GOURMET 297: NEVER-ENDING SIEGE!!
CHOO CHOO CHOMPER!
GET US OUT OF HERE, QUICKLY!

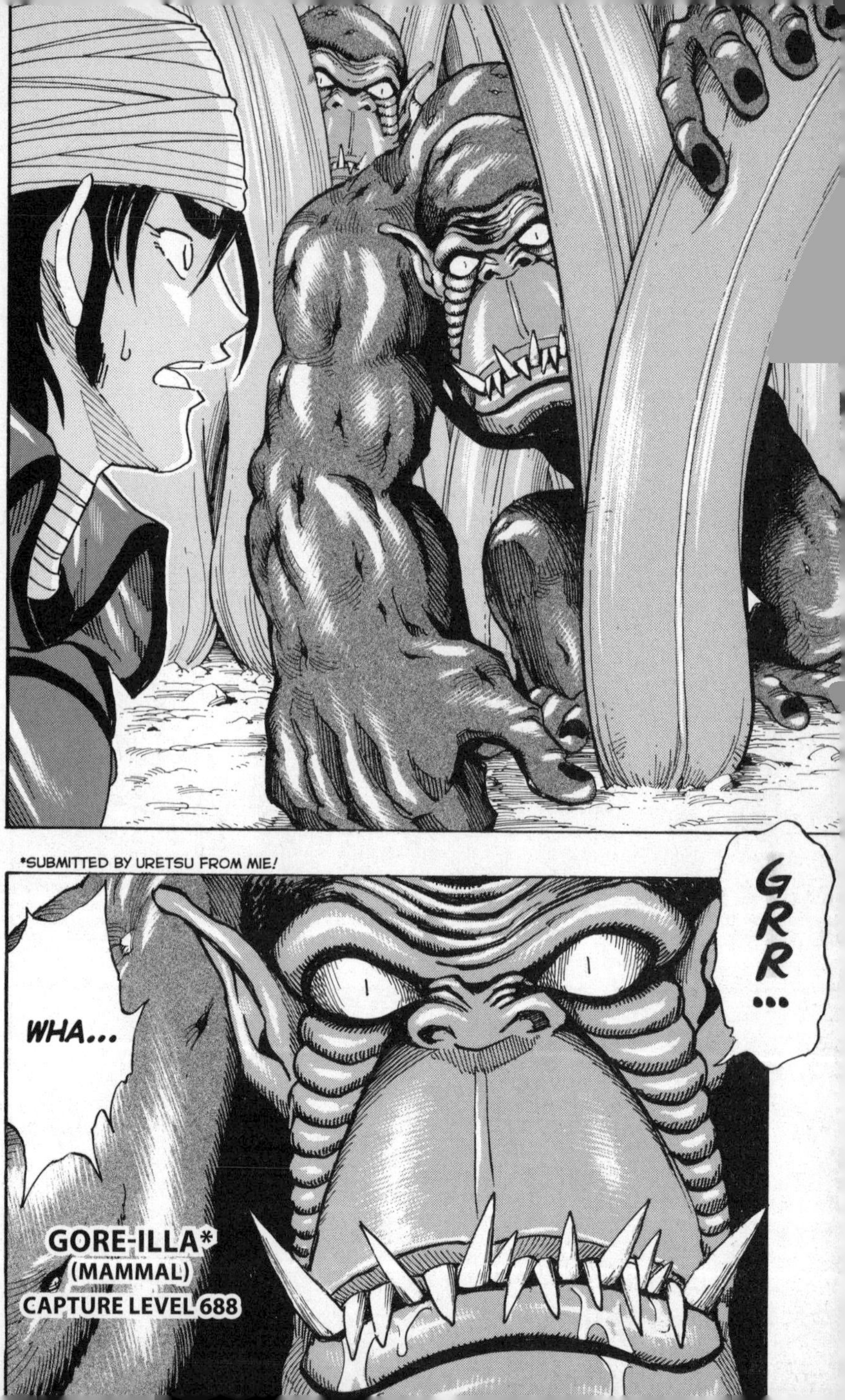
*SUBMITTED BY URETSU FROM MIE!
GRR...
WHA...
GORE-ILLA*
(MAMMAL)
CAPTURE LEVEL 688

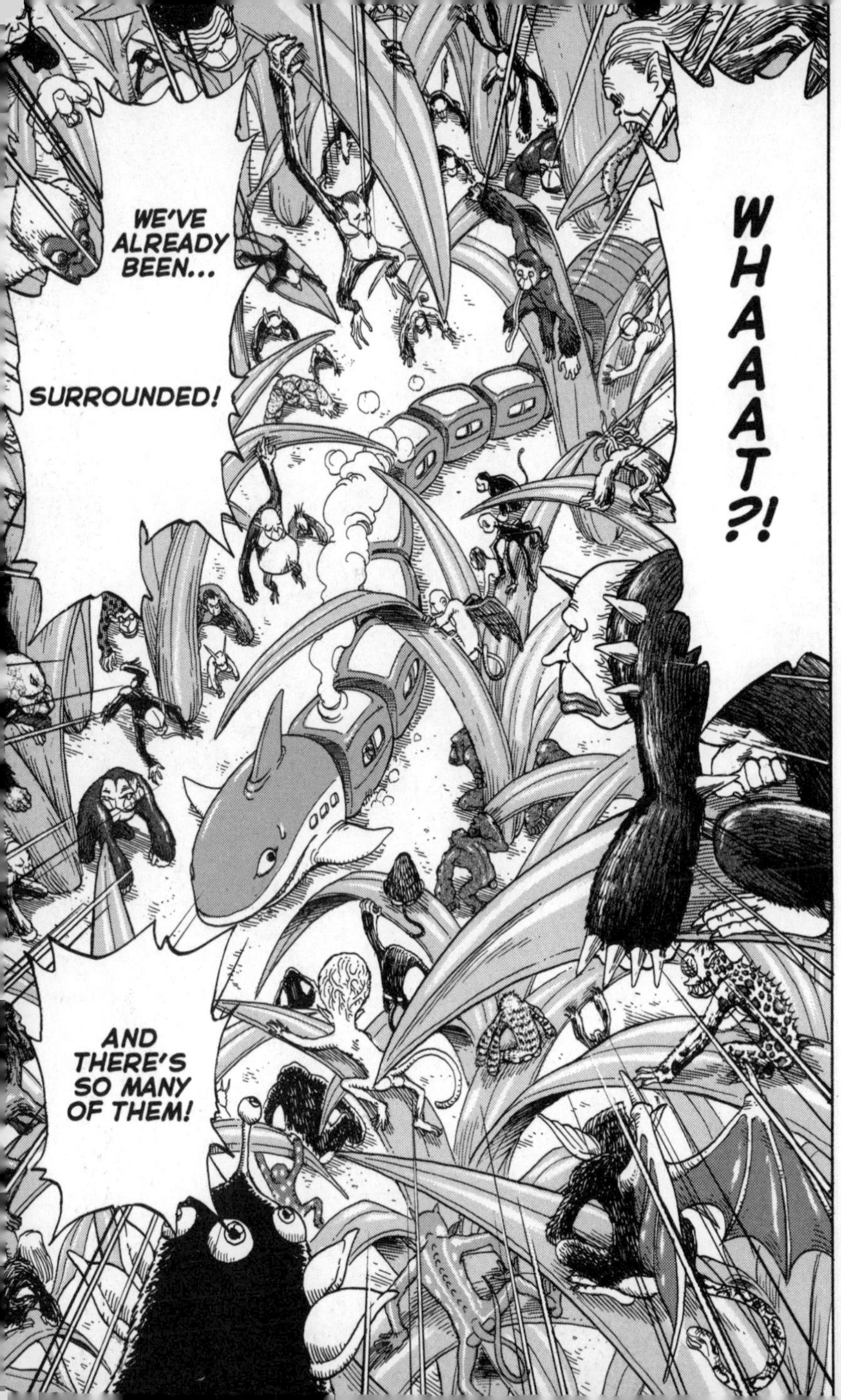
WHAAAAT?!
WE'VE ALREADY BEEN...
SURROUNDED!
AND THERE'S SO MANY OF THEM!

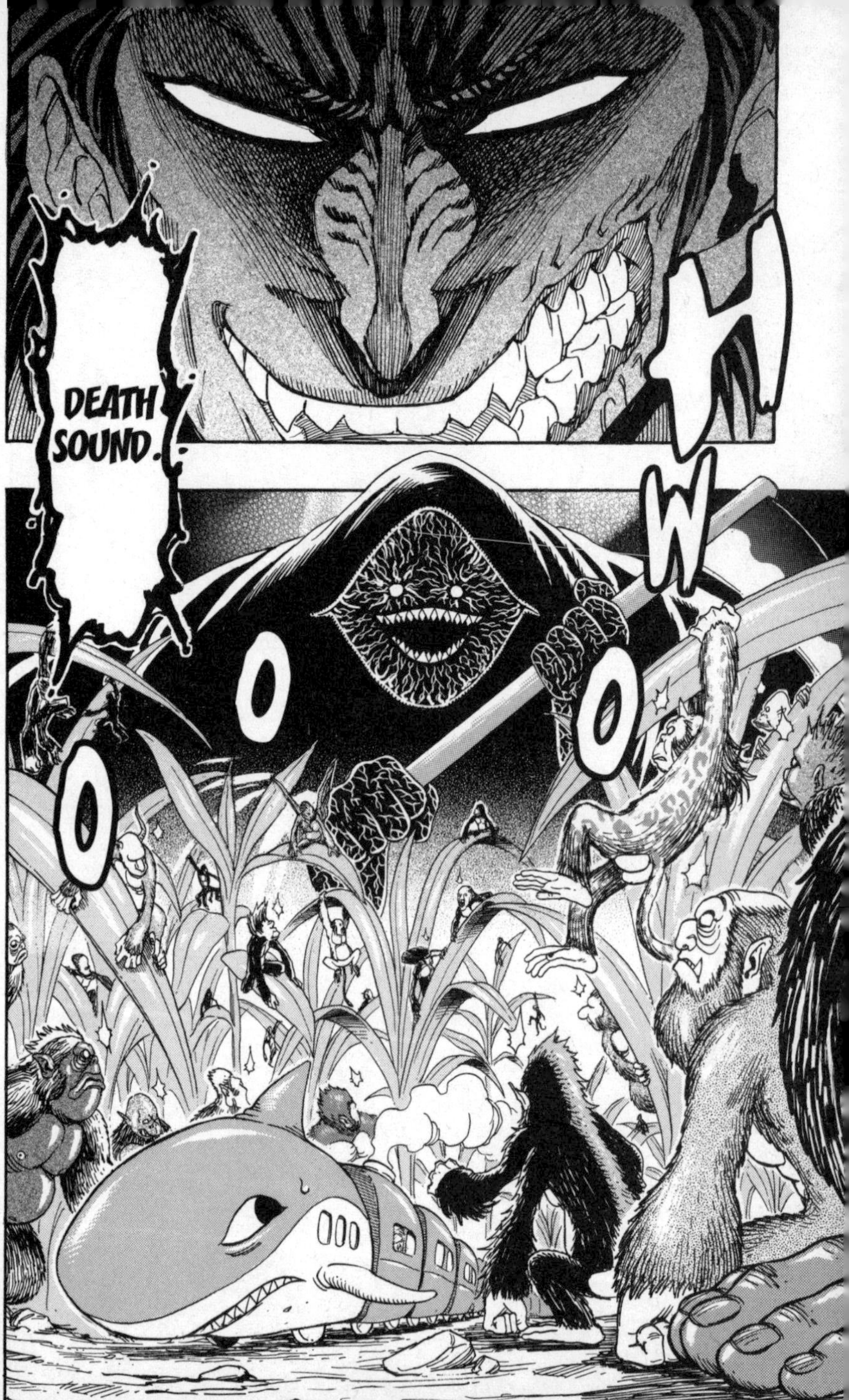
DEATH SOUND.
WOOOOOH

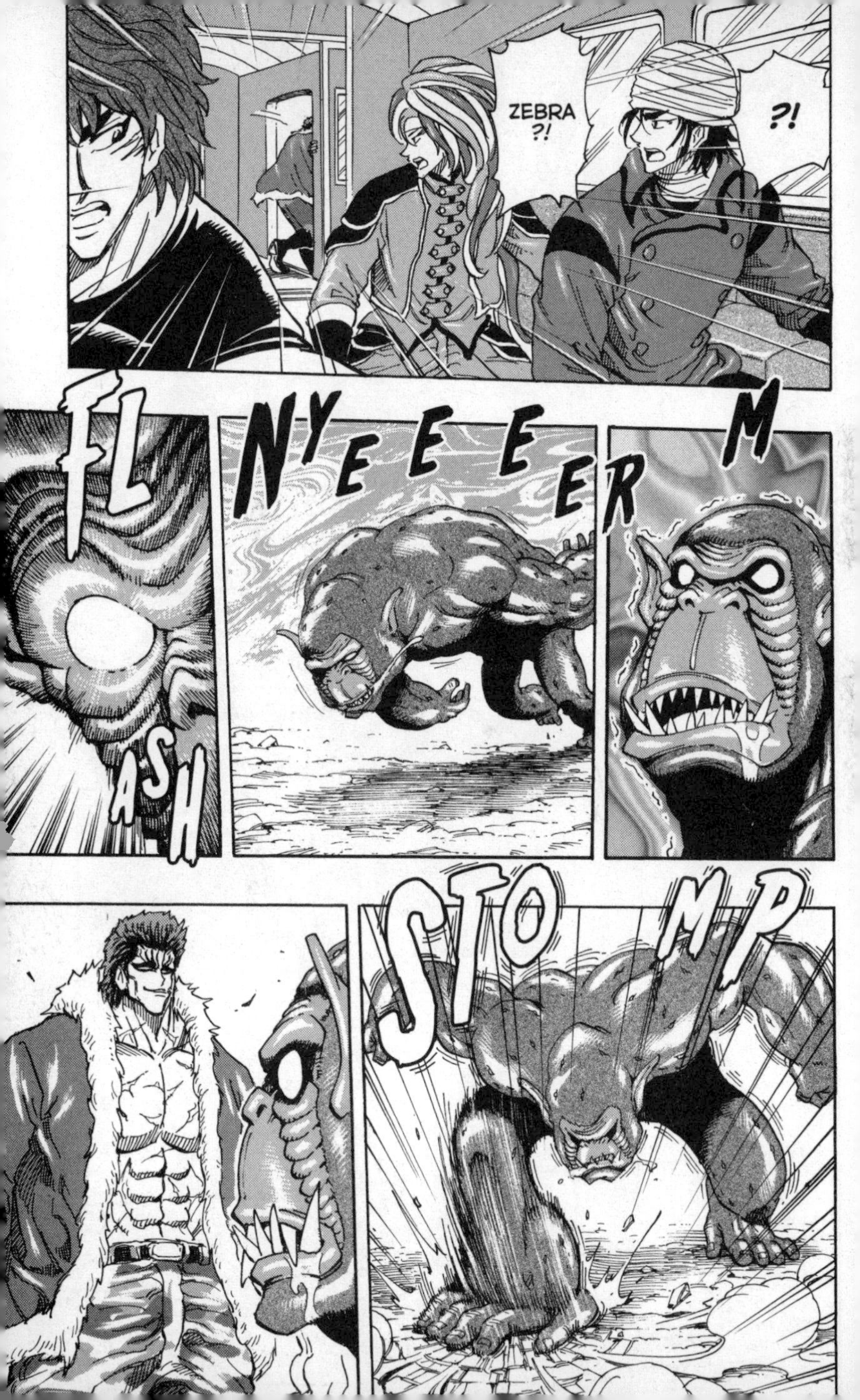
?!
ZEBRA ?!
NYEEEERM
FLASH
STOMP

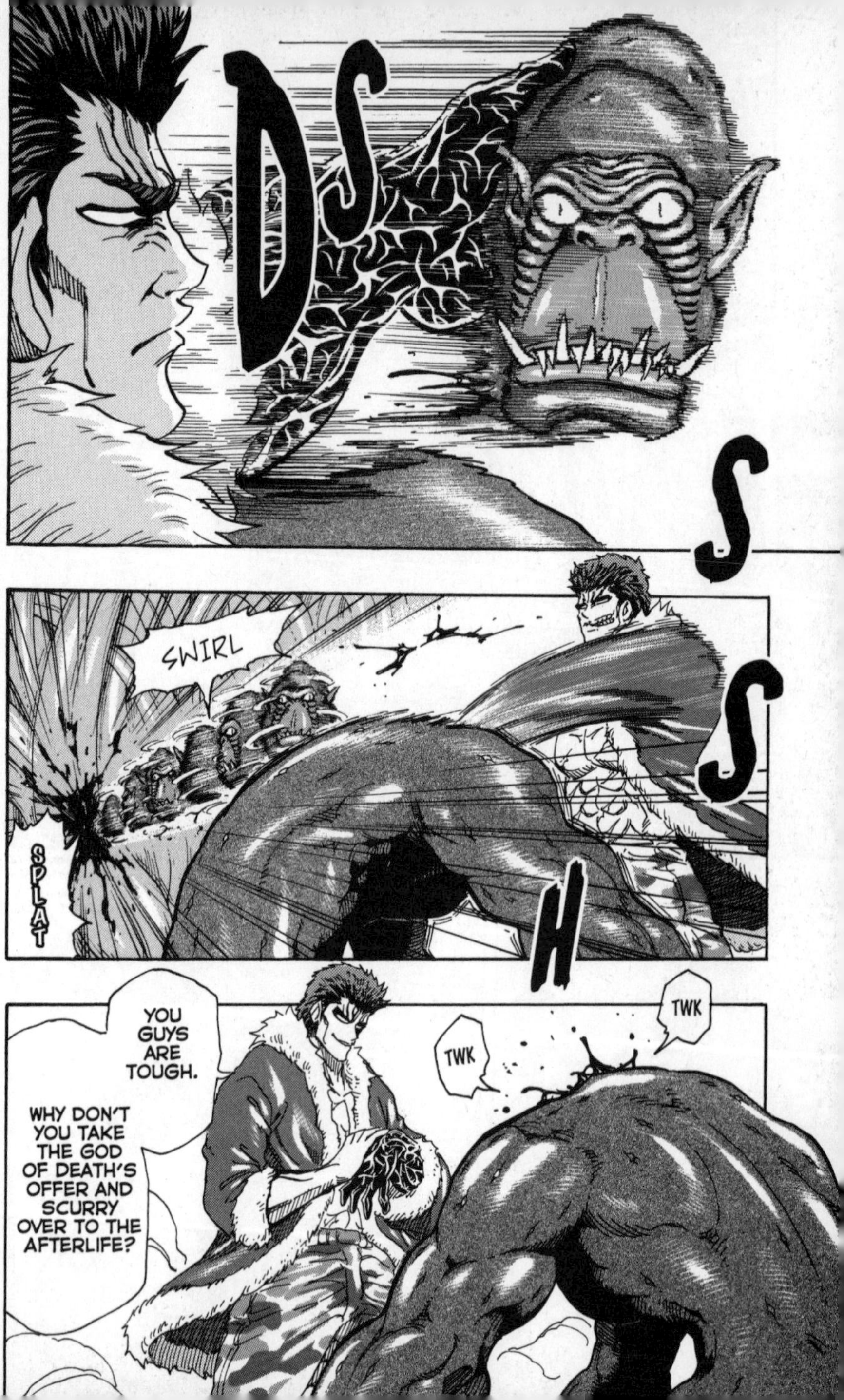
DS
SSSH
SWIRL
SPLAT
YOU GUYS ARE TOUGH.
WHY DON'T YOU TAKE THE GOD OF DEATH'S OFFER AND SCURRY OVER TO THE AFTERLIFE?
TWK
TWK

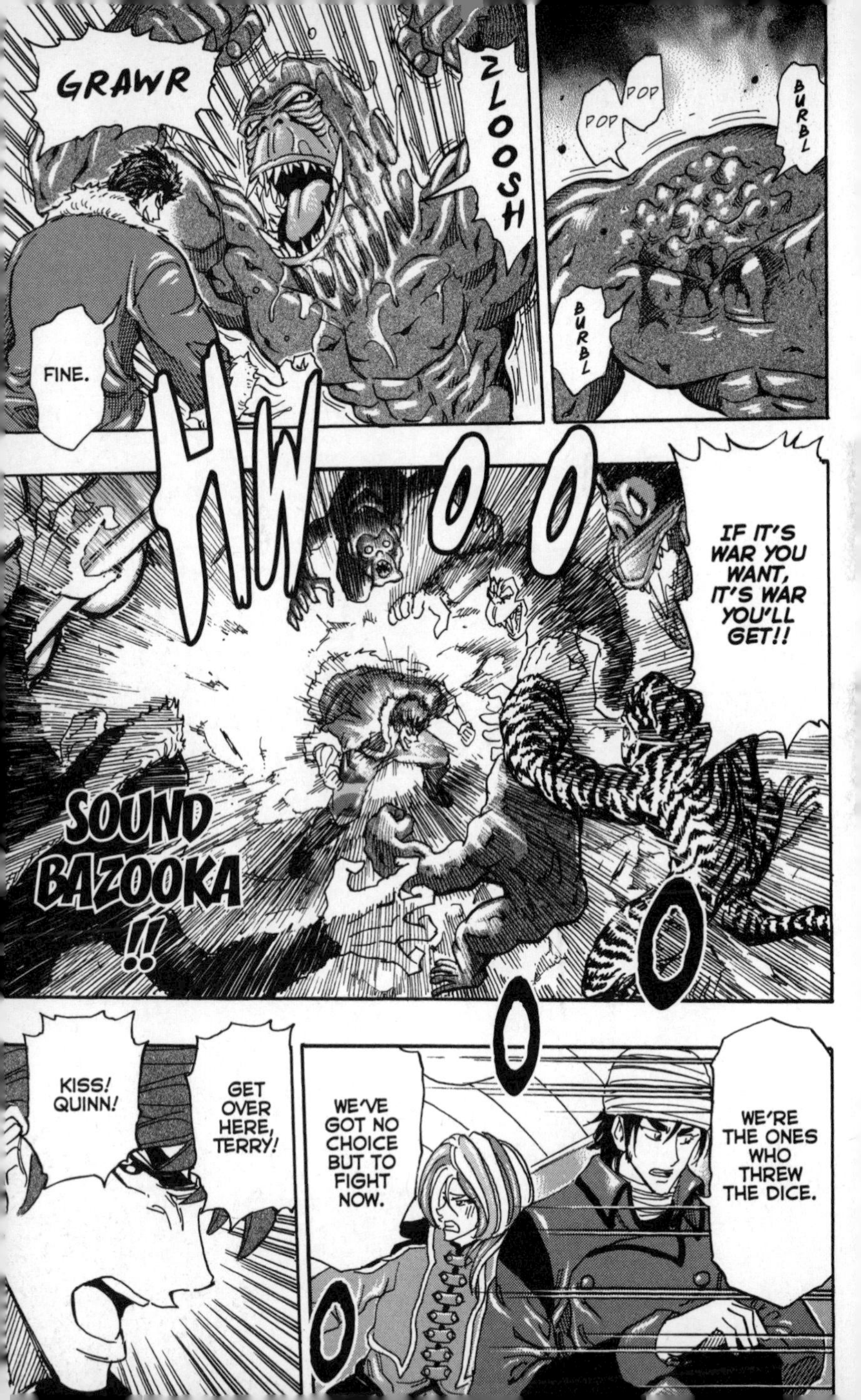
POP
POP
BURBL
BURBL
GRAWR
ZLOOSH
FINE.
HWOOOO
IF IT'S WAR YOU WANT, IT'S WAR YOU'LL GET!!
SOUND BAZOOKA!!
WE'RE THE ONES WHO THREW THE DICE.
WE'VE GOT NO CHOICE BUT TO FIGHT NOW.
GET OVER HERE, TERRY!
KISS! QUINN!

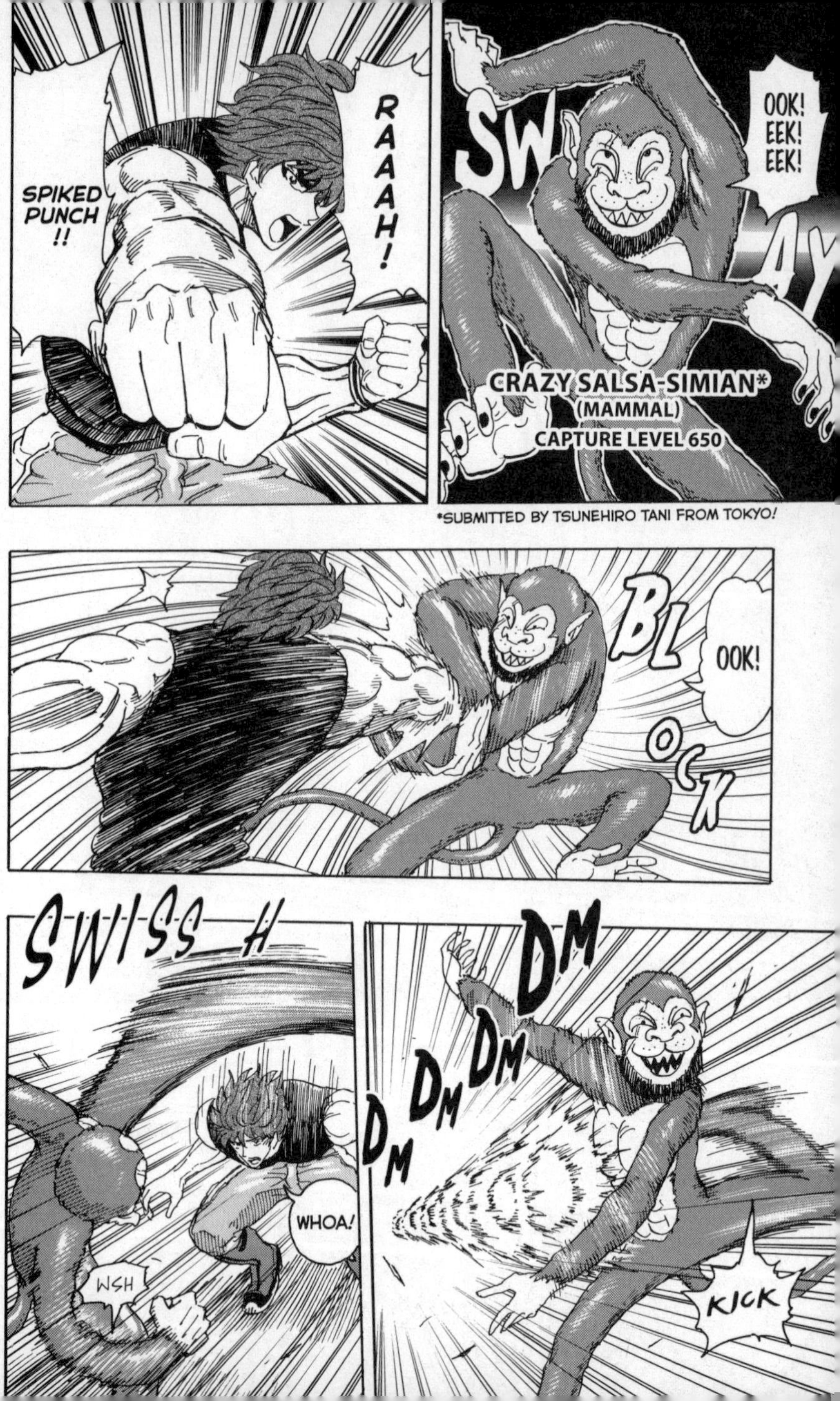
SW
AY
OOK! EEK! EEK!
CRAZY SALSA-SIMIAN* (MAMMAL) CAPTURE LEVEL 650
RAAAAH!
SPIKED PUNCH !!
BLOCK
OOK!
DM DM DM DM DM
KICK
SWISS H
WHOA!
WSH

*SUBMITTED BY TSUNEHIRO TANI FROM TOKYO!

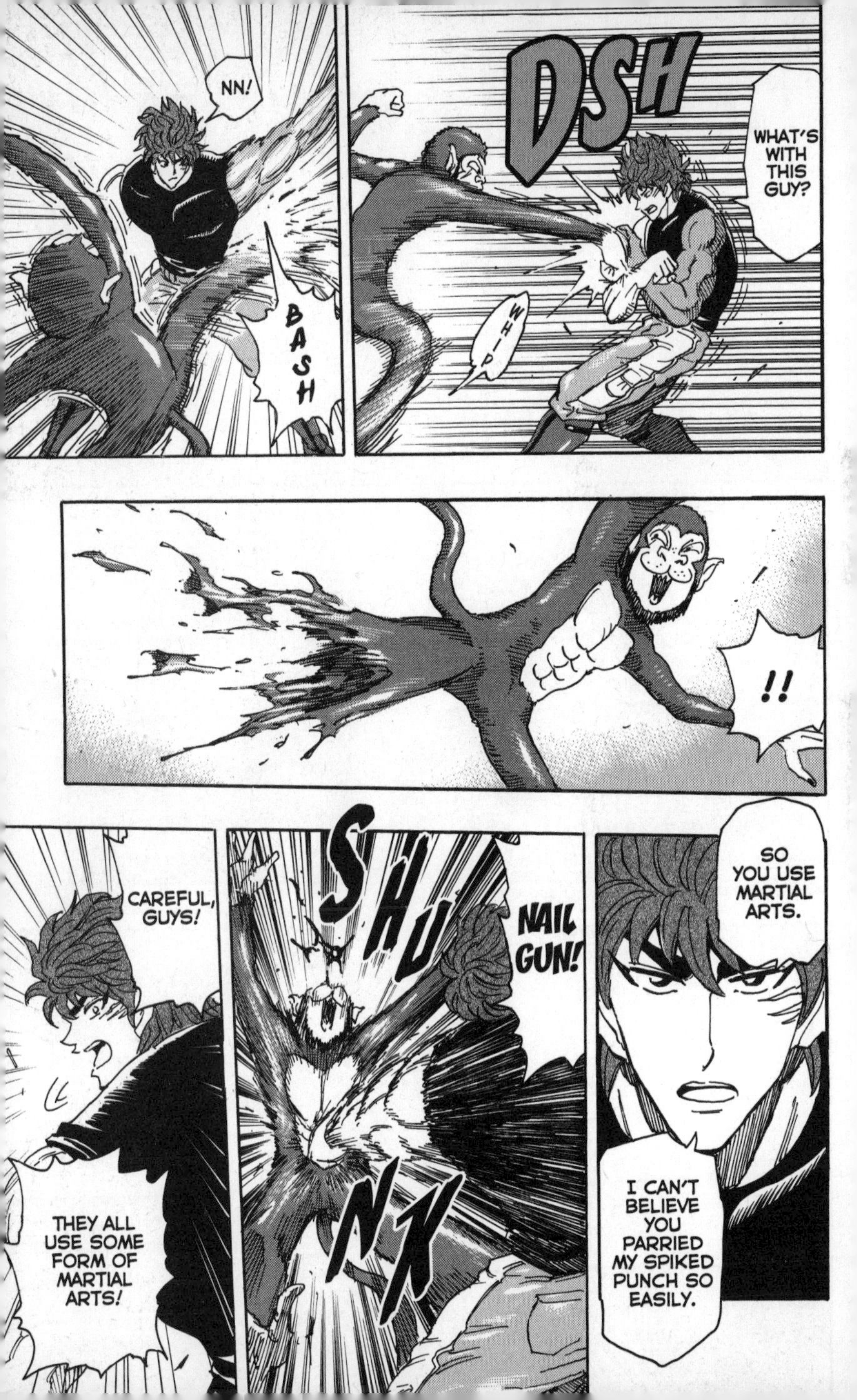
DSH
WHAT'S WITH THIS GUY?
WHIP
NN!
BASH
!!
SO YOU USE MARTIAL ARTS.
I CAN'T BELIEVE YOU PARRIED MY SPIKED PUNCH SO EASILY.
SHUNK
NAIL GUN!
CAREFUL, GUYS!
THEY ALL USE SOME FORM OF MARTIAL ARTS!

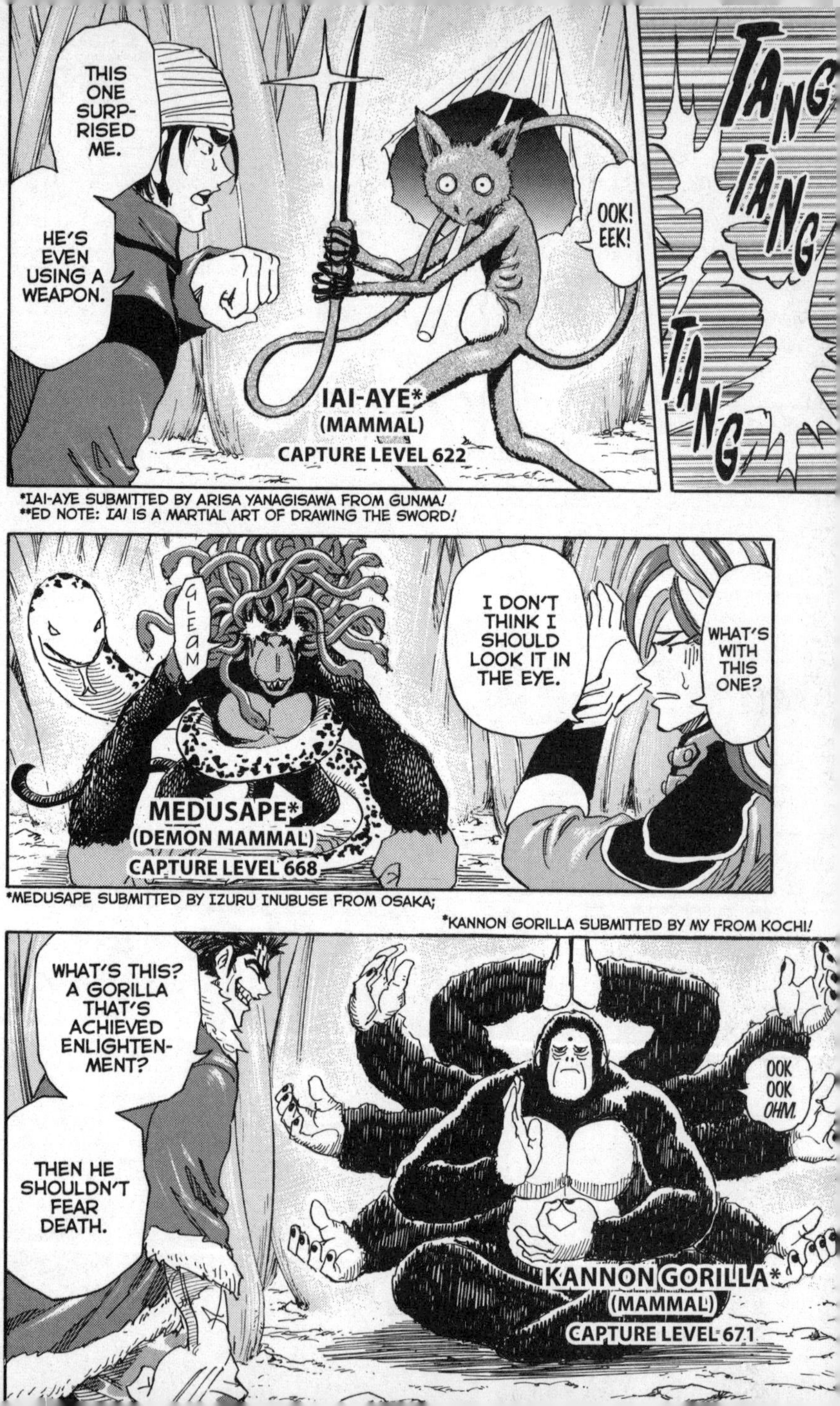
TANG TANG TANG TANG
THIS ONE SURPRISED ME.
HE'S EVEN USING A WEAPON.
OOK! EEK!
IAI-AYE* (MAMMAL) CAPTURE LEVEL 622
WHAT'S WITH THIS ONE?
I DON'T THINK I SHOULD LOOK IT IN THE EYE.
GLEAM
MEDUSAPE* (DEMON MAMMAL) CAPTURE LEVEL 668
OOK OOK OHM.
WHAT'S THIS? A GORILLA THAT'S ACHIEVED ENLIGHTENMENT?
THEN HE SHOULDN'T FEAR DEATH.
KANNON GORILLA* (MAMMAL) CAPTURE LEVEL 671

*IAI-AYE SUBMITTED BY ARISA YANAGISAWA FROM GUNMA!
**ED NOTE: *IAI* IS A MARTIAL ART OF DRAWING THE SWORD!

*MEDUSAPE SUBMITTED BY IZURU INUBUSE FROM OSAKA;

*KANNON GORILLA SUBMITTED BY MY FROM KOCHI!

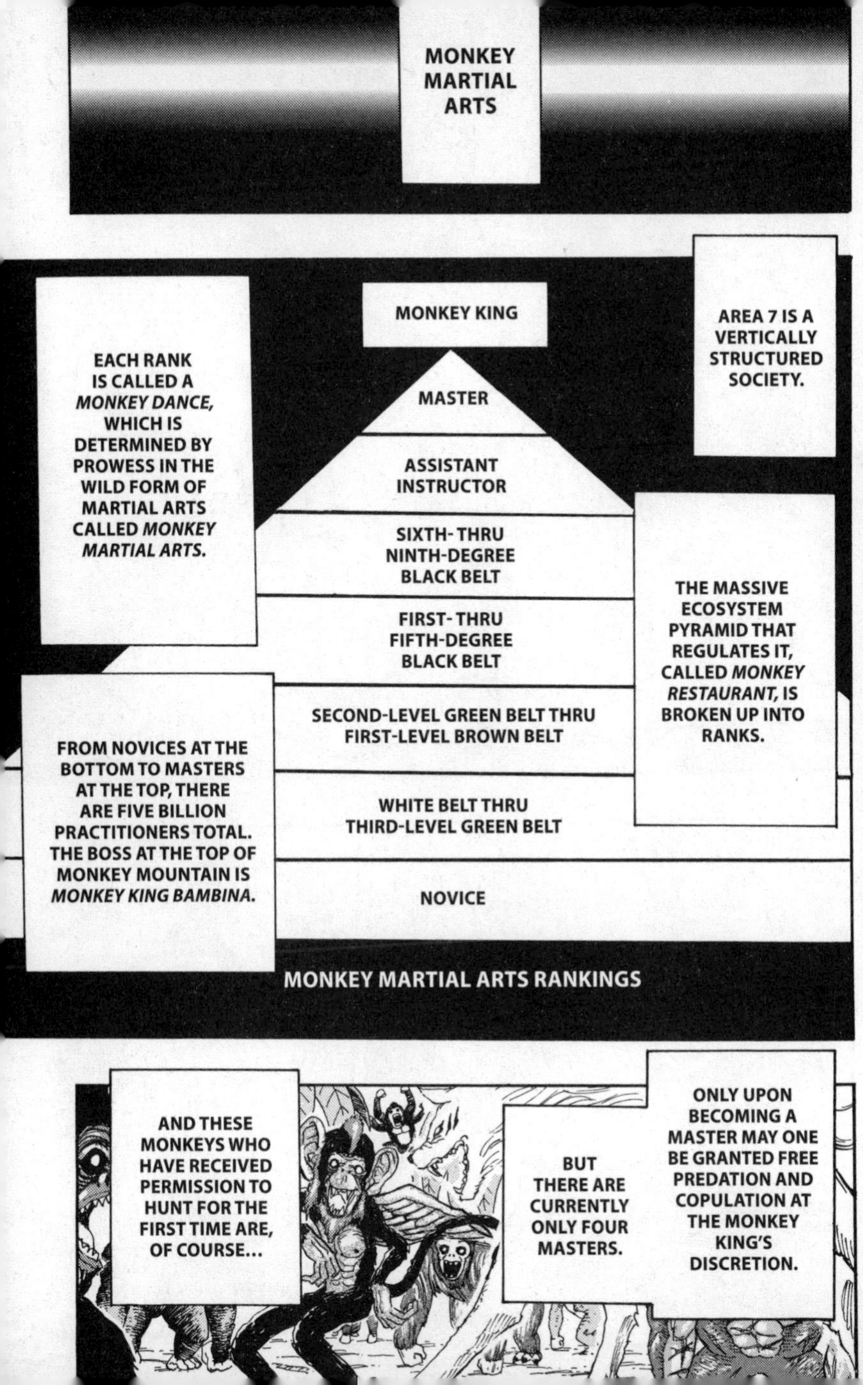

MONKEY MARTIAL ARTS
AREA 7 IS A VERTICALLY STRUCTURED SOCIETY.
THE MASSIVE ECOSYSTEM PYRAMID THAT REGULATES IT, CALLED *MONKEY RESTAURANT,* IS BROKEN UP INTO RANKS.
MONKEY KING
MASTER
ASSISTANT INSTRUCTOR
SIXTH- THRU NINTH-DEGREE BLACK BELT
FIRST- THRU FIFTH-DEGREE BLACK BELT
SECOND-LEVEL GREEN BELT THRU FIRST-LEVEL BROWN BELT
WHITE BELT THRU THIRD-LEVEL GREEN BELT
NOVICE
MONKEY MARTIAL ARTS RANKINGS
EACH RANK IS CALLED A *MONKEY DANCE,* WHICH IS DETERMINED BY PROWESS IN THE WILD FORM OF MARTIAL ARTS CALLED *MONKEY MARTIAL ARTS.*
FROM NOVICES AT THE BOTTOM TO MASTERS AT THE TOP, THERE ARE FIVE BILLION PRACTITIONERS TOTAL. THE BOSS AT THE TOP OF MONKEY MOUNTAIN IS *MONKEY KING BAMBINA.*
ONLY UPON BECOMING A MASTER MAY ONE BE GRANTED FREE PREDATION AND COPULATION AT THE MONKEY KING'S DISCRETION.
BUT THERE ARE CURRENTLY ONLY FOUR MASTERS.
AND THESE MONKEYS WHO HAVE RECEIVED PERMISSION TO HUNT FOR THE FIRST TIME ARE, OF COURSE...

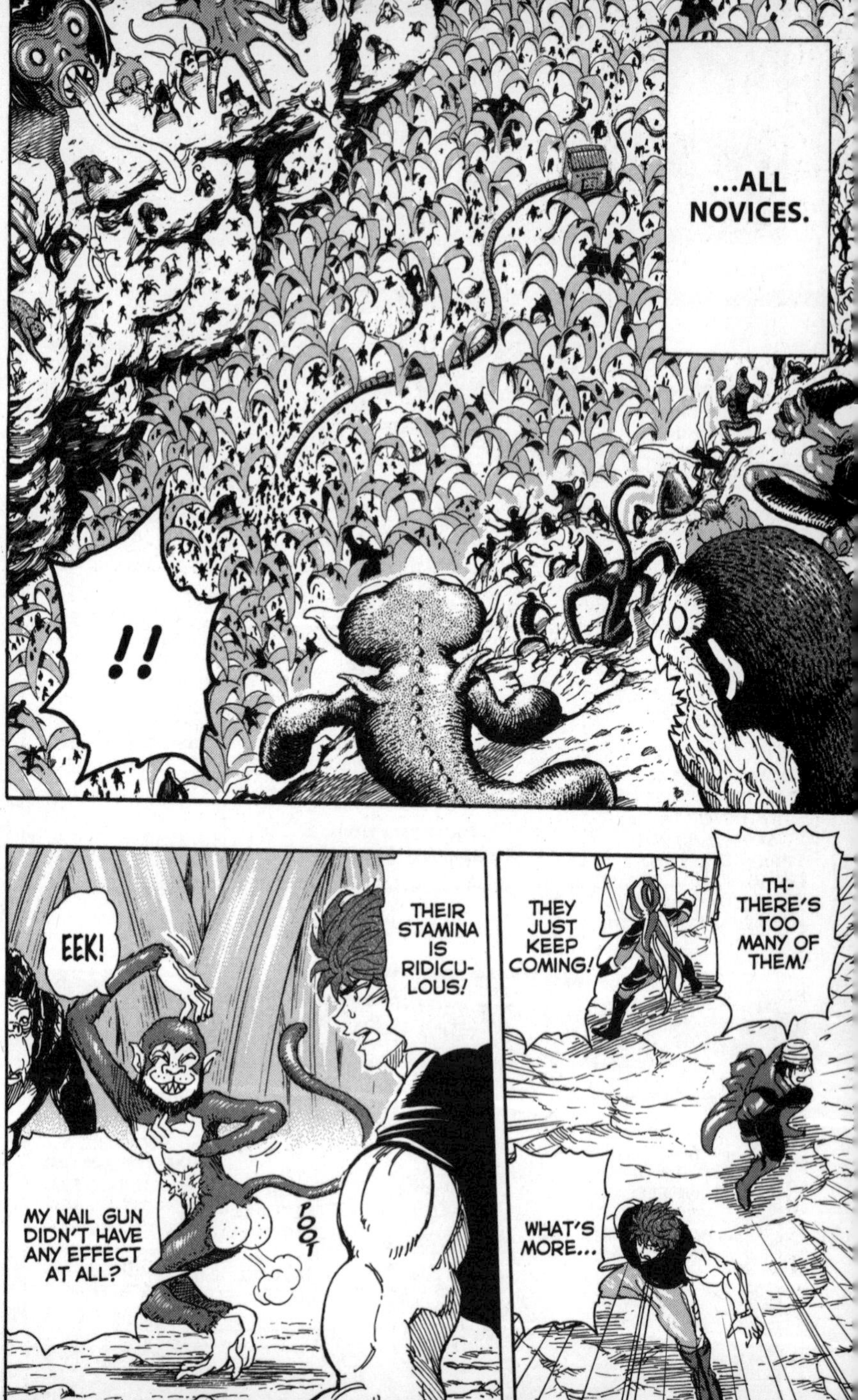
...ALL NOVICES.
!!
TH-THERE'S TOO MANY OF THEM!
THEY JUST KEEP COMING!
WHAT'S MORE...
THEIR STAMINA IS RIDICU-LOUS!
EEK!
POOT
MY NAIL GUN DIDN'T HAVE ANY EFFECT AT ALL?

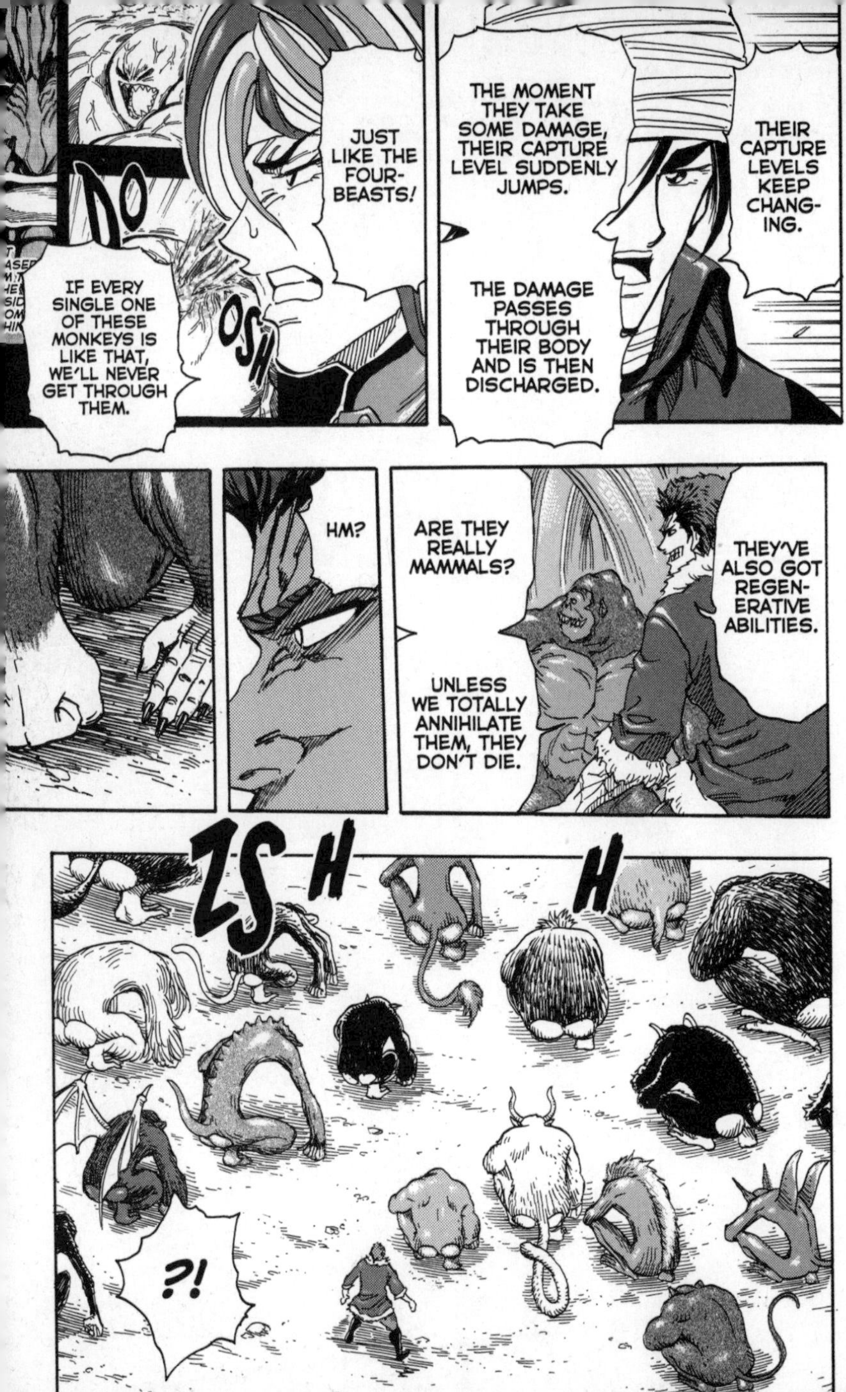
THEIR CAPTURE LEVELS KEEP CHANG-ING.
THE MOMENT THEY TAKE SOME DAMAGE, THEIR CAPTURE LEVEL SUDDENLY JUMPS.
THE DAMAGE PASSES THROUGH THEIR BODY AND IS THEN DISCHARGED.
JUST LIKE THE FOUR-BEASTS!
DOOSH
IF EVERY SINGLE ONE OF THESE MONKEYS IS LIKE THAT, WE'LL NEVER GET THROUGH THEM.
THEY'VE ALSO GOT REGEN-ERATIVE ABILITIES.
ARE THEY REALLY MAMMALS?
UNLESS WE TOTALLY ANNIHILATE THEM, THEY DON'T DIE.
HM?
ZSH H
?!

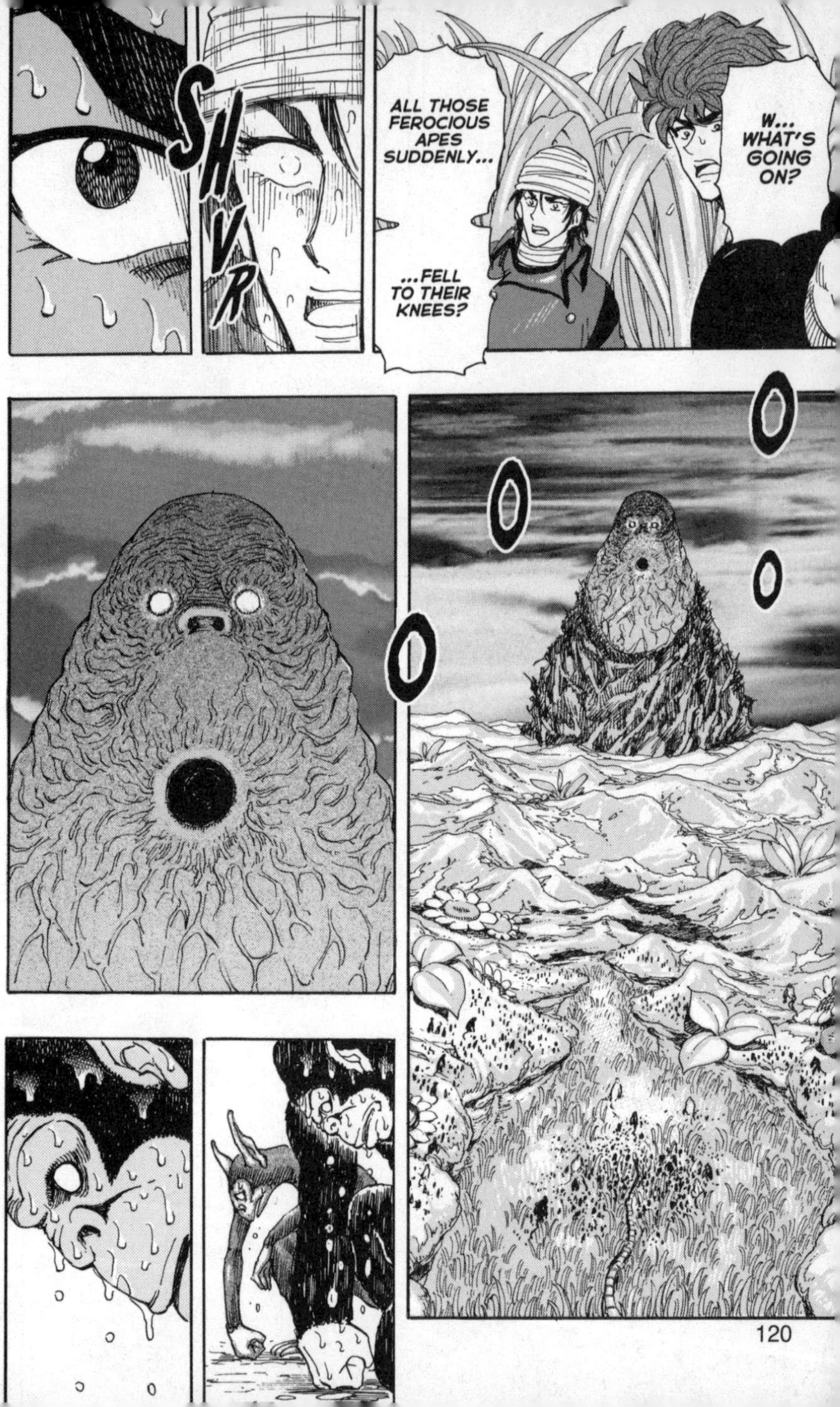
W... WHAT'S GOING ON?
ALL THOSE FEROCIOUS APES SUDDENLY...
...FELL TO THEIR KNEES?
SHVR

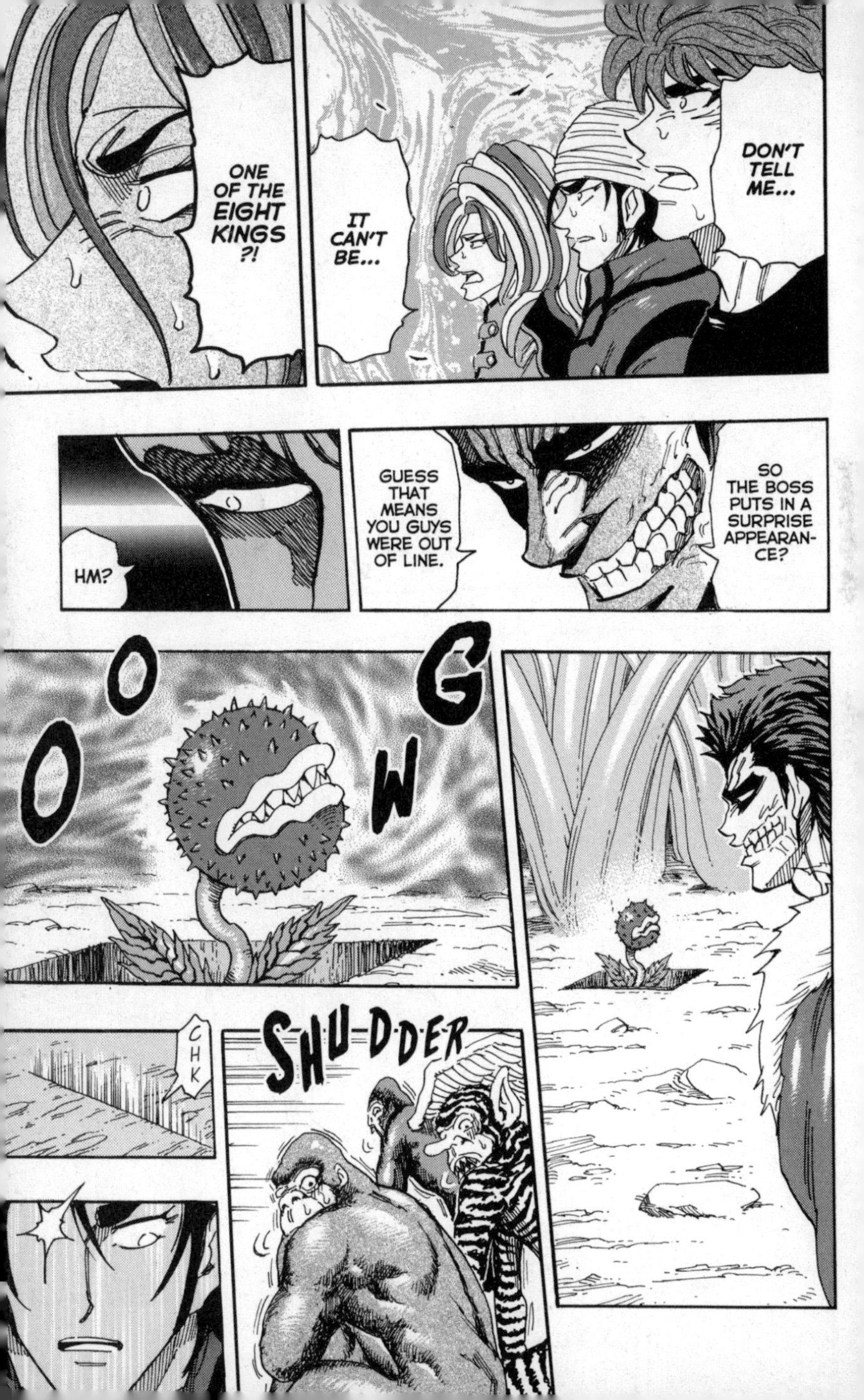
DON'T TELL ME...
IT CAN'T BE...
ONE OF THE EIGHT KINGS?!
SO THE BOSS PUTS IN A SURPRISE APPEARANCE?
GUESS THAT MEANS YOU GUYS WERE OUT OF LINE.
HM?
OOGW
SHUDDER
CHK

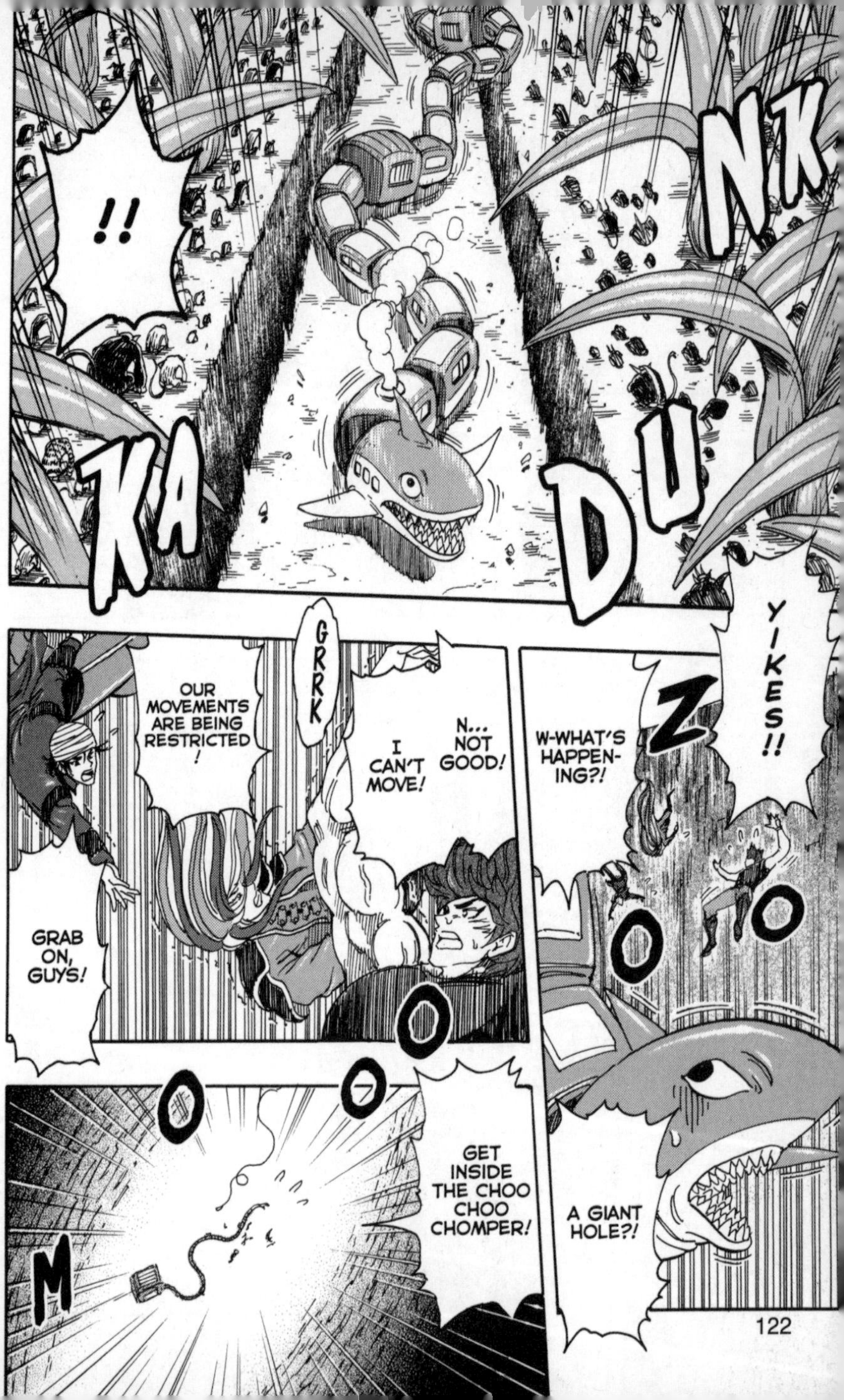
KA DU NK
!!
YIKES!!
W-WHAT'S HAPPEN-ING?!
ZOOOOOM
A GIANT HOLE?!
N... NOT GOOD!
I CAN'T MOVE!
GRRK
OUR MOVEMENTS ARE BEING RESTRICTED!
GRAB ON, GUYS!
GET INSIDE THE CHOO CHOO CHOMPER!

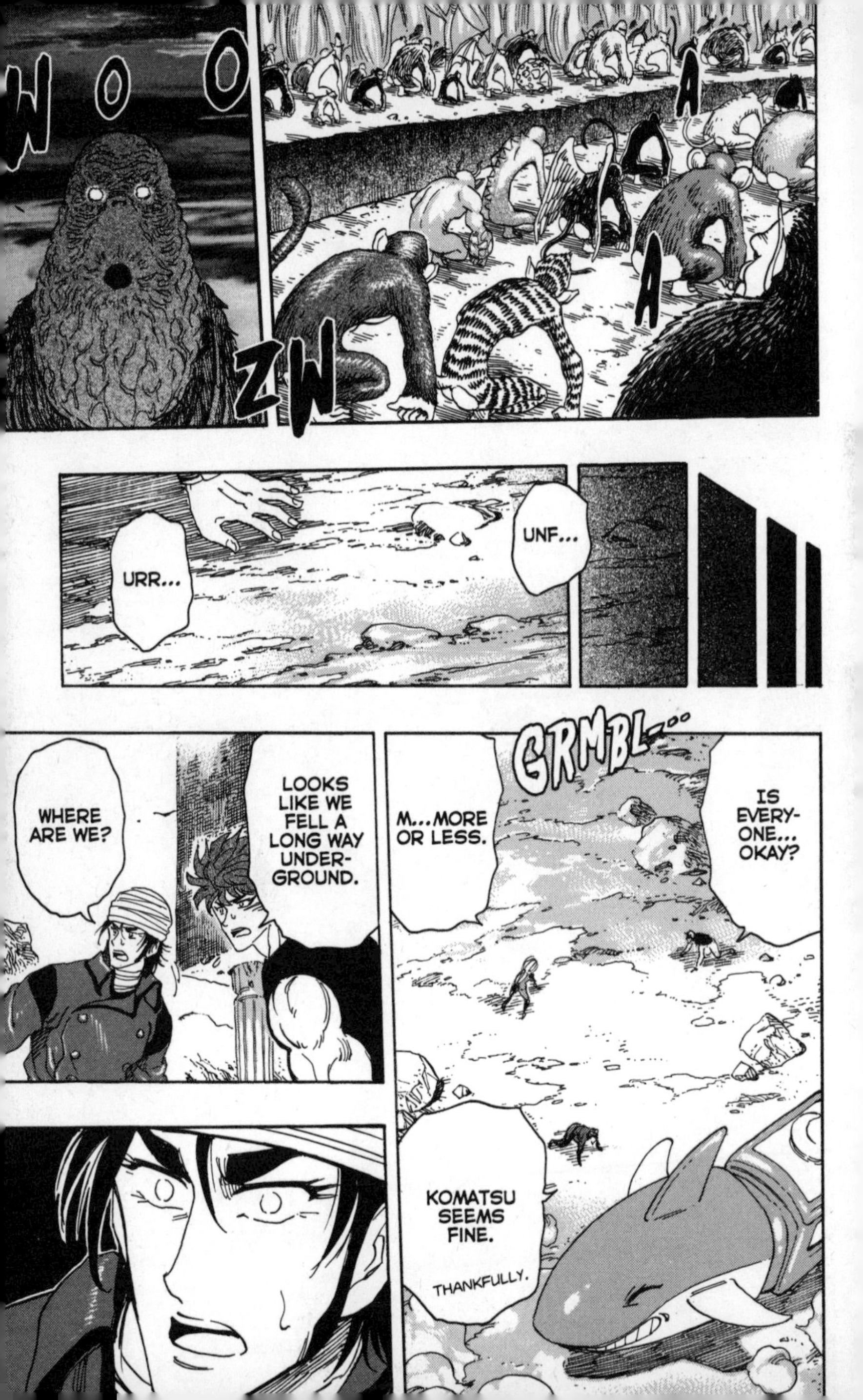
AAA
WOO
ZW
UNF...
URR...
GRMBL...
IS EVERYONE... OKAY?
M...MORE OR LESS.
KOMATSU SEEMS FINE.
THANKFULLY.
LOOKS LIKE WE FELL A LONG WAY UNDERGROUND.
WHERE ARE WE?

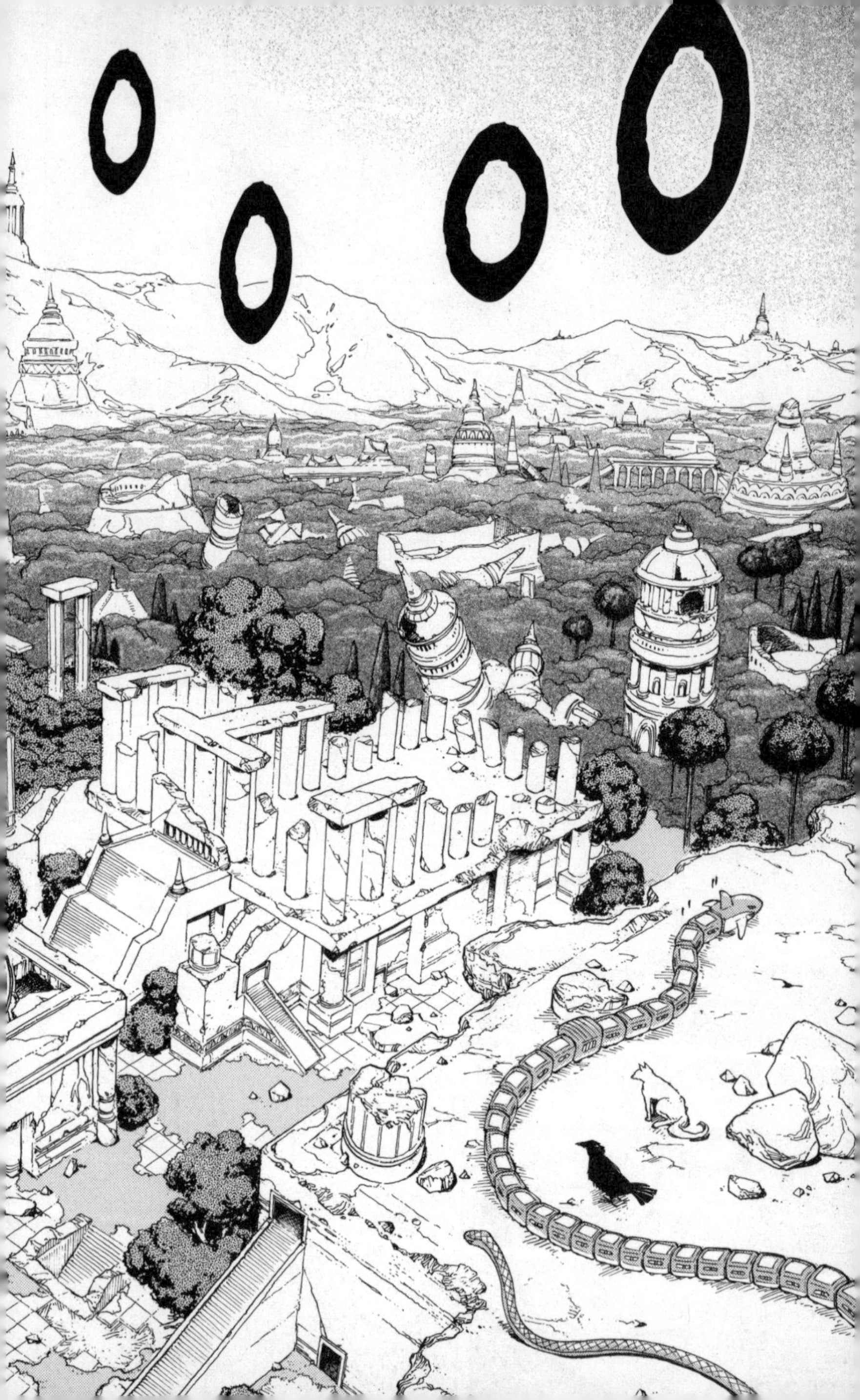

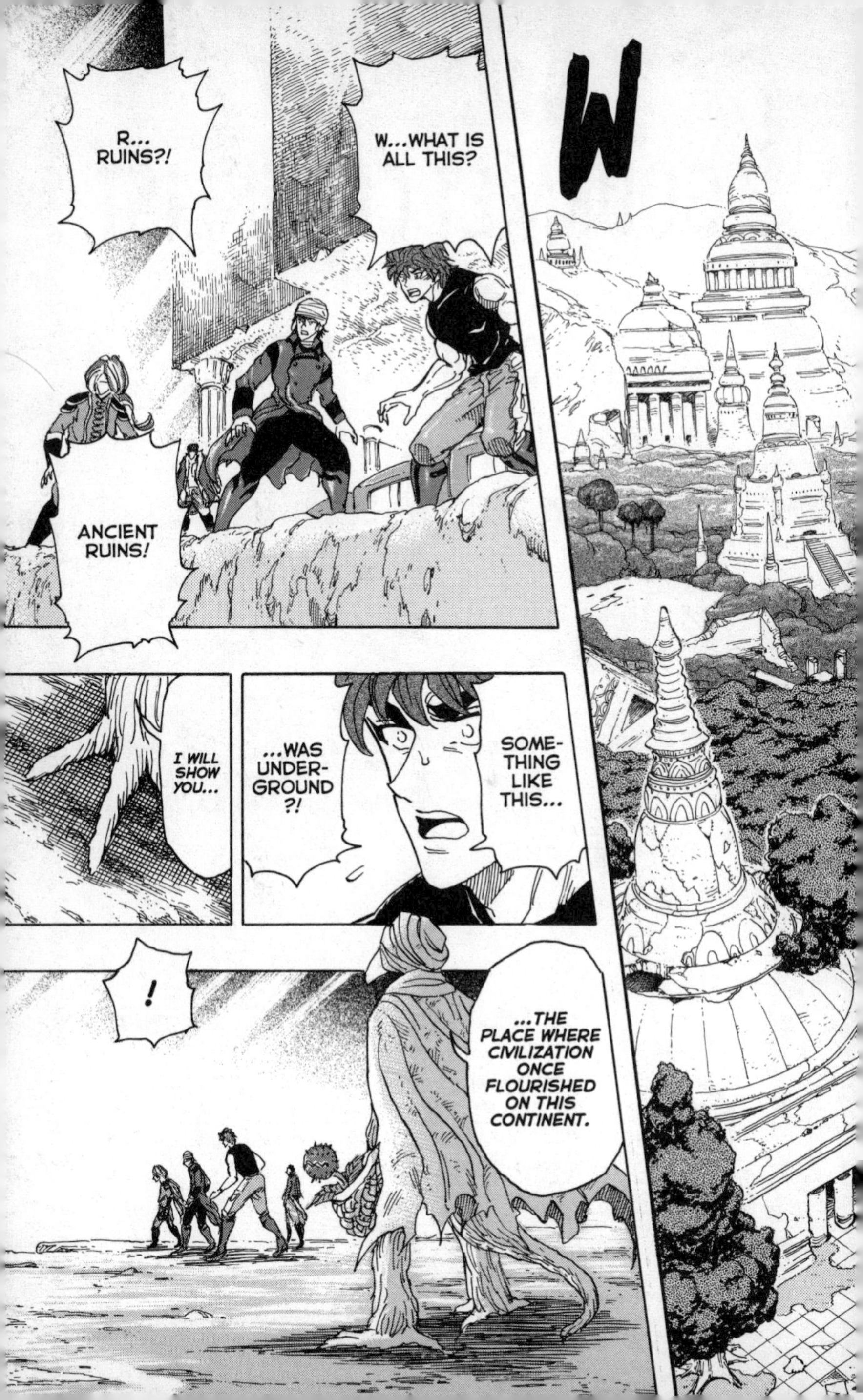
W
W...WHAT IS ALL THIS?
R... RUINS?!
ANCIENT RUINS!
SOME-THING LIKE THIS...
...WAS UNDER-GROUND?!
I WILL SHOW YOU...
...THE PLACE WHERE CIVILIZATION ONCE FLOURISHED ON THIS CONTINENT.
!

GOURMET CHECKLIST

Vol. 322

MELON BREAD TURTLE
(REPTILE)

CAPTURE LEVEL: 25
HABITAT: DEEP WOODS
SIZE: 40 CM
HEIGHT: ---
WEIGHT: 7 KG
PRICE: 500 YEN PER ROLL

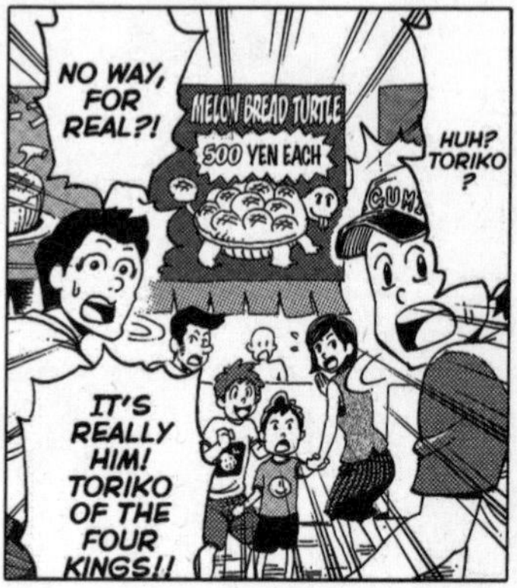
HUH? TORIKO?
MELON BREAD TURTLE
500 YEN EACH
NO WAY, FOR REAL?!
IT'S REALLY HIM! TORIKO OF THE FOUR KINGS!!

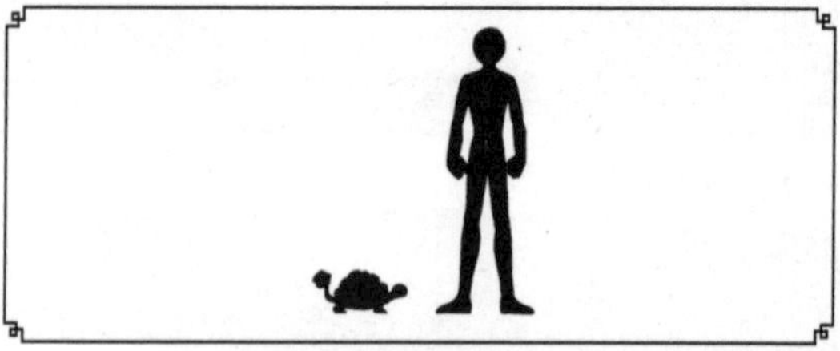

SCALE

A MYSTERIOUS TURTLE THAT CONTINUOUSLY GROWS HIGH-QUALITY MELON BREAD FRESH BAKED OFF ITS SHELL. IF YOU TRY TO APPROACH IT, IT WILL QUICKLY RUN AWAY SO IT'S ACTUALLY REALLY DIFFICULT TO CATCH. IT'S A COMMON INGREDIENT SOLD BY FOOD VENDORS AT EVENTS. YOU CAN EVEN FIND IT AT STALLS AT THE GOURMET FESTIVAL! IT COMES IN FIRST OR SECOND IN TERMS OF POPULARITY.

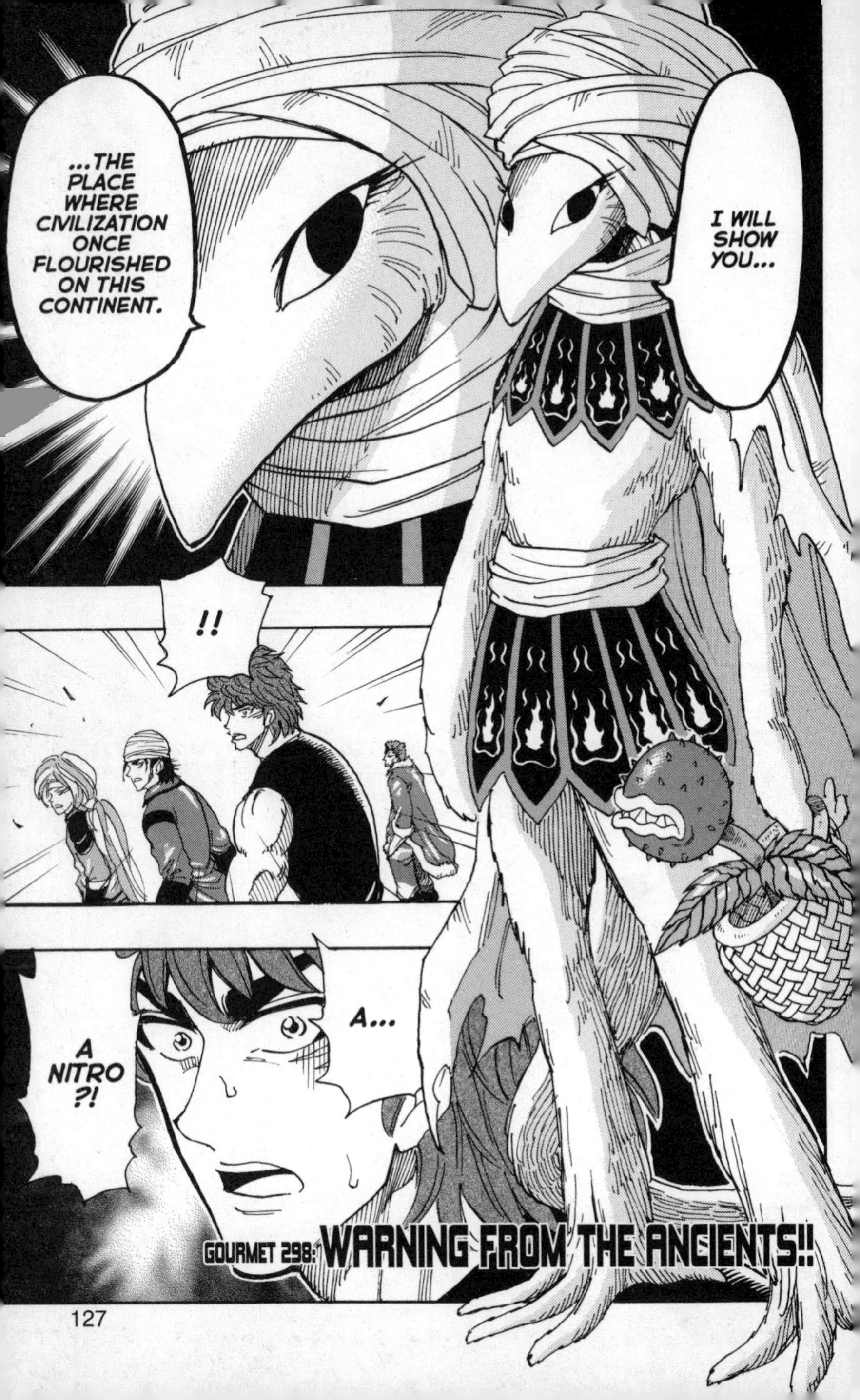
I WILL SHOW YOU...
...THE PLACE WHERE CIVILIZATION ONCE FLOURISHED ON THIS CONTINENT.
!!
A...
A NITRO?!
GOURMET 298: WARNING FROM THE ANCIENTS!!

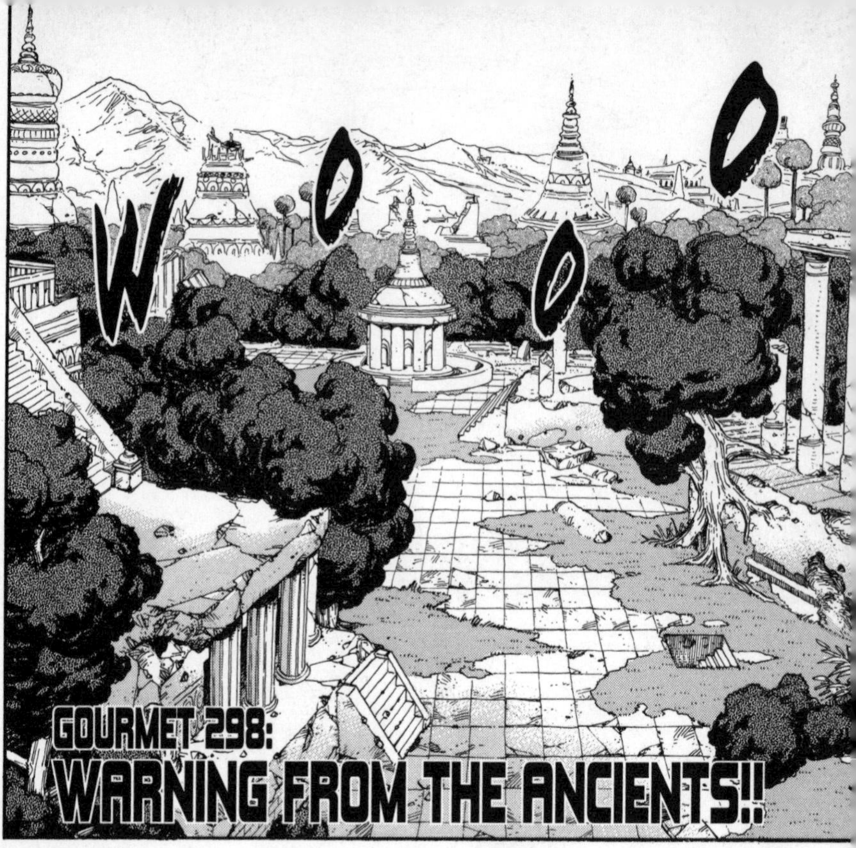
WOOOO
GOURMET 298:
WARNING FROM THE ANCIENTS!!

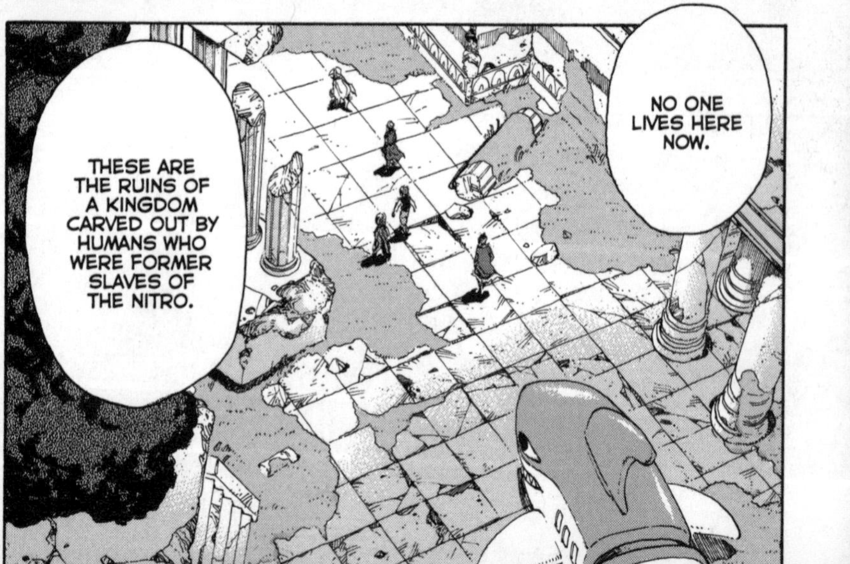
NO ONE LIVES HERE NOW.
THESE ARE THE RUINS OF A KINGDOM CARVED OUT BY HUMANS WHO WERE FORMER SLAVES OF THE NITRO.

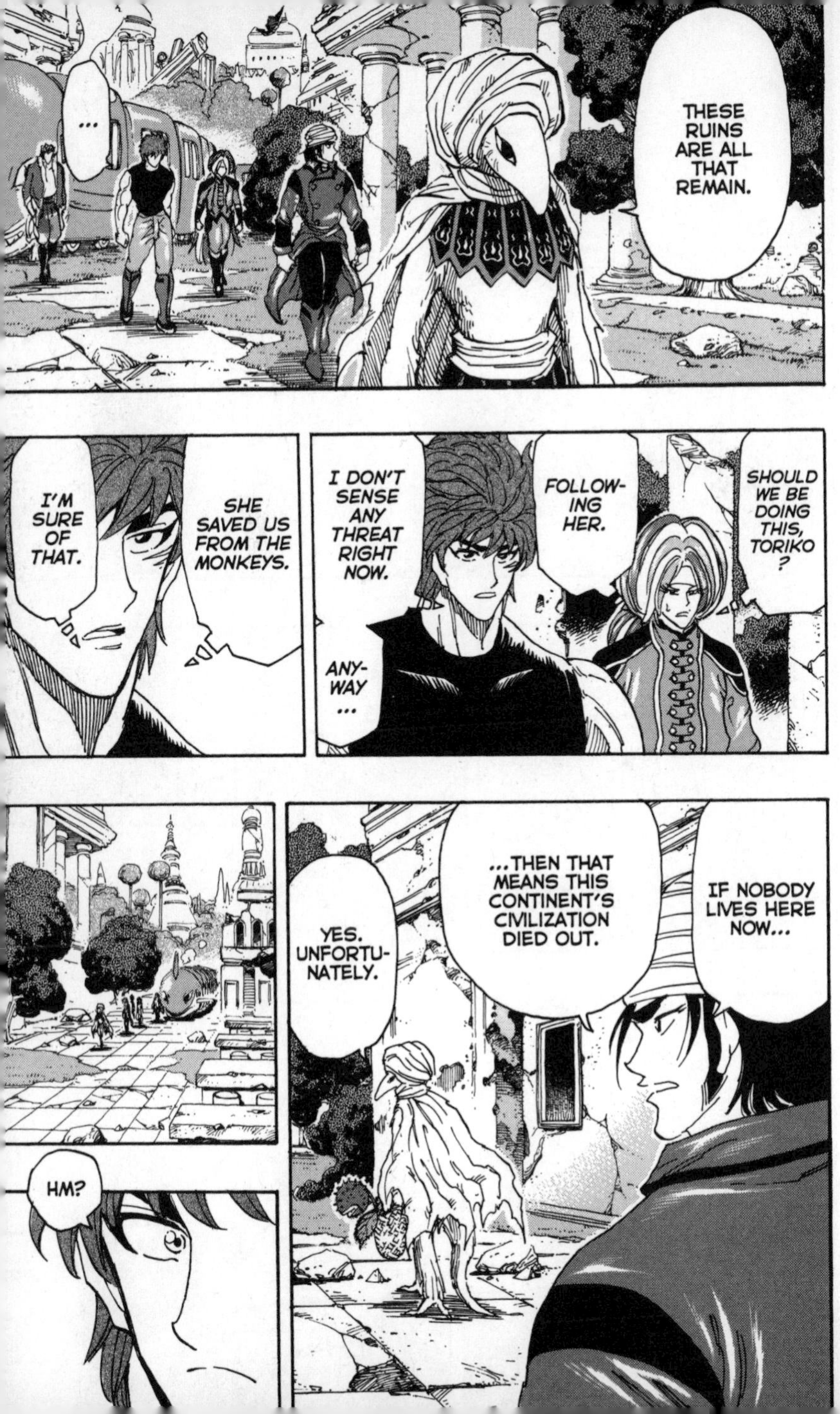
THESE RUINS ARE ALL THAT REMAIN.
...
SHOULD WE BE DOING THIS, TORIKO?
FOLLOW-ING HER.
I DON'T SENSE ANY THREAT RIGHT NOW.
ANY-WAY...
SHE SAVED US FROM THE MONKEYS.
I'M SURE OF THAT.
IF NOBODY LIVES HERE NOW...
...THEN THAT MEANS THIS CONTINENT'S CIVILIZATION DIED OUT.
YES. UNFORTU-NATELY.
HM?

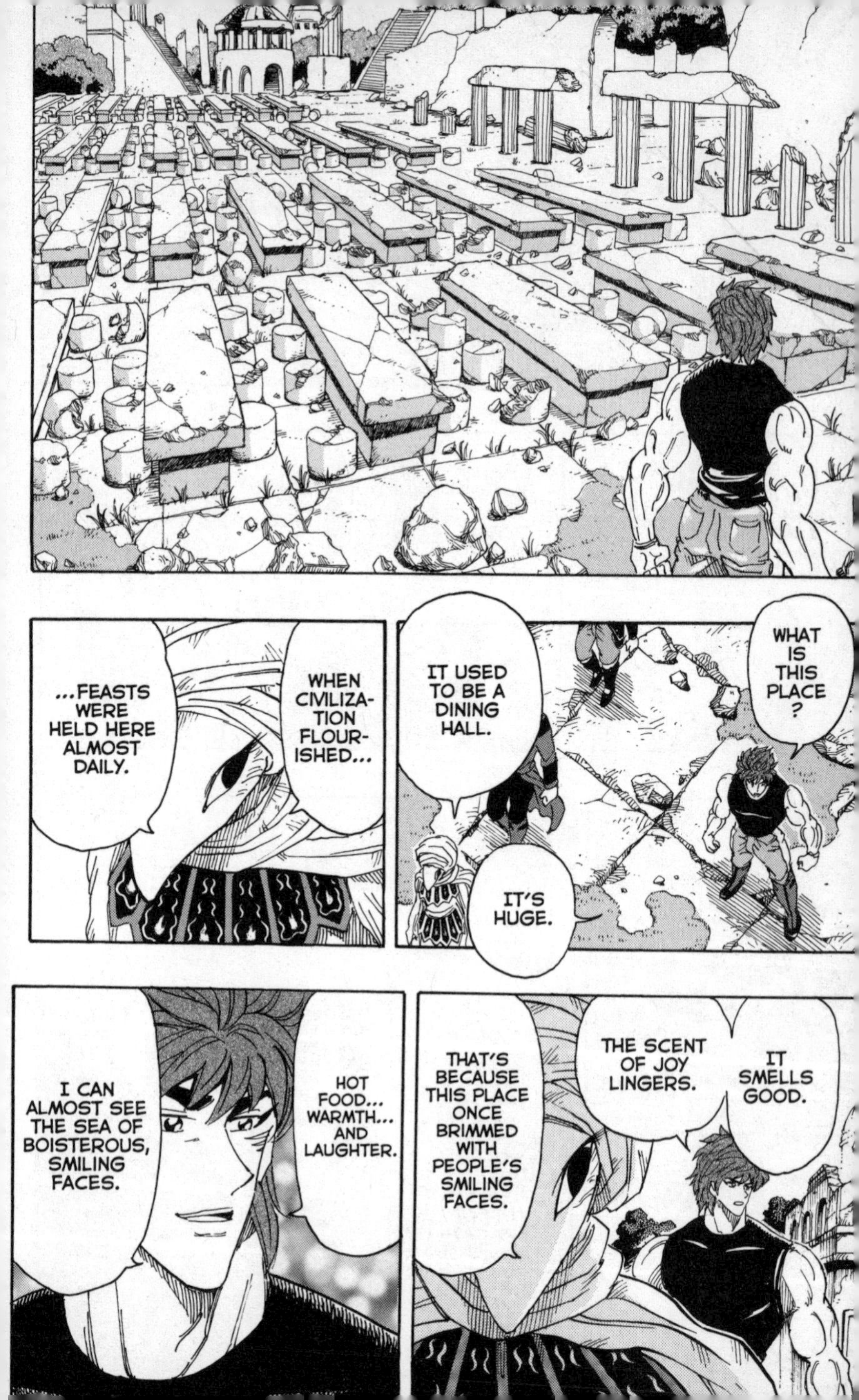
WHAT IS THIS PLACE?
IT USED TO BE A DINING HALL.
IT'S HUGE.
WHEN CIVILIZATION FLOURISHED...
...FEASTS WERE HELD HERE ALMOST DAILY.
IT SMELLS GOOD.
THE SCENT OF JOY LINGERS.
THAT'S BECAUSE THIS PLACE ONCE BRIMMED WITH PEOPLE'S SMILING FACES.
HOT FOOD... WARMTH... AND LAUGHTER.
I CAN ALMOST SEE THE SEA OF BOISTEROUS, SMILING FACES.

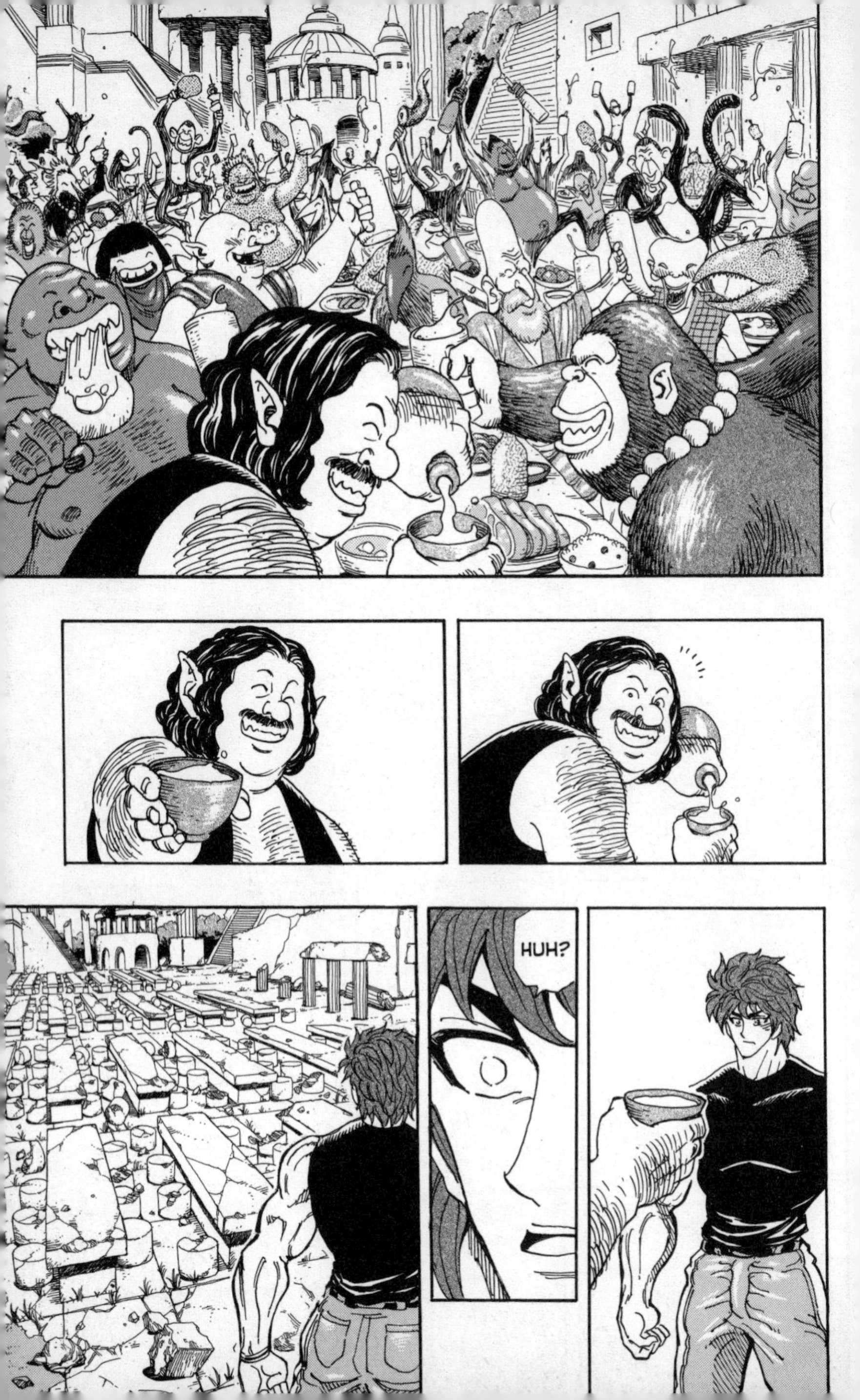
HUH?

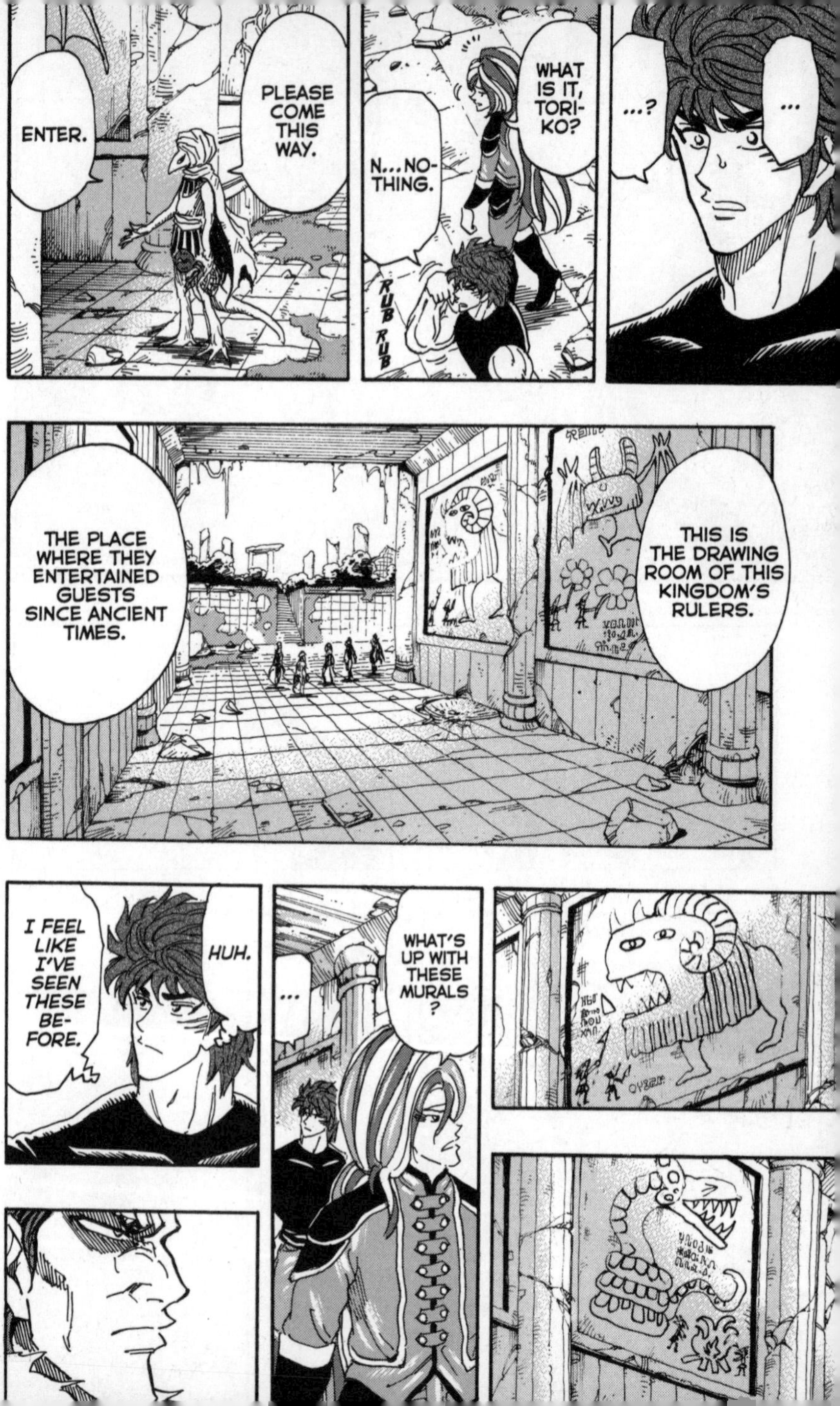
...
...?
WHAT IS IT, TORIKO?
N...NO-THING.
RUB RUB
PLEASE COME THIS WAY.
ENTER.
THIS IS THE DRAWING ROOM OF THIS KINGDOM'S RULERS.
THE PLACE WHERE THEY ENTERTAINED GUESTS SINCE ANCIENT TIMES.
WHAT'S UP WITH THESE MURALS?
...
HUH.
I FEEL LIKE I'VE SEEN THESE BE-FORE.

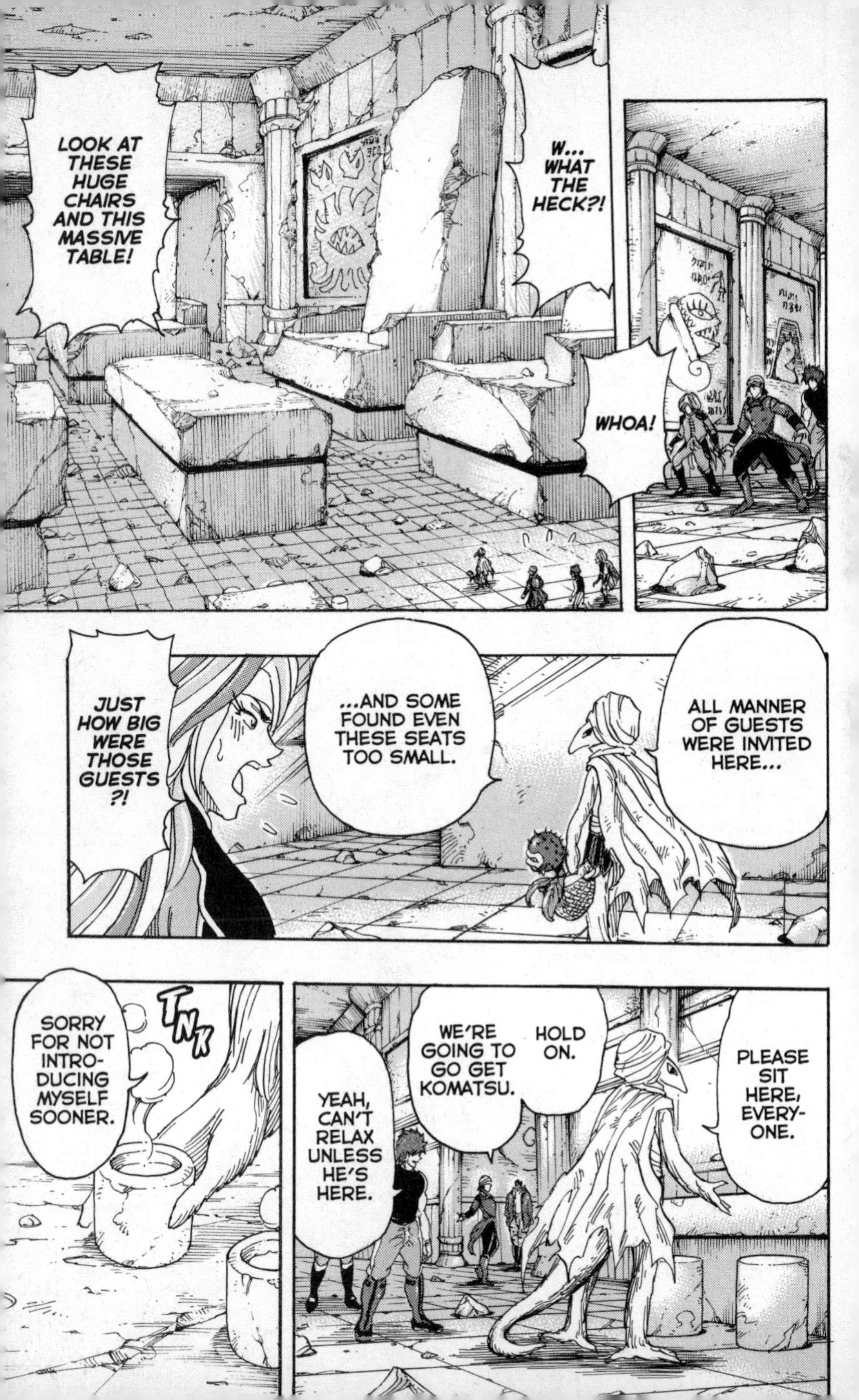
WHOA!
W... WHAT THE HECK?!
LOOK AT THESE HUGE CHAIRS AND THIS MASSIVE TABLE!
ALL MANNER OF GUESTS WERE INVITED HERE...
...AND SOME FOUND EVEN THESE SEATS TOO SMALL.
JUST HOW BIG WERE THOSE GUESTS ?!
PLEASE SIT HERE, EVERY-ONE.
HOLD ON.
WE'RE GOING TO GO GET KOMATSU.
YEAH, CAN'T RELAX UNLESS HE'S HERE.
TNK
SORRY FOR NOT INTRO-DUCING MYSELF SOONER.

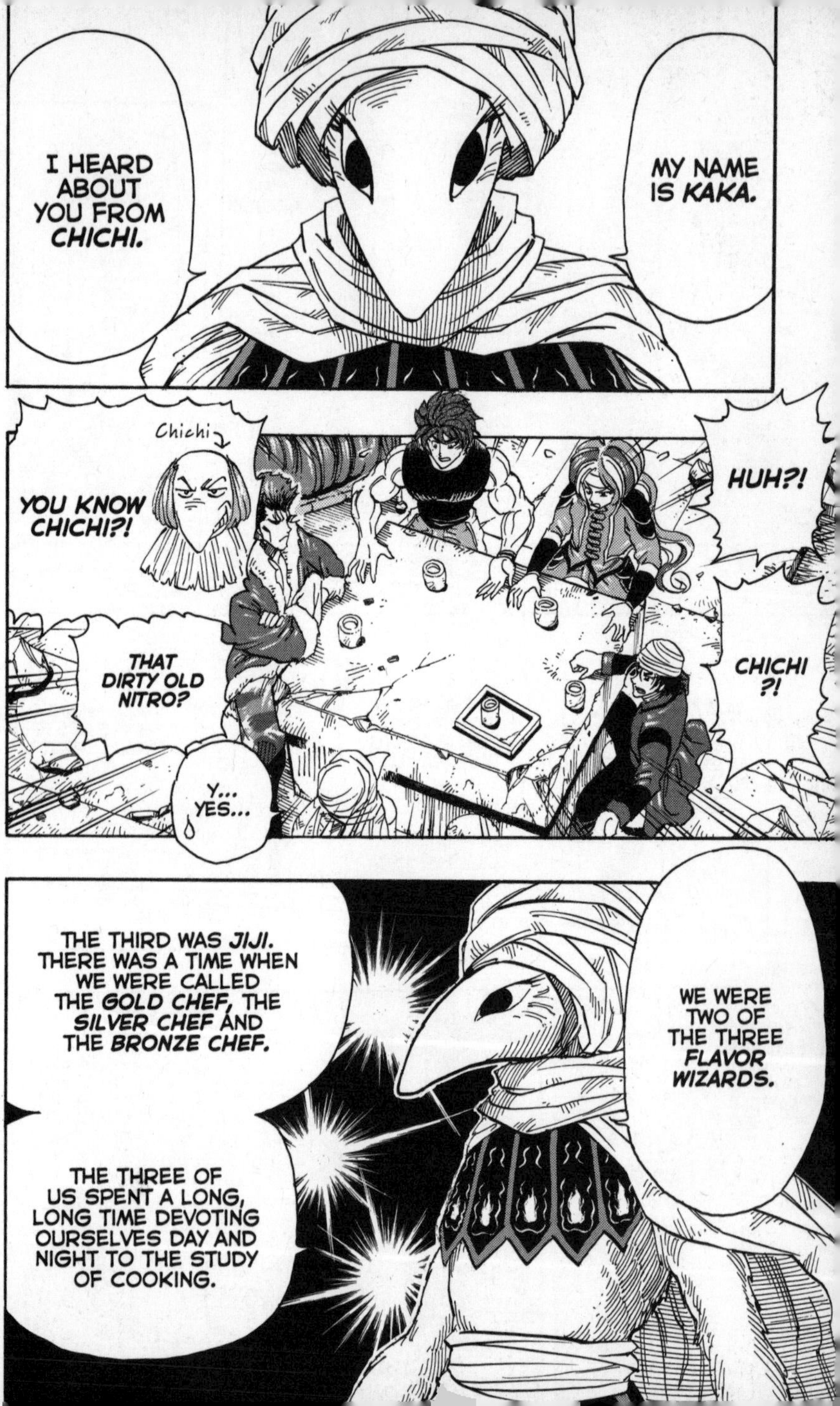
MY NAME IS KAKA.
I HEARD ABOUT YOU FROM CHICHI.
HUH?!
CHICHI ?!
YOU KNOW CHICHI?!
Chichi
THAT DIRTY OLD NITRO?
Y... YES...
WE WERE TWO OF THE THREE FLAVOR WIZARDS.
THE THIRD WAS JIJI. THERE WAS A TIME WHEN WE WERE CALLED THE GOLD CHEF, THE SILVER CHEF AND THE BRONZE CHEF.
THE THREE OF US SPENT A LONG, LONG TIME DEVOTING OURSELVES DAY AND NIGHT TO THE STUDY OF COOKING.

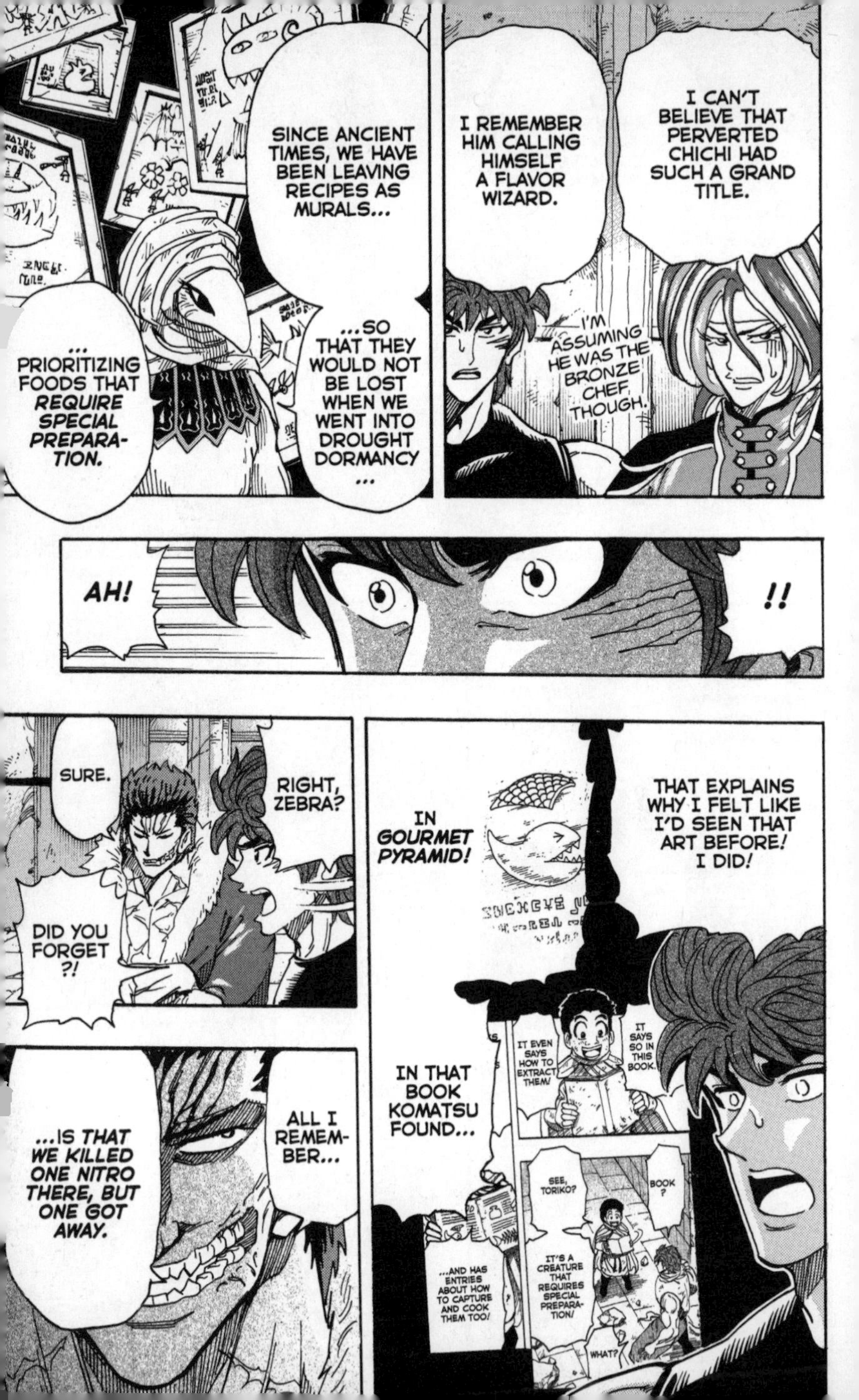
I CAN'T BELIEVE THAT PERVERTED CHICHI HAD SUCH A GRAND TITLE.
I REMEMBER HIM CALLING HIMSELF A FLAVOR WIZARD.
I'M ASSUMING HE WAS THE BRONZE CHEF THOUGH.
SINCE ANCIENT TIMES, WE HAVE BEEN LEAVING RECIPES AS MURALS...
...SO THAT THEY WOULD NOT BE LOST WHEN WE WENT INTO DROUGHT DORMANCY ...
... PRIORITIZING FOODS THAT *REQUIRE SPECIAL PREPARATION.*
!!
AH!
THAT EXPLAINS WHY I FELT LIKE I'D SEEN THAT ART BEFORE! I DID!
IN *GOURMET PYRAMID!*
IN THAT BOOK KOMATSU FOUND...
IT SAYS SO IN THIS BOOK.
IT EVEN SAYS HOW TO EXTRACT THEM!
BOOK?
SEE, TORIKO?
IT'S A CREATURE THAT REQUIRES SPECIAL PREPARATION!
...AND HAS ENTRIES ABOUT HOW TO CAPTURE AND COOK THEM TOO!
WHAT?
RIGHT, ZEBRA?
SURE.
DID YOU FORGET ?!
ALL I REMEMBER...
...IS *THAT* WE KILLED ONE NITRO THERE, BUT ONE GOT AWAY.

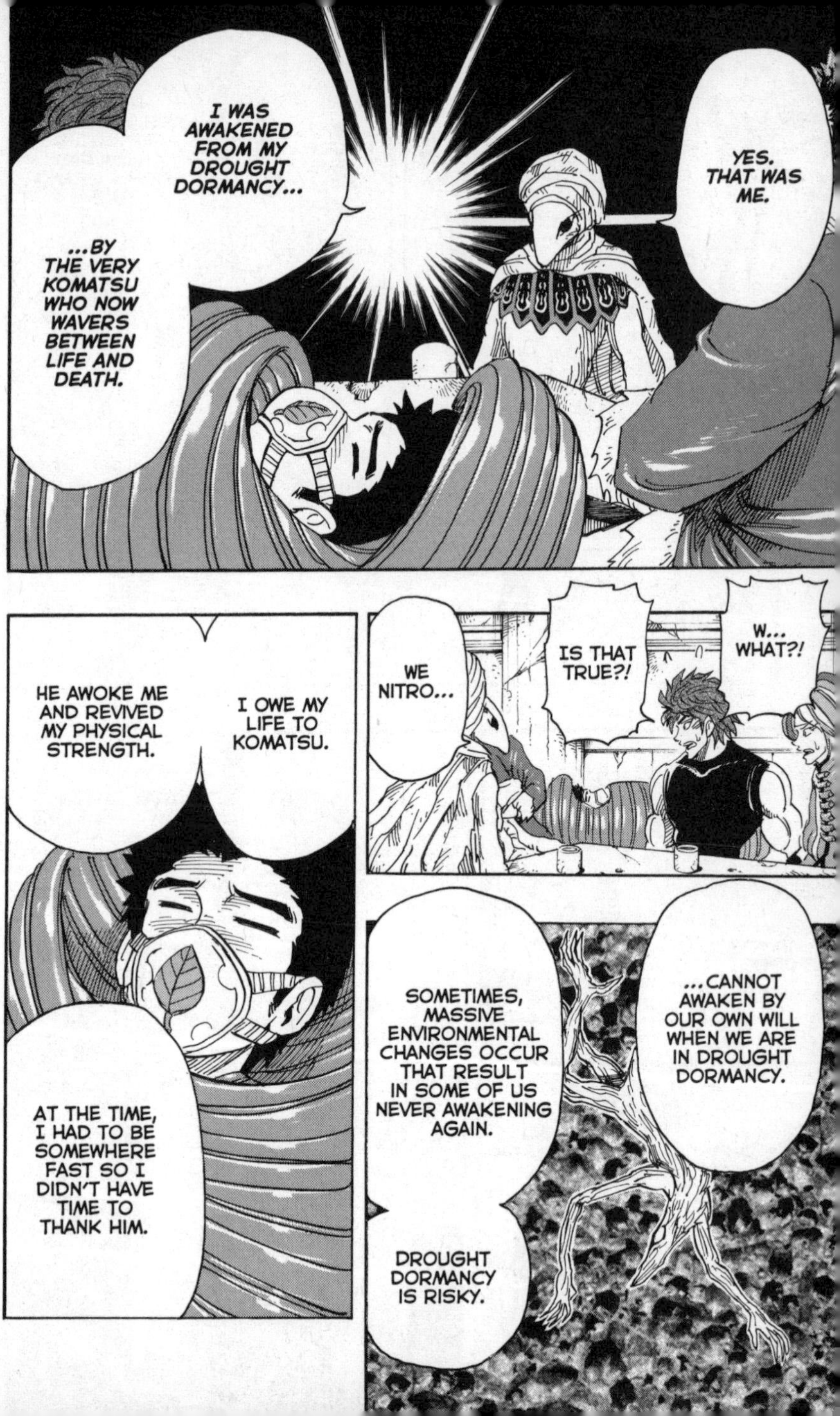
YES. THAT WAS ME.
I WAS AWAKENED FROM MY DROUGHT DORMANCY...
...BY THE VERY KOMATSU WHO NOW WAVERS BETWEEN LIFE AND DEATH.
W... WHAT?!
IS THAT TRUE?!
WE NITRO...
...CANNOT AWAKEN BY OUR OWN WILL WHEN WE ARE IN DROUGHT DORMANCY.
SOMETIMES, MASSIVE ENVIRONMENTAL CHANGES OCCUR THAT RESULT IN SOME OF US NEVER AWAKENING AGAIN.
DROUGHT DORMANCY IS RISKY.
I OWE MY LIFE TO KOMATSU.
HE AWOKE ME AND REVIVED MY PHYSICAL STRENGTH.
AT THE TIME, I HAD TO BE SOMEWHERE FAST SO I DIDN'T HAVE TIME TO THANK HIM.

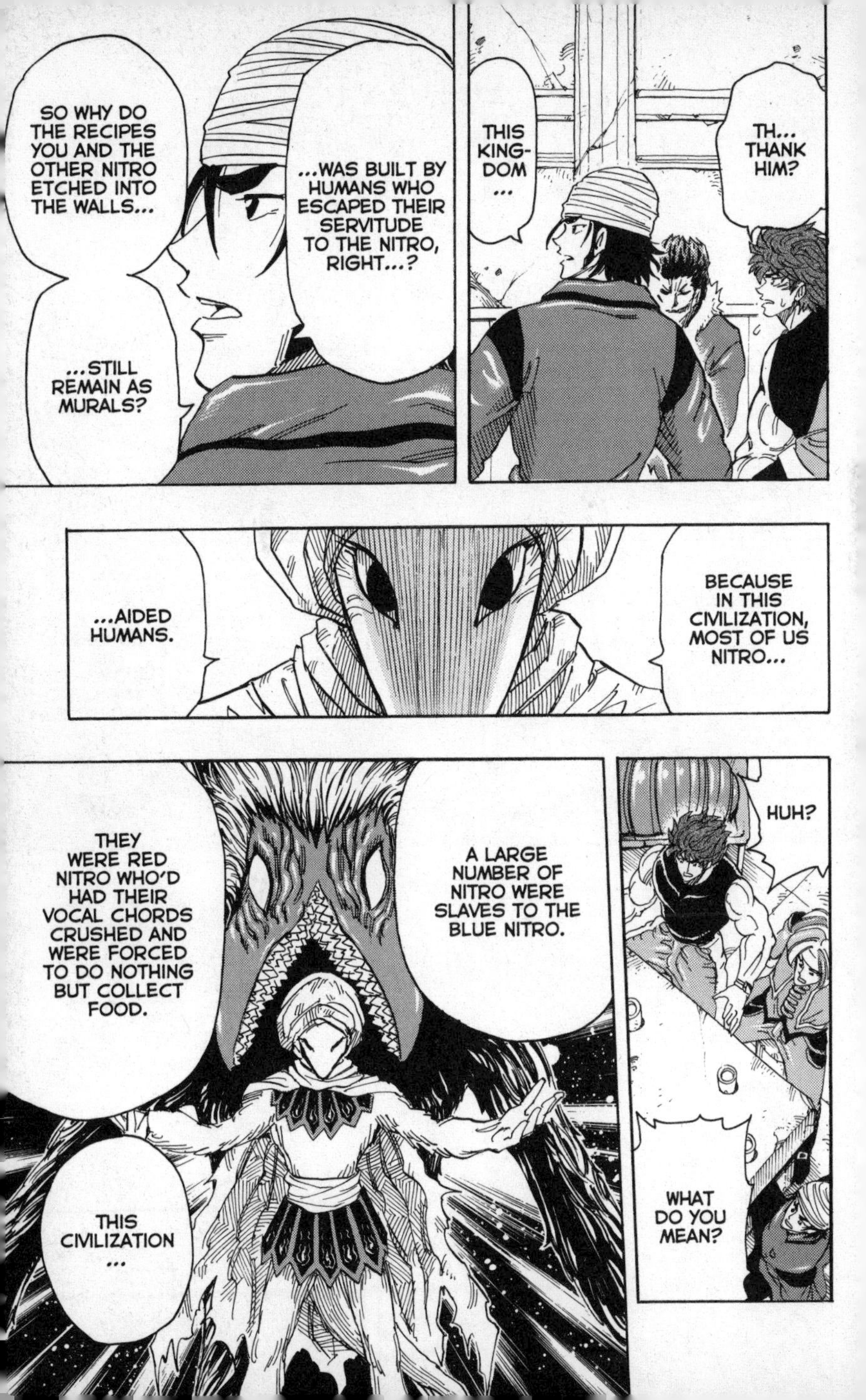
TH... THANK HIM?
THIS KING-DOM...
...WAS BUILT BY HUMANS WHO ESCAPED THEIR SERVITUDE TO THE NITRO, RIGHT...?
SO WHY DO THE RECIPES YOU AND THE OTHER NITRO ETCHED INTO THE WALLS...
...STILL REMAIN AS MURALS?
BECAUSE IN THIS CIVILIZATION, MOST OF US NITRO...
...AIDED HUMANS.
HUH?
WHAT DO YOU MEAN?
A LARGE NUMBER OF NITRO WERE SLAVES TO THE BLUE NITRO.
THEY WERE RED NITRO WHO'D HAD THEIR VOCAL CHORDS CRUSHED AND WERE FORCED TO DO NOTHING BUT COLLECT FOOD.
THIS CIVILIZATION...

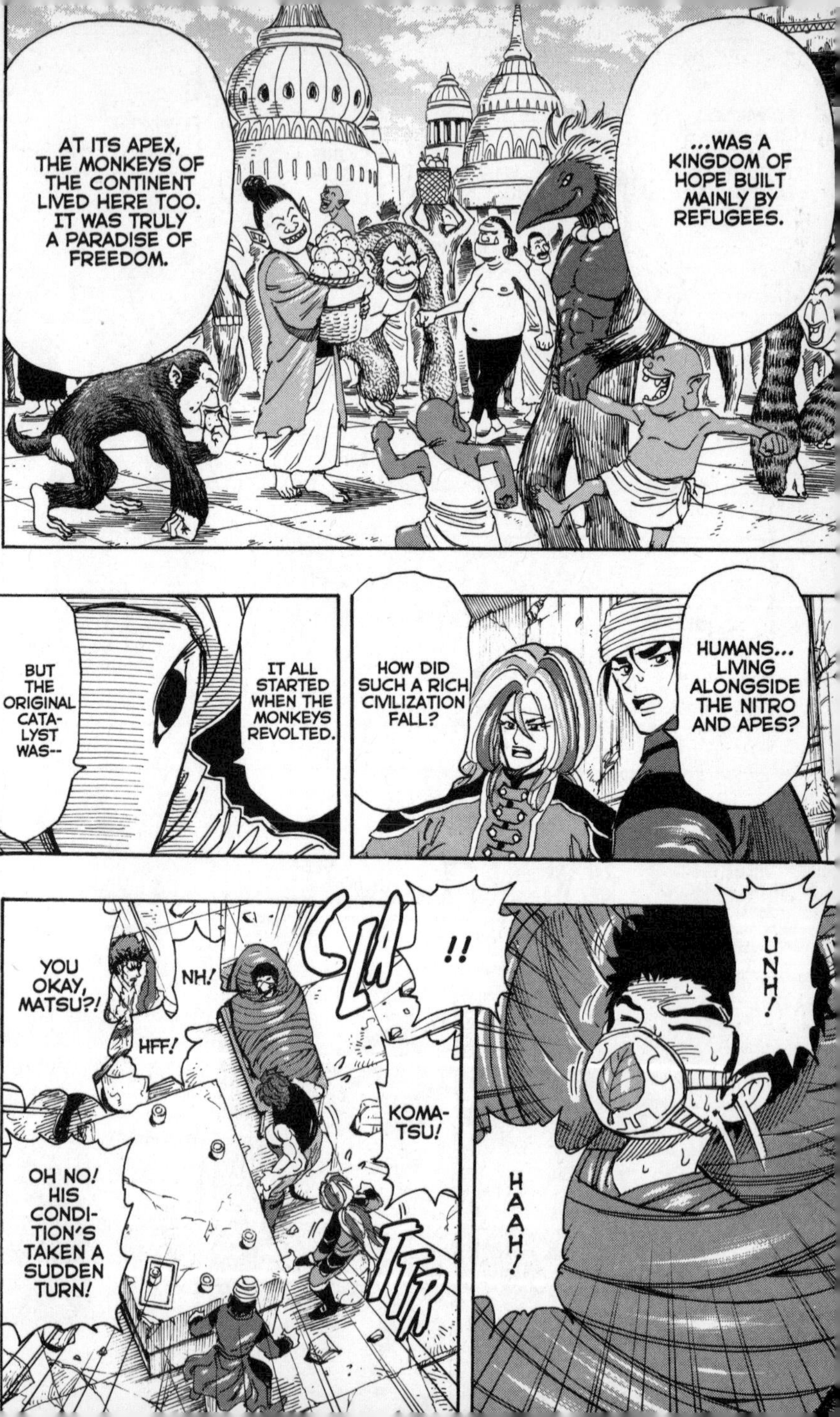
...WAS A KINGDOM OF HOPE BUILT MAINLY BY REFUGEES.
AT ITS APEX, THE MONKEYS OF THE CONTINENT LIVED HERE TOO. IT WAS TRULY A PARADISE OF FREEDOM.
HUMANS... LIVING ALONGSIDE THE NITRO AND APES?
HOW DID SUCH A RICH CIVILIZATION FALL?
IT ALL STARTED WHEN THE MONKEYS REVOLTED.
BUT THE ORIGINAL CATALYST WAS--
UNH!
HAAAH!
!!
CLATTR
NH!
YOU OKAY, MATSU?!
HFF!
KOMATSU!
OH NO! HIS CONDITION'S TAKEN A SUDDEN TURN!

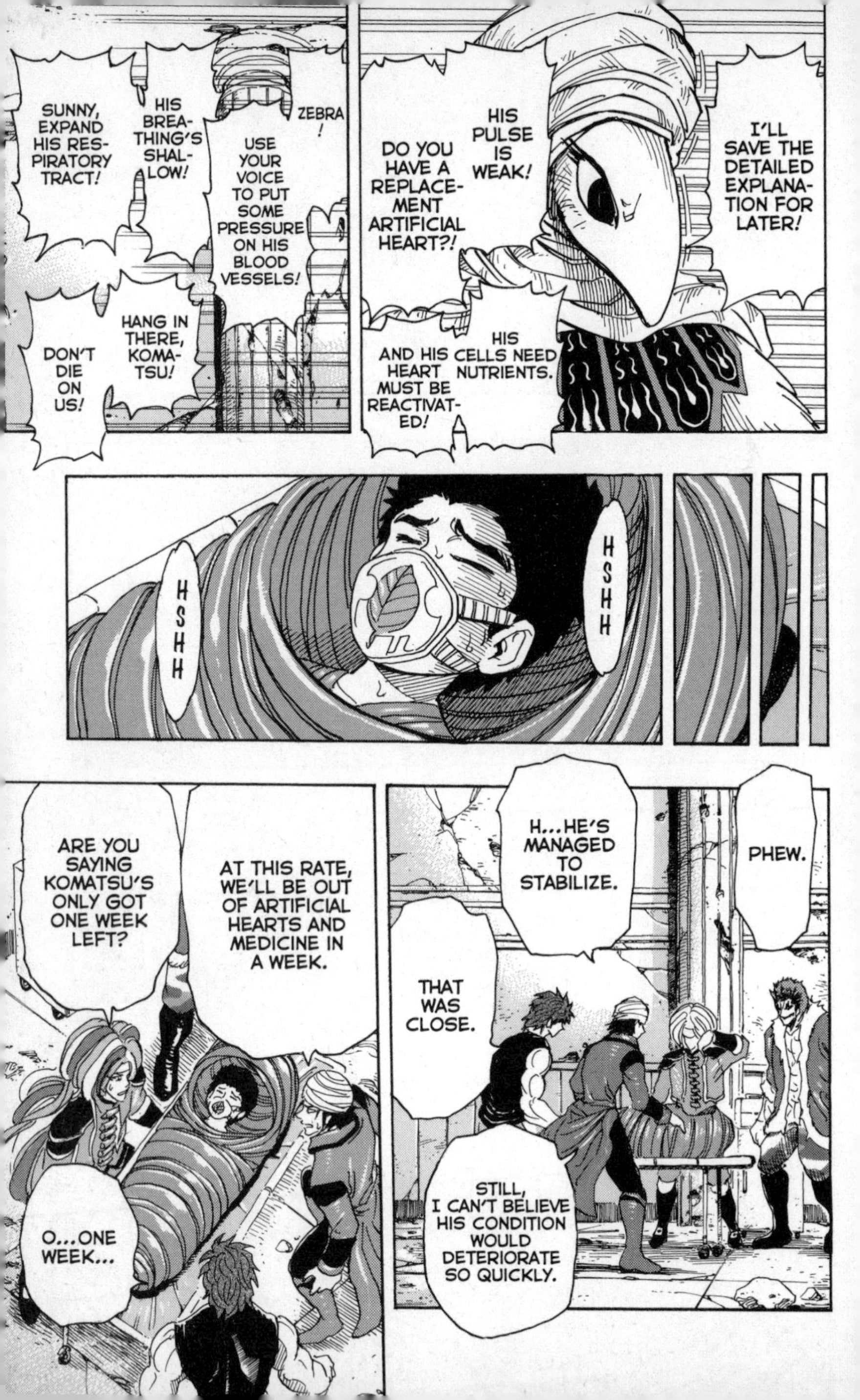
I'LL SAVE THE DETAILED EXPLANATION FOR LATER!
HIS PULSE IS WEAK!
DO YOU HAVE A REPLACEMENT ARTIFICIAL HEART?!
HIS CELLS NEED NUTRIENTS.
AND HIS HEART MUST BE REACTIVATED!
ZEBRA!
USE YOUR VOICE TO PUT SOME PRESSURE ON HIS BLOOD VESSELS!
HIS BREATHING'S SHALLOW!
SUNNY, EXPAND HIS RESPIRATORY TRACT!
HANG IN THERE, KOMATSU!
DON'T DIE ON US!
HSHH
HSHH
PHEW.
H...HE'S MANAGED TO STABILIZE.
THAT WAS CLOSE.
STILL, I CAN'T BELIEVE HIS CONDITION WOULD DETERIORATE SO QUICKLY.
AT THIS RATE, WE'LL BE OUT OF ARTIFICIAL HEARTS AND MEDICINE IN A WEEK.
ARE YOU SAYING KOMATSU'S ONLY GOT ONE WEEK LEFT?
O...ONE WEEK...

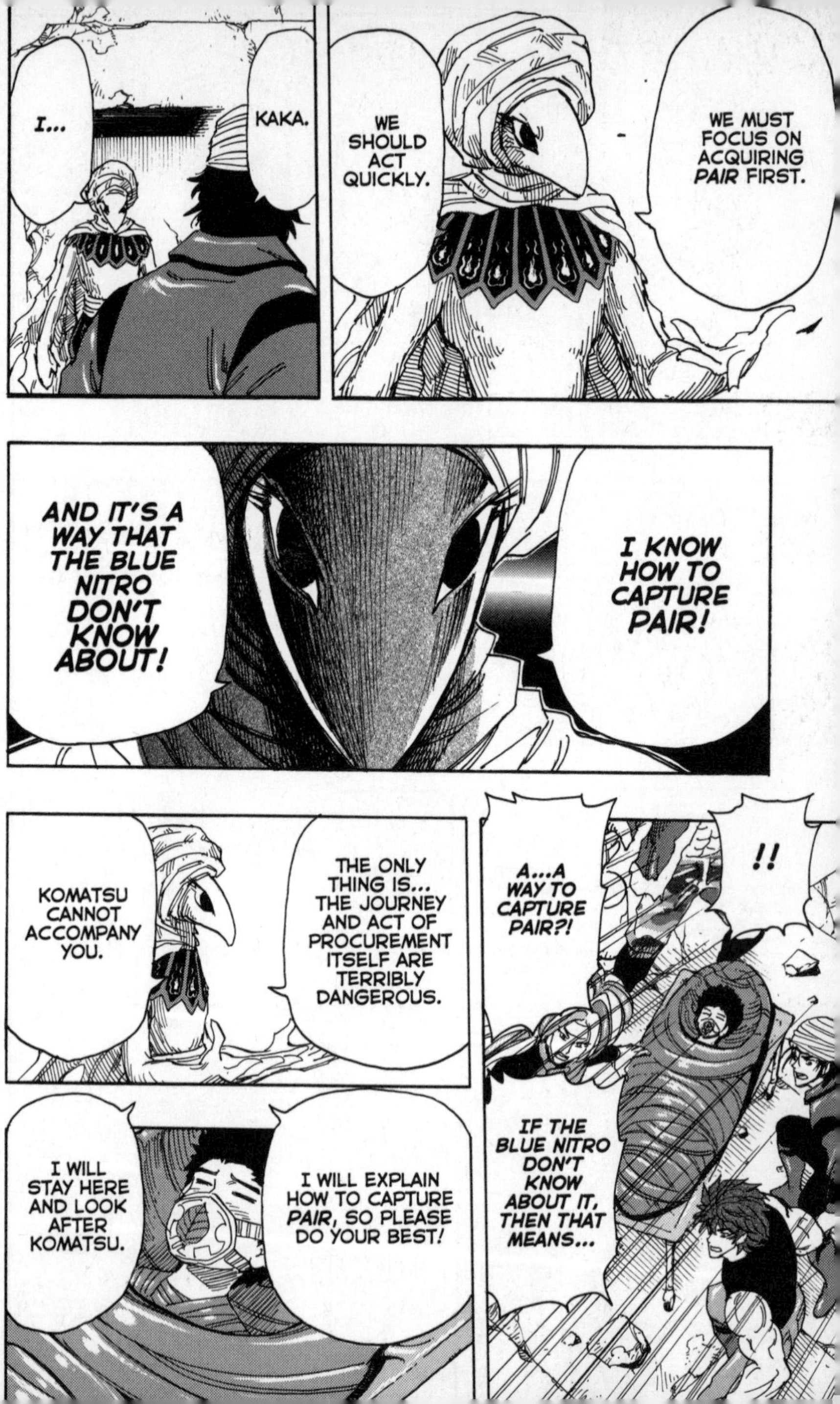
WE MUST FOCUS ON ACQUIRING *PAIR* FIRST.
WE SHOULD ACT QUICKLY.
KAKA.
I...
I KNOW HOW TO CAPTURE PAIR!
AND IT'S A WAY THAT THE BLUE NITRO DON'T KNOW ABOUT!
!!
A...A WAY TO CAPTURE PAIR?!
IF THE BLUE NITRO DON'T KNOW ABOUT IT, THEN THAT MEANS...
THE ONLY THING IS... THE JOURNEY AND ACT OF PROCUREMENT ITSELF ARE TERRIBLY DANGEROUS.
KOMATSU CANNOT ACCOMPANY YOU.
I WILL EXPLAIN HOW TO CAPTURE *PAIR*, SO PLEASE DO YOUR BEST!
I WILL STAY HERE AND LOOK AFTER KOMATSU.

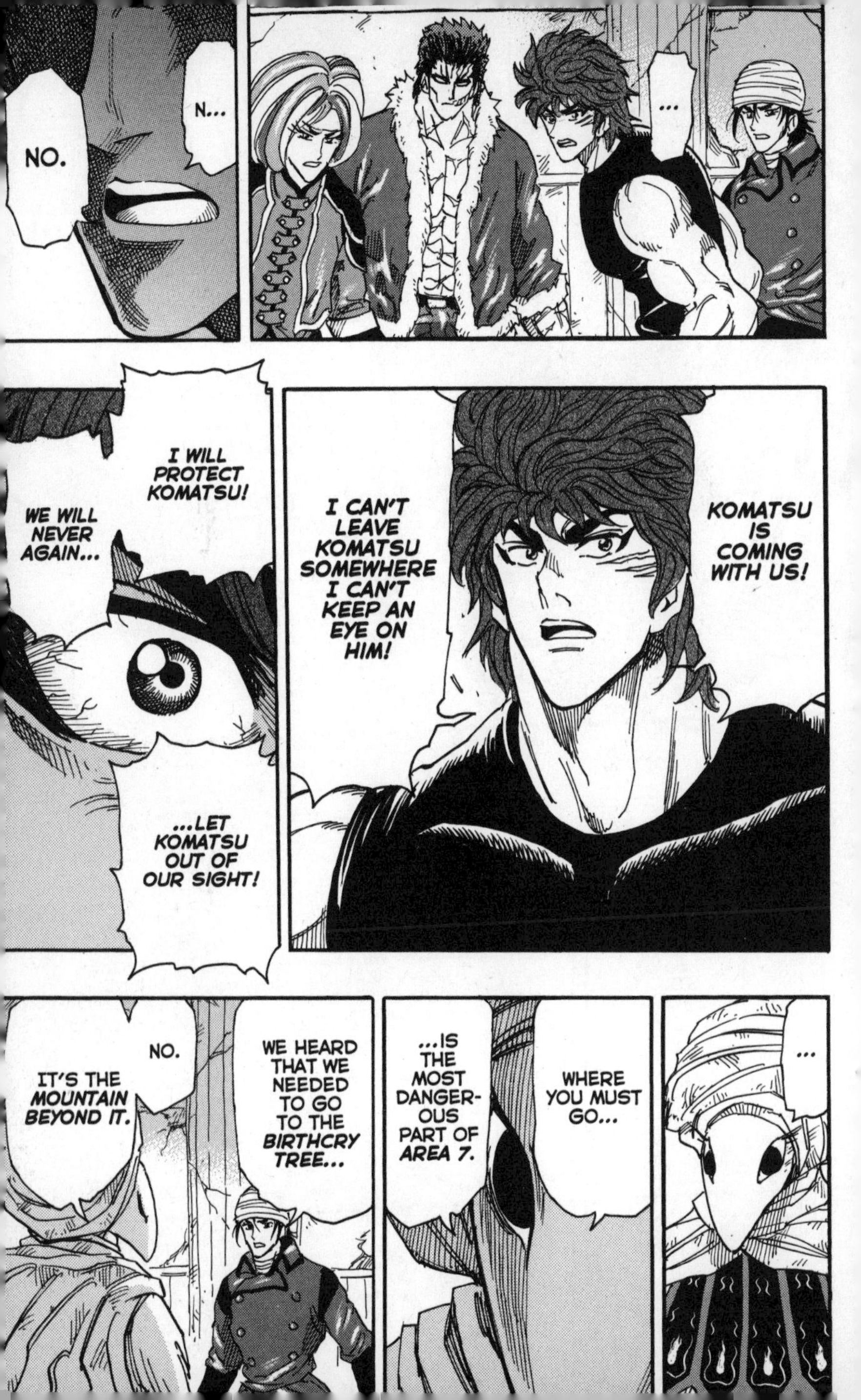
...
N...
NO.
KOMATSU IS COMING WITH US!
I CAN'T LEAVE KOMATSU SOMEWHERE I CAN'T KEEP AN EYE ON HIM!
I WILL PROTECT KOMATSU!
WE WILL NEVER AGAIN...
...LET KOMATSU OUT OF OUR SIGHT!
...
WHERE YOU MUST GO...
...IS THE MOST DANGER-OUS PART OF AREA 7.
WE HEARD THAT WE NEEDED TO GO TO THE BIRTHCRY TREE...
NO.
IT'S THE MOUNTAIN BEYOND IT.

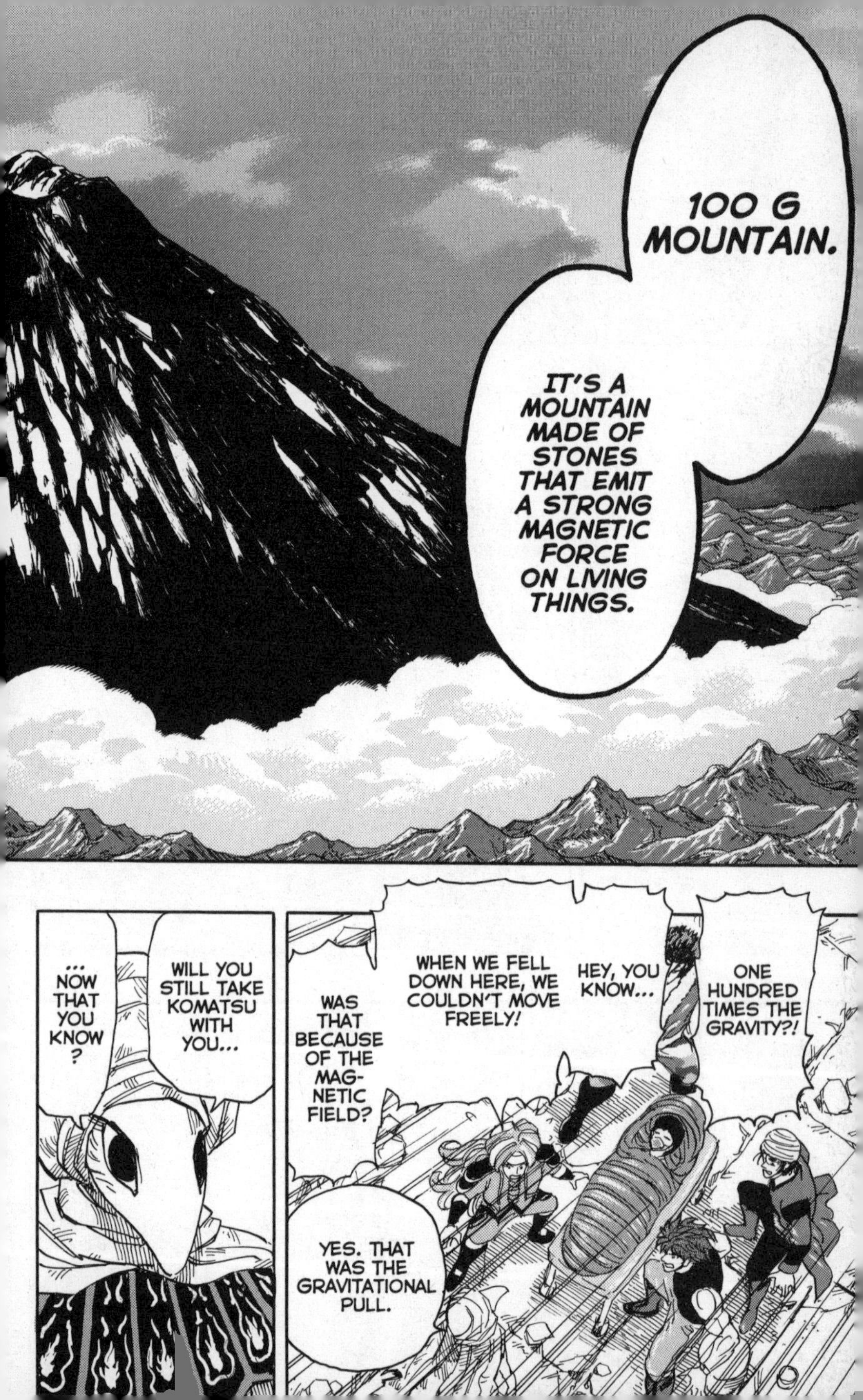
100 G MOUNTAIN.
IT'S A MOUNTAIN MADE OF STONES THAT EMIT A STRONG MAGNETIC FORCE ON LIVING THINGS.
ONE HUNDRED TIMES THE GRAVITY?!
HEY, YOU KNOW...
WHEN WE FELL DOWN HERE, WE COULDN'T MOVE FREELY!
WAS THAT BECAUSE OF THE MAG-NETIC FIELD?
YES. THAT WAS THE GRAVITATIONAL PULL.
WILL YOU STILL TAKE KOMATSU WITH YOU...
...NOW THAT YOU KNOW?

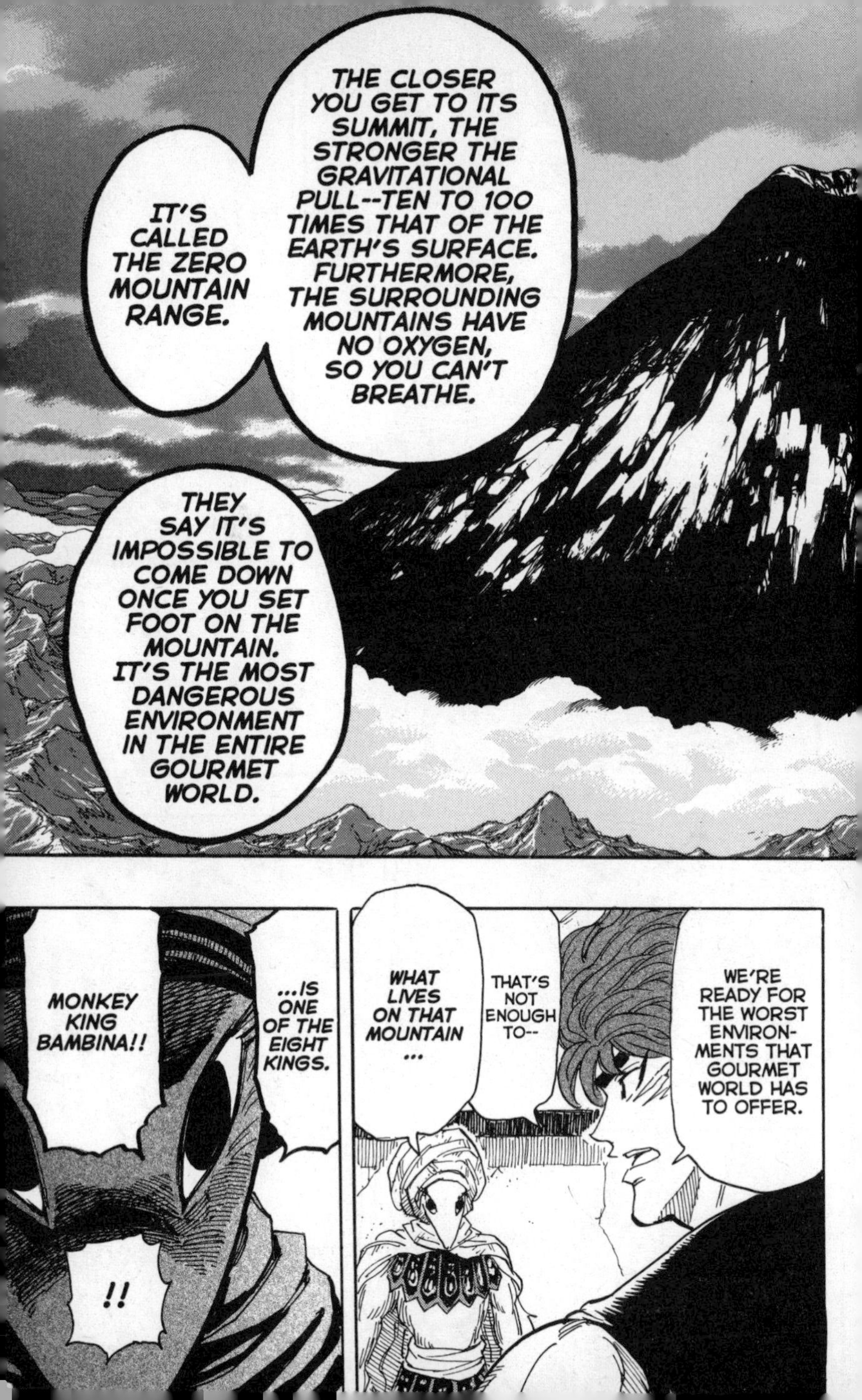
IT'S CALLED THE ZERO MOUNTAIN RANGE.
THE CLOSER YOU GET TO ITS SUMMIT, THE STRONGER THE GRAVITATIONAL PULL--TEN TO 100 TIMES THAT OF THE EARTH'S SURFACE. FURTHERMORE, THE SURROUNDING MOUNTAINS HAVE NO OXYGEN, SO YOU CAN'T BREATHE.
THEY SAY IT'S IMPOSSIBLE TO COME DOWN ONCE YOU SET FOOT ON THE MOUNTAIN. IT'S THE MOST DANGEROUS ENVIRONMENT IN THE ENTIRE GOURMET WORLD.
WE'RE READY FOR THE WORST ENVIRON-MENTS THAT GOURMET WORLD HAS TO OFFER.
THAT'S NOT ENOUGH TO--
WHAT LIVES ON THAT MOUNTAIN ...
...IS ONE OF THE EIGHT KINGS.
MONKEY KING BAMBINA!!
!!

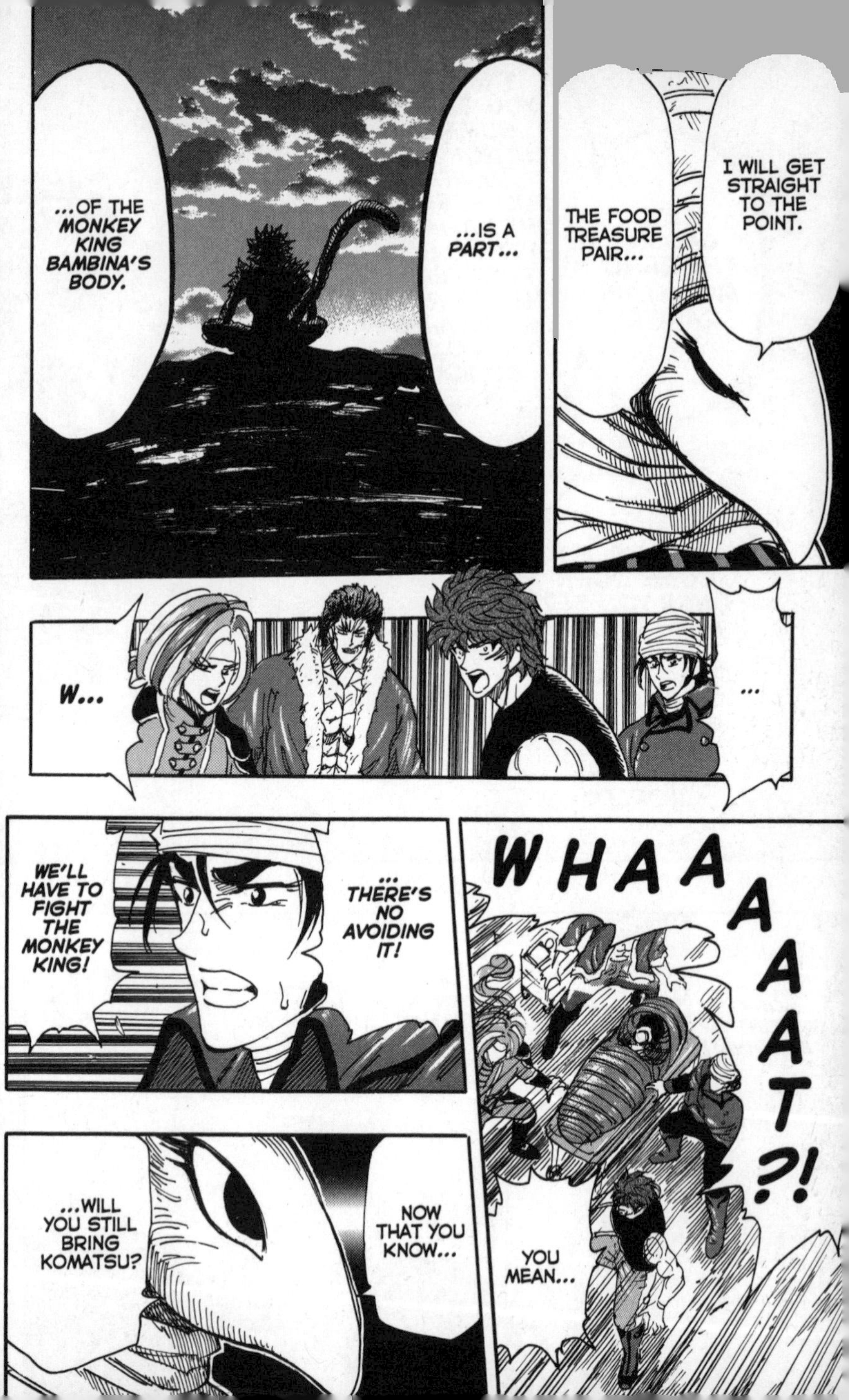
I WILL GET STRAIGHT TO THE POINT.
THE FOOD TREASURE PAIR...
...IS A PART...
...OF THE MONKEY KING BAMBINA'S BODY.
...
W...
WHAAAAAAT?!
YOU MEAN...
...THERE'S NO AVOIDING IT!
WE'LL HAVE TO FIGHT THE MONKEY KING!
NOW THAT YOU KNOW...
...WILL YOU STILL BRING KOMATSU?

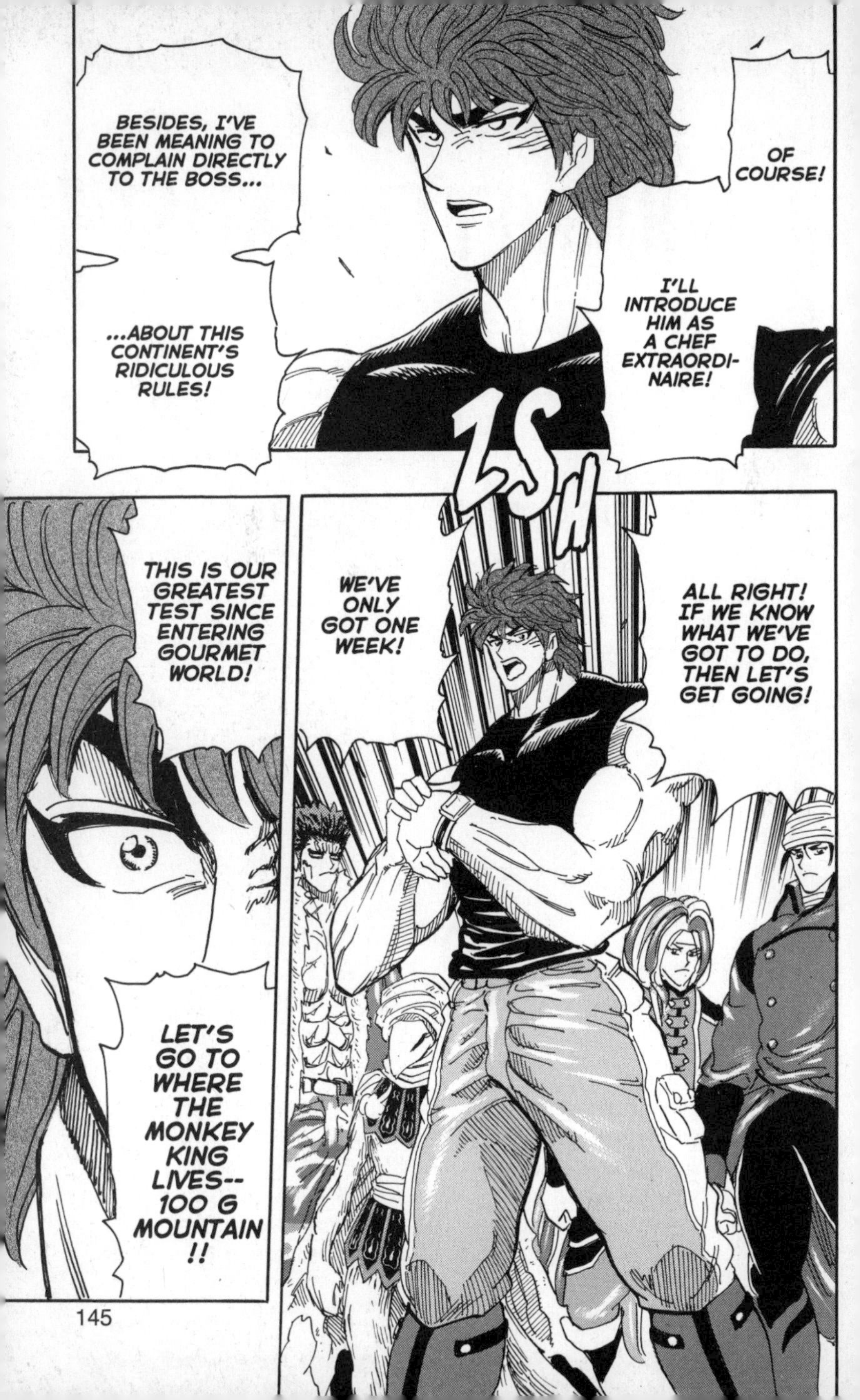
OF COURSE!
I'LL INTRODUCE HIM AS A CHEF EXTRAORDINAIRE!
BESIDES, I'VE BEEN MEANING TO COMPLAIN DIRECTLY TO THE BOSS...
...ABOUT THIS CONTINENT'S RIDICULOUS RULES!
ZSH
ALL RIGHT! IF WE KNOW WHAT WE'VE GOT TO DO, THEN LET'S GET GOING!
WE'VE ONLY GOT ONE WEEK!
THIS IS OUR GREATEST TEST SINCE ENTERING GOURMET WORLD!
LET'S GO TO WHERE THE MONKEY KING LIVES-- 100 G MOUNTAIN !!

TORIKO

GOURMET CHECKLIST
Vol. 323

GIRAFFE BIRD
(MAMMAL)

CAPTURE LEVEL: 90
HABITAT: GOURMET LAB (HYBRID CLONE)
SIZE: ---
HEIGHT: 120 M
WEIGHT: 400 TONS
PRICE: MEAT IS INEDIBLE

BFFT

GIRAFFE BIRD*
(MAMMAL)
CAPTURE LEVEL 90

SCALE

A HYBRID CLONE MADE UP OF SEVERAL SPECIES OF HERBIVORES THAT POSSESSES
SUPERIOR OFFENSIVE AND DEFENSIVE CAPABILITIES, AN EXCELLENT SENSE OF SMELL
AND THE OFFENSIVE CAPABILITIES OF A CARNIVOROUS MONSTER. WHEN ANYBODY
SUSPICIOUS CROSSES ITS PATH, IT NOTICES THEM RIGHT AWAY. IF THE SUSPICIOUS
PERSON ATTACKS IT, IT WILL TURN INTO A CARNIVIOROUS MONSTER AND FIGHT TO ITS
LAST BREATH! IT WAS DEVELOPED BY THE IGO FOR BATTLE AGAINST GOURMET CORP.

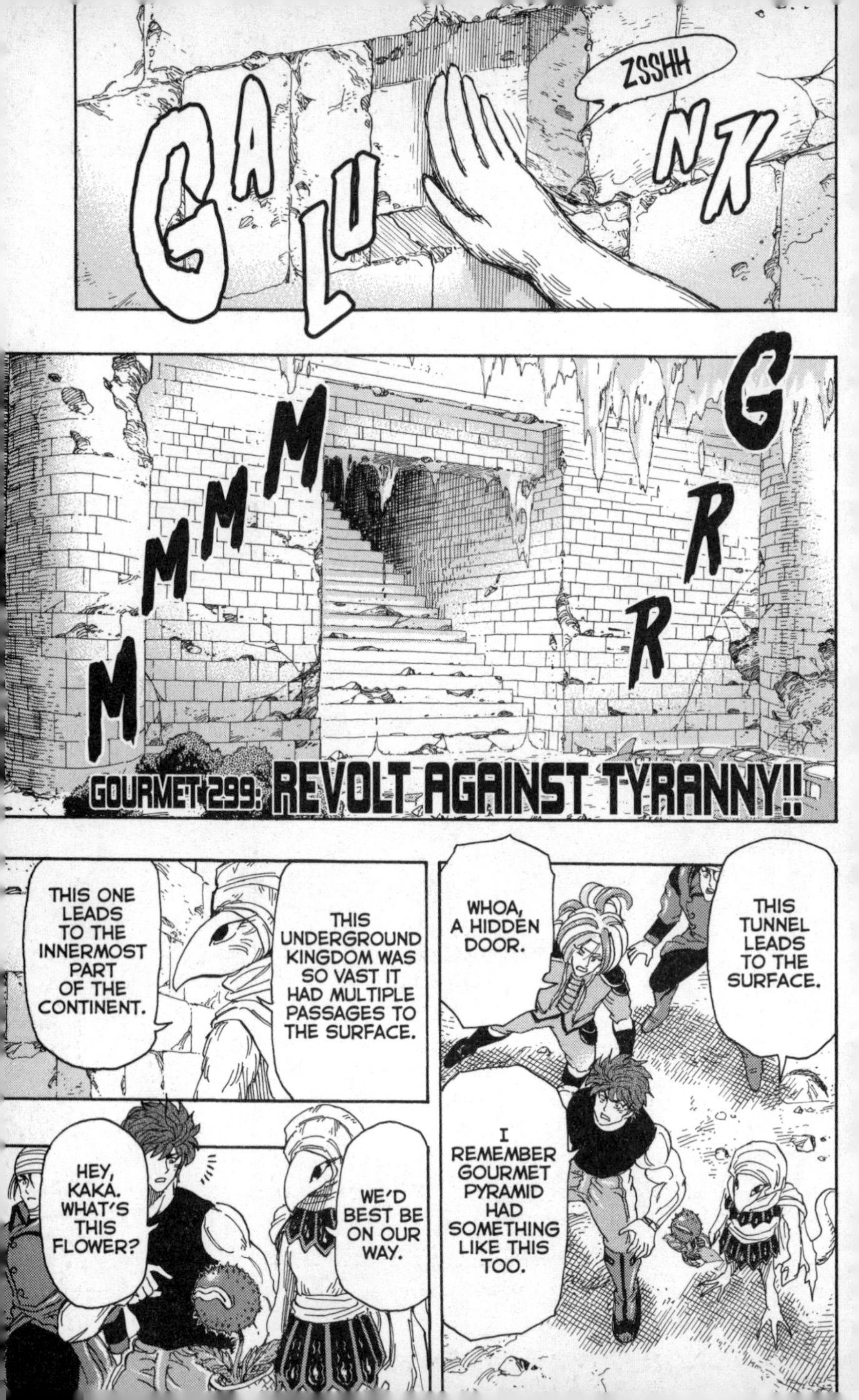
ZSSHH
GALUNK
GRRR
MMMMM
GOURMET 299: REVOLT AGAINST TYRANNY!!
THIS TUNNEL LEADS TO THE SURFACE.
WHOA, A HIDDEN DOOR.
I REMEMBER GOURMET PYRAMID HAD SOMETHING LIKE THIS TOO.
THIS UNDERGROUND KINGDOM WAS SO VAST IT HAD MULTIPLE PASSAGES TO THE SURFACE.
THIS ONE LEADS TO THE INNERMOST PART OF THE CONTINENT.
WE'D BEST BE ON OUR WAY.
HEY, KAKA. WHAT'S THIS FLOWER?

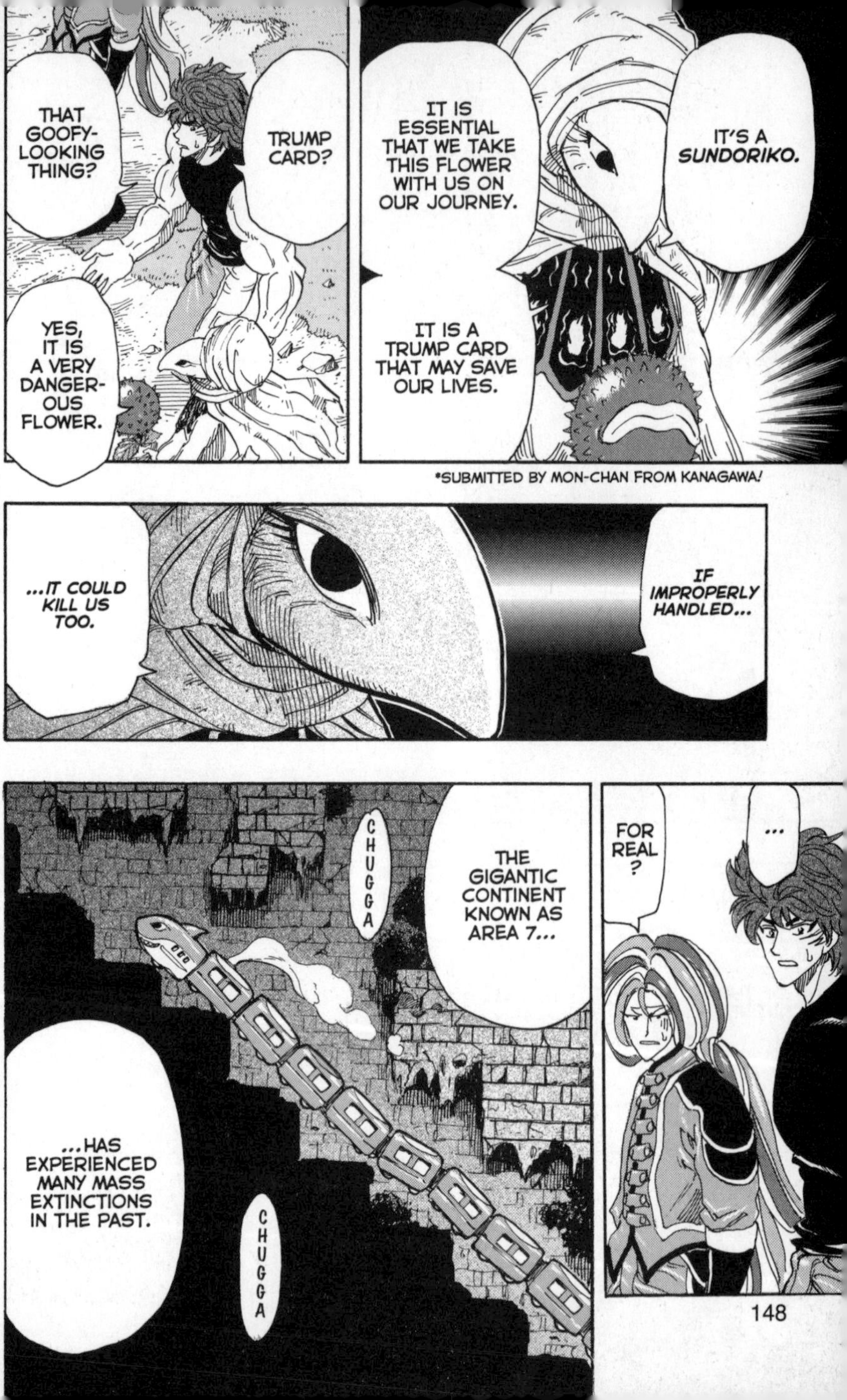
IT'S A *SUNDORIKO.*
IT IS ESSENTIAL THAT WE TAKE THIS FLOWER WITH US ON OUR JOURNEY.
IT IS A TRUMP CARD THAT MAY SAVE OUR LIVES.
TRUMP CARD?
THAT GOOFY-LOOKING THING?
YES, IT IS A VERY DANGER-OUS FLOWER.
*SUBMITTED BY MON-CHAN FROM KANAGAWA!
IF IMPROPERLY HANDLED...
...IT COULD KILL US TOO.
...
FOR REAL?
THE GIGANTIC CONTINENT KNOWN AS AREA 7...
CHUGGA
...HAS EXPERIENCED MANY MASS EXTINCTIONS IN THE PAST.
CHUGGA

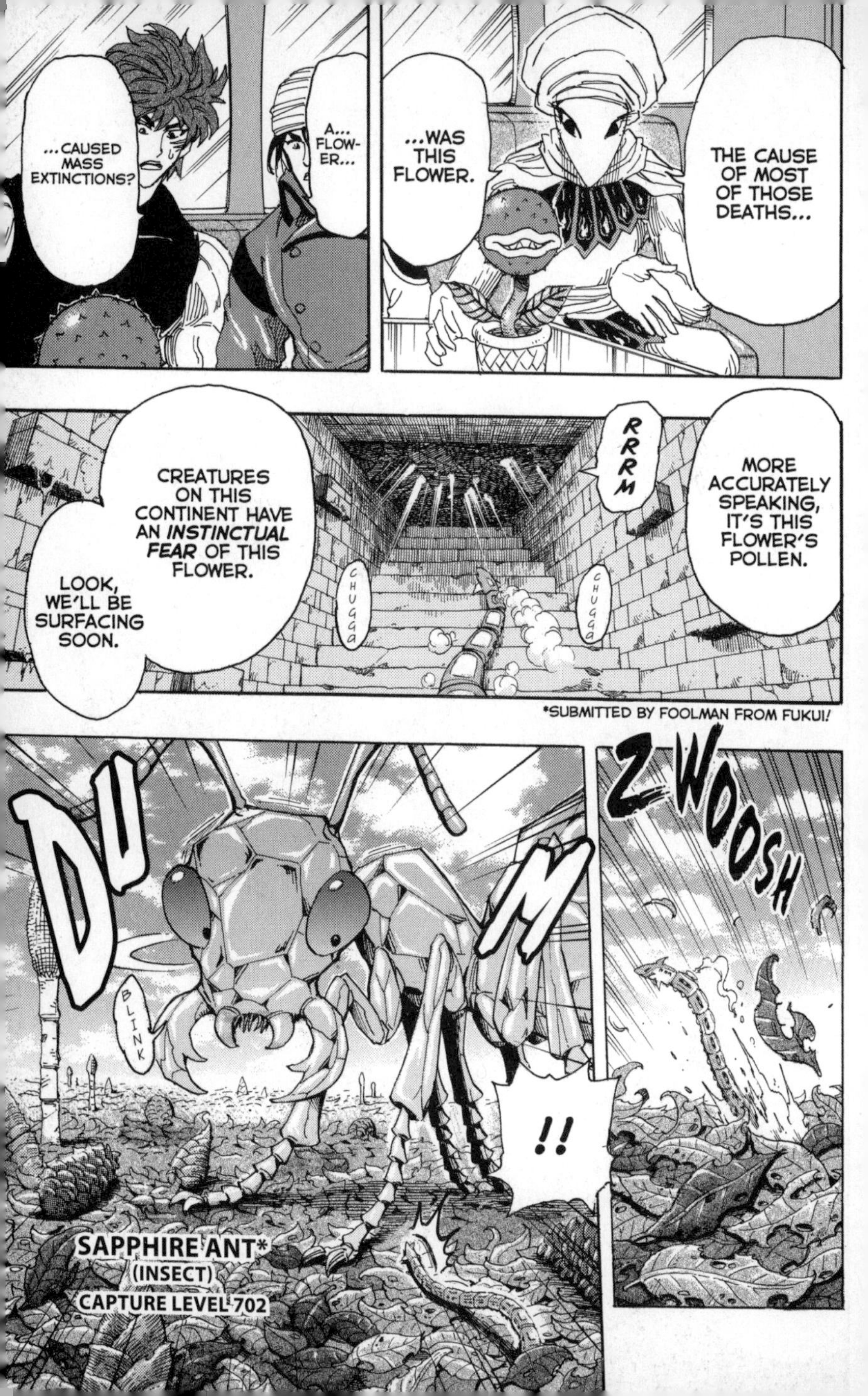
THE CAUSE OF MOST OF THOSE DEATHS...
...WAS THIS FLOWER.
A... FLOWER...
...CAUSED MASS EXTINCTIONS?
MORE ACCURATELY SPEAKING, IT'S THIS FLOWER'S POLLEN.
RRRM
CHUGGA
CHUGGA
CREATURES ON THIS CONTINENT HAVE AN *INSTINCTUAL FEAR* OF THIS FLOWER.
LOOK, WE'LL BE SURFACING SOON.
ZWOOSH
!!
DUM
BLINK
SAPPHIRE ANT*
(INSECT)
CAPTURE LEVEL 702
*SUBMITTED BY FOOLMAN FROM FUKUI!

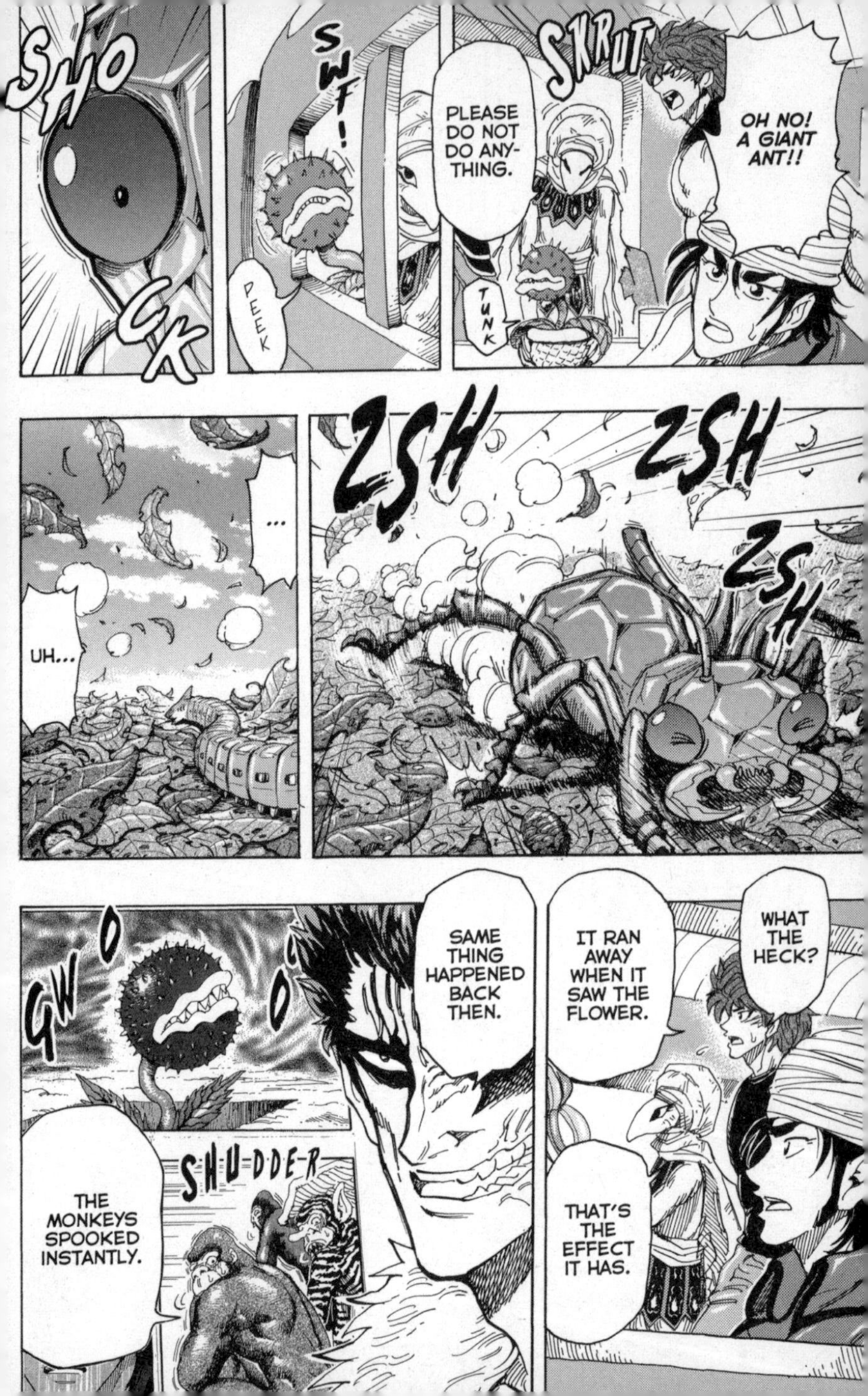
SKRUT
OH NO! A GIANT ANT!!
PLEASE DO NOT DO ANY-THING.
TUNK
SWF!!
PEEK
SHOCK
ZSH
ZSH
ZSH
...
UH...
WHAT THE HECK?
IT RAN AWAY WHEN IT SAW THE FLOWER.
THAT'S THE EFFECT IT HAS.
SAME THING HAPPENED BACK THEN.
GWOO
THE MONKEYS SPOOKED INSTANTLY.
SHUDDER

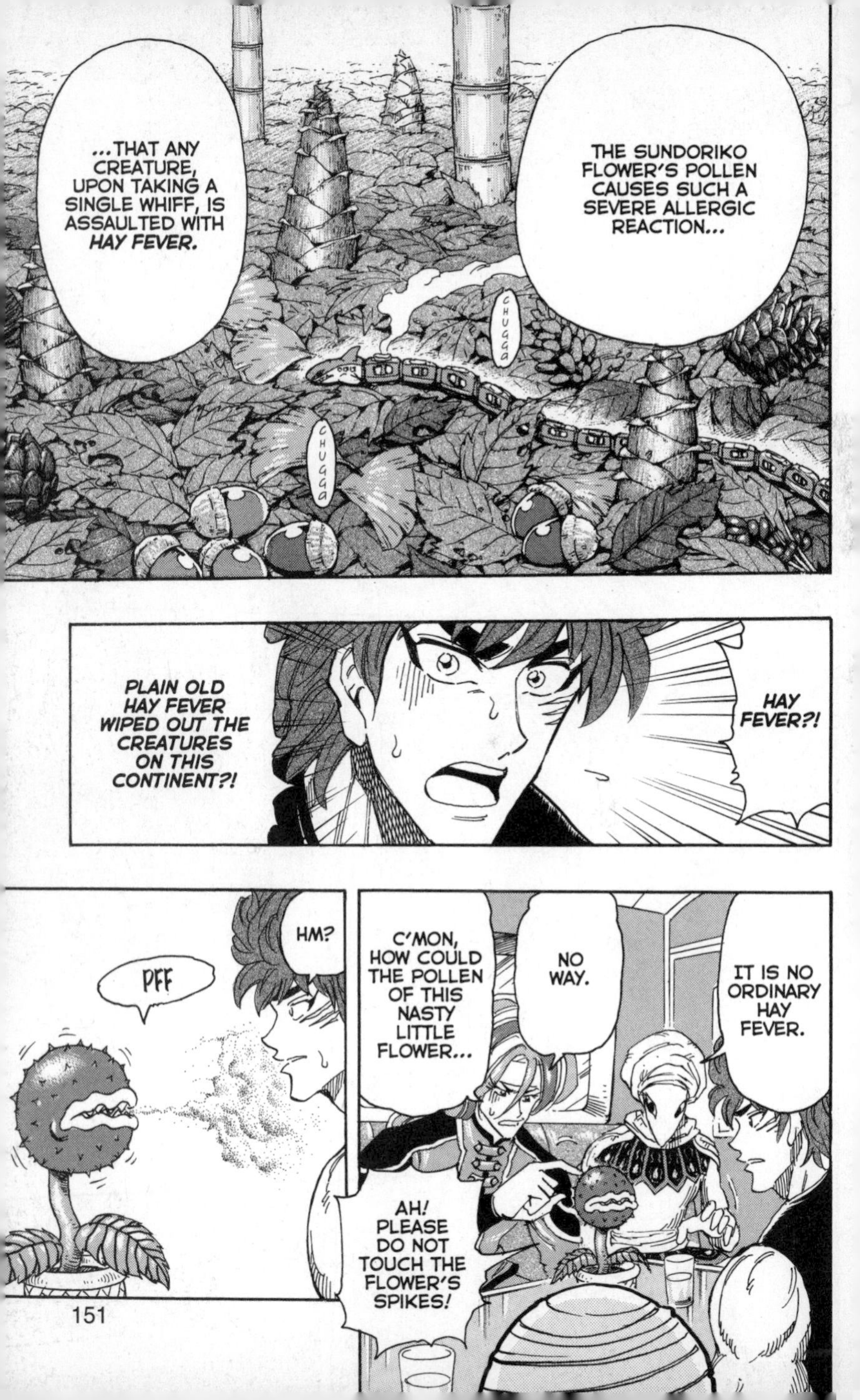
THE SUNDORIKO FLOWER'S POLLEN CAUSES SUCH A SEVERE ALLERGIC REACTION...
...THAT ANY CREATURE, UPON TAKING A SINGLE WHIFF, IS ASSAULTED WITH HAY FEVER.
CHUGGA
CHUGGA
HAY FEVER?!
PLAIN OLD HAY FEVER WIPED OUT THE CREATURES ON THIS CONTINENT?!
IT IS NO ORDINARY HAY FEVER.
NO WAY.
C'MON, HOW COULD THE POLLEN OF THIS NASTY LITTLE FLOWER...
AH! PLEASE DO NOT TOUCH THE FLOWER'S SPIKES!
HM?
PFF

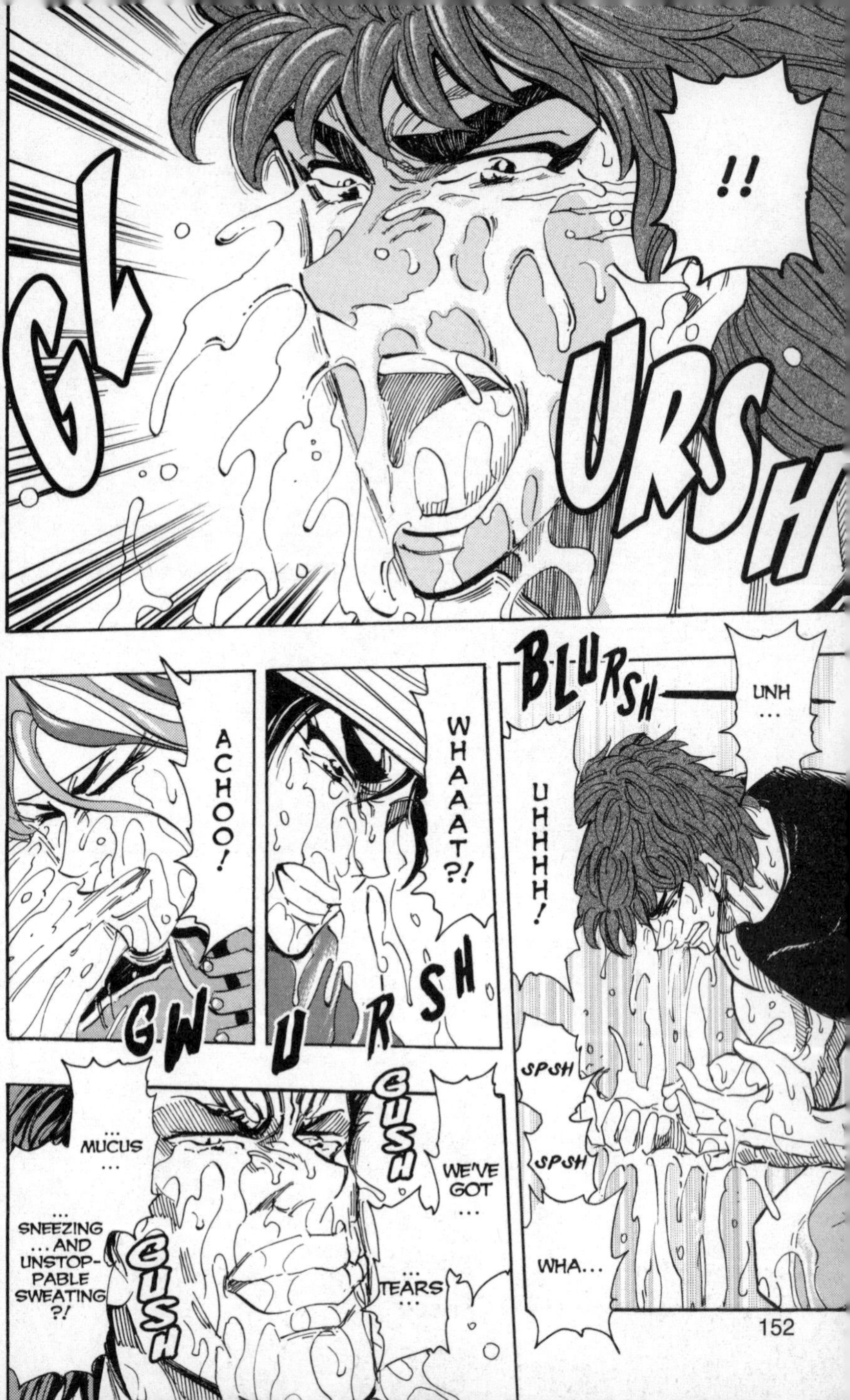
!!
GL
URSH
BLURSH
UNH …
UHHHHH!
SPSH
SPSH
WHA…
WHAAAT?!
ACHOO!
GWURSH
GUSH
WE'VE GOT …
… MUCUS …
… TEARS …
… SNEEZING … AND UNSTOP-PABLE SWEATING ?!
GUSH

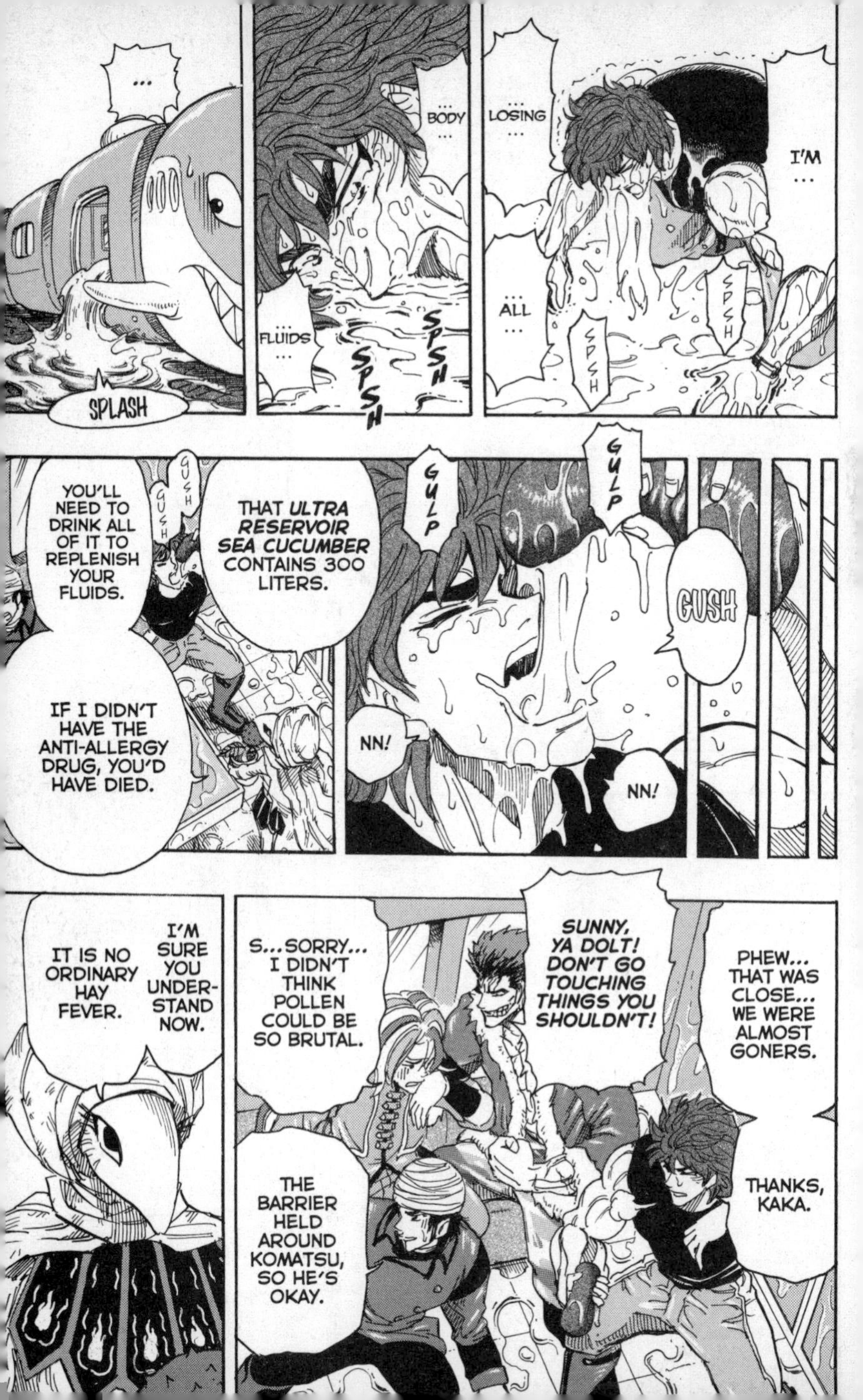
I'M ...
... LOSING ...
... ALL ...
SPSH
SPSH
... BODY ...
... FLUIDS ...
SPSH
SPSH
...
SPLASH
GULP
GULP
GUSH
NN!
NN!
THAT *ULTRA RESERVOIR SEA CUCUMBER* CONTAINS 300 LITERS.
YOU'LL NEED TO DRINK ALL OF IT TO REPLENISH YOUR FLUIDS.
GUSH
GUSH
IF I DIDN'T HAVE THE ANTI-ALLERGY DRUG, YOU'D HAVE DIED.
PHEW... THAT WAS CLOSE... WE WERE ALMOST GONERS.
SUNNY, YA DOLT! DON'T GO TOUCHING THINGS YOU SHOULDN'T!
S...SORRY... I DIDN'T THINK POLLEN COULD BE SO BRUTAL.
THANKS, KAKA.
THE BARRIER HELD AROUND KOMATSU, SO HE'S OKAY.
I'M SURE YOU UNDERSTAND NOW.
IT IS NO ORDINARY HAY FEVER.

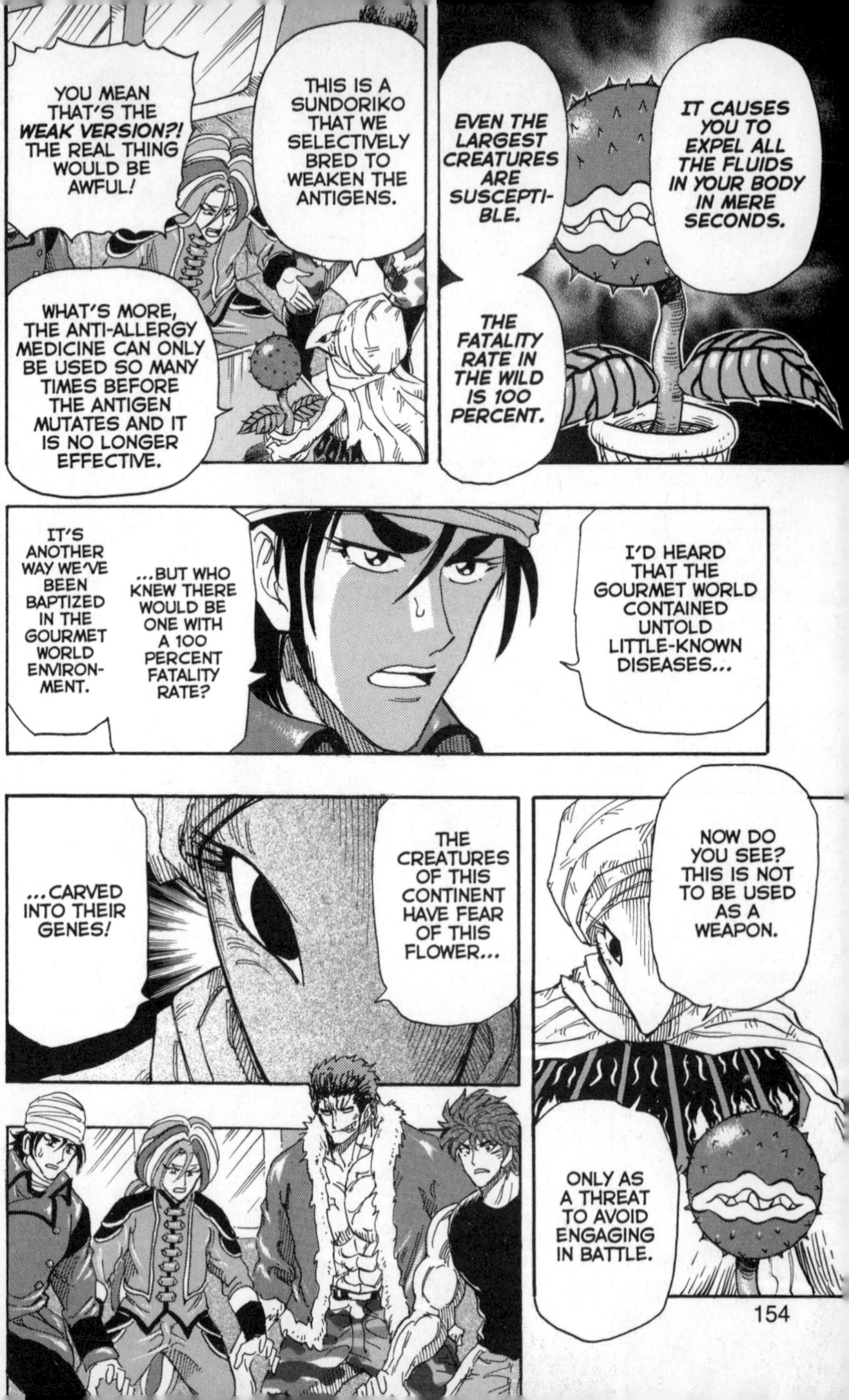

IT CAUSES YOU TO EXPEL ALL THE FLUIDS IN YOUR BODY IN MERE SECONDS.
EVEN THE LARGEST CREATURES ARE SUSCEPTI-BLE.
THE FATALITY RATE IN THE WILD IS 100 PERCENT.
THIS IS A SUNDORIKO THAT WE SELECTIVELY BRED TO WEAKEN THE ANTIGENS.
YOU MEAN THAT'S THE WEAK VERSION?! THE REAL THING WOULD BE AWFUL!
WHAT'S MORE, THE ANTI-ALLERGY MEDICINE CAN ONLY BE USED SO MANY TIMES BEFORE THE ANTIGEN MUTATES AND IT IS NO LONGER EFFECTIVE.
I'D HEARD THAT THE GOURMET WORLD CONTAINED UNTOLD LITTLE-KNOWN DISEASES...
...BUT WHO KNEW THERE WOULD BE ONE WITH A 100 PERCENT FATALITY RATE?
IT'S ANOTHER WAY WE'VE BEEN BAPTIZED IN THE GOURMET WORLD ENVIRON-MENT.
NOW DO YOU SEE? THIS IS NOT TO BE USED AS A WEAPON.
ONLY AS A THREAT TO AVOID ENGAGING IN BATTLE.
THE CREATURES OF THIS CONTINENT HAVE FEAR OF THIS FLOWER...
...CARVED INTO THEIR GENES!

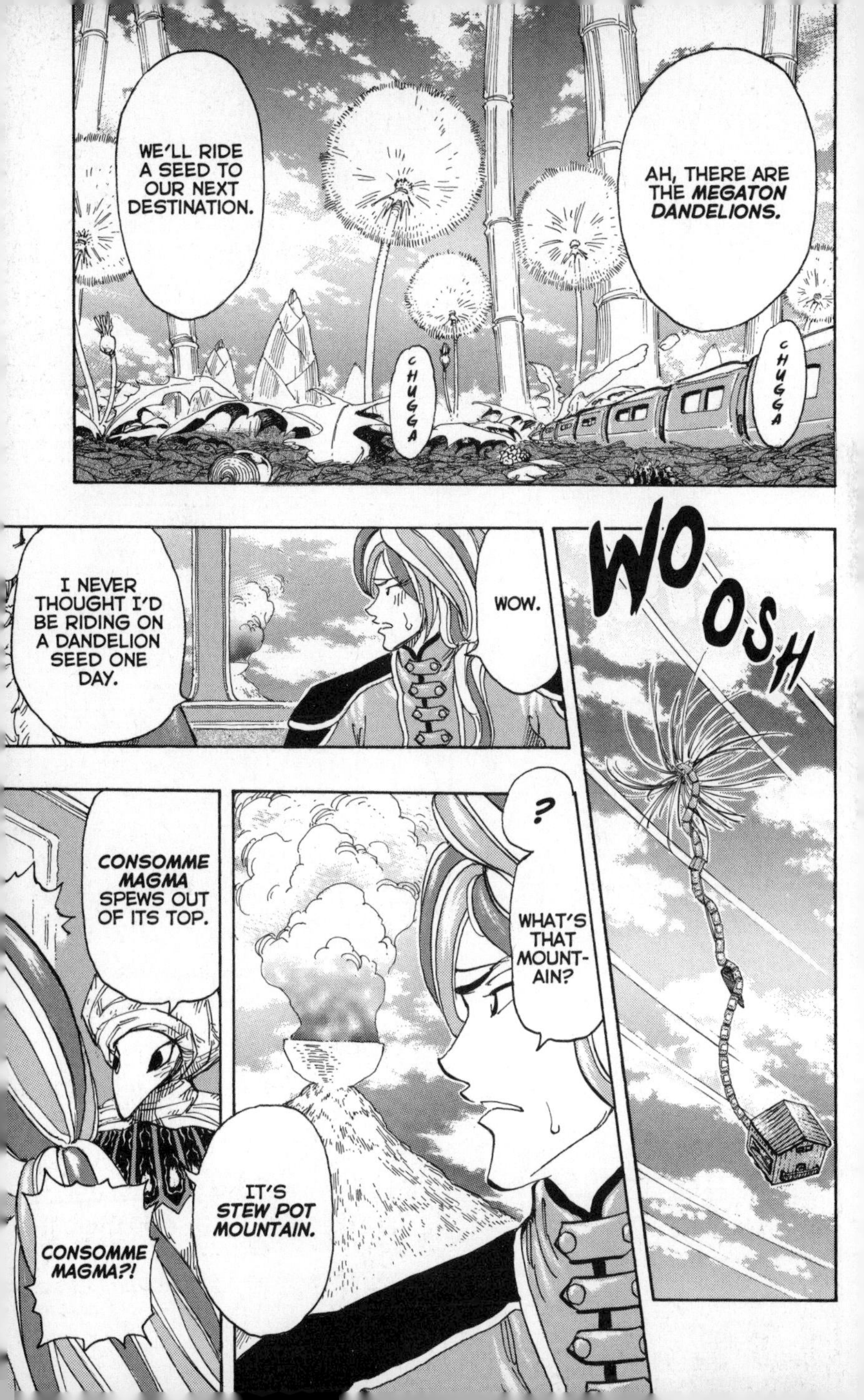
AH, THERE ARE THE *MEGATON DANDELIONS.*
WE'LL RIDE A SEED TO OUR NEXT DESTINATION.
CHUGGA
CHUGGA
WOOSH
WOW.
I NEVER THOUGHT I'D BE RIDING ON A DANDELION SEED ONE DAY.
?
WHAT'S THAT MOUNT-AIN?
IT'S *STEW POT MOUNTAIN.*
CONSOMME MAGMA SPEWS OUT OF ITS TOP.
CONSOMME MAGMA?!

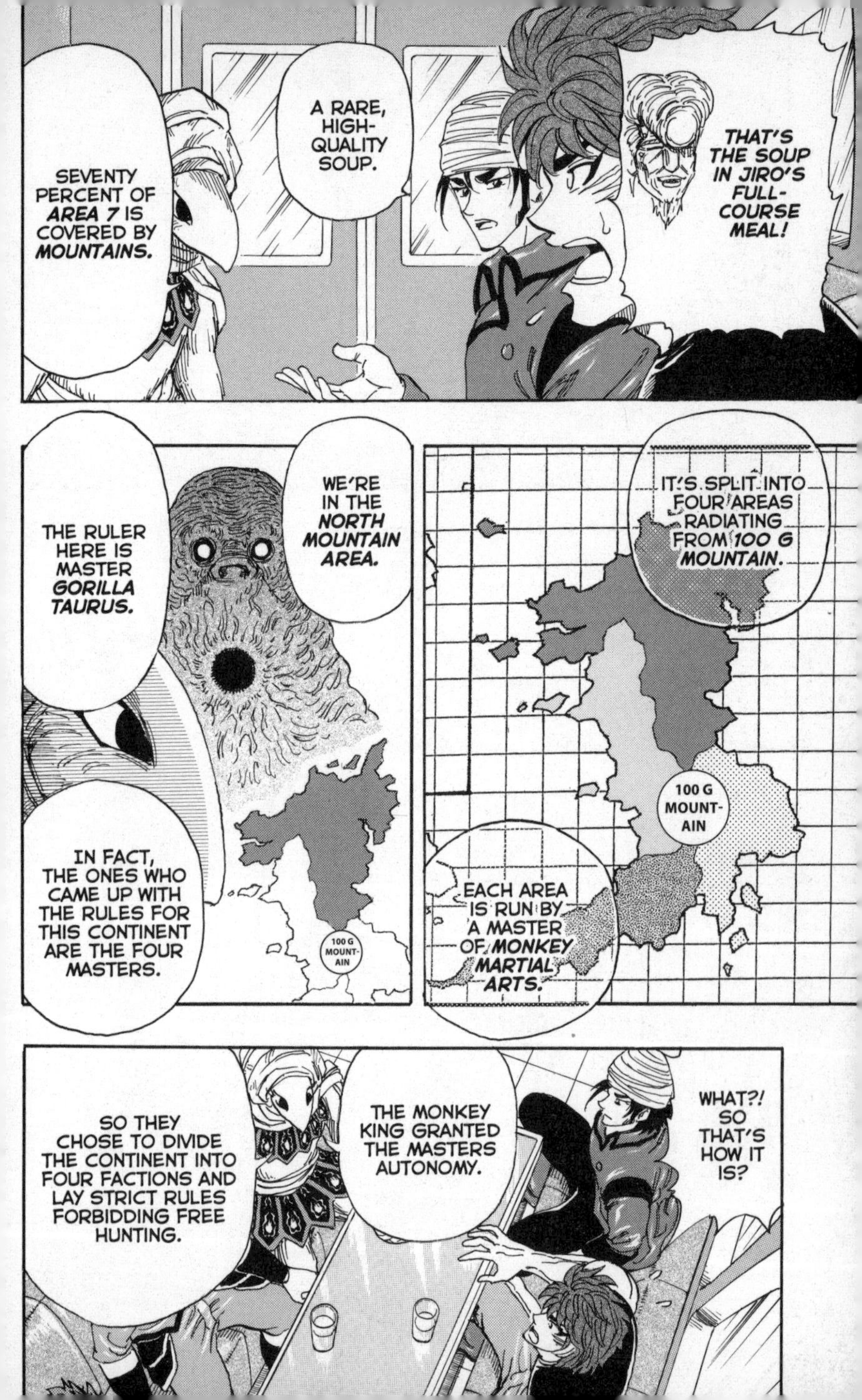
THAT'S THE SOUP IN JIRO'S FULL-COURSE MEAL!
A RARE, HIGH-QUALITY SOUP.
SEVENTY PERCENT OF AREA 7 IS COVERED BY MOUNTAINS.
IT'S SPLIT INTO FOUR AREAS RADIATING FROM 100 G MOUNTAIN.
100 G MOUNTAIN
EACH AREA IS RUN BY A MASTER OF MONKEY MARTIAL ARTS.
WE'RE IN THE NORTH MOUNTAIN AREA.
THE RULER HERE IS MASTER GORILLA TAURUS.
100 G MOUNTAIN
IN FACT, THE ONES WHO CAME UP WITH THE RULES FOR THIS CONTINENT ARE THE FOUR MASTERS.
WHAT?! SO THAT'S HOW IT IS?
THE MONKEY KING GRANTED THE MASTERS AUTONOMY.
SO THEY CHOSE TO DIVIDE THE CONTINENT INTO FOUR FACTIONS AND LAY STRICT RULES FORBIDDING FREE HUNTING.

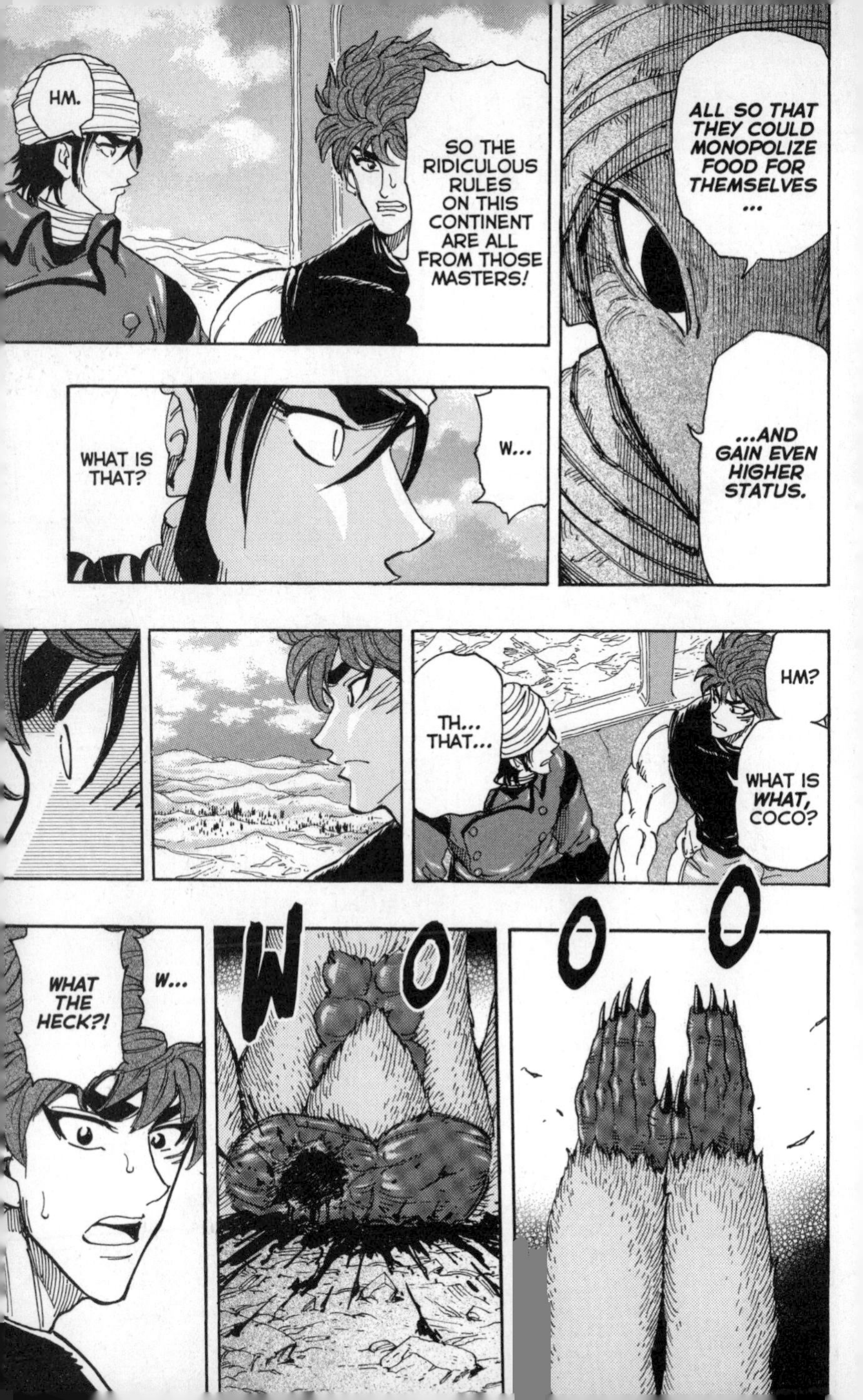

ALL SO THAT THEY COULD MONOPOLIZE FOOD FOR THEMSELVES...
...AND GAIN EVEN HIGHER STATUS.
SO THE RIDICULOUS RULES ON THIS CONTINENT ARE ALL FROM THOSE MASTERS!
HM.
W...
WHAT IS THAT?
HM?
WHAT IS WHAT, COCO?
TH... THAT...
WOOO
W...
WHAT THE HECK?!

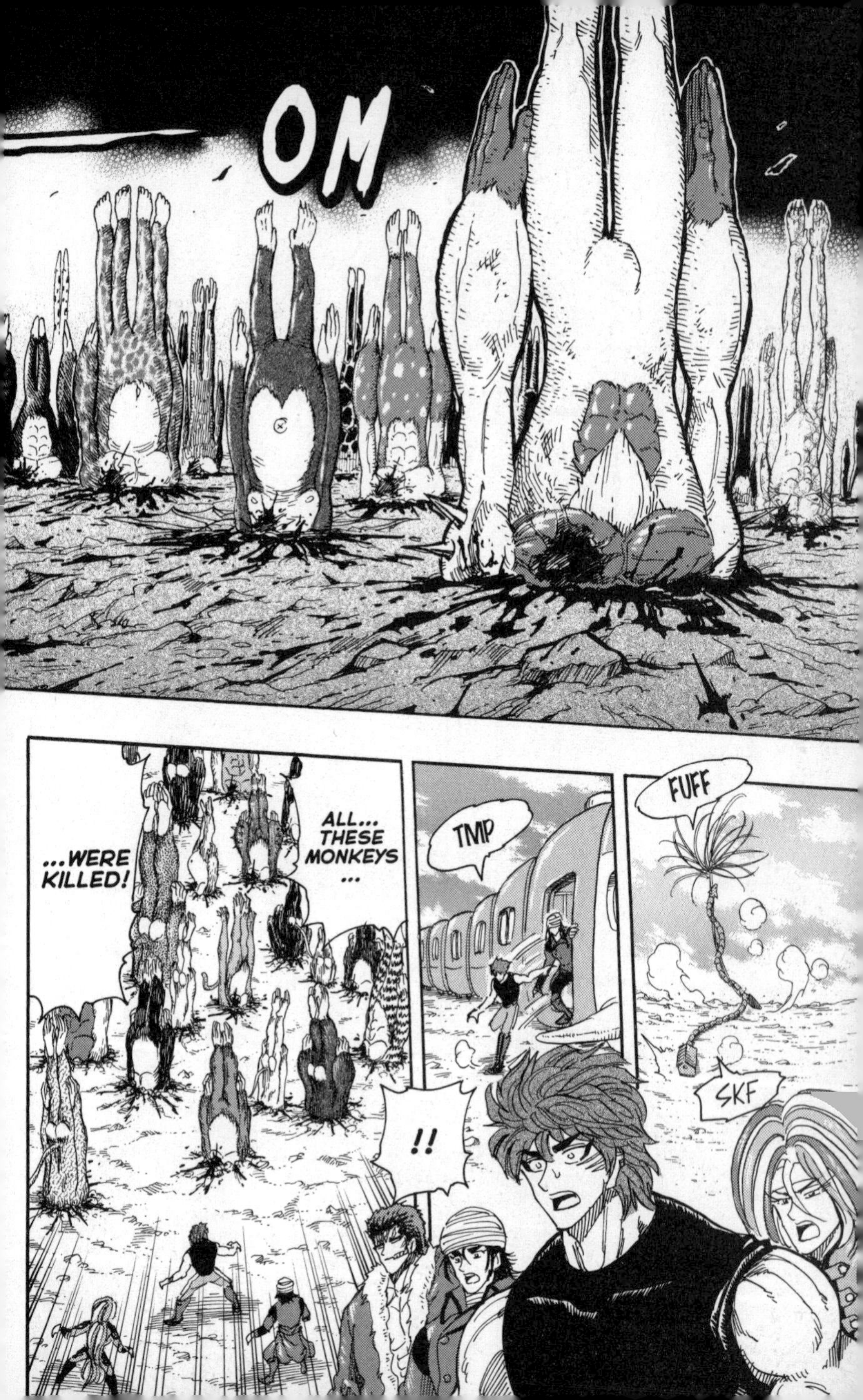
OM
FUFF
SKF
TMP
!!
ALL... THESE MONKEYS ...
...WERE KILLED!

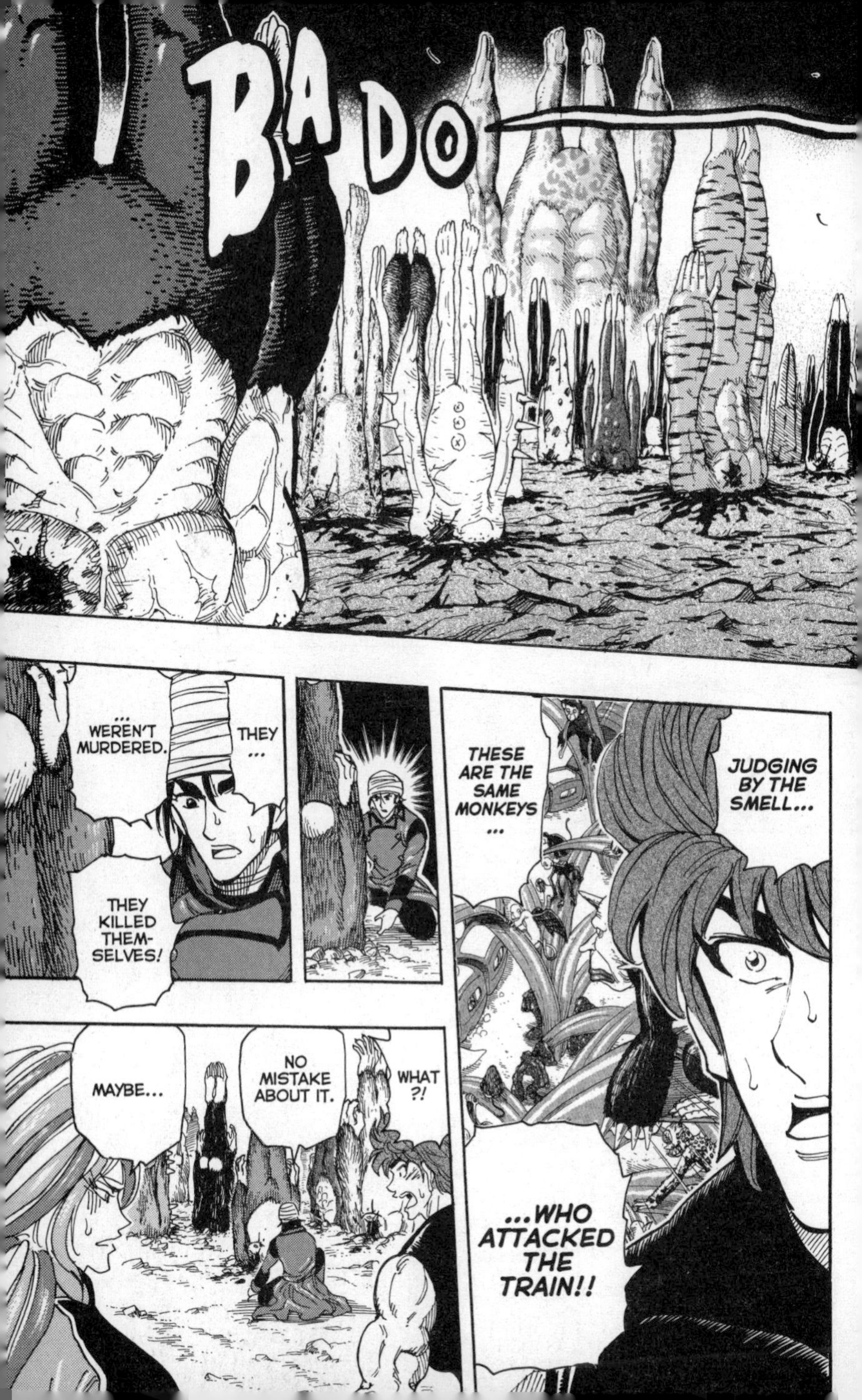
BADO
JUDGING BY THE SMELL...
THESE ARE THE SAME MONKEYS...
...WHO ATTACKED THE TRAIN!!
THEY...
...WEREN'T MURDERED.
THEY KILLED THEM-SELVES!
WHAT?!
NO MISTAKE ABOUT IT.
MAYBE...

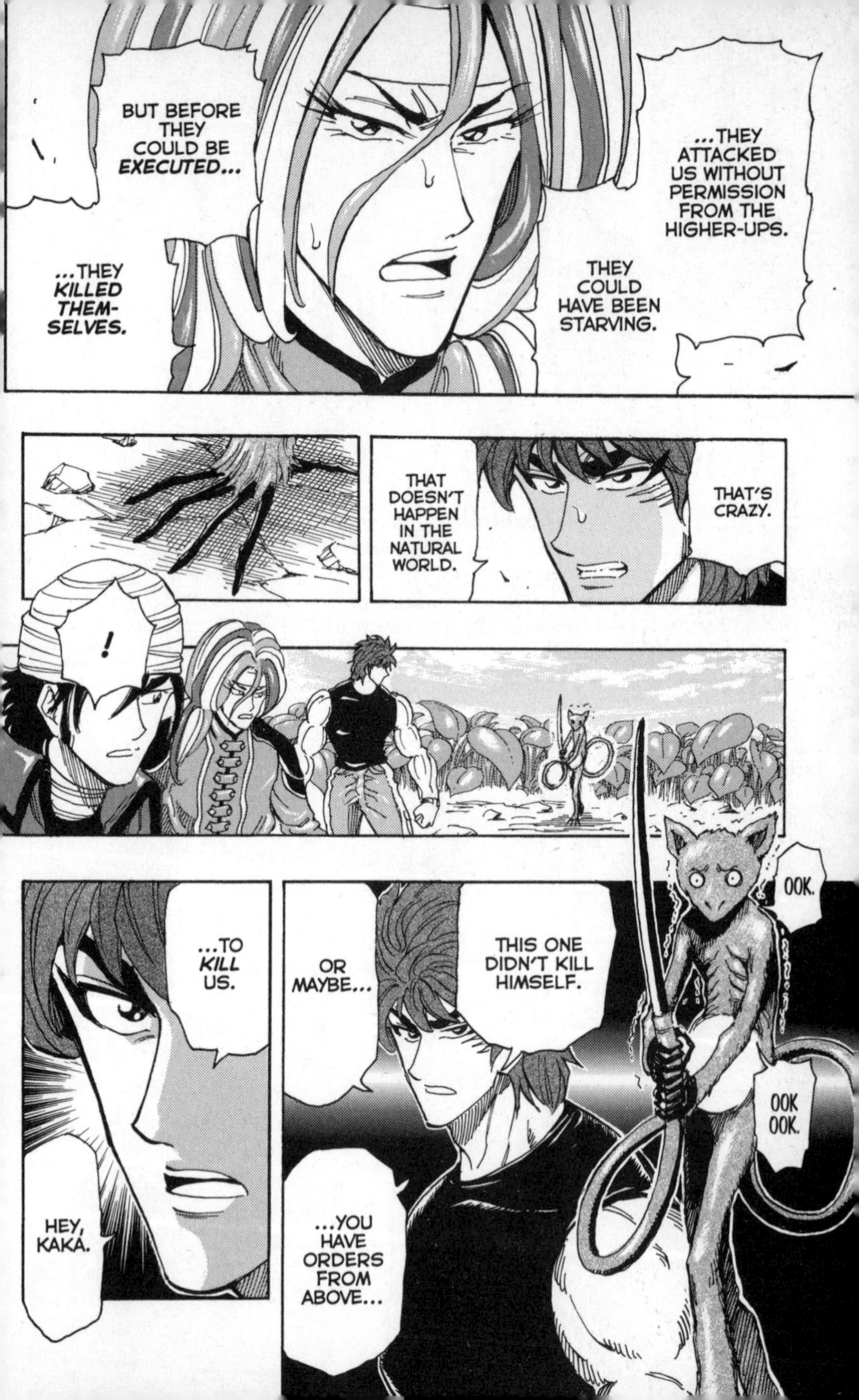
...THEY ATTACKED US WITHOUT PERMISSION FROM THE HIGHER-UPS.
THEY COULD HAVE BEEN STARVING.
BUT BEFORE THEY COULD BE *EXECUTED*...
...THEY *KILLED THEMSELVES.*
THAT'S CRAZY.
THAT DOESN'T HAPPEN IN THE NATURAL WORLD.
!
OOK.
OOK OOK.
THIS ONE DIDN'T KILL HIMSELF.
OR MAYBE...
...YOU HAVE ORDERS FROM ABOVE...
...TO *KILL* US.
HEY, KAKA.

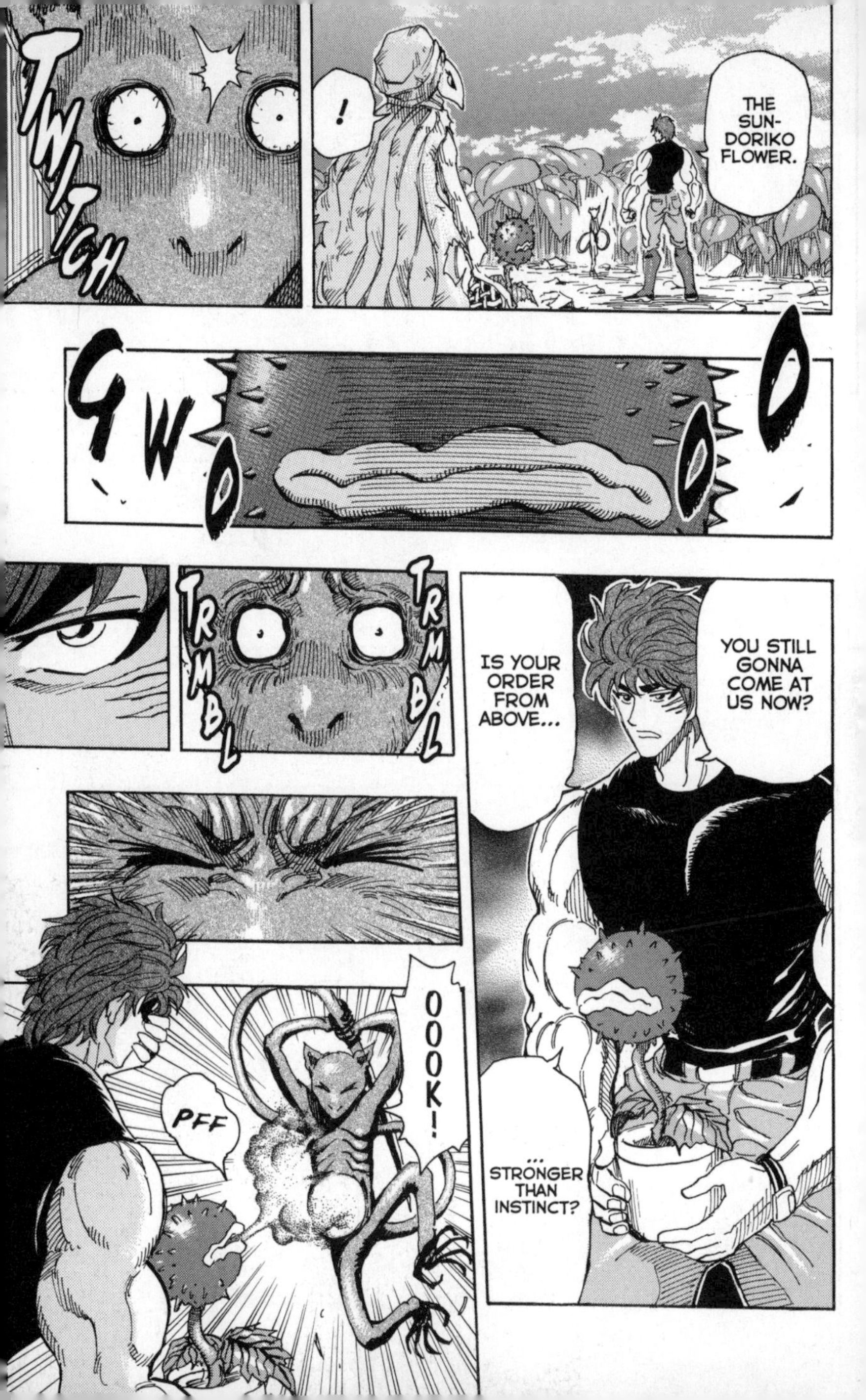
THE SUN-DORIKO FLOWER.
!
TWITCH
GWOOO
YOU STILL GONNA COME AT US NOW?
IS YOUR ORDER FROM ABOVE...
... STRONGER THAN INSTINCT?
TRMBL
TRMBL
OOOOK!
PFF

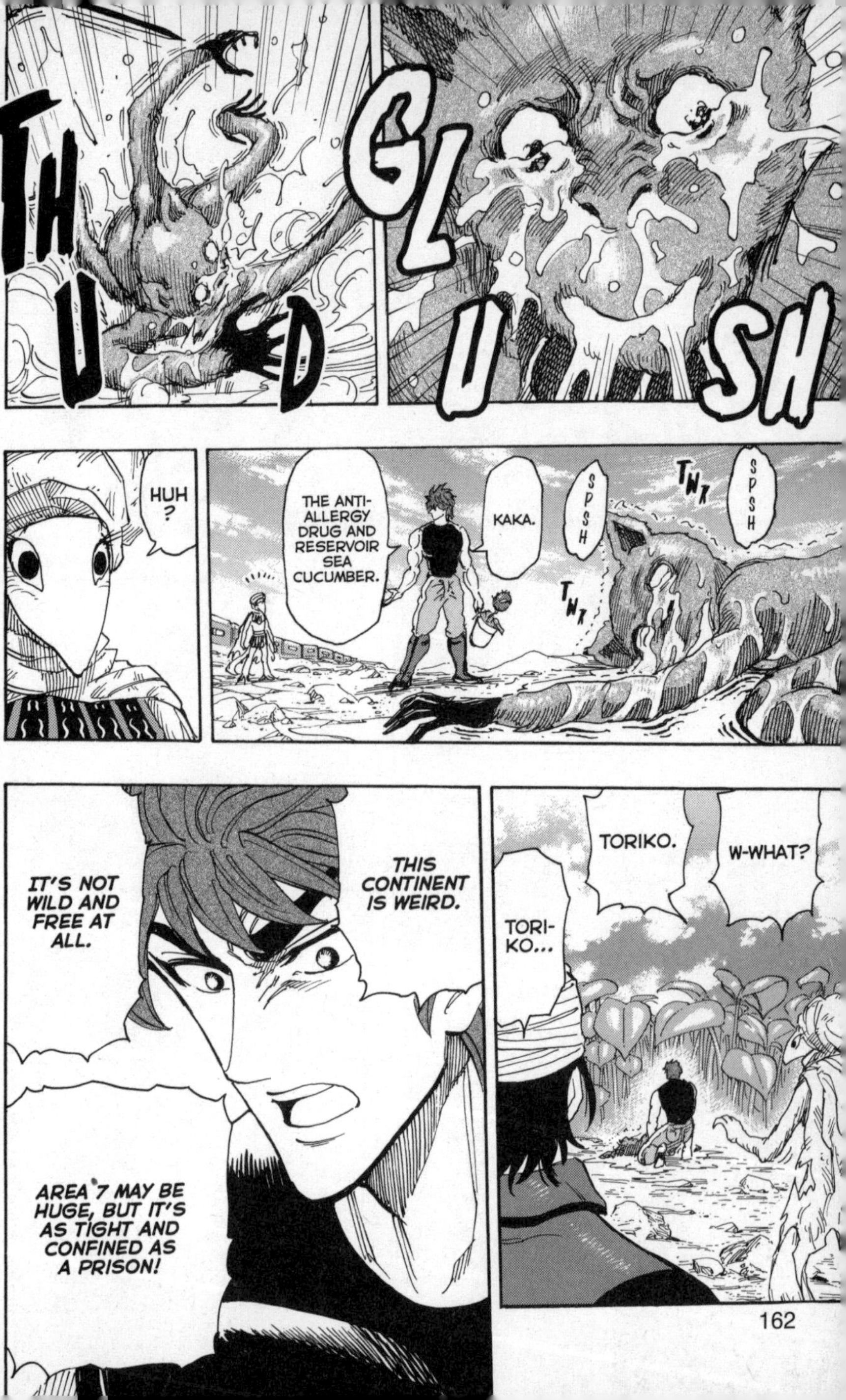
GLUSH
THUD
SPSH
TWK
SPSH
KAKA.
THE ANTI-ALLERGY DRUG AND RESERVOIR SEA CUCUMBER.
TWK
HUH?
W-WHAT?
TORIKO.
TORI-KO...
THIS CONTINENT IS WEIRD.
IT'S NOT WILD AND FREE AT ALL.
AREA 7 MAY BE HUGE, BUT IT'S AS TIGHT AND CONFINED AS A PRISON!

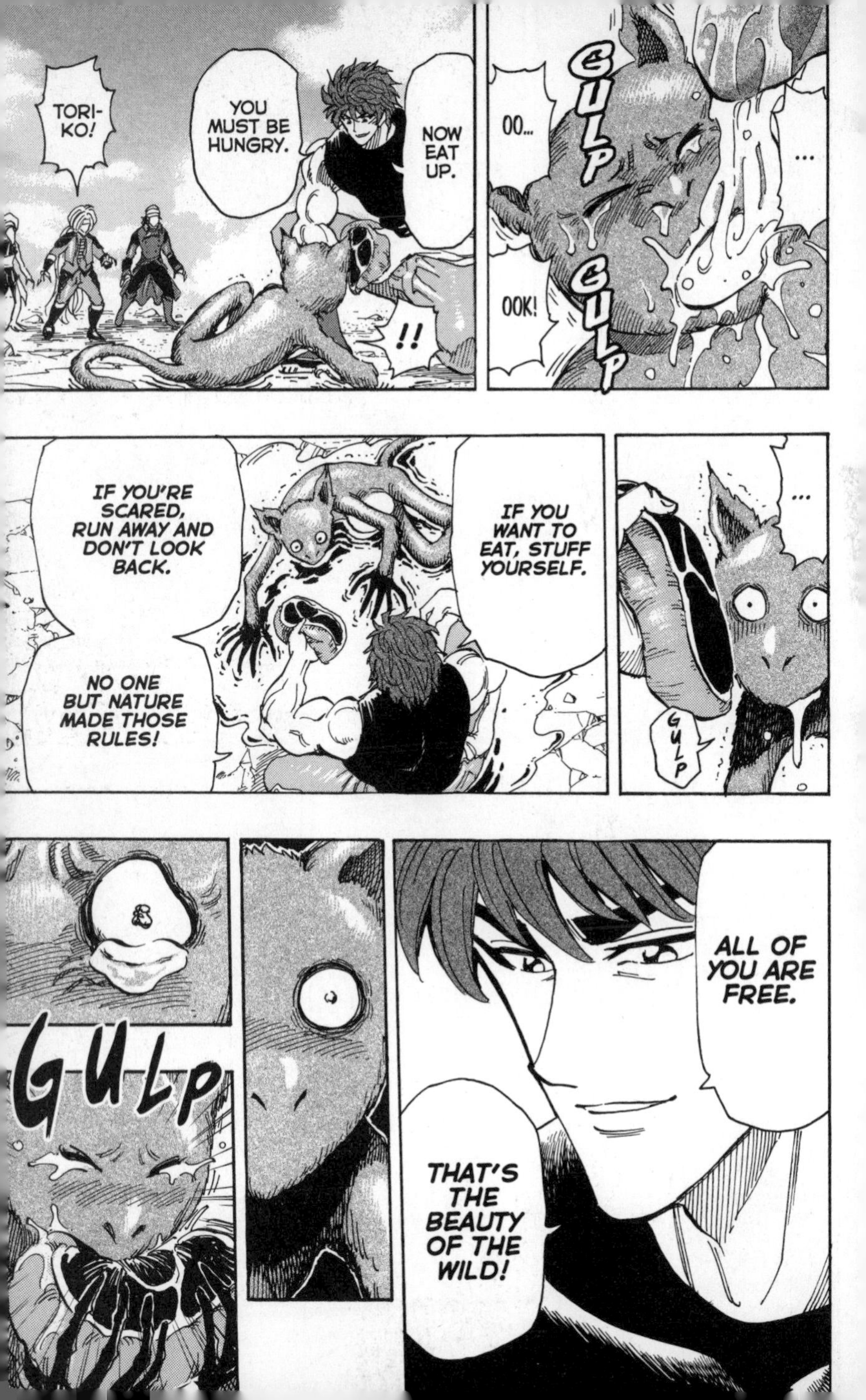
...
GULP
OO...
GULP
OOK!
NOW EAT UP.
YOU MUST BE HUNGRY.
TORI-KO!
!!
...
GULP
IF YOU WANT TO EAT, STUFF YOURSELF.
IF YOU'RE SCARED, RUN AWAY AND DON'T LOOK BACK.
NO ONE BUT NATURE MADE THOSE RULES!
ALL OF YOU ARE FREE.
THAT'S THE BEAUTY OF THE WILD!
GULP

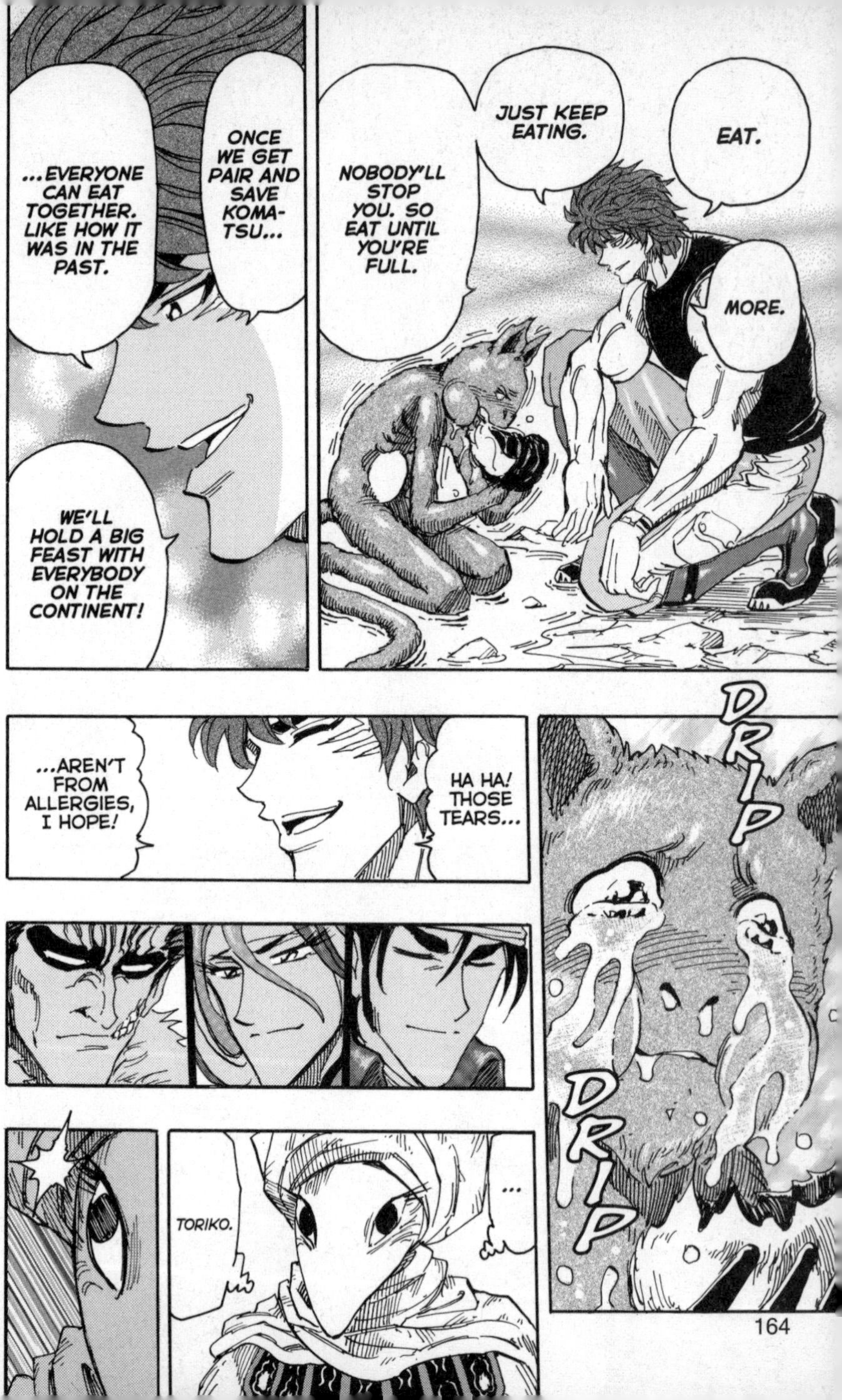
EAT.
JUST KEEP EATING.
MORE.
NOBODY'LL STOP YOU. SO EAT UNTIL YOU'RE FULL.
ONCE WE GET PAIR AND SAVE KOMA-TSU...
...EVERYONE CAN EAT TOGETHER. LIKE HOW IT WAS IN THE PAST.
WE'LL HOLD A BIG FEAST WITH EVERYBODY ON THE CONTINENT!
DRIP
DRIP
HA HA! THOSE TEARS...
...AREN'T FROM ALLERGIES, I HOPE!
...
TORIKO.

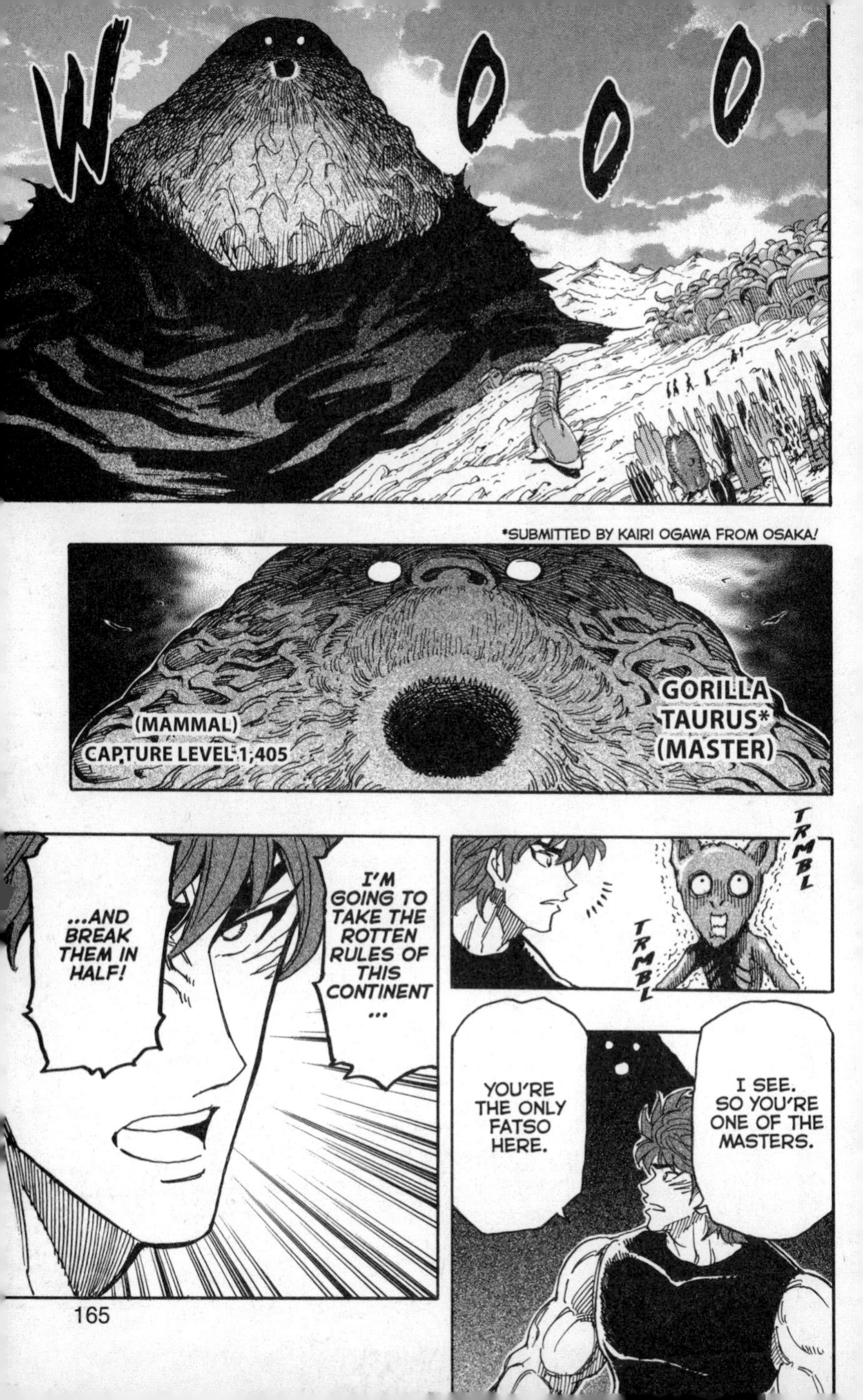
WOOOO
*SUBMITTED BY KAIRI OGAWA FROM OSAKA!
GORILLA TAURUS* (MASTER)
(MAMMAL) CAPTURE LEVEL 1,405
TRMBL
TRMBL
I SEE. SO YOU'RE ONE OF THE MASTERS.
YOU'RE THE ONLY FATSO HERE.
I'M GOING TO TAKE THE ROTTEN RULES OF THIS CONTINENT ...
...AND BREAK THEM IN HALF!

TORIKO

GOURMET CHECKLIST

Vol. 324

PAPER CROCODILE

(MAMMAL)

CAPTURE LEVEL: 28

HABITAT: COOKING ISLAND

SIZE: 10M

HEIGHT: ---

WEIGHT: 1 TON

PRICE: 4,000 YEN PER 100 GRAMS

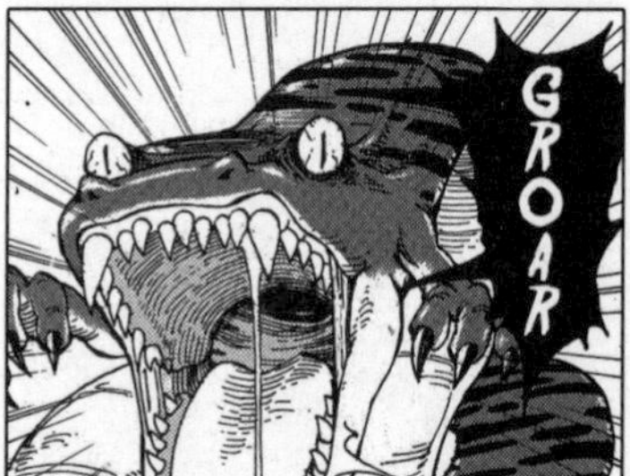
GROAR
PAPER CROCODILE*
(MAMMAL)
CAPTURE LEVEL 28

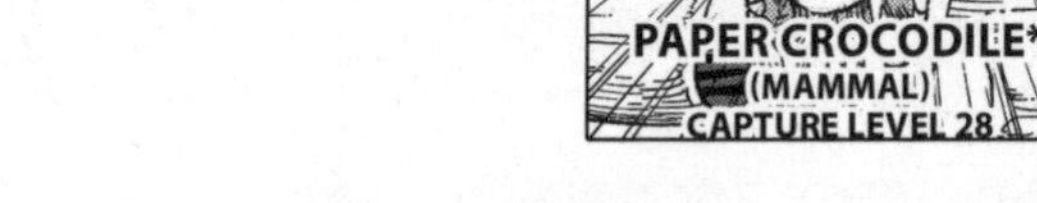

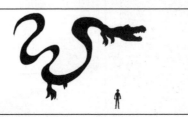

SCALE

INHABITS THE TRIATHLON COURSE OF COOKING ISLAND. USING ITS MASTERFUL CAMOUFLAGE POWERS, IT HIDES ITSELF AND ATTACKS WHEN YOU LEAST EXPECT IT! ITS PAPER-THIN SKIN IS SUPER FLAVORFUL AND IS STEEPED WITH COLLAGEN. STRONGER CONTENDERS TEND TO GO AFTER THEM MID-RACE TO USE THEM IN THEIR COOKING MATCHES AFTERWARD..

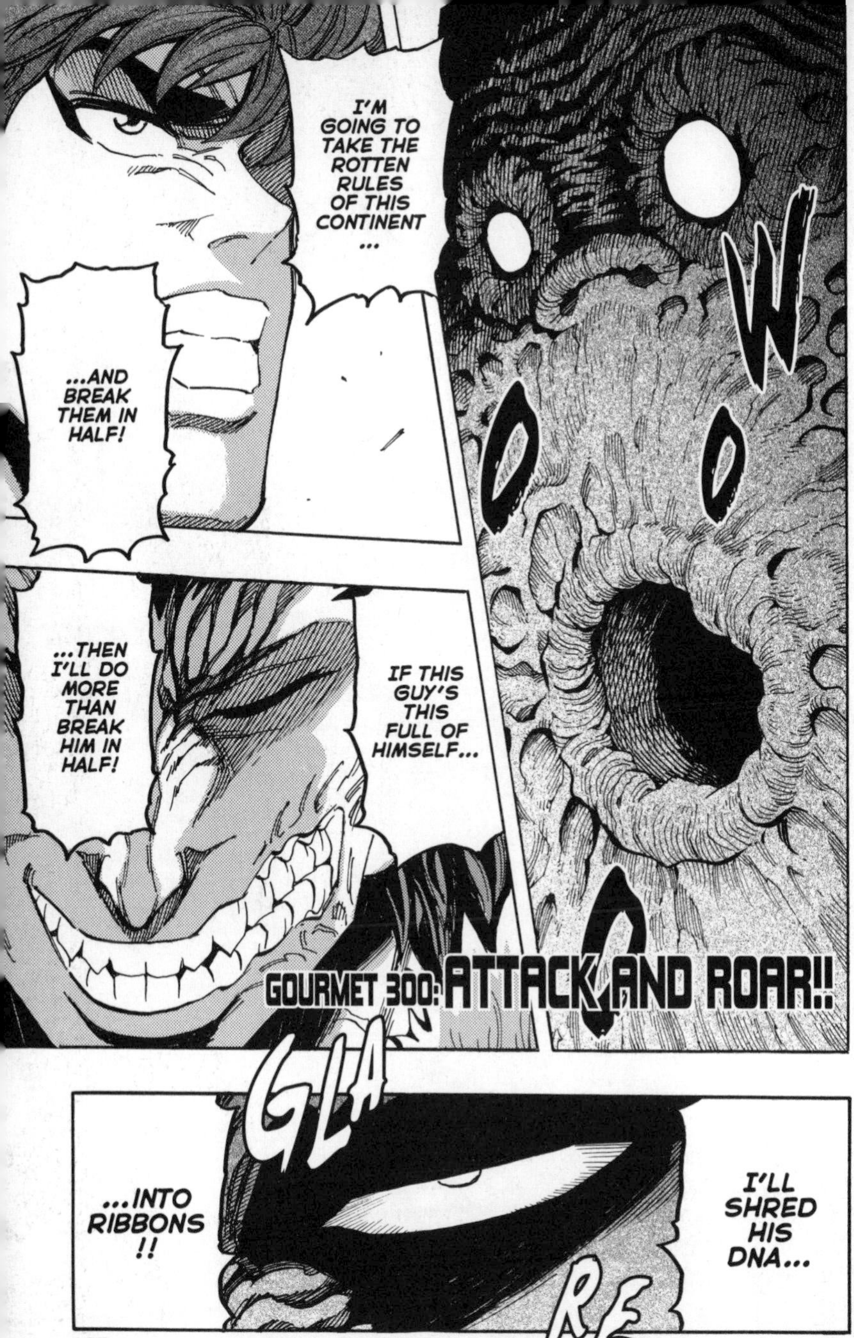
GOURMET 300: ATTACK AND ROAR!!
I'M GOING TO TAKE THE ROTTEN RULES OF THIS CONTINENT...
...AND BREAK THEM IN HALF!
IF THIS GUY'S THIS FULL OF HIMSELF...
...THEN I'LL DO MORE THAN BREAK HIM IN HALF!
I'LL SHRED HIS DNA...
...INTO RIBBONS!!
GLA RE

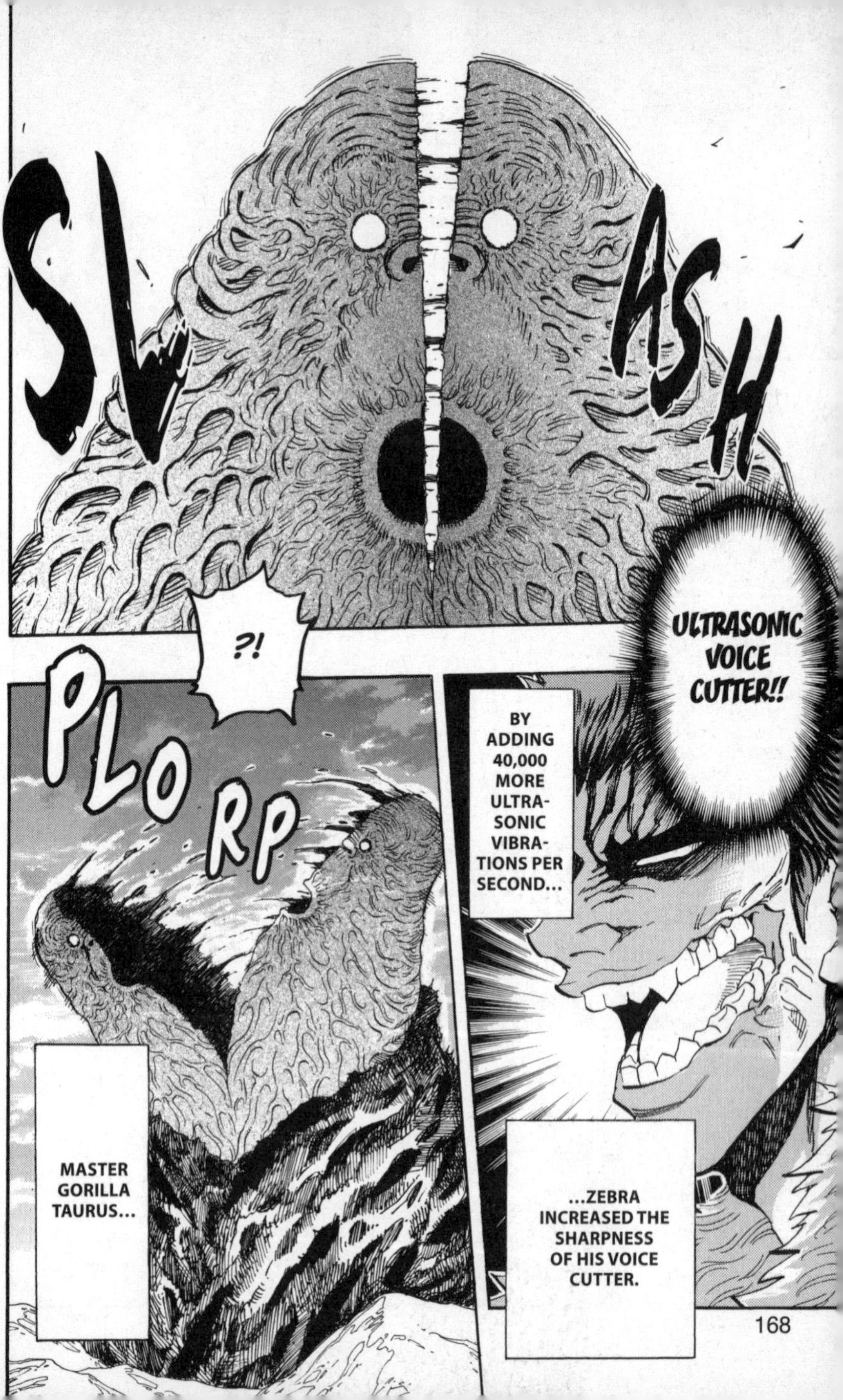
SLASH
ULTRASONIC VOICE CUTTER!!
?!
BY ADDING 40,000 MORE ULTRA-SONIC VIBRA-TIONS PER SECOND...
...ZEBRA INCREASED THE SHARPNESS OF HIS VOICE CUTTER.
PLORP
MASTER GORILLA TAURUS...

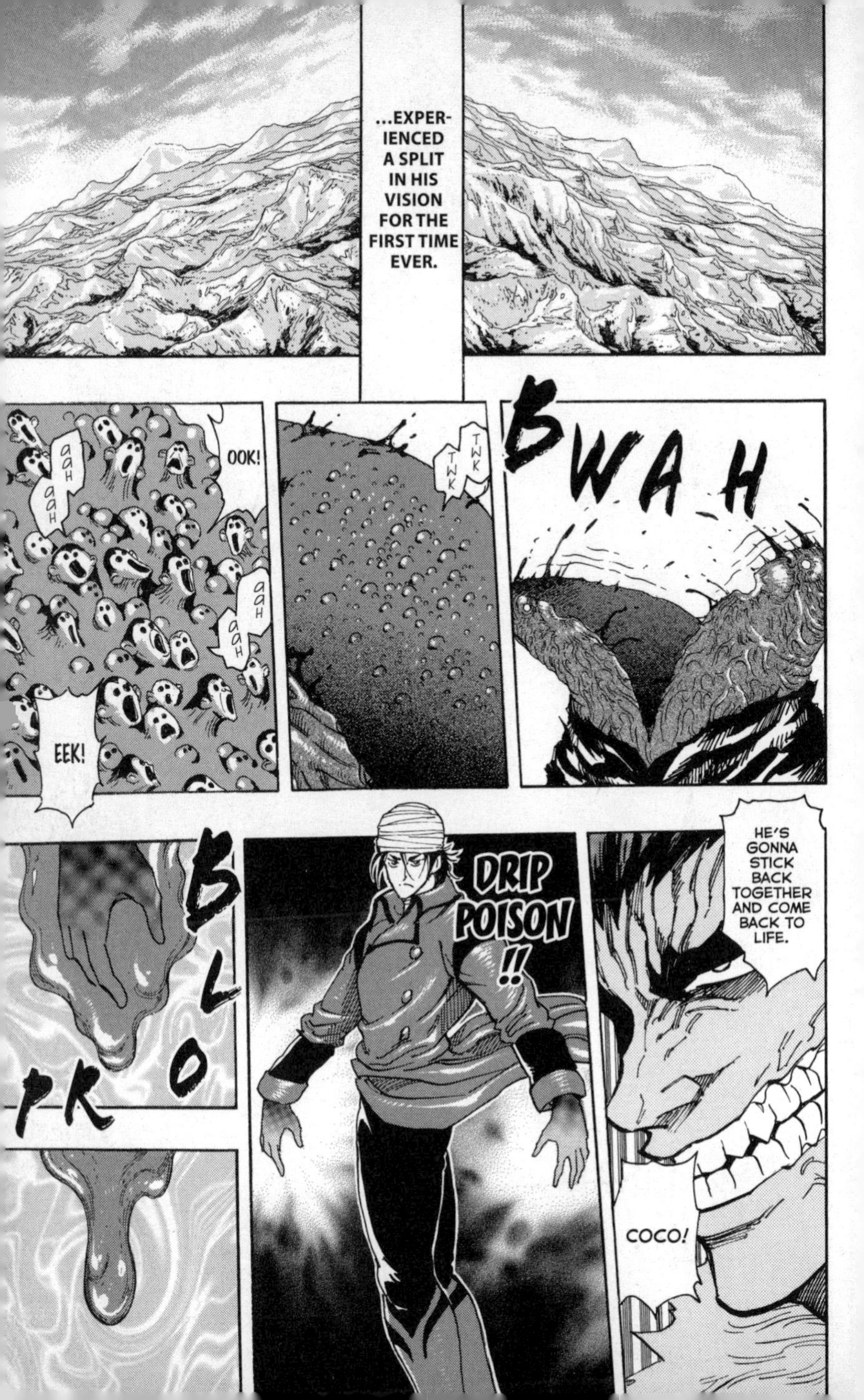
...EXPER-IENCED A SPLIT IN HIS VISION FOR THE FIRST TIME EVER.
BWAH
TWK TWK
OOK!
aah aah
aah aah
EEK!
HE'S GONNA STICK BACK TOGETHER AND COME BACK TO LIFE.
COCO!
DRIP POISON!!

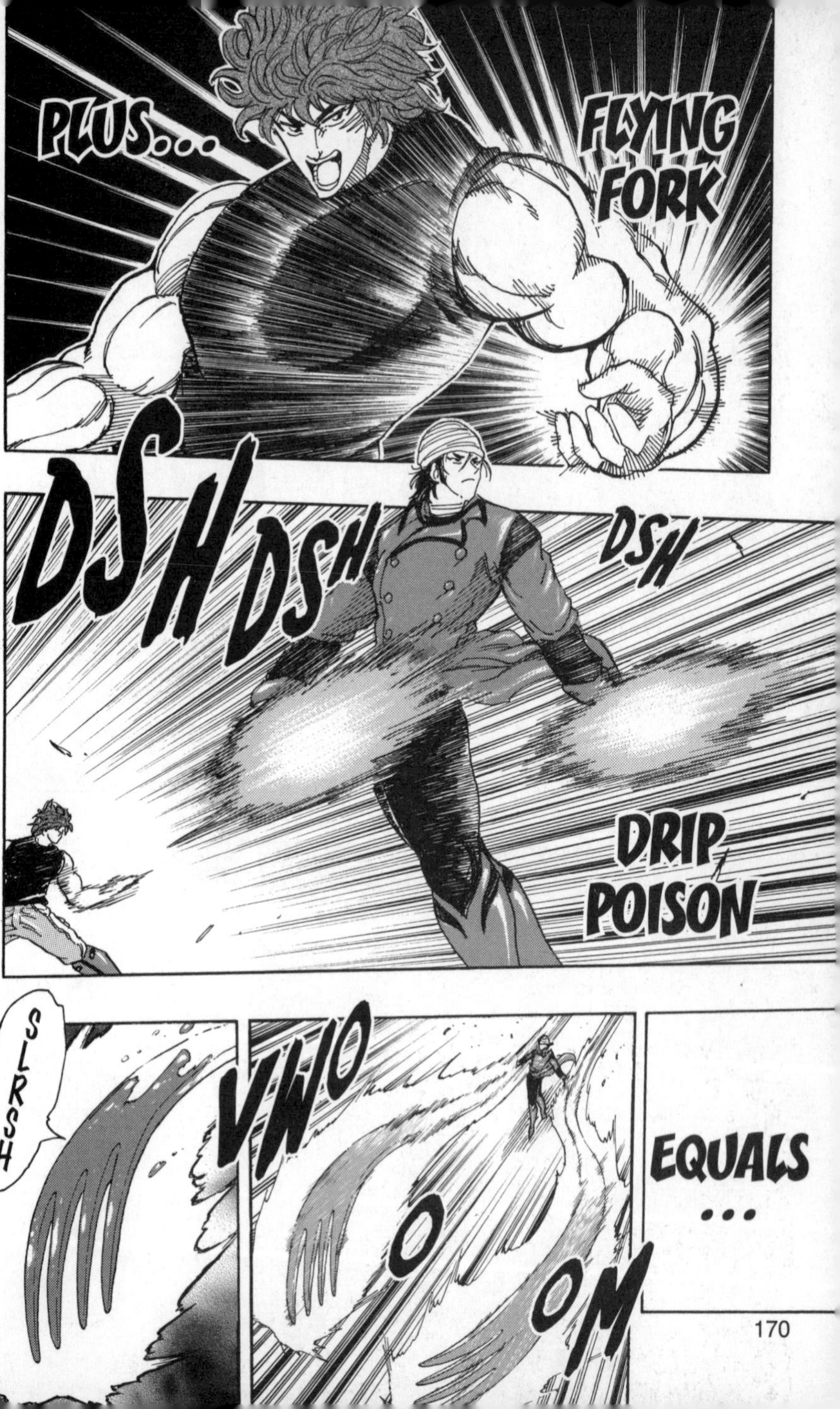
FLYING FORK
PLUS...
DSH
DSH
DSH
DRIP POISON
EQUALS...
VWOOOM
SLRSH

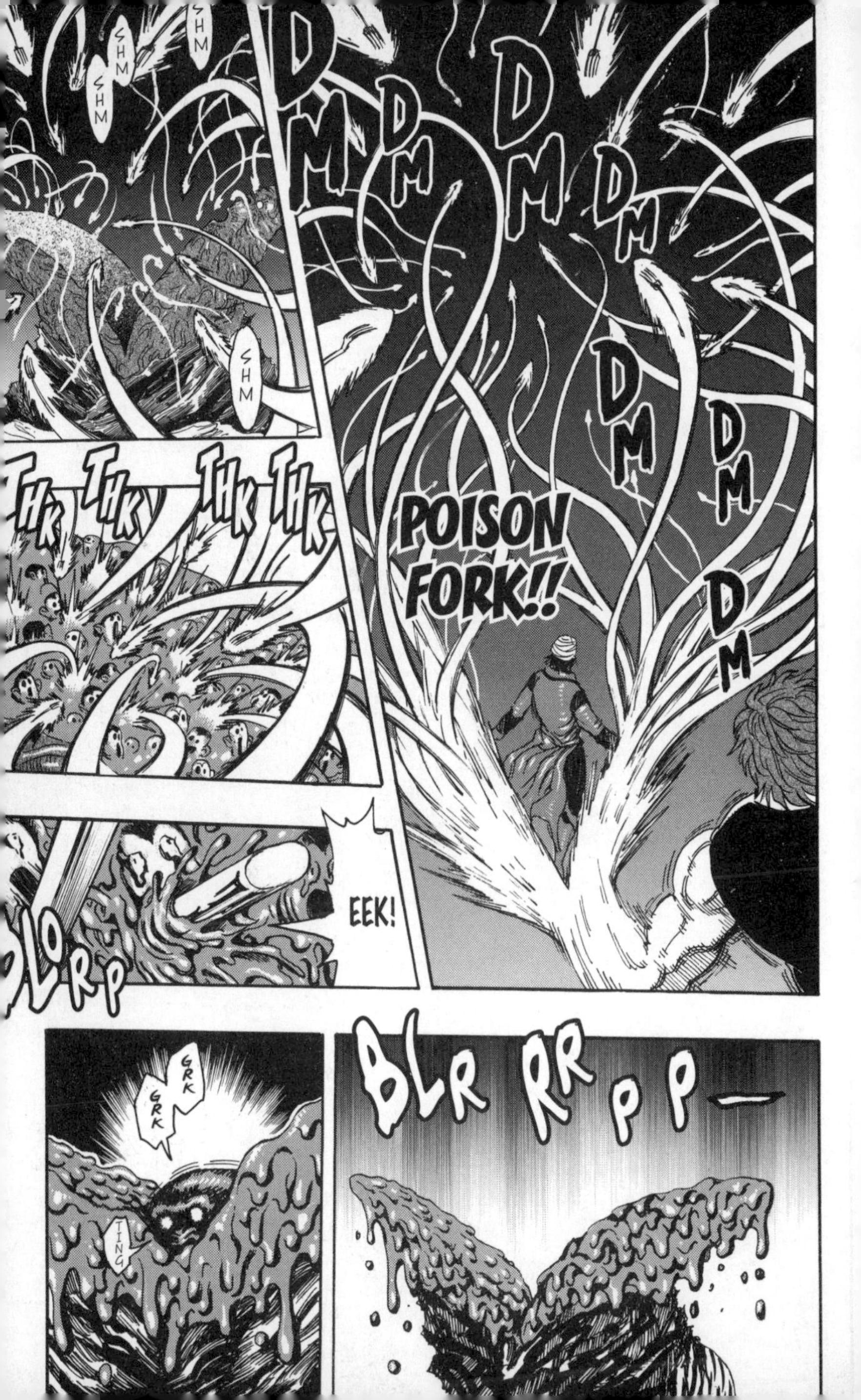
D M
D M
D M
D M
D M
D M
D M
POISON FORK!!
SHM
SHM SHM
SHM
THK
THK
THK
THK
EEK!
BLORP
BLR RR P P—
GRK GRK
TING

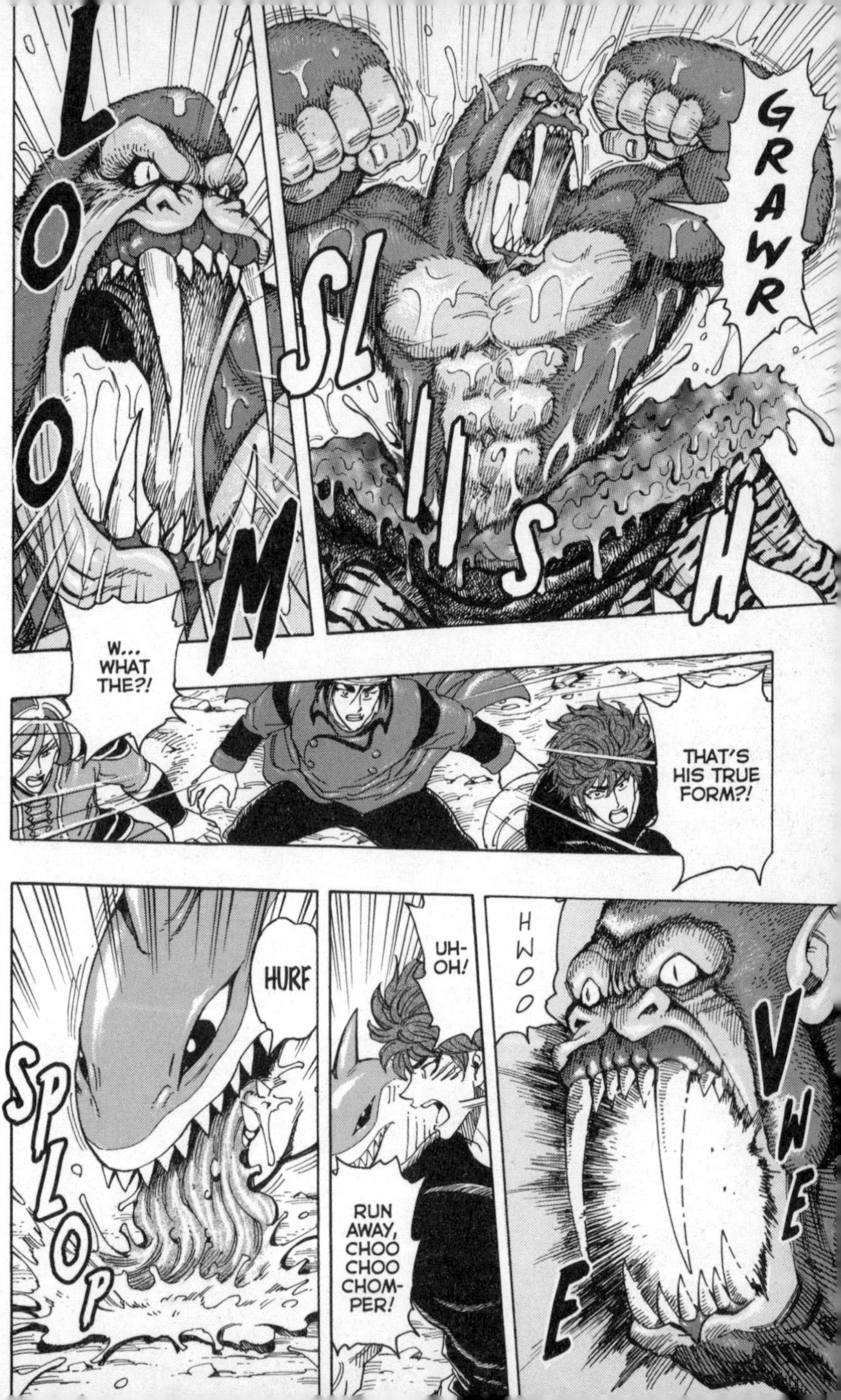
GRAWR
SLIISH
LOOM
THAT'S HIS TRUE FORM?!
W... WHAT THE?!
HWOO
VWEE
UH-OH!
RUN AWAY, CHOO CHOO CHOMPER!
HURF
SPLOP

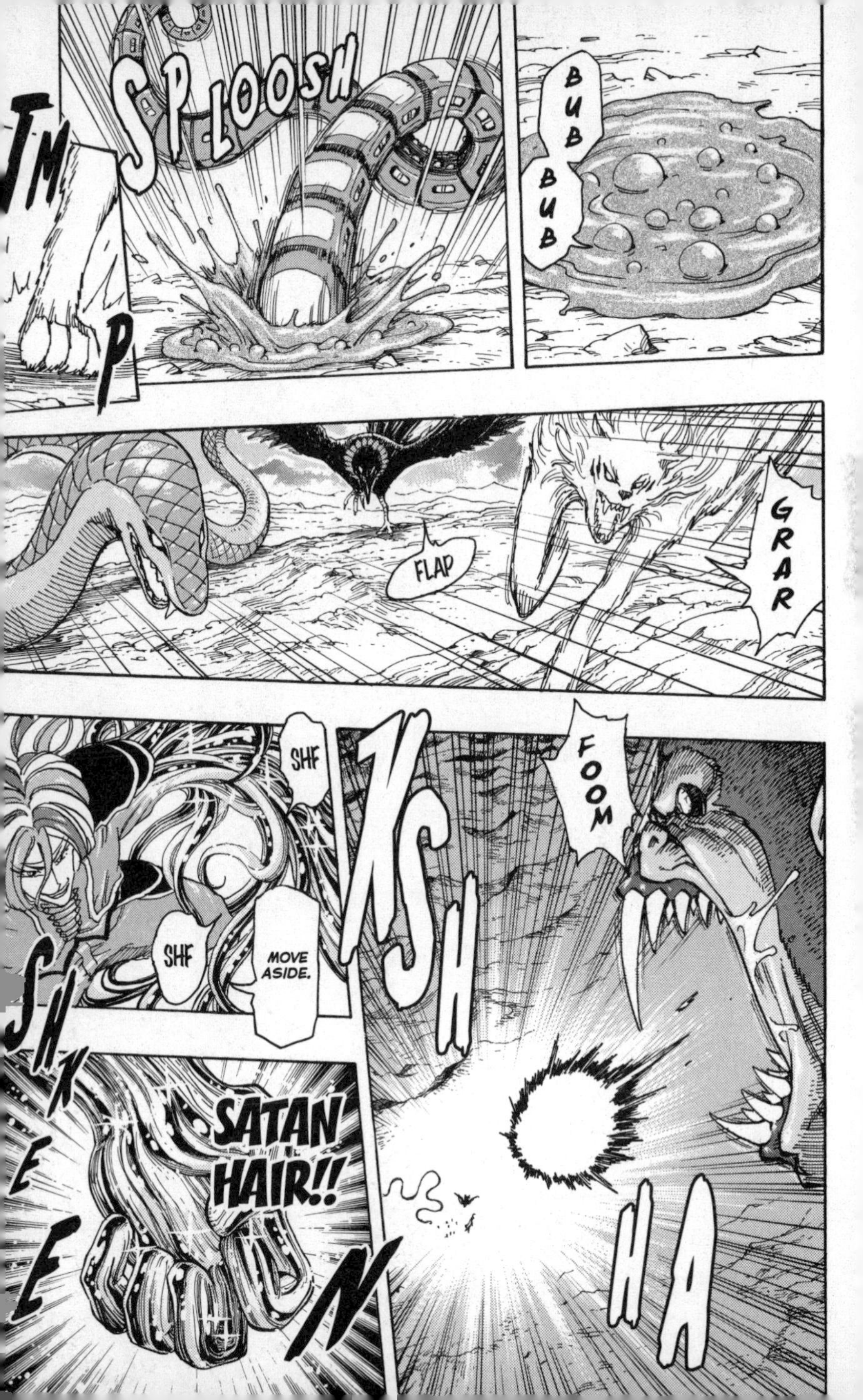
BUB BUB
SPLOOSH
TMP
GRAR
FLAP
FOOM
KSH
HA
SHF
MOVE ASIDE.
SHF
SATAN HAIR!!
SHKEEN

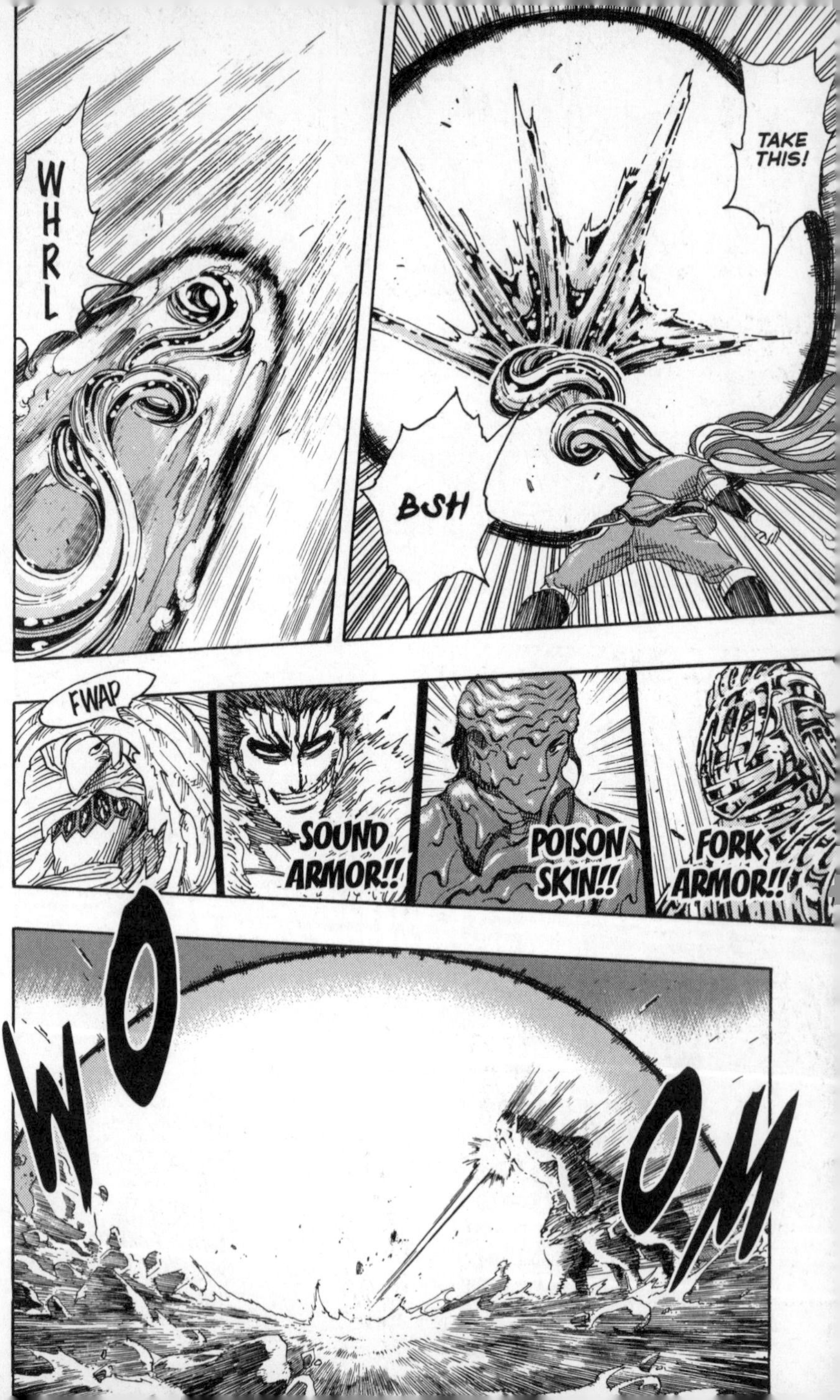
TAKE THIS!
BSH
WHRL
FORK ARMOR!!
POISON SKIN!!
SOUND ARMOR!!
FWAP
WOOM

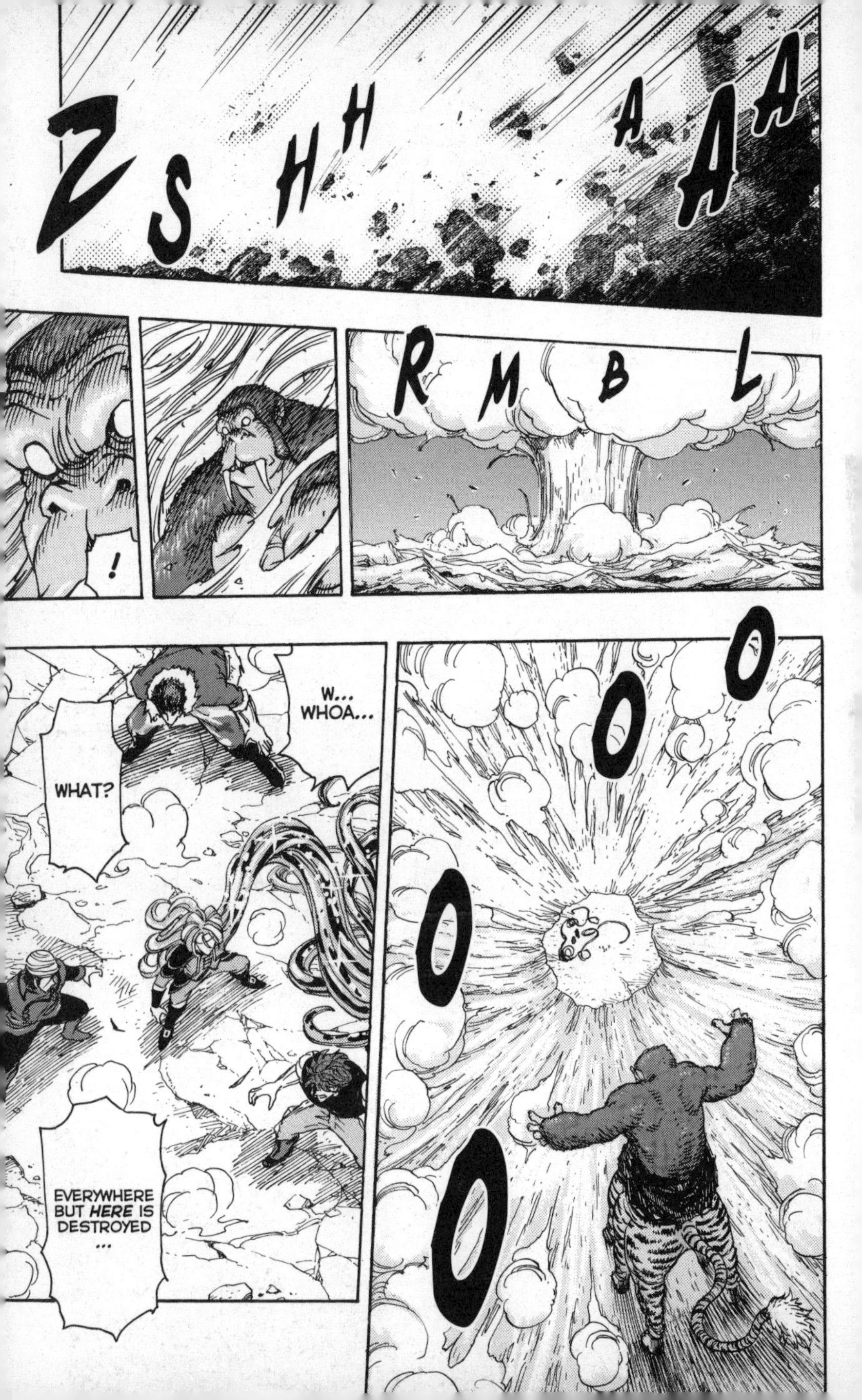
ZSHHAAAA
RMBL
!
OOOO
W... WHOA...
WHAT?
EVERYWHERE BUT *HERE* IS DESTROYED...

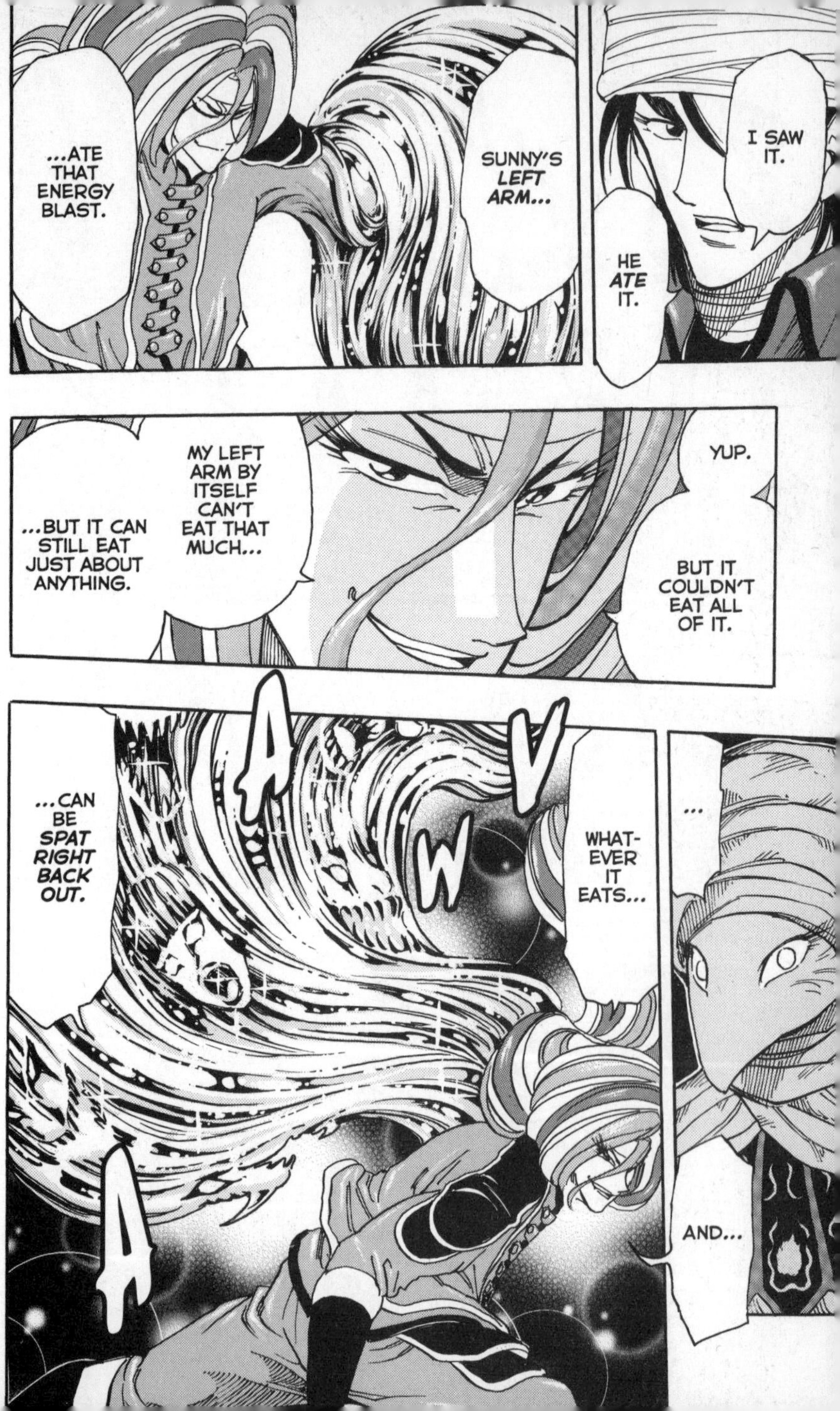
I SAW IT.
HE *ATE* IT.
SUNNY'S *LEFT ARM...*
...ATE THAT ENERGY BLAST.
YUP.
BUT IT COULDN'T EAT ALL OF IT.
MY LEFT ARM BY ITSELF CAN'T EAT THAT MUCH...
...BUT IT CAN STILL EAT JUST ABOUT ANYTHING.
...
AND...
WHATEVER IT EATS...
...CAN BE *SPAT RIGHT BACK OUT.*

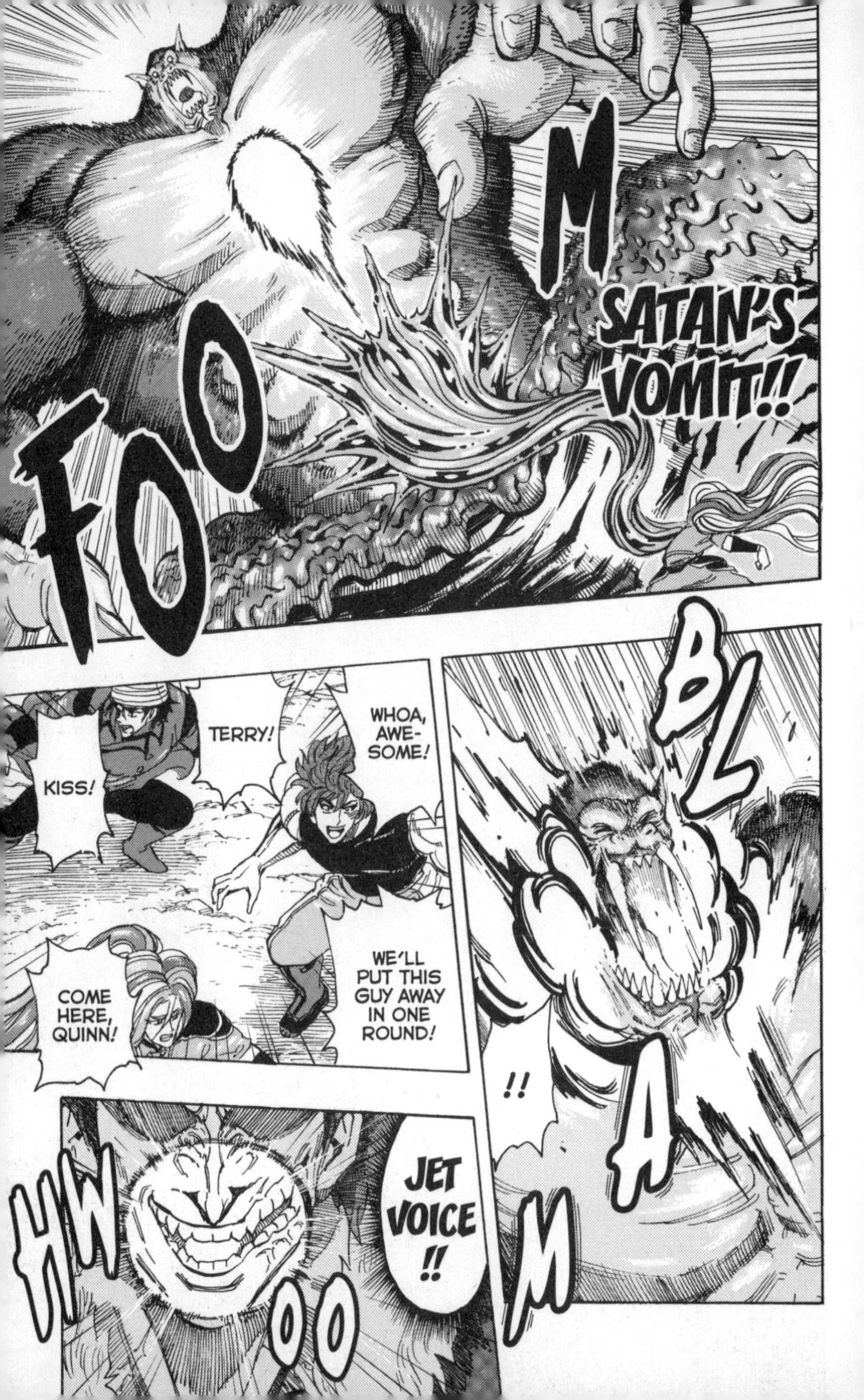
SATAN'S VOMIT!!
FOOM
BLAM
!!
WHOA, AWESOME!
TERRY!
KISS!
WE'LL PUT THIS GUY AWAY IN ONE ROUND!
COME HERE, QUINN!
JET VOICE!!
HWOOM

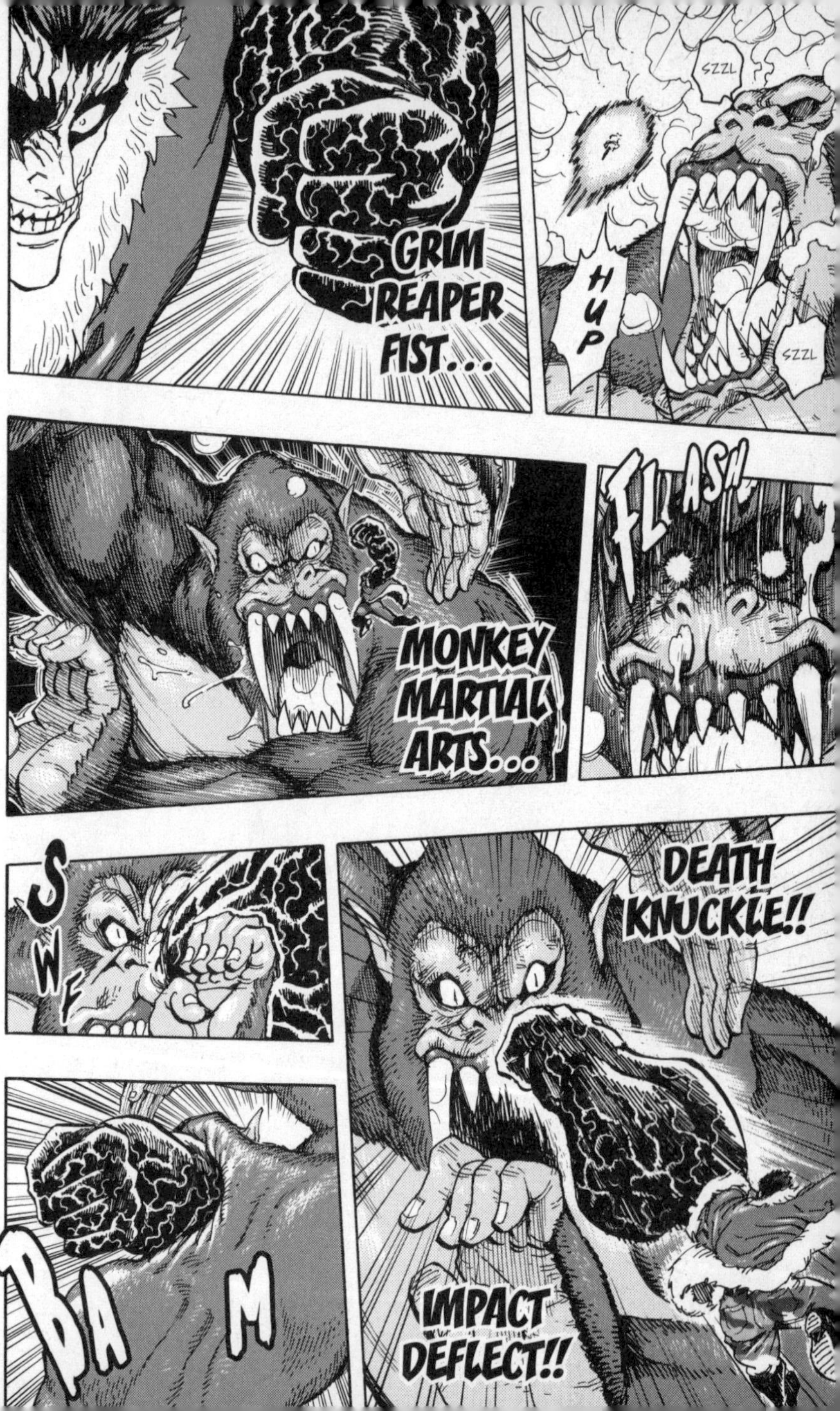
SZZL
HUP
SZZL
GRIM REAPER FIST...
FLASH
MONKEY MARTIAL ARTS...
DEATH KNUCKLE!!
IMPACT DEFLECT!!
SWF
BAM

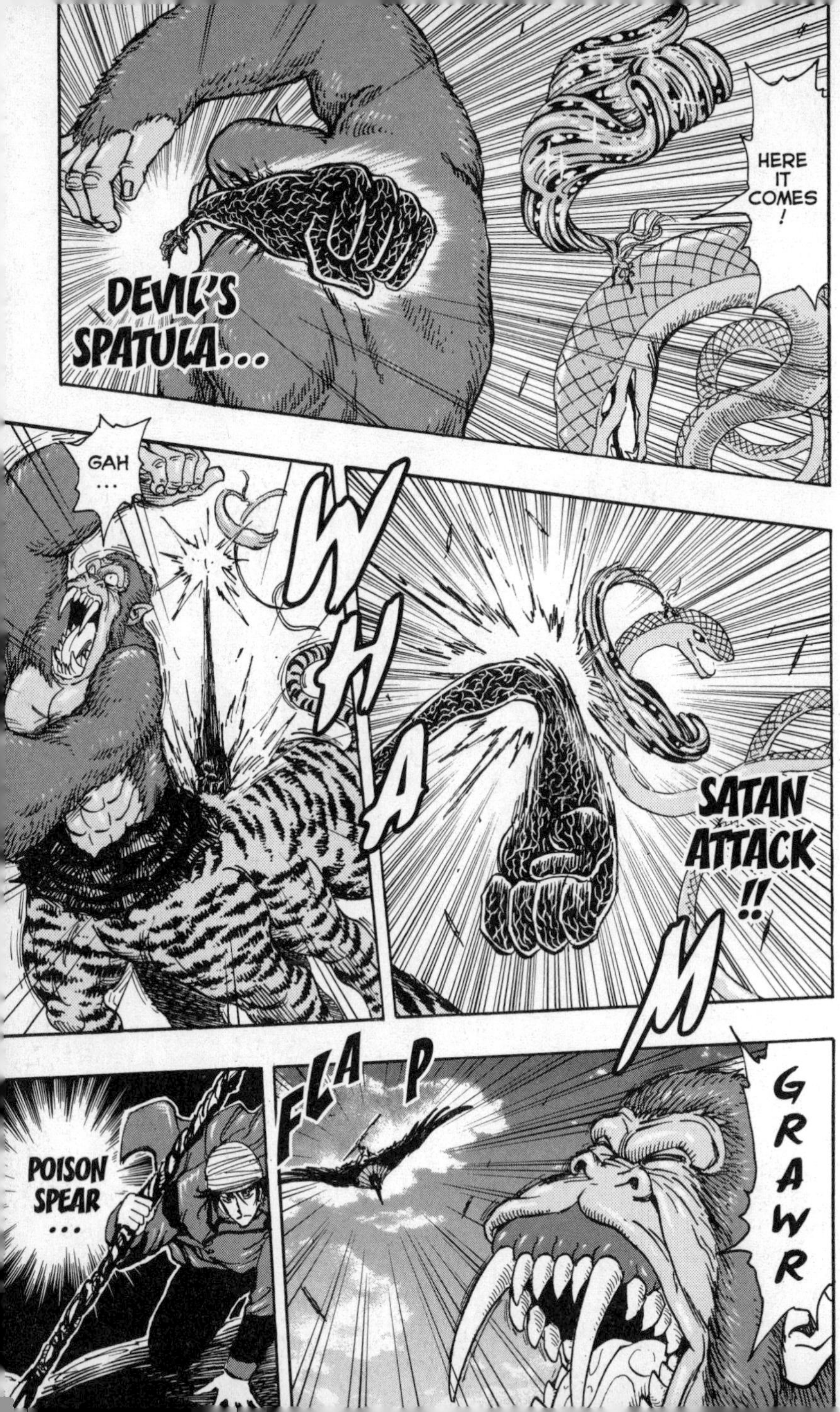
HERE IT COMES!
DEVIL'S SPATULA...
WHAM
SATAN ATTACK!!
GAH...
GRAWR
FLAP
POISON SPEAR...

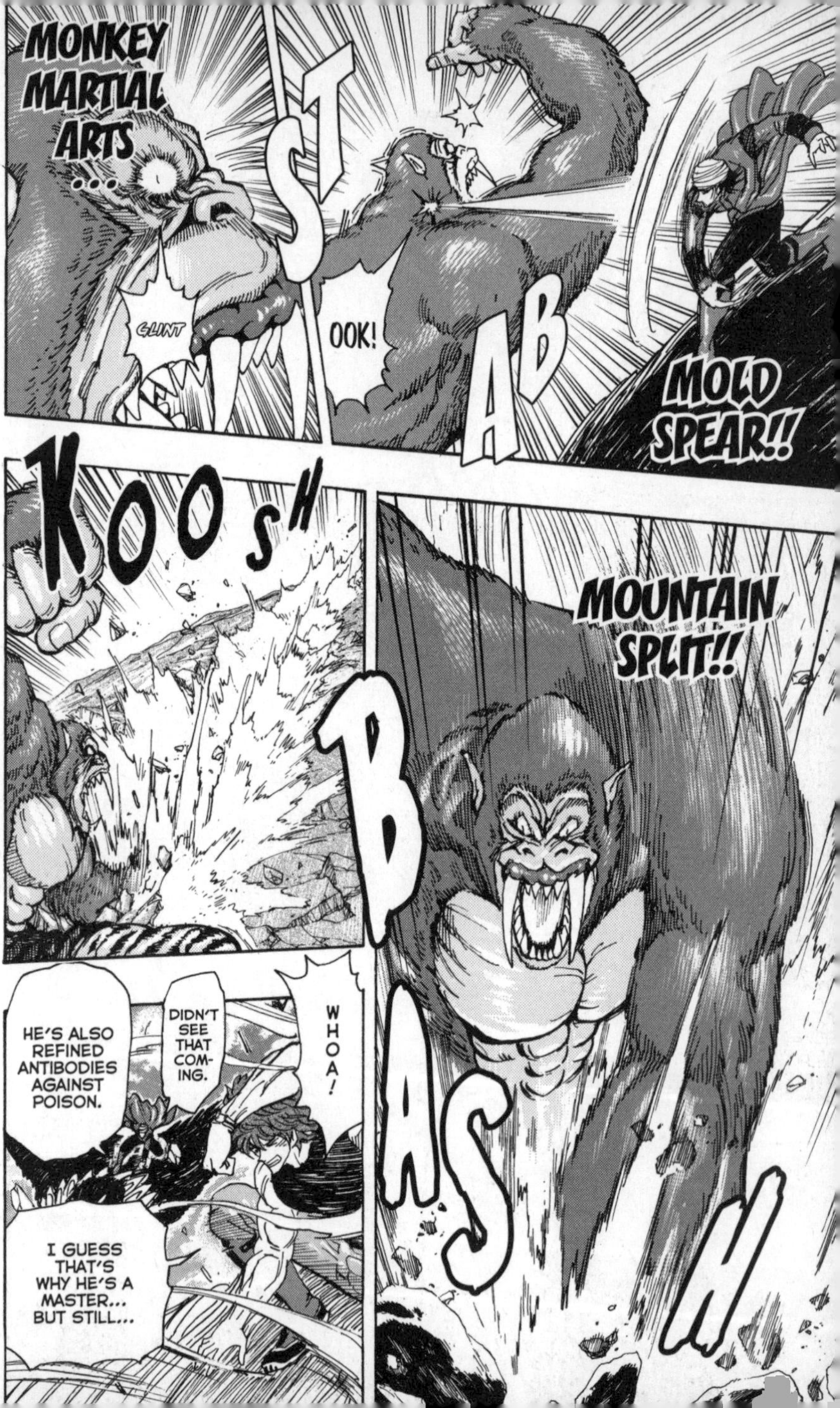
MONKEY MARTIAL ARTS...
STAB
OOK!
GLINT
MOLD SPEAR!!
MOUNTAIN SPLIT!!
BASH
KOOSH
WHOA!
DIDN'T SEE THAT COMING.
HE'S ALSO REFINED ANTIBODIES AGAINST POISON.
I GUESS THAT'S WHY HE'S A MASTER... BUT STILL...

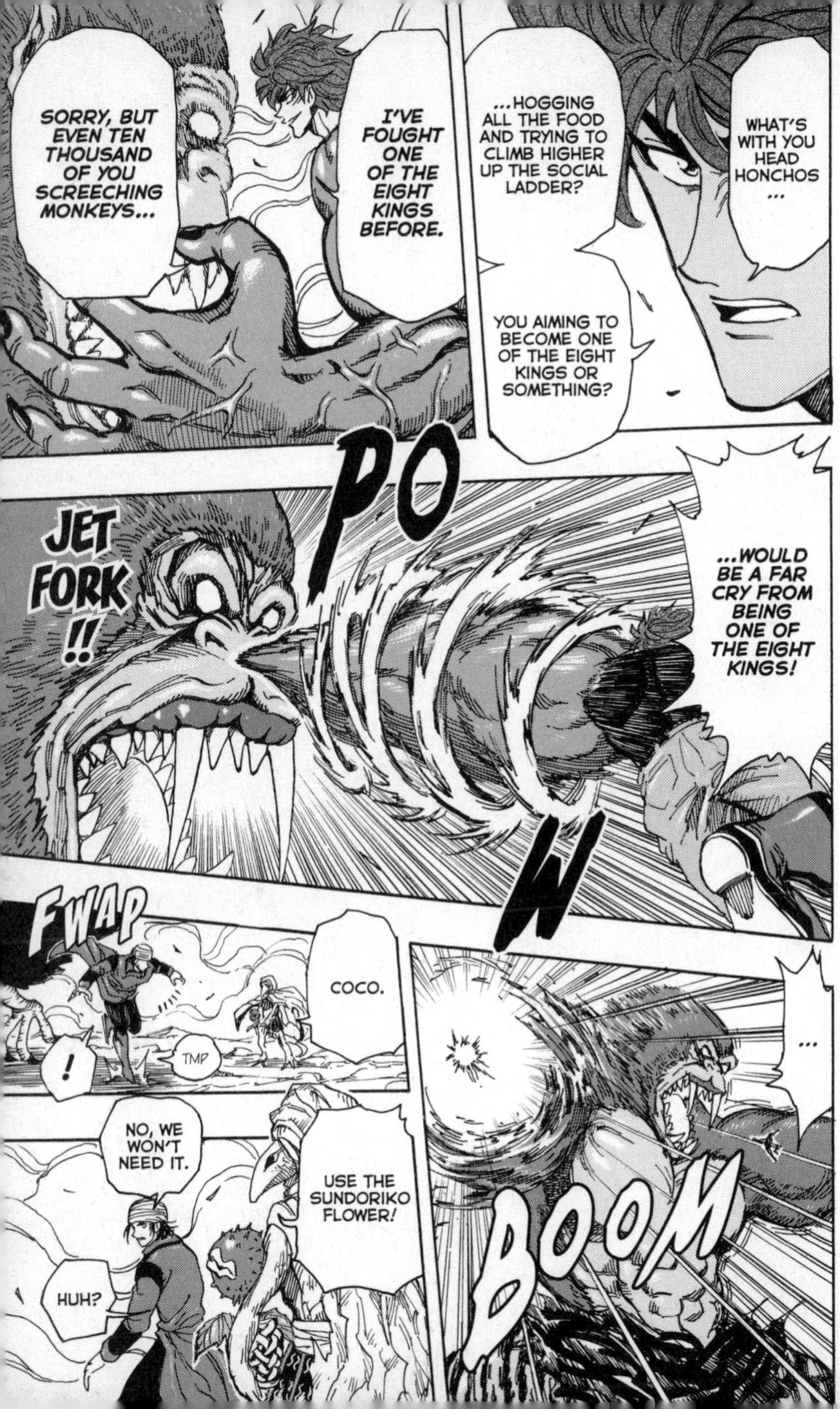
WHAT'S WITH YOU HEAD HONCHOS...
...HOGGING ALL THE FOOD AND TRYING TO CLIMB HIGHER UP THE SOCIAL LADDER?
YOU AIMING TO BECOME ONE OF THE EIGHT KINGS OR SOMETHING?
I'VE FOUGHT ONE OF THE EIGHT KINGS BEFORE.
SORRY, BUT EVEN TEN THOUSAND OF YOU SCREECHING MONKEYS...
...WOULD BE A FAR CRY FROM BEING ONE OF THE EIGHT KINGS!
POW
JET FORK!!
...
BOOM
COCO.
FWAP
TMP
!
USE THE SUNDORIKO FLOWER!
NO, WE WON'T NEED IT.
HUH?

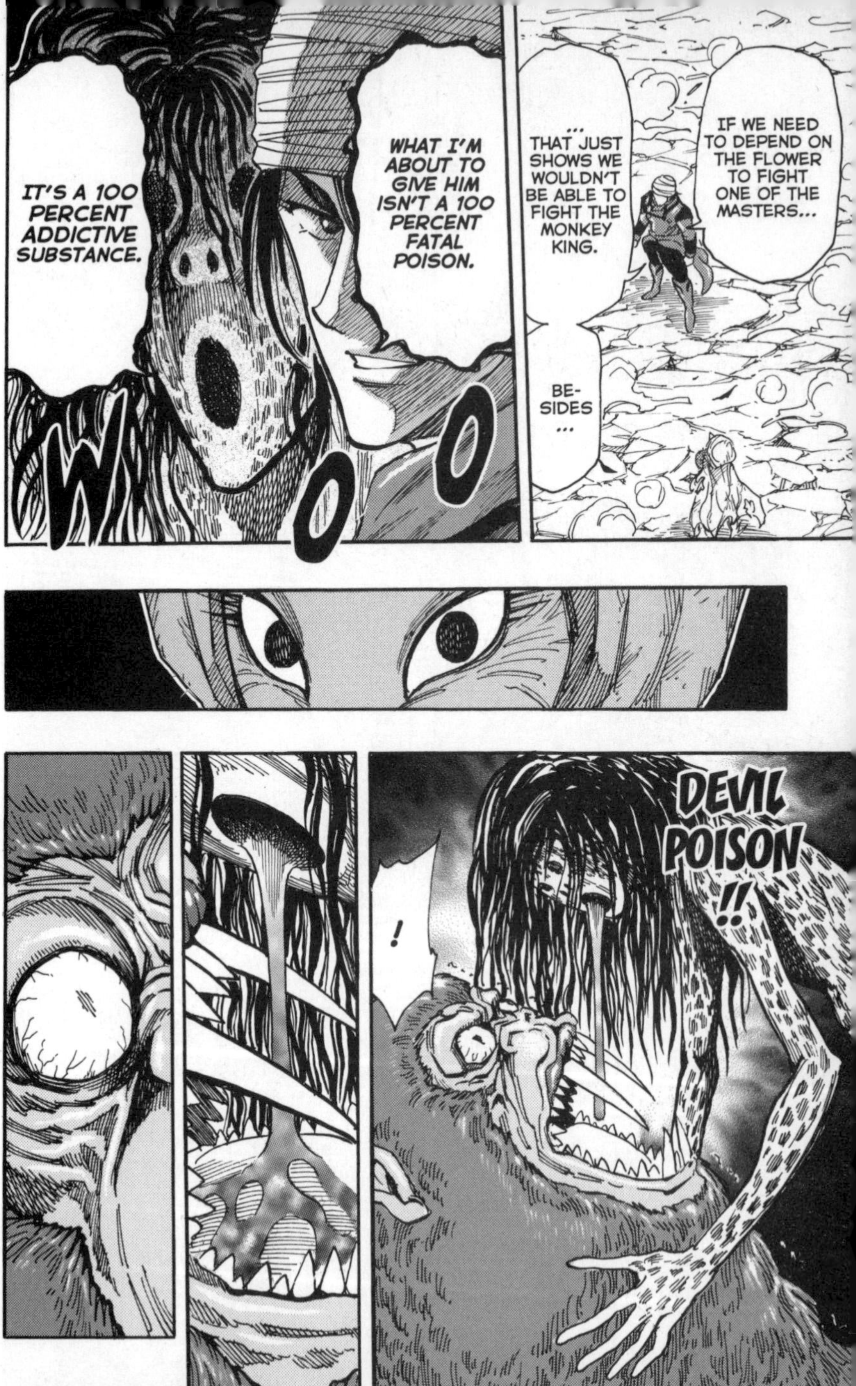
IF WE NEED TO DEPEND ON THE FLOWER TO FIGHT ONE OF THE MASTERS...
... THAT JUST SHOWS WE WOULDN'T BE ABLE TO FIGHT THE MONKEY KING.
BE-SIDES ...
WHAT I'M ABOUT TO GIVE HIM ISN'T A 100 PERCENT FATAL POISON.
IT'S A 100 PERCENT ADDICTIVE SUBSTANCE.
WOO
DEVIL POISON!!
!

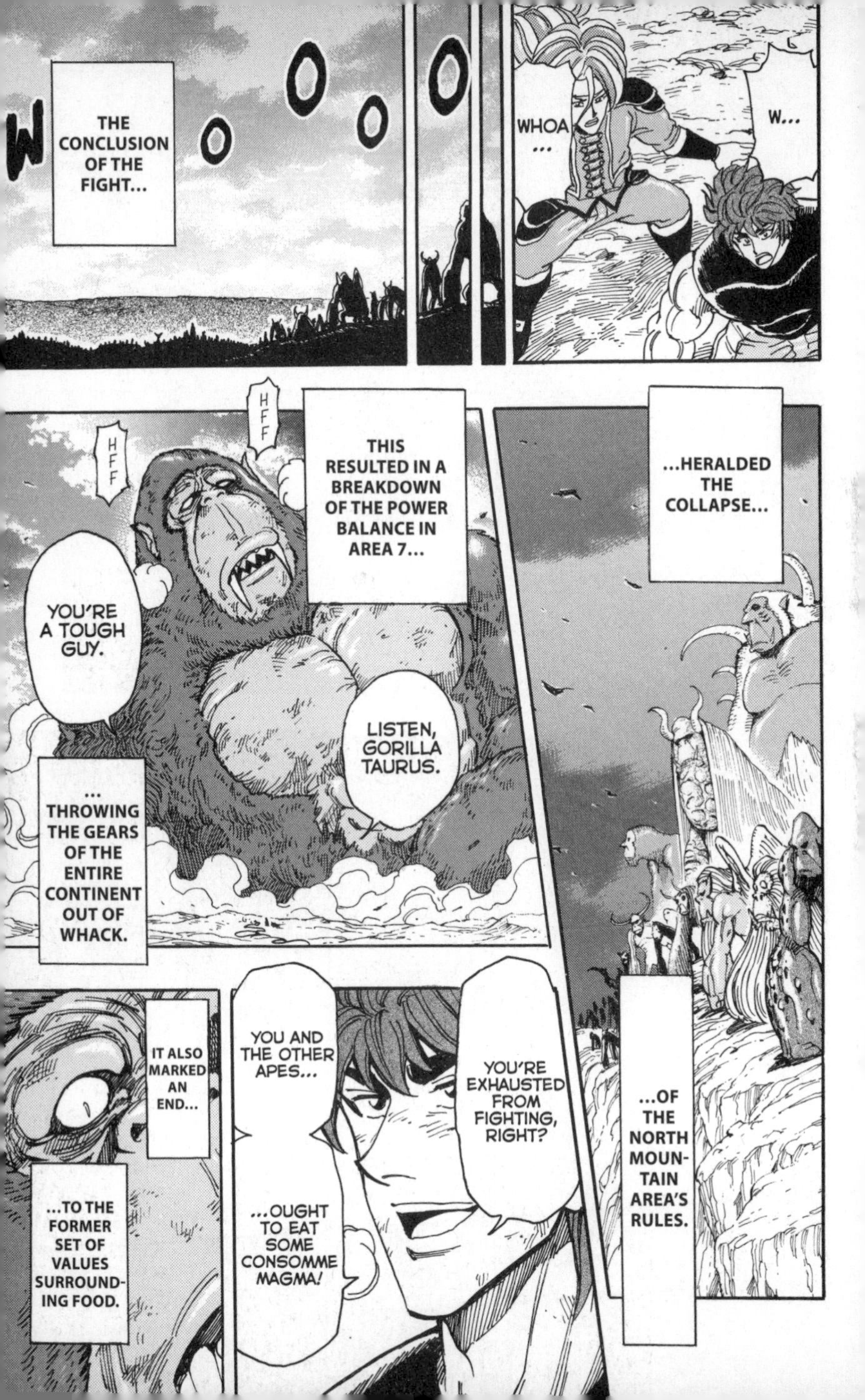
W...
WHOA ...
WOOOOO
THE CONCLUSION OF THE FIGHT...
...HERALDED THE COLLAPSE...
...OF THE NORTH MOUN-TAIN AREA'S RULES.
THIS RESULTED IN A BREAKDOWN OF THE POWER BALANCE IN AREA 7...
HFF
HFF
LISTEN, GORILLA TAURUS.
YOU'RE A TOUGH GUY.
... THROWING THE GEARS OF THE ENTIRE CONTINENT OUT OF WHACK.
YOU'RE EXHAUSTED FROM FIGHTING, RIGHT?
YOU AND THE OTHER APES...
...OUGHT TO EAT SOME CONSOMME MAGMA!
IT ALSO MARKED AN END...
...TO THE FORMER SET OF VALUES SURROUND-ING FOOD.

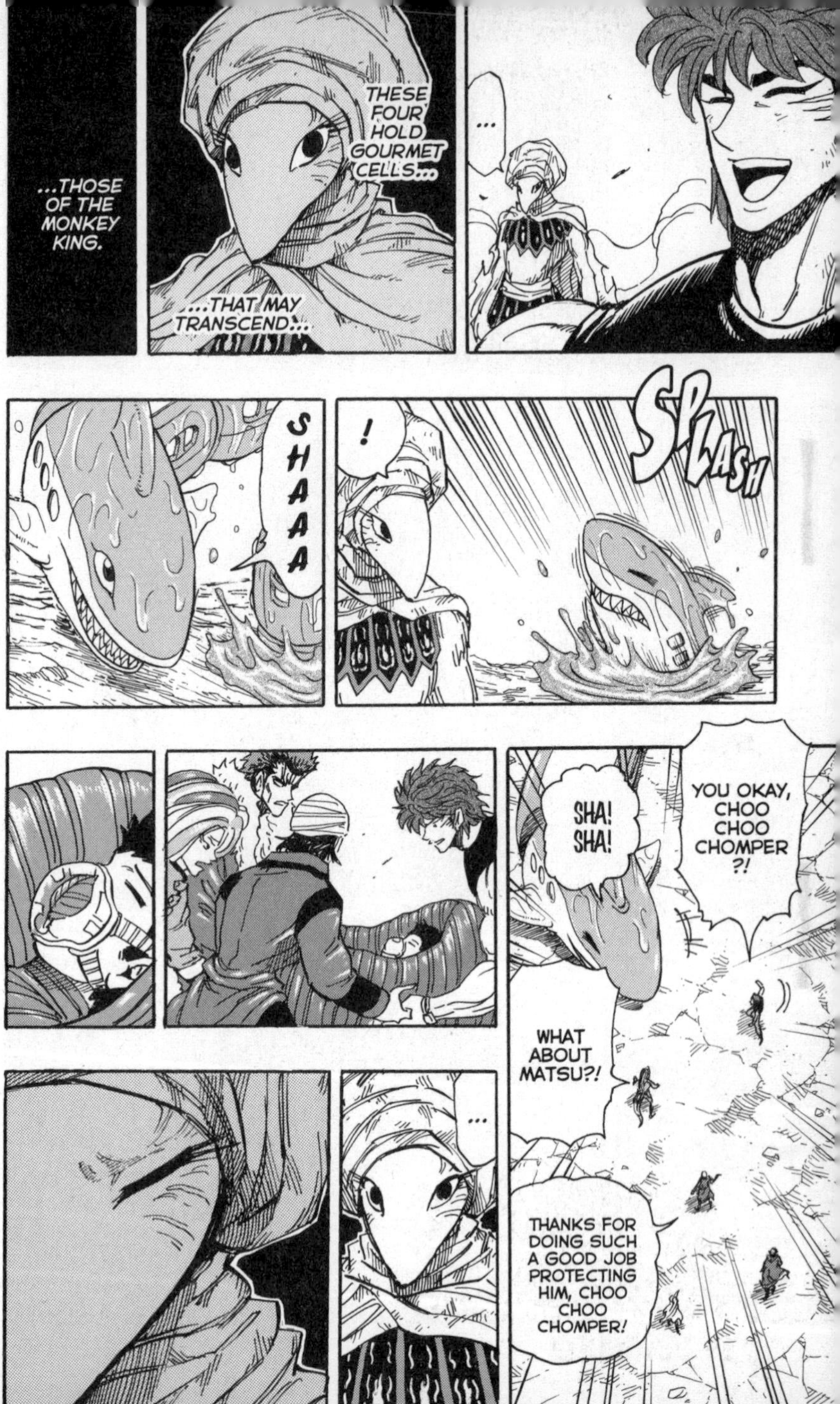
...
THESE FOUR HOLD GOURMET CELLS...
...THAT MAY TRANSCEND...
...THOSE OF THE MONKEY KING.
SPLASH
!
SHAAAA
YOU OKAY, CHOO CHOO CHOMPER?!
SHA! SHA!
WHAT ABOUT MATSU?!
THANKS FOR DOING SUCH A GOOD JOB PROTECTING HIM, CHOO CHOO CHOMPER!
...

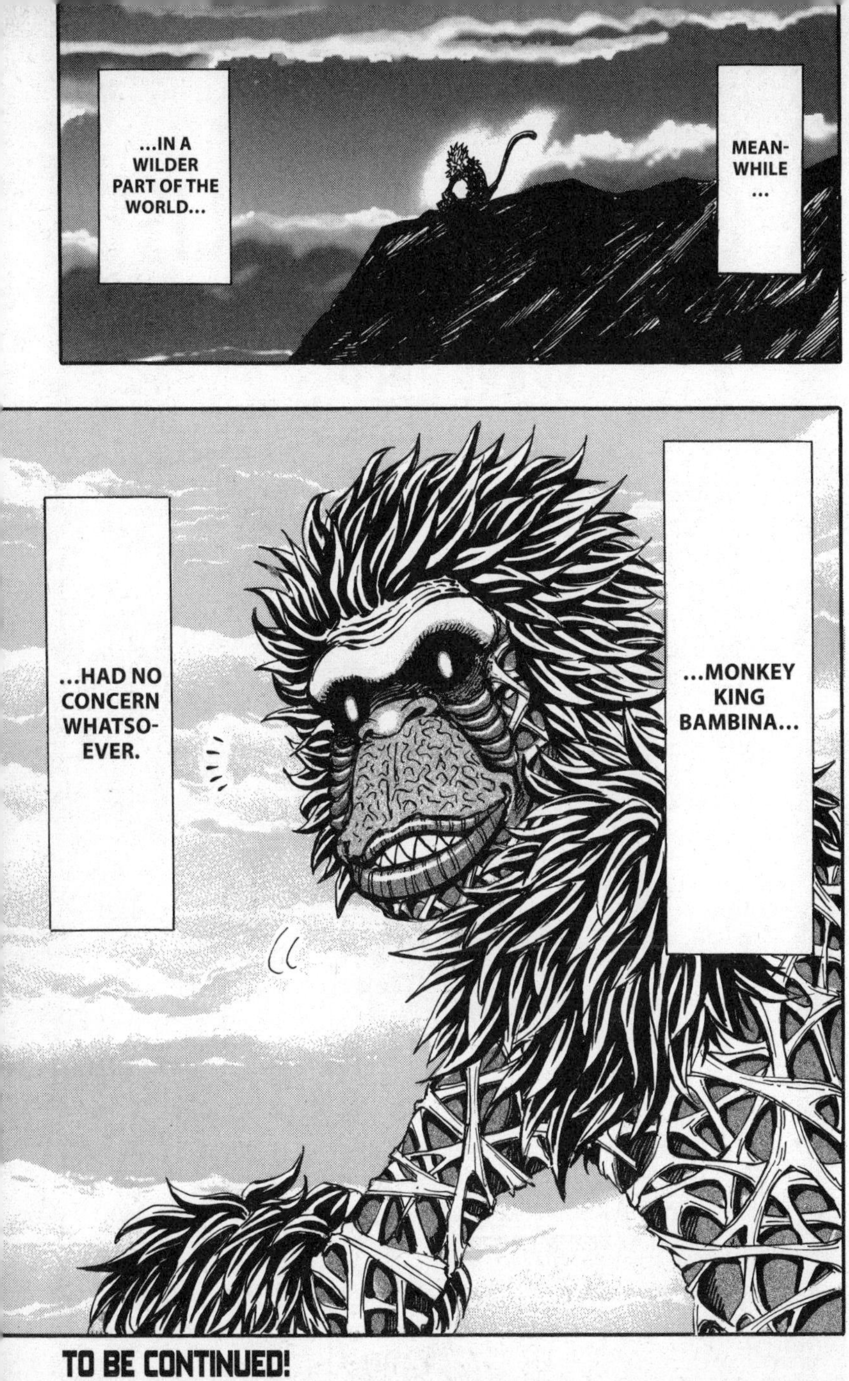
MEAN-WHILE...
...IN A WILDER PART OF THE WORLD...
...MONKEY KING BAMBINA...
...HAD NO CONCERN WHATSO-EVER.

TO BE CONTINUED!

TORIKO

GOURMET CHECKLIST
Vol. 325

SPARE RIB PIG
(MAMMAL BEAST)

CAPTURE LEVEL: 20
HABITAT: COOKING ISLAND
SIZE: 5 M
HEIGHT: ---
WEIGHT: 10 TONS
PRICE: 40,000 YEN PER 100 G

OOOINK!

SPARE RIB PIG*
(MAMMAL)
CAPTURE LEVEL 20

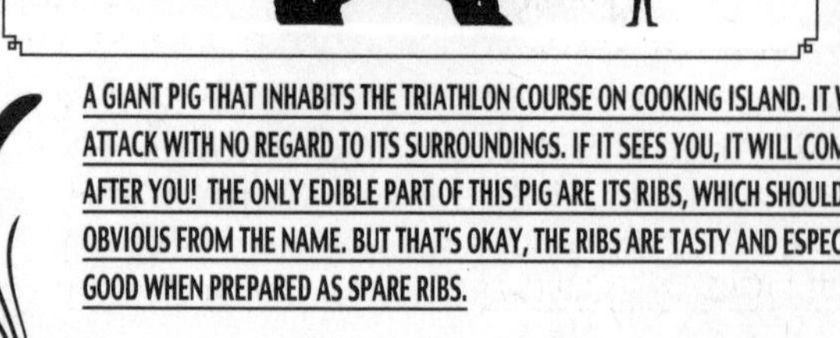

SCALE

A GIANT PIG THAT INHABITS THE TRIATHLON COURSE ON COOKING ISLAND. IT WILL ATTACK WITH NO REGARD TO ITS SURROUNDINGS. IF IT SEES YOU, IT WILL COME AFTER YOU! THE ONLY EDIBLE PART OF THIS PIG ARE ITS RIBS, WHICH SHOULD BE OBVIOUS FROM THE NAME. BUT THAT'S OKAY, THE RIBS ARE TASTY AND ESPECIALLY GOOD WHEN PREPARED AS SPARE RIBS.

TORIKO

GOURMET CHECKLIST

Vol. 326

SAND HAMSTER
(MAMMAL)

CAPTURE LEVEL: 22

HABITAT: COOKING ISLAND

SIZE: 2M

HEIGHT: ---

WEIGHT: 150KG

PRICE: 1,200 YEN PER 100G

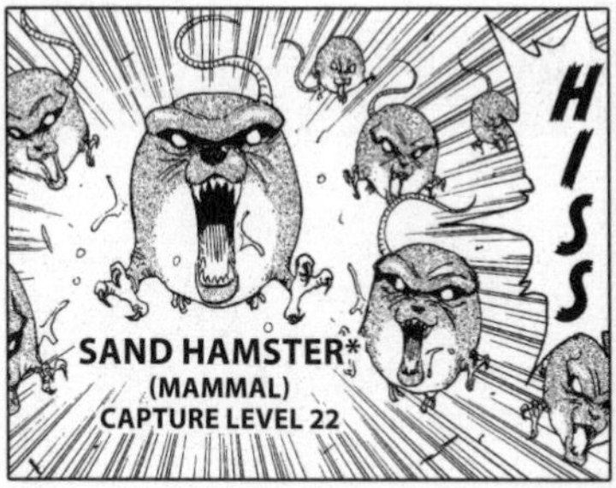
HISS
SAND HAMSTER*
(MAMMAL)
CAPTURE LEVEL 22

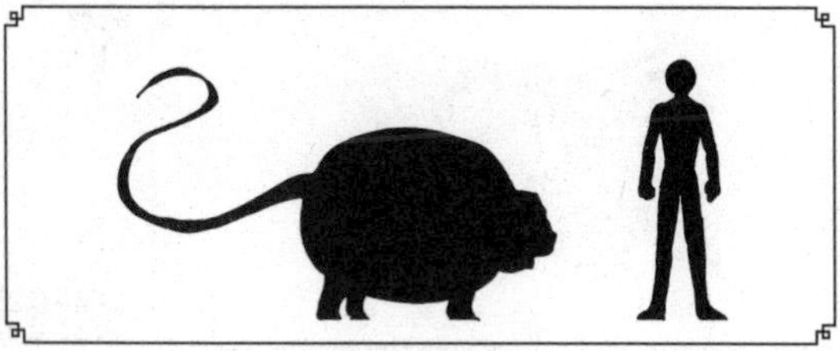

SCALE

A FEROCIOUS HAMSTER THAT INHABITS THE TRIATHLON COURSE ON COOKING ISLAND. ITS APPETITE IS SO GREAT THAT IT WILL EVEN EAT THE BONES OF ITS PREY! THEY ARE ESPECIALLY SCARY IN HERDS. WHEN THESE GUYS TEAM UP, EVEN THE MOST SKILLED CONTESTANTS WILL BE FIGHTING FOR THEIR LIVES! THEY'RE SMALL BUT THEY PACK A BIG BITE, LITERALLY! THESE LITTLE GUYS WILL SEND YOU THROUGH HELL AND BACK!

TORIKO

GOURMET CHECKLIST
Vol. 327

VILE DUNG FLY
(INSECT)

CAPTURE LEVEL: 82
HABITAT: INSIDE TOMMYROD
SIZE: 1.5M
HEIGHT: ---
WEIGHT: 80KG
PRICE: INEDIBLE

SCALE

IT HUNG OUT INSIDE THE BODY OF TOMMYROD, A VICE-CHIEF OF GOURMET CORP. IT'S A DISGUSTING INSECT THAT WILL ATTACK ITS PREY WITH ITS AWFUL STENCH. ONE WHIFF COULD KNOCK A MAN OUT! ITS REVOLTING APPEARANCE AND ODOR WILL MAKE YOU LOSE YOUR WILL TO FIGHT. IT'S SO VILE THAT IT'LL JUST MAKE AN OPPONENT WANT TO RUN AWAY.

COMING NEXT VOLUME

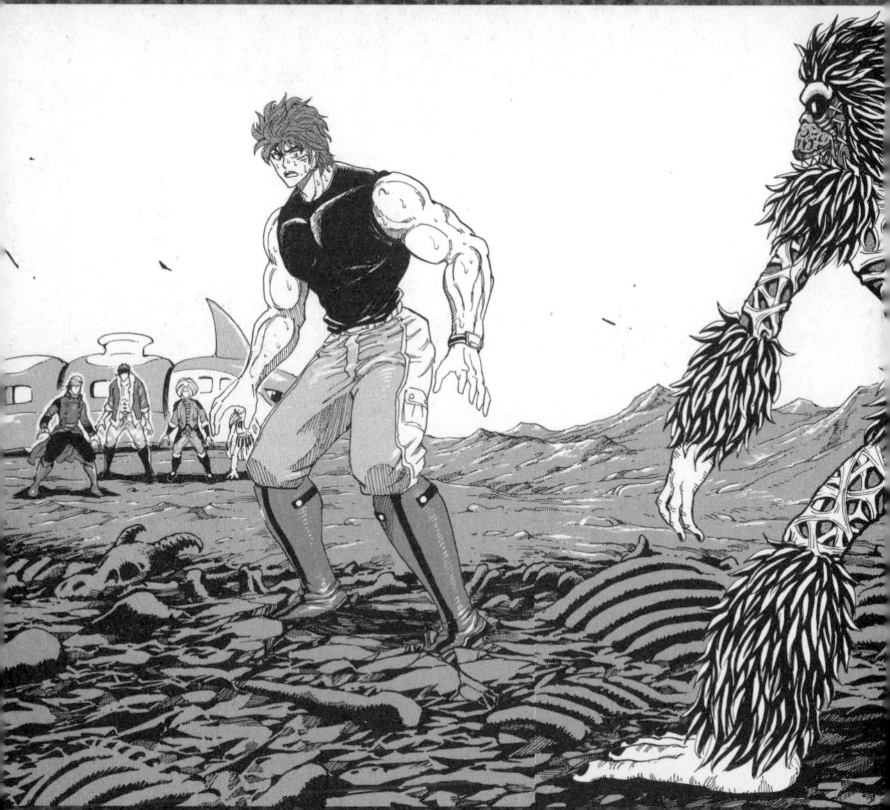

KING AT PLAY!!

Toriko and the gang travel to Area 7 to capture Acacia's Soup, Pair, to save Komatsu. There's no room for monkey business, but what are they supposed to do when the Monkey King wants to play? Toriko and the gang must learn to unify their Gourmet Cells and best the mischievous monster at his own game and obtain Pair. There's no foul play allowed, even if they have to reach below the belt for their prize.

AVAILABLE JUNE 2016!

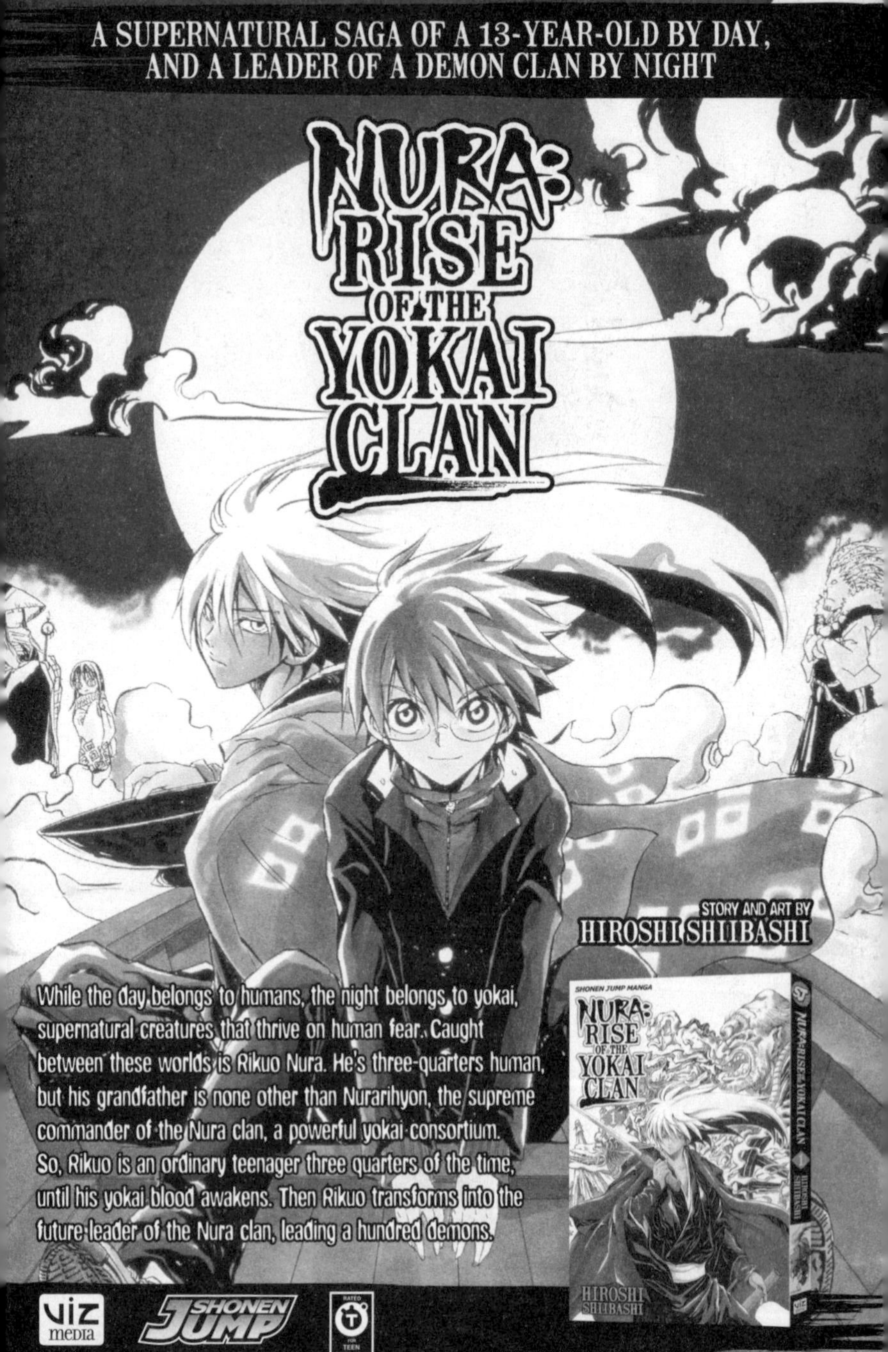
A SUPERNATURAL SAGA OF A 13-YEAR-OLD BY DAY, AND A LEADER OF A DEMON CLAN BY NIGHT
NURA: RISE OF THE YOKAI CLAN
STORY AND ART BY
HIROSHI SHIIBASHI
While the day belongs to humans, the night belongs to yokai, supernatural creatures that thrive on human fear. Caught between these worlds is Rikuo Nura. He's three-quarters human, but his grandfather is none other than Nurarihyon, the supreme commander of the Nura clan, a powerful yokai consortium. So, Rikuo is an ordinary teenager three quarters of the time, until his yokai blood awakens. Then Rikuo transforms into the future leader of the Nura clan, leading a hundred demons.
SHONEN JUMP MANGA
NURA: RISE OF THE YOKAI CLAN
HIROSHI SHIIBASHI
viz media
www.viz.com
SHONEN JUMP
www.shonenjump.com
RATED T FOR TEEN
ratings.viz.com
NURARIHYON NO MAGO © 2008 by Hiroshi Shiibashi/SHUEISHA Inc.

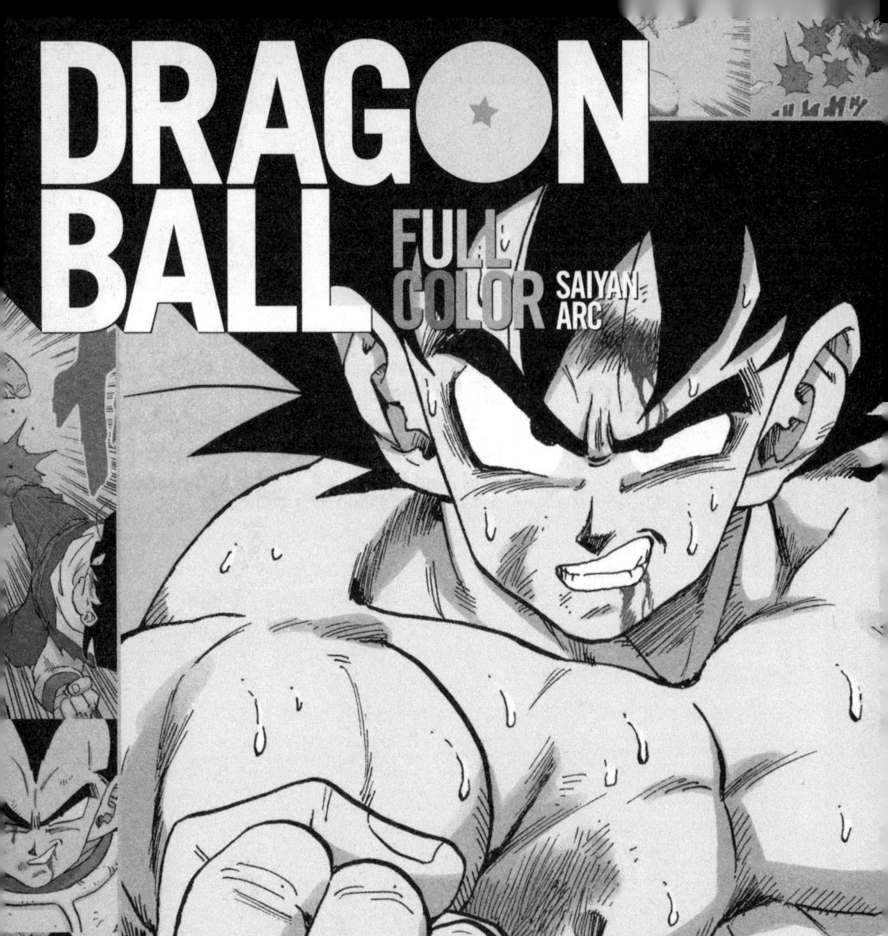
DRAGON BALL
FULL COLOR
SAIYAN ARC
ARRH

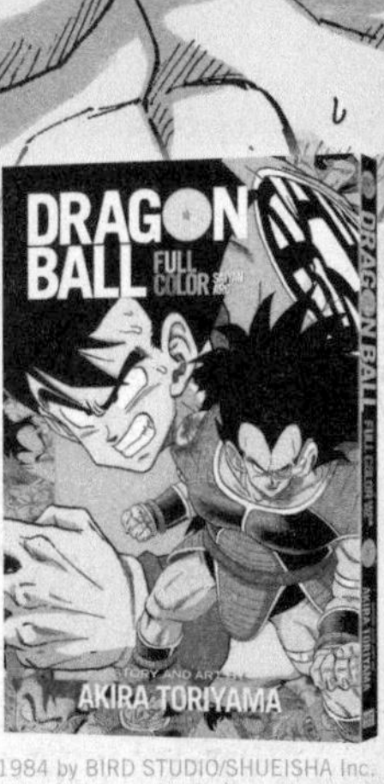
DRAGON BALL
FULL COLOR
STORY AND ART BY
AKIRA TORIYAMA

You're Reading in the Wrong Direction!!

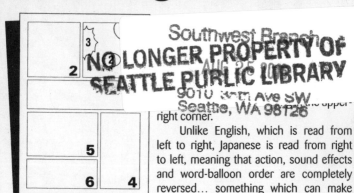

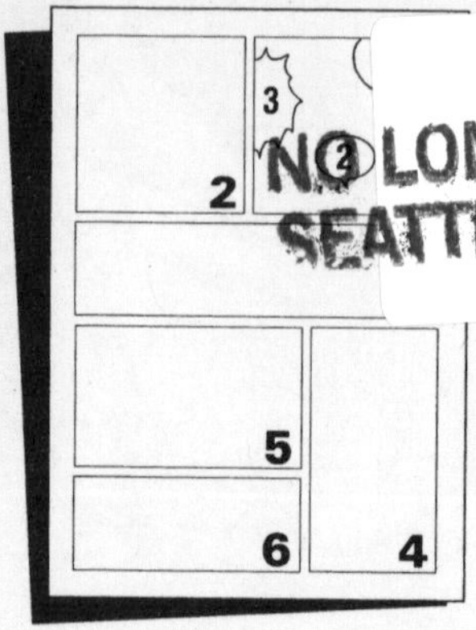
3
2
2
5
6
4

...right corner.

Unlike English, which is read from left to right, Japanese is read from right to left, meaning that action, sound effects and word-balloon order are completely reversed... something which can make readers unfamiliar with Japanese feel pretty backwards themselves. For this reason, manga or Japanese comics published in the U.S. in English have sometimes been published "flopped"—that is, printed in exact reverse order, as though seen from the other side of a mirror.

By flopping pages, U.S. publishers can avoid confusing readers, but the compromise is not without its downside. For one thing, a character in a flopped manga series who once wore in the original Japanese version a T-shirt emblazoned with "M A Y" (as in "the merry month of") now wears one which reads "Y A M"! Additionally, many manga creators in Japan are themselves unhappy with the process, as some feel the mirror-imaging of their art skews their original intentions.

We are proud to bring you Mitsutoshi Shimabukuro's **Toriko** in the original unflopped format. For now, though, turn to the other side of the book and let the adventure begin...!

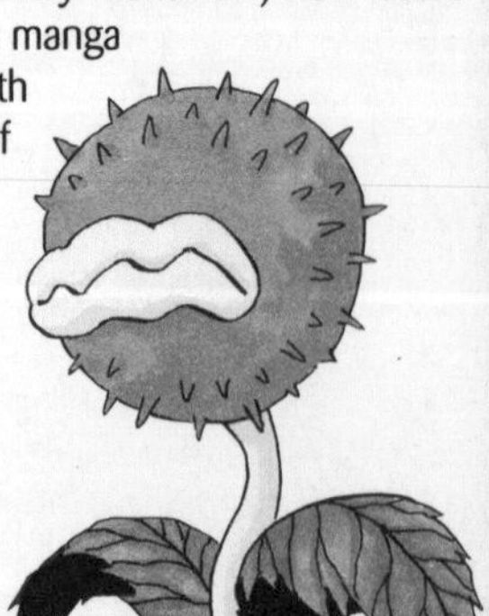

—Editor